An Eye for Hitchcock

To Dean:
with much esteem
and sincere gratitude.

[signature]

December 2008
Toronto

An Eye for

Murray Pomerance

Hitchcock

Rutgers University Press

New Brunswick, New Jersey, and London

Library of Congress Cataloging-in-Publication Data

Pomerance, Murray, 1946–
  An eye for Hitchcock / Murray Pomerance.
    p. cm.
  Includes bibliographical references and index.
    ISBN 0-8135-3394-5 (alk. paper)—ISBN 0-8135-3395-3 (pbk. : alk. paper)
    1. Hitchcock, Alfred, 1899—Criticism and interpretation. I. Title.
  PN1998.3.H58P66 2004
  791.43'0233'092—dc21 2003014221

British Cataloging-in-Publication information for this book is available from the
British Library.

Design by Karolina Harris

Photograph of Alfred Hitchcock on p. 260 courtesy Photofest Film Archive.

Manufactured in the United States of America

To
Nellie,
night and day

Contents

Acknowledgments

I am grateful to the Society for Cinema and Media Studies for entertaining readings of early drafts of some material contained here, and to Wheeler Winston Dixon, Gwendolyn Audrey Foster, Jon Lewis, and John Sakeris, who were responsible for the publication of small excerpts from the essays on *North by Northwest*, *Vertigo*, and *Torn Curtain* in a different form.

One accepts a great deal of help in writing a book such as this. I would like to express thanks to my students, who always permitted me to spiel; and to my friends and colleagues, especially Jean-Paul Chavy, Toronto; James Clark Jr., Ottawa; Saul Cooper, Santa Barbara; Barbara D'Arcy, San Francisco; Michael DeAngelis, Austin and Chicago; David Desser, Champaign, Hong Kong, and Ann Arbor; Rufus Dickinson, Santa Barbara and Toronto; Wheeler Winston Dixon, Lincoln; Ann Dooley, Toronto; Louis Feldhammer, Toronto; Blake Fitzpatrick, Peterborough; Mike Frank, Boston; Lester Friedman, Chicago; Andrew Furman, Toronto; Krin Gabbard, New York; Frances Gateward, Champaign and Ann Arbor; C. T. Gillin, Toronto; Peter Glassgold, Brooklyn and Pleasant Valley; Jay Glickman, Silver City, New Mexico; C. Keith Hampson, Toronto; Robert Harlow, Toronto; Jane Hoehner, Detroit; Norman Holland, Gainesville; Nathan Holmes, Toronto; Andrew Hunter, Toronto; Garth Jowett, Houston; Kathleen Kellett-Betsos, Toronto; the late Nina Leibman, Santa Clara; Nick Lopez-Aragon, Toronto; Jim MacLachlan, Toronto; Curtis Maloley, Toronto; Marianne McKenna, Toronto; Douglas Messerli, Los Angeles; Ken Mogg, Victoria, Australia; Doug Nicholson, Toronto; Charles Oberdorf, Toronto; Christopher Olsen, Orange County; Stephen Paul, New York; William Rothman, Miami; Skip Schwartz, Toronto; Jane Sloan, New Brunswick, New Jersey; Shaun Smith, Toronto; Eric Smoodin, Oakland; Jonathan and Rolf Soja, Toronto and Bracebridge; Brad Spurgeon, Asnières-sur-Seine; David Sterritt, New York; Lorne Tepperman, Toronto; John Turtle, Toronto; Sean Valentini, Toronto; Eugene Weiner, Haifa and Moscow; and Eric Zinner, New York.

Particular kindnesses and illuminations were offered by Lewis M. Allen and Jay Presson Allen, New York, whose generosity and lively spirit helped me travel back to the 1960s while living in the 1990s, no easy task. I am grateful, too, to Ted Anthony; David S. Azzolina and Dan Traister, Franklin Library of the University of Pennsylvania; the late Wayne Barker, Amagansett; Larry Billman, Los Angeles; Peter Bogdanovich, Beverly Hills; Susanna Bonetti, San Francisco Psychoanalytic Institute Library; Bob Boyle, Los Angeles; Henry Bumstead, San Marino; Fred Burchsted, Harvard College Library; Michel Chion, Paris; James Clark, Ottawa; the late Herbert Coleman, Los Angeles; C. O. "Doc" Erickson, Los Angeles; Ann Kaplan, New York; Kristine Kreuger, The Margaret Herrick Library of the Academy of Motion Picture Arts and Sciences, Beverly Hills; Meghann Matwichuk, University of Illinois at Urbana-Champaign Library; Uday Mohan, Washington, D.C.; Ellie Peck, New York Public Library for the Performing Arts at Lincoln Center, New York; Debbie Randorf, the New-York Historical Society; Suzanne Meyers Sawa, Edward Johnson Music Library, the University of Toronto; Jennifer Sayre, Northwest Airlines, Minneapolis–St. Paul; Rosemary Ullyot, Cinémathèque Ontario, Toronto; Elisabeth Weis, New York; Mark J. Wolf, Mequon, Wisconsin; Susanna Woods, the Free Library of Philadelphia; and Carolyn Zeifman, Toronto.

I am thankful for support from the Office of Research Services at Ryerson University, especially Robert Dirstein, Mary Jane Curtis, and Rose Jackson.

Three colleagues have championed my efforts here, and in so doing have given me to feel the warmth of shelter against what has often felt like a storm: Barry Keith Grant, St. Catharines; William Rothman, Miami; and Vivian Sobchack, Los Angeles. To express encouragement is always a virtue, I believe, but these three have gone beyond virtue into amity.

To my compadres at Rutgers University Press, Leslie Mitchner, Molly Baab, Anne Hegeman, Marilyn Campbell, and Eric Schramm, I extend my warmest salute and gratitude for their energy, their excitement, and their genuine stewardship.

My parents, Mike and Syd Pomerance, may they rest in peace, brought me first to Hitchcock, specifically to *The Man Who Knew Too Much*, when I was 10. I wonder whether they imagined what effect that would have one day. One of my regrets is that while they were alive I never said thank you in the proper way for the movies they gave me unstintingly as part of my birthright. My friend Paul Levy pointed me to *Vertigo* in the early 1960s: much, much, much, much, much later I finally recognized what he had been trying to do. Reginald Bedford and Evelyn Eby taught me to hear, Dave Heath to trust my eyes. And in more ways than he knows I have benefited from the extreme generosity and warmheartedness of Steven Alan Carr.

Last, but most profoundly, I thank my companion, teacher, and wisest friend Nellie Perret, who has endured my wanderings through Hitchcock with an astute humor, a sharp eye, and a caring heart. And a continuing inspiration have been the astute curiosity and quick wit of my son, Ariel, for whom the world of film is a marvel, too.

An Eye for Hitchcock

After a certain measure of recognized achievement . . . all subsequent artistic work by the same author should enjoy the benefit of the doubt, even, where necessary, to the point of a suspension of judgement, provisionally considering apparent defects as virtues that we do not yet know how to appreciate.

Pere Gimferrer, *Giorgio de Chirico*

I think that I know how to look, if it's something I know, and also that every looking oozes with mendacity, because it's that which expels us furthest outside ourselves, without the least guarantee.

Julio Cortázar, "Blow-Up"

Introduction: His Master's Voice

In this book of meditations upon six very great symphonic works of a very great composer, I am surely, as Norman O. Brown once put it, "turning and turning in the animal belly, the mineral belly, the belly of time. To find the way out: the poem."[1]

Hitchcock's films, too, are turning and turning. They continue to delight and profoundly intrigue the patient viewer, like all classical works that speak beyond the boundaries of their time and place. Inquiry, not statement, motivates me. The form of my action is play, not analysis. My question, if you like, is the pleasure of the Hitchcockian moment.

I have been privileged to speak with a number of generous people who helped Alfred Hitchcock make some of the films I write about in this book, to hear them, who knew him from such proximity, say his name. One of these, a writer of great charm, gently chided me for an observation I had made about her screenplay, and that tickled her, and brought as well a chill of self-doubt and self-recognition to my spine: "It doesn't connect with anything, darling, truly! Don't be such an academic." All my life I have struggled to balance a revealing discourse with an understanding of what artists do, a conundrum that has been my curse. I am myself, and have long been, an artist: I was an artist long before I was a detective. My instinctual response in that capacity to the work of Alfred Hitchcock is a tremulous embrace. Nor is he the first artist for whom I have felt this strange brotherhood (I am an only child): Claude Debussy has moved me the way Hitchcock does; at moments Constant Lambert; the Nicholas Ray of *On Dangerous Ground*. Fantin-Latour's grapes. E. M. Forster. But Hitchcock, I think it fair to say, has plagued me, since his riddles are so incommensurate with the proportions of everyday experience, and since his technique is so vast. I don't want to be an "academic" here, if out of imaginary molehills an "academic" makes real claims of mountains. But regardless of whether Hitchcock or his collaborators would see these films as I have seen them, I have been true in these pages to what I have seen. That is the challenge that has been paramount to me: to say, if not all then enough of what I find when I look at Hitchcock's films, yet in particular the six films that occupy this book.

This is an unconventional book about Alfred Hitchcock. It does not make the claim to recount the filmmaker's life as the motive, or explanation, of the work, or his working style, his passions, his opinions, his pranks, his obsessions, or his gamut of themes—the provocative blonde woman, the innocent man mistakenly perceived as guilty, the alluring villain. Instead it takes a very personal approach to films chosen because I find them in particular ways fascinating and rich. Indeed, the films here are seen with some intensity and at relatively great length as film essays go. I follow Taggard's approach to Emily Dickinson: rather than attempting to tell my view from left to right, as if I were drawing a line, I may seem instead to be turning a relic over and over in my hands.[2] Often, instead of following the story in a linear fashion, I leap across moments, rather in the way that memory does when we recollect films and try to map them against our experience. As much as these pieces are about particular films, then, they are about recollection. My recollection—as much as I can hope to share it with you.

This attempt to make sense of, and also relish, the complexity of what Hitchcock put on the screen openly flies in the face of much contemporary "received wisdom" about the "death" of the author in general, what is sometimes termed anti-auteurism. John Belton nicely encapsulates the central postulate of this practice when he writes of the evolution of technique as the product of

> an ideological demand that is, in turn, constituted by socioeconomic determinants. Neither techniques nor technologies are natural, nor do they evolve naturally. Contrary to André Bazin's idealist notions of the history of technology and of cinematic forms, their evolution is not natural but "cultural," responding to the pressures of ideology.[3]

While ideological critique fascinates me, indeed absorbs me to some degree, it leaves me feeling empty in the case of Hitchcock. My conviction is that even the anti-auteurist critics of Hitchcock, such as Belton or, occasionally, Ina Rae Hark or, rather persistently, Robert Corber,[4] to name only three of many, are, in the production of a critical view, authorial—a kind of critical *auteur*. What they author is a coherent, even stylish, argument that sets film in a social context—a context, by the way, no more social than the one in which they write that critique. Their auteurism itself is social, and so, I try to argue here some of the time, is Hitchcock's—sociological, even, and especially sensitive to cultural factors, particularly those of social class and the structure of knowledge. He had been born (in 1899) and raised, after all, in Victorian England, as dense and rigid a class structure as can be imagined. Anti-auteurism tends to privilege audience reception in its analysis, taking the film as a code to be translated and understood in terms of cultural practices; but I do not think that in order to be interested in doing that it is necessary to deny the complexity of the production process, the aesthetic accomplishments of the filmmaker, or the filmmaking as a philosophical act.

At each juncture here, I try very hard to show evidence on the screen for my assertions and conclusions. I believe both scholarship and popular adoration have paid insufficient attention to that screen, have but glossed its contents, neglected the deep backgrounds of shots, skipped the small stuff (by which I do not necessarily mean the small items lying upon the tables, such as Rebecca's hair brush, but perhaps *do* mean the fact that we are never shown the hair brush of the woman who is looking at that hair brush), and have, indeed, elided whole scenes when they have blemished the clear analysis we have wanted to make. The reader unfamiliar with Hitchcock's work may come away from these essays with a strong desire to see the films. The reader who knows a Hitchcock film or two may be surprised to see me pay considerable attention to moments viewers do not normally bother to mention, such as Father Michael Logan's foray into housepainting in *I Confess*. The reader who knows Hitchcock well will, perhaps, have the ticklish feeling there is still more to be seen and will want to see the films again. Hitchcock's work repays vigilance and devoted viewing, and I cannot imagine having the feeling of having seen any one of these works "enough."[5] And we may recall what one of Godard's characters says in *L'Amour*: "*Non les images mentent jamais*" (images never lie).

Because I think these films are riddles, and complex ones, I make no apology for going on about them. And while I have some interest in dramaturgy as a basis for making analysis, I very much wanted in writing this not to be forcing the work into the perspective of any single theoretical mode developed a long way from Hitchcock and not for the purpose of interpreting material like this. Psychoanalytically based literary criticism, for example, is popular among some scholars (especially when mixed with a feminist theoretical language): while I am fascinated by psychoanalysis, as I think the essay on *Spellbound* will show, I don't believe it solves all the riddles of film, especially since the very few (and very precise) essays Freud actually wrote about creative work, such as "The Relation of the Poet to Daydreaming," almost never get quoted or used as the basis of filmic analysis.[6] This is not to say psychoanalytically based scholarship has not made intriguing observations—for example, Harvey R. Greenberg's study of *Psycho*, or Slavoj Žižek's treatment of *Saboteur*.[7] Yet to take psychoanalysis very seriously as a basis for understanding Hitchcock in general is surely to rely upon the humanism of his characters, to imagine them, indeed, as people rather than as constructions he shaped to fit onto his screen. For instance, often a critic will talk about a character's gaze (following Laura Mulvey).[8] But characters do not have a gaze so much as an orientation of the eye; this functions to lead *the viewer's gaze*, and also to lead the viewer into imagining that she is watching a gazer gazing.[9]

One may haul Hitchcock onto any theoretical band wagon without being committed to Hitchcock—a problem, in my view, both moral and philosophical. He can be seen so nicely to illustrate something one already wanted to say—yet something one could have said just as well without the Hitchcockian pretext and that, indeed, one would have said quite happily about another filmmaker, or another subject entirely. Any theoretical project is, of course, only a project; it doesn't explain everything about anything; and what leaves me feeling hungry about considerable theory as it approaches Hitchcock is that it neglects his irony, his wit, his paradoxes, his visual work, the blunt expressive fact of his casting, and more. Much of the scholarship that suggests Hitchcock's films merely fit into broader trends and cultural developments— for instance, that many of his heroes exemplify the middle-class search for mastery, that neo-Victorianism permeates the films, or that there is a relentless misogyny in Hitchcock's treatment of women—does not account for the pervasive cultural influence of such themes on all filmmaking in the twentieth century and, indeed, for Hitchcock's rather idiosyncratic qualities: that his films, emerging from neo-Victorianism, are actually modernist; that his women are actually heroes; that he goes to lengths to show middle-class existence in the context of other social possibilities. If it is bourgeois sentiment, misogyny, and prurience one seeks, it is easier to find these in Ford, Hawks, Minnelli, Cukor, and Wilder, but I think Hitchcock plays with these themes more, makes them more interesting and more provocative, even less hidden, and so he gets pointed at. But what is most troubling to me about criticism that fits Hitchcock into prevailing themes or extrinsic theoretical constructs is its lack of genuine love for the Hitchcockian oeuvre, a sign not of well-illuminated objectivity but, I think, of exploitation. If the films are not strictly autobiographical, still they speak to their condition as products of a man's artistic obsession and perduring philosophical concerns. That he was master of his medium should alone persuade us to view him much more carefully.

Biography pleases many people as a motive, an explanation, for behavior. There is no really satisfactory biography of Hitchcock. That is to say, there is no biography that answers the questions that plague me when I watch the films. John Russell Taylor's *Hitch* has less filigree, and an opinion less angular, than Donald Spoto's *The Dark Side of Genius*,[10] but neither book takes me into the alleyways I desire to search, his fondness for particular American scenes, for example, his musical and painterly interests and references. Dan Auiler's *Hitchcock's Notebooks* is, similarly, rich and often fascinating,[11] but cannot possibly satisfy, based as it is on a limited reproduction of records from a limited supply to which Auiler, or anyone, could have had access. I have read many of Hitchcock's letters, and seen his notes and his drawings as well as production files from his films—they open gateways, but do not take one far inside the palace. At least as intriguing, and surely as unresolved, are the favorite family menus included by Pat Hitchcock O'Connell in her *Alma Hitchcock: The Woman behind the Man*.[12] Why among the recipes is there none for watercress rolls that he apparently adored so much? Might not the watercress roll help us digest the films?

The artists I have spoken with who knew and worked with him tend (quite sensibly) not to be as carried away by the films as I am; their job was to help him get what he wanted, not figure out what he was trying to do onscreen. Or they have anecdotes, charming and engaging, to be sure, but always technical and operational, not creative: what happened when we were setting up for such and such a shot. How wonderful it would have been, I have thought over and over, to sit at his side while he was making these films, but with the consciousness of a person who already knew the work, so that we could chat about particular details and move along day by day to see the pieces come together on the screen. I would not have wanted the kind of chat François Truffaut had, exhaustive in scope but perfunctory in depth. I want, glutton that I am, to know everything. At the end of Sam Shepard's play *Angel City*, a Hollywood producer transmogrifies into a reel of celluloid; perhaps one must become the films one loves.

The films I have approached in this book, in a writing that persistently circles around toward itself, take the contemporary viewer and reader on a voyage through time, back fifty years to a period from which many records have been destroyed or lost. (A friend of mine wanted to research a particularly obscure director at a major studio and consulted the archivist. "Oh," he was told, "we took all our files from the 1940s, 1950s, and 1960s, hauled them out back, and threw them in a dumpster. What you want is probably underneath one of our expressways.") These six motion pictures were made in, and are visions of, a vanished era—the particular one, indeed, in which I was born and grew up. I attempt here to recapture the past, but also to discuss what it is to do that, since the struggle to recapture the past is itself a frequent pre-occupation of Hitchcock's characters—not, I hasten to say, because Hitchcock was Proustian, although one may say he was; but because like Proust, and Forster, and James, and Ford Madox Ford, and so many other artists and philosophers of his time, Hitchcock wanted to understand his time, his living, and his experience. I think it is possible that Hitchcock's dream-fascination with the past is part of what made him so appealing to Truffaut, whose estimate I share that Hitchcock is the greatest filmmaker of the twentieth century.[13]

Since his works are symphonic, and since I am a failed musician (if such a creature is possible), each essay in this book has been created with the form of the relevant film in mind; perhaps in some small and respectful way they mirror the works they study. Such a process involved reconstituting not only the narrative but also a social fabric that was directly apparent to me and yet was unintelligible, since it was my world. John Knowles wrote in *A Separate Peace*, "There is no stage you comprehend better than the one you have just left," but I waited far too long after the 1960s to address these films and so they became riddles to me again, much as some of them were when first I saw them. More: in looking at Hitchcock one has to learn to recognize. His films are full of shockingly precise references to places, artifacts, habits, nuances of feeling, moral codes, routes, and strands of character, that have to be brought forward intact if the stories are to be fully meaningful for us as they originally were. A tiny example that I do not discuss in these pages: near the beginning of *Rear Window*, a young ballerina, "Miss Torso," practices a dance routine while L. B. "Jeff" Jefferies gawks at her from his apartment across the court-yard and speaks on the telephone. Since his boss does not want him back on the job yet——Jeff's leg is still in a cast, as it has been for weeks—and he is sending another photographer on an important mission to the other side of the world, Jeff is frustrated at being tied to his wheelchair. But the music Miss Torso is dancing to is Leonard Bernstein's *Fancy Free* (later *On the Town*, 1944), a ballet celebrating three sailors who explore New York, pick up some girls, and have a wonderful time. Jeff is expressly prevented from doing exactly these kinds of things in this film, notwithstanding his romantic difficulties. In a scene like this, any ballet music might have done for Miss Torso's little exercises, since (as every writer about this films tells us) she is (only) a dancer practicing a routine, but *Fancy Free* adds a special nuance. Its happy jive taunts Jeff on many levels—as music, as story, as basis for Miss Torso's inestimable exertions. Without knowing what the music is, we don't have quite the same sense that this man who watches the lives of strangers across the way, and intercedes in their affairs, is feeling mocked. All the films I explore here are studded with references of this specificity and preciseness that open dimensions of appreciation otherwise not available to us.

Hitchcock's films are not precisely texts, although one can address their scripts and stories, their language and exposition. Most critiques of Hitchcock films have been produced, in fact, by scholars in literature, many of them so eminent in my estimation that I have hesitated in this endeavor to tap even lightly at their doors. Yet because the subject matter here is film, not writing, a certain knowledge of visual practice, visual thought, visual form, and filmic technique is beneficial to the erstwhile critic.[14] Impressive and meaningful in Hitchcock is not just the composition of the frame but the precise distancing of the camera from the subject, the lighting, the use of color, the choice of lens. My passion was to approach the visual material as directly as possible, to give a reading of it congruent with my own experience of the world and with the structure of the films themselves. The essays were conceived, then, as homages, and in watching the films and writing about them my overwhelming desire was to see as much as possible of what had been put on the screen to see.

There is no doubt that my approach led me away from some beautiful and valuable works of criticism, such as Lesley Brill's dense and engaging *The Hitchcock Romance* and Robin Wood's challenging *Hitchcock's Films Revisited*.[15] In these books I have been awakened in some places, turned away in others, but altogether overwhelmed by the sharp penetrations and cogent arguments these scholars put forward. Yet, while feeling a debt of gratitude to the writers on whose shoulders I stand, I am left by the literary style of criticism to feel a discomfort that brings me again and again to the original works, not the books about them. Robin Wood, for instance, finds himself affected by *Marnie* much as I do, believing that this film, "though now widely (but by no means universally) respected, has still not achieved the recognition it deserves as one of Hitchcock's finest, most realized, most personal, most intense and disturbing works. Anyone who doesn't love *Marnie* doesn't really love Hitchcock."[16] This extremely unguarded and accurate adoration seems to me precisely as personal and as affecting a stance as could be desired, and the enthusiasm it reveals seems just the quality so much Hitchcock criticism lacks, yet Wood's analysis of *Marnie*, meticulous in its way, and pointing to a great deal that conventional criticism abandoned, pays no attention at all to many moments in the film that strike me as emphatic and unavoidable. To cite just two: that the nuts spilling on the kitchen floor should be pecans, and that at the tea party at Wykwyn Marnie is forced to pour. More about this anon.

Lesley Brill's technique is to see the Hitchcock oeuvre in a chiaroscuro of symbols,[17] noting significance in similarities between passages and moments in various films as they similarly reflect mythopoetic light. For example, he compares the conclusion of the opening sequence of *Vertigo* to the finale of *North by Northwest*, in an observation that is stunning and certainly apposite, yet for me problematic:

> "Give me your hand," says Roger Thornhill as he stretches down for Eve Kendall. She reaches up for him in return, and a close-up of their meeting hands is soon followed by the famous dissolve into the upper berth of the 20th Century Limited. *Vertigo* has the same words and the same shot; but the hands do not meet because Scottie, almost fainting from his acrophobia, cannot reach for the proffered help.[18]

While this vision fascinates, it also neglects. As I try to suggest below, Eve Kendall is not exactly brought to salvation by Roger's lift, as Scottie would be if his policeman friend succeeded. And it is not paralysis that keeps Scottie from grasping the policeman's hand; but deafness—Hitchcock muffles the cop's offer of help to help us appreciate how Scottie is acoustically displaced from the world. While Brill goes on to note that "downwardness in Hitchcock's movies is almost always associated with an imagery that suggests infernal regions, the land of the dead," I find myself seeing in Hitchcock instead an astute social consciousness bred in London life and aware at every moment of class as a structuring force in human relations. Looking down also suggests superciliousness, or perhaps nostalgia. While literary texts allude to and represent the social, films present and constitute it, and this is a different relation requiring more than stylistic, metaphorical, linguistic, and thematic analysis.

With the William Rothman who wrote the eye-opening and galvanizing *Hitchcock—The Murderous Gaze* and *The "I" of the Camera*[19] I find myself deeply sympathetic, and so I must be willing to share his fate of being lambasted, as he was by Fredric Jameson, for his idealism that made "a formal structure or feature into a type of content."[20] If disregard from such as Jameson is the price of the kind of careful attention to features and structures Rothman gives, so be it. What I share with Rothman is both the conviction that Hitchcock was a builder, and the desire to experience his architecture fully—more fully, I think, than do the anti-auteurists who, satisfied to place Hitchcock's work in terms of a genre theory that has little to do with it, deprecate Rothman for what he "finds" there. In his struggle to bring Hitchcock to alignment with Stanley Cavell, Rothman writes (and I nod enthusiastically as I read), "I find myself continually called on to make discoveries, to see things that viewers do not ordinarily see, or to see familiar things in an unfamiliar light, to discover unsuspected connections. . . . To read a Hitchcock film is to understand that Hitchcock is the most unknown as well as the most popular of filmmakers. His films are meditations on unknownness."[21] They are also meditations on knowing, believing, doubting, remembering, being. I believe the present essays depart from Rothman only in a particular obsessiveness—a desire to clarify not only "things that viewers do not ordinarily see" in much-analyzed scenes but whole scenes and configurations that criticism has had a habit of passing by. The auction scene in *North by Northwest* is one example of the kind of material I refer to, and so is the policeman's confabulation in Prof. Brulov's house in *Spellbound*. Likewise the scenes in the bathroom in *Marnie*, the acoustic references in *Vertigo*, the rectory painting in *I Confess*, or the role played by academic life in *Torn Curtain*. If my explorations of these films elaborate too much, I hope they share, in however elementary a fashion, the spirit of Rothman's work.

It is essential to pay very strict attention to the Hitchcockian frame: as it is so rich, such observation is a daunting task and it is perhaps the greatest reward of any attempt that at the end one feels a stinging frustration at the wealth of material one has perforce neglected, failed to catch, lost hold of. I find the Hitchcockian frame so philosophically dense and provocative, indeed, that it is impossible for me to imagine behind it the "sponge, eager to adapt the point of view that would sell, and open to any idea that seemed good, insistent only that it fit his design" that Jane Sloan claims Hitchcock to have been.[22] What, indeed, was that *design*, into which "any idea that seemed good" might fit? By implying Hitchcock's filmic ideas needed only to fit his design, Sloan sees the design as a simple catch-all. But on the elusively complex design of any one of the films I address here—and many more—a monograph could be written without addressing every angle and form, and surely without inspiring agreement with Jean Narboni's observation, adduced by Sloan, that Hitchcock's work consists of "many signs, no facts."[23] How fashionable it has become to look for signs, to find what one looks for, to suspect nothing but signs exist in the world!

Admittedly, one could be less idiosyncratic than I have been—many writers have—but I want to be true to the fact that these films are first and foremost experiences, and idiosyncratic ones: to my mind, for instance, the theme of espionage, interesting enough as a diversion, is insufficient to account for *Torn Curtain*; *Spellbound* is much more than a story of murder and neurosis; *I Confess*, it may take a Canadian to show, is a Canadian film.[24]

Received wisdom has blinded many observers of these films. *Vertigo* has been revered as a film about a man's obsession with love and death, but observers have declined to ask why Hitchcock (a director who loved to travel) bought a book set in Paris and then reset his action in San Francisco (near his farm).[25] Or, indeed, why the viewer must be placed *inside* the car with Scottie as he pursues Madeleine through the San Francisco streets. And why, indeed, *these* streets, driven in this particular order? *North by Northwest* has generally been acclaimed as a light film; yet its fans have mostly neglected to write in depth about Roger Thornhill's curious profession and its relation to the plot. *Marnie*, consistently misperceived, has been treated over and over in terms of thieving frigidity with no regard to the palpable play of social class in a story about women's liberation.

Recurring is the currently unfashionable idea that these films, being about verticality in some manifestation, reflect the class hierarchy. (Postmodernism, for example, has all of us duped by simulacra; therefore all of us are equals in a strange democracy of phantasmagoria.) But rather than treating class as a simplistic theme for statement and recapitulation, Hitchcock gives it elaborate and often shattering development. There is vital verticality, then, in all of the films I treat here, but not, surely, in only these. We may be on the lookout for social scales in which powerlessness struggles under power; climbing; falling; precarious rest in gravity; architectures suggesting, and founded upon, upward thrust; camera movement in the vertical line, especially shooting from above and below;[26] geographical upness and downness; the moral scale. Nor is there only verticality. Hitchcock was keenly interested in the play of surfaces and presentations, thus, dramaturgy. And I have tried to include here a range of films: some that everyone seems to acknowledge as masterpieces, *Vertigo* and *North by Northwest;* some that are saddled with lighter reputations, *Marnie* and *Spellbound;* and some, *Torn Curtain* and *I Confess,* that have caused even Hitchcock's most loving admirers to turn away in revulsion or disappointment—because, I hope to show, they have not loved enough.

Why these six films and not others? Only because these have carried me on fabulous journeys. Six different films could have filled this book, or six still different. Nor have I said about these all that I need to say, but that gives me something to write about tomorrow.

Viewing the films, one by one, before (or while) reading the essays about them won't hurt a bit. In constructing these pieces I have taken care not to spell out the action of the plots in any detail (although a short endnote giving the "plot" is placed in each essay), since my whole point is that a great deal more is going on in Hitchcock's work than can be revealed by a pedestrian attempt at spelling out the "story." If the reader really desires a plain, straightforward, verbal account of the action in Hitchcock's films, an acceptable source would be Jane Sloan's *Alfred Hitchcock: A Filmography and Bibliography*.[27] In terms of its tone, the present book is intended as a serious discourse upon Hitchcock's work, but not one that excludes a general reader unfamiliar with sociology, cinema studies, academic analysis, or, indeed, critical exegesis more generally. Anyone who finds these films engaging, touching, riddling, charming, or memorable is imagined as my companion in this discovery. Some will claim I have "found" in Hitchcock what is not really there, and to these readers I can say only that my meditations are prompted by an extremely close reading and rereading of what is on the screen. I took as model Truffaut's reminiscences of watching the "Good Mornin'!" routine from *Singin' in the Rain* over and over on a Movieola until he had seen the finest nuance of a gesture Debbie Reynolds executed at one moment in history to cause her skirt, in mid-step, to cover a naked knee.[28] This kind of discreet moment is the stuff of film. To stand back oblivious, to run over it by trying to follow the story, to glide past it in order to see yet another and still another film, are all ways of being blinded. As Jean Starobinski said, "I saw no need to decide whether these intentions were conscious or unconscious. The fact that they were evident was enough."[29]

But I am concerned about another possibility suggested by Starobinski:

> I may have given the impression of claiming to decipher him better than he was able to do himself, from a superior position and as if it were up to the critic to unearth secrets that no one else had ever discovered. The dominating vantage of the critic is merely that privilege he derives from being a spectator who arrives on the scene after the fact, in a new age of knowledge and in the name of greater enlightenment.[30]

Dominating vantages should have no place in this confession. Hitchcock's films are elegant ciphers of his ability to decipher himself. If, perhaps, here I am, as Starobinski says again, "availing myself of the device of identification so often used by Poulet, which involves mingling (for a moment) the voice of the critic with the voice of the author," it is not to make a ladder that I do this, but to surrender.

Toronto-Firle-Trouville-Los Angeles-La Jolla-
Lake St. Nora-Amagansett-Boston-Toronto
June 1997–December 2003

A Great Fall:

Action North by Sincerity Northwest

It's not a man. . . !
The Man Who Knew Too Much

GAMBITS

Are we, after all, what we seem to be? At least since the Greeks sang of the visit of Amphitryon, the God who descended to walk hidden among men, and if only in the context of narrative, we have been wondering this, with special urgency perhaps as we contemplate film. Are we to be recognized, named, and judged by an audience, that most circumspect and unyielding of entities? Or does our existence spring from within, from before? If we live, like the Red King, in others' dreams of us, in others' eyes, they can surely be wrong from time to time, as we can be wrong in thinking to recognize people who are not there. The history of confused identity has been plaited with both the history of situational ambiguity and the history of the development of the technology of disguise, not to mention the history of identificatory photography.[1]

In capitalism—film has always resided in the age of capitalism—identity is a form of property both in its profession and in its confusion. Previously, in feudal society, identity was already a means of location and placement, literally a mise-en-scène—as though preparation for a film. And while the technology of disguise is sometimes objective and material—a suit waiting in a

hotel room closet to be pressed, a hair brush, a mask of shaving cream seen in the mirror of a railway station men's room—it is just as often stylistic and evanescent, a way of recounting a story, a choice of words, a careful circumlocution, a tone of voice. There are many ways to hide, in life and onscreen; onscreen, perhaps, especially, as I hope to show by taking a somewhat circuitous but methodical route toward a vision of *North by Northwest*.

Harold Garfinkel discusses a technique he calls "anticipatory following," which is essentially learning by imitating.[2] How to frame answers to potentially threatening questions, we deduce by paying careful attention to the structure of the questions themselves. We take cues from others as to the behavior they expect or the frame within which reasonable action can be set, and thus contrive how to "be" the person observers assume we naturally, automatically, simply, merely, and wholeheartedly are and always have been. But which comes first with anticipatory following, the gesture or the cue for the gesture? We all do anticipatory following, particularly as young children but often later in life as well. We all know how to simulate what we hope others will take us for, guessing quickly from their behavior toward us who "we" are and what it is that "we" are supposed to do in order to simulate "ourselves" correctly. For instance, I don't recall a single moment in my childhood (when I was taken to see *Beneath the 12 Mile Reef* at the Tivoli on James Street in Hamilton, Ontario, or else *The Greatest Show on Earth* [which I know I saw ten times on ten successive Saturdays in 1956], or *The Man Who Knew Too Much*, or *Boy on a Dolphin*, or *His Majesty O'Keefe* with that amazing performer, Abraham Sofaer, or *The Road to Bali*) when anybody actually gave me the instructions, "Sit down in this plush chair. Watch that sparkling screen. Be quiet, listen, and see everything that is there. Eat this popcorn without making any noise." But I did manage to learn to be the movie watcher my parents and babysitters thought I already and simultaneously was or had the potential to be, and I have been that watcher all my life since. I can even remember having been that watcher the other day, while yet another motion picture was spun out in front of my eyes, but now instead of popcorn I had my decaf Starbucks. I am that watcher now, as I write this book.

Alfred Hitchcock's Roger O. Thornhill (Cary Grant) is an anticipatory follower, too. There are virtually no analyses of his escapades in *North by Northwest* that do not somehow recognize this elemental fact, if not necessarily in these words, although relatively few of those who have written about the film find it especially interesting, being charmed instead by his predicament as the butt of a profound existential joke.[3] Once Roger has been kidnapped at the Plaza, however, our protagonist is a man who can learn to survive only from those who fail to acknowledge him as Roger O. Thornhill (the person *he* supposes himself naturally, automatically, simply, merely, and wholeheartedly to be), persistently recognizing him instead as a person *they* believe him naturally, automatically, simply, merely, and wholeheartedly to be, George Kaplan.[4] Even though he insists that he is *not* Kaplan (and one of the lovely ironies of the film early on is that we tend to agree with him), his denials must be directed toward a small and powerful audience convinced that he *is*. He is therefore in trouble, and it is only through the aperture of Kaplan—by learning how to "be" that man—that he can possibly find safety when he is in their presence. In order to escape from his kidnappers and survive their malevolent attentions, he sets out on a journey of discovery, northnorthwest, to find out just who George Kaplan is, learning at each stage in the process what his tormentors expect of him without giving them evidence that he is learning it or that they are his teachers. I should say here as well that the kidnappers are extremely nasty, if courteous, types engaged in serious business: should they realize that they have captured the wrong man (i.e., that it is a mere Roger Thornhill who is desperately learning from them), they will kill him; while Kaplan, the individual they zealously seek and believe they have come upon, the man Roger steadfastly refuses to be, is worth keeping alive. Roger's *pas de deux*, as it were, with the invisible cipher Kaplan I take as a central conundrum of this film.

North by Northwest is a profoundly social film, by which I mean it reveals social structure and power. Because the kidnappers' "recognition" of Thornhill as Kaplan, in the Oak Bar at the Plaza Hotel, is performed more or less under the gun, at issue in it are both personal influence and social control—thus vertical ascendancy. The gun at Roger's ribs will influence him to walk along with men who wish to redirect him against his will, since it is to a telephone in the lobby he is taking himself, not their mauve limousine parked outside at the curb. The kidnapping is brutality at its most elegant—social power, in fact: a force that legitimates every assumption these men make, and tilts the balance of probability away from the victim who can muster no force of his own. The power of the gunmen is manifested in the scene through an astonishing directorial coup. A bellboy is circling the room with a call: "Paging Mr. George Kaplan!" This is smooth and mannerly social behavior in the restricted bar of a glamorous New York hotel—all completely *comme il faut*. Roger is at a table taking drinks with some business associates and has suddenly remembered that although a few minutes before, outside on 59th Street, he had asked his secretary to call his mother at a certain telephone number, mother is in fact elsewhere. He urgently now wants to send a wire.[5] A suave barfly, he turns to look for the bellboy and raises a hand to signal at the exact moment the boy has put out the call for Kaplan, a call loud enough and musical enough to have caught our ears but one Roger didn't detect, being uninterested in the space outside his little microecological preserve. He is not expecting to be paged here and is preoccupied talking to gentlemen, one of whom happens to be hard of hearing. The deaf man raises a hand to his ear, diegetically scooping Roger's cocktail jibberish but extradiegetically signaling us to pay attention to sounds in general, that is, sounds beyond the periphery of this table. That Roger is taken for Kaplan (literally) by the men who initiated the bellboy's page is itself a social nicety (although not a nice nicety) since he made a signal and the signal was enthusiastically read. What more need ever be accomplished beyond making a sign that is read? That he did not intend to make the sign is surely immaterial, for what is an intention to an audience but a sign of an intention, and he has made a sign! That a person can inadvertently signal, can possess an audience unwittingly, suggests that the power of identification is in the field characters inhabit, not in characters themselves. The bellboy, seeing the signal too, and being innocent (though dangerous), has no reason for thinking the man answering his call is anybody other than the George Kaplan he is calling. He directs Roger to the phone in the lobby, where the gunmen intercept him. This kidnapping scene—in truth it does not seem like one until the action is well along—is a bold statement of the fragility of identification, since it is through an unintended temporal juxtaposition of signs, the hand in the air and the vocal call, that Roger innocently forsakes himself here and plunges into another man's life. If Hitchcock was intrigued all his life by the imbalance of consciousness and power that enables human influence, we may not be surprised to find considerable attention to class, dominance, and social order in his dramatic settings of taken and mistaken identity: *The Lady Vanishes*, for instance, or *North by Northwest*.[6]

We can explore this film in terms of matters not being quite what they seem. A scene in the dining car of the Twentieth-Century Limited, as Thornhill and Eve Kendall (Eva Marie Saint) first formally meet, is especially interesting in this regard. Roger is in flight from New York, incriminated as a murderer in a purely coincidental newspaper photograph—in short, a man who has been taken to really be what he only looks like he is (but on the front page, a fixing frame). Eve is ostensibly enjoying a business trip. "I'm an industrial designer," says she, not exactly lying since industry is intense and devoted activity and she is indeed engaged in design. Which industry she serves, we shall discover only later. Similarly true and nothing but true (as far as ever we are positioned to discover while watching this film) is her self-revelation as being "twenty-six and unmarried," although it is not (we may suspect soon) the whole truth: she is unmarried but does not seem unattached. Yet she caps her statement with a definitive, "Now you know everything." Eventually, I believe, the viewer concludes that Eve's attachments to other men are really not real, and that Roger does "know everything," even if it will be some time before he sheds enough fear or cynicism to see this himself. What I wish to point out here, at any rate, is that dialogue that has a slightly fishy smell when we hear it is in fact completely straight; and therefore things are not what they seem.

At any rate Roger, very much attached to a cynical view, now consciously and purposively adopts a pseudonym for the only time in the film—although he is not palpably endangered at this moment. Eve catches him in his deception, smoothly and imperturbably giving "correction" by insisting he is the person we have all along been recognizing—not "Jack Phillips" of "Kingby Electronics" but Roger O. Thornhill of Madison Avenue. Even though he would under other circumstances eagerly claim it for himself (most of his eager contribution to the Lester Townsend library scene is just such a claiming), the name "Roger Thornhill" is used in this circumstance as a label forced upon him by a person he is a little afraid of; a name—a label—in alignment with which he is now forced to reestablish himself. Further, it is a name connected to an identity vulnerable to transformation by others, such as the headline- and caption-writers of the newspaper Eve is carrying. Not just false identities can be laid upon us, then. What we might call authentic ones can, too. And so it is that even in being ourselves we may be compelled to do anticipatory following, orienting our activity toward others and taking clues from them as to how we should contrive to be. To some real extent, this taking of clues and reacting sensibly to the information that clues contain is the social life of which Roger Thornhill is such an adept.

Roger's social life, embedded as it is in his career as an advertising executive, focuses on communication and, therefore, potential ambiguity, construction, and conceit. Most people most of the time are not involved professionally in the fabrication of illusion, and make the assumption that the world should be interpreted at face value. This is precisely the assumption Roger typically capitalizes upon. To the same extent that the facile (and disingenuous) advertisements he concocts are taken as straightforward messages by consumers not in the know, messages to be attended to eagerly, the carefully edited "reports" in the daily newspaper—for instance, a headline story labeling Roger as a "murderer"—are taken as straightforward accounts by the same credulous audience. Roger, however, is not one of these gullibles, but a man fully informed about the possibilities of ideological manipulation—he gets paid very well for producing it—and he is therefore dismayed, yet not at all shocked, to find the compromising photograph of himself-as-killer on the front page of Eve's paper when he believes that in truth he killed nobody. Eve cannot yet be presumed by Roger to be in the same sort of show business. She must be taken as a woman who will tend to believe what she reads, so camouflage is necessary, and also useful, in the face of her prodding. That she doesn't take that newspaper any more seriously than he does is something Roger doesn't know yet.

Regarding Roger's camouflage, one delicious irony of the film is that it is not a necessary prop for dealing with the archvillain Vandamm (James Mason), since Vandamm's man did commit the murder of Townsend, on Vandamm's instructions, and Vandamm therefore shares with Roger a knowledge "above" that in the popular press. More: like Roger, and like the Eve Roger hasn't really met yet, Vandamm does not typically lower himself to read the news in newspapers,[7] and thus his utile fantasy that Roger is George Kaplan is not dissipated by the caption under that photograph definitively labeling the face as belonging to "Roger O. Thornhill." In this layer of the tissue of the plot lies something of an essay on social class, since in general those persons, like Vandamm and Thornhill, who make news are in no need of populist organs to bring it to their attention. They tend to own those organs, and

to shape the reporting. If in this case the newspaper is powerfully informative, leading the police to connect Roger with the murder knife, it is also low
enough an organ to escape the snobbish eye of Vandamm, who won't trouble
to think of Roger as Roger.[8]

Roger is not himself (neither real nor authentic nor whole), in fact, so long
as he is identified only on a front page, a pulp too palpably digestible by the
police and too far beneath the notice of Vandamm. His deep identity as a
non-murderous non-Kaplan can be established only by a higher and more
discreet power, the sort that endows the press with the ability to rename, or
at least reclassify, people who get written about in news stories because it represents the class interests that own the press, not the readers who are manipulated by it. Hitchcock knew that for substantiating, or at least regrounding,
a belief that Roger is who he says he is rather than the person he very clearly
seems to be to anyone looking at the pose in the photograph—that he is
Roger the innocent advertising man, not Roger the killer; indeed that he is
Roger, not George—it would be necessary to include an unimpeachable la-
beler, a mother (Jessie Royce Landis) with at least as much social clout as
Vandamm or the *New York Times* and a person for whom Roger can hardly be
anybody else than what she has named him. It is no accident that Mrs. Thornhill emphasizes her maternity and seems to look down her nose at the world.
Any other sort of mother would never manage to relieve us from the haunting worry that the dignified and erudite Vandamm might be correct, that
somehow without his knowing it (a completely believable eventuality, given
his blithe goofiness),[9] Roger might be Kaplan in truth. And this is a first clue
to the film's architecture. Once we have the vagaries of identification, we have
the power of appearance; once we have the power of appearance we have the
ability of the press, and of persons suitably placed, to miscast people (by mis-
displaying them). As miscasting is one particular way of looking down, it is
domination, and so once we have miscasting we have the possibility of snobbery. To trump the snobbery of Vandamm nothing will do but the greater,
and more authentic, snobbery of a matron who would sniffle at even him.
Mrs. Thornhill contributes to this film no other material weight and performs no function that could not be handled instead by a minor functionary.
She must be here in order to give some grounding to Roger's identity. Without mother, he is absolutely at sea.

He is surely at sea in the dining car with Eve. Eve puts him uptight, at least
because she finds him stimulating and says so. Though it is hardly ostensible
to us at this moment that Eve should imperil him—principally because as
moviegoers we are prepared, even eager, for the show of romantic coupling
these two are notably equipped to provide [10]—nevertheless Roger is afraid, at

least in posture. "Honest women frighten me," he admits. "Somehow they seem to put me at a disadvantage." The disadvantage Roger is talking about is sexual, presumably, because he hasn't mentioned "honest people" (and nothing of his behavior seems to queer him), but whether or not Eve Kendall also constitutes a threat to his survival is a central issue of the plot more broadly (one that can hardly have been framed for him at this moment), not really a sexual matter at all. Here in the dining car, as he waits for his rainbow trout, he has no reason to shrink from her beyond the simple fact of her femininity as a kind of nonmasculine otherness. If as a mother's boy he is (and presumably long was) accustomed to being overprotected, dominated, and lovingly demeaned, he has also learned to manipulate people and situations successfully. So his skillfully rendered trepidation, his Jack-Phillipsing, may be nothing other than a covert from which masterfully to take aim at this bird, his "fear" a kind of foreplay. Later, Hitchcock will give us to worry that Kendall really does threaten Thornhill (the Chicago station phone booth scene); and, later still, to recognize that Thornhill threatens her (the cafeteria at Mount Rushmore).

If we are not who we seem to be, if our genuine essence is inner and unknown; if others, indeed, cannot quite understand us, do we at least know ourselves? The game of hide-and-seek that proceeds from Roger's gambit at the dining car table (who is he really and who is his companion?), through Eve's gambit with her note to Vandamm (what side is she playing on?), through her collaboration with Roger in the train escape (can her relationship with Vandamm be fake, or has she set Roger up for a great fall?), through her telephone call to Leonard at Chicago Union Station (is she pretending to set Roger up for assassination, or really doing it?), through her behavior at the Ambassador East Hotel (what is her ultimate purpose for Roger?) and her performance later at Shaw & Oppenheim Galleries (how far, morally, is she willing to go to pursue her ends?), is about secret apprenticeship (as Garfinkel calls it) in the construction of identity, a dramatized Follow the Leader. Of this film we might ask, who is being, and who is merely apprenticing? Who experiences situations, and who, while apparently experiencing, is only subtly responding to cues being given by people who do not imagine themselves to be giving cues? Where, therefore, is performance?

And whose? It is worth considering that Roger is not alone onstage. Even as Vandamm has been manipulating and setting up the act called "George Kaplan" (as played out, embodied, by Roger), he has apparently, too, been manipulating and producing the nefarious "Eve Kendall" (played out by the patriotic Eve Kendall). She is also a desperate apprentice, and not only her identity but her life depends upon her skill. Roger gives her someone new to follow in her relentless surveillance just as she gives him someone new to pursue in his relentless search for mastery. (Before they met one another, these two were already on trajectories.) By the time the train pulls into Chicago, the woman's life has become a survival dance between the two Eves, Vandamm's and Roger's.

But there is a third face of Eve, belonging—or perhaps, appertaining—to a man we come to know only as the Professor (Leo G. Carroll).[11] This Eve is invoked with moral passion on the tarmac at Midway Airport, and also played to by Roger on a kind of stage at the cafeteria at Mount Rushmore, and also actually encountered, directly and face-to-face, for a few precious moments in the pine grove. In Vandamm's mountain aerie, Kendall is Vandamm's Eve planning to fly away, then Roger's Eve during the secret confabulation in the upstairs bedroom, ostensibly Vandamm's Eve but deeply Roger's Eve as she bravely marches to the landing strip, Roger's Eve fleeing in the car and running through the woods, drawn to the edge of the precipice, crawling upon the faces of the presidents, hanging on for her life, then raised up into the cramped "sardine can" (Roger's analogy) of the (matrimonial) upper berth in the finale. When I say she is Roger's, I do not mean, as Tania Modleski does, to suggest he wishes to own her, that throughout the film he is "hanging over precipices, scaling walls, and clinging, as it were, to nothing as he attempts to gain possession of the woman";[12] I mean she is the Eve he would recognize and comprehend, and therefore that in our own recognition and comprehension of her we adopt Roger's point of view. There is also, presumably, Eve's Eve, but *that* woman is not sufficiently rendered in the narrative that we may see her (this *lack of rendition* hardly to be taken as evidence that she is not her own woman, anymore than our not meeting Roger's father is to be taken as evidence that he did not have one). If, indeed, Eve's diegetic plasticity in the hands of men seems to make her the least dignified female in Hitchcock's American films, we may also estimate that her responsiveness, both political and moral, is dominant in order to give Hitchcock a needed center to his deep story, which is about neither love, nor espionage, nor flight, but appearance and how we learn to produce it. It is hardly just romantic submission to Roger that strains her. Like him, she is masterful at anticipatory following, but since her tutors keep changing, her apprenticeship is a torturous dance, one we are put in position to watch. Vandamm's Eve is a vamp, and should Roger end up with her his innocence will surely be corrupted. But his own Eve is a provocateuse, who may tickle him but will surely drag him down. Of all the Eves, the Professor's is the most tranquil, the most comforting, the wisest, the least strained, and the only one we can feel happy with for him. But Roger is a trained dominator: he liberates her from her thralldom to the government, privatizes her, appropriates her for his own glorification and use. This dynamic motif is spelled out in an elaborate verticality on the screen, with Eve hanging from the cliff, Vandamm hovering high above her, scornful, aloof; his henchmen, wounded or killed, all fallen beneath; and Roger just above her head holding her from the drop and then raising her up.

The Professor, at the end, is not with Roger but with Vandamm, founding a partnership in the rejection of—and by—Eve. Roger's appropriation of Eve is in his vertical lift, his "bringing her to his own level," his acknowledging her and redeeming her by strength. That Vandamm and the Professor look on from above—a little wiser, and resigned—is narratively possible because, though on opposite "sides" of the "political conflict" (that we never see elaborated onscreen), they share a rarefaction of intelligence, an urbanity, a worldliness that Roger, in his aggressiveness and purposiveness, lacks. The two are half-brothers, and in the Professor's cold and calculating abandonment of his fictive agent George Kaplan early in the film we can see the same steely, skillful utility of wit and manner by which the villain Vandamm is characterized throughout.

INTERMEZZO: THE EDGE OF THE WOODS

But this discussion, rationalizing a good bit of the dialogue and action of *North by Northwest*, leaves unaddressed the delirious sensation of excitement, and the precocity, of a film that even after being seen over and over persists in trapping us if we but glance at it from the corner of an eye. One never escapes being captured by jabbering Roger O. Thornhill as he emerges from that elevator with his secretary (Doreen Lang) and patters hello to the doorman whose wife isn't talking to him anymore. Though we can have calculated his every step and memorized his every word and gesture, to see him is to be caught by his preoccupations, to be enticed to overhear the tattoo of his conversation, to sneak into that taxicab and ride across town with him, to enter the Plaza for a drink in his company without having realized a thirst, and there, of course, to be snared. What is the spirit that resides beyond the mere explication of this story, the ambiguous substrate that is evident in, say, the sweeping, too-green vista of the Townsend estate as the limousine bearing Roger as prisoner glides into it; the syrupy bath of Vandamm's voice questioning Roger in the Townsend library; the microecology of postures in the elevator of the Plaza as Roger and his mother are bookended by the killers; the curious necking scene in the train compartment where Roger and Eve embrace one another with arms that seem to be separated from their bodies; the fact that Roger flees the attacking cropduster in a gray silk business suit;

the intoxicating tranquility of the pine grove *liebeslied*, with the perfectly pro-
portioned trees marking space upon the screen as Roger and Eve make an approach to one another; Eve's suit, in which with Roger she flees Vandamm's
house and hangs from the presidential monument—at twilight it is a radiant
apricot color that makes her swim in the air before our eyes. The *North by
Northwest* we must come to terms with, somehow, contains all these rich moments and touches, and hearing what characters say to one another, or noting what becomes of them, hardly helps.

One moment is especially stunning, even overwhelming, and no verbal
configuration of the story can do it justice. The filmic exposition utterly
dwarfs the narrative facts, and for a moment the screen vision makes the plot
disappear.

Roger and Eve are running for their lives through the woods:

> 1223.[13] LS: *Roger and Eve reach the edge of the woods, where several trees have been
> cut. They run forward across a bare space, into MS. Suddenly they stop, looking off-
> screen to the right rear of the camera.*
> 1224. ELS (*matte*): *Roger and Eve's POV. In the distance are the tops of three gi-
> gantic stone heads, perched on the edge of a mountain.*
> 1225. MS, *as at end of 1223.*
> ROGER: This is no good, we're on top of the monument!

The stunning moment I am referring to is in shot 1224. Let me try to de-
scribe it in a kind of reconstructive freeze. With Eve in tow, and with the music thundering, Roger has been fleeing two of Vandamm's thugs, Leonard
(Martin Landau) and Valerian (Adam Williams), through the dense woods
that abut the villain's property just outside Rapid City, South Dakota. Suddenly Eve has snagged her wrap on a tree. It is the lip of night, and an eerie
twilight highlights and metallicizes the apricot color of it enchantingly. The
music, in a 6/8 *agitato*, is frenetic, desperate, wild. But now two things happen, the first (in characteristic Hitchcockian fashion) an artful preparation for
the second. As (in shot 1223) the heroic fugitives hurl themselves forward
through the woods in our direction, because we have anticipated their
progress and are looking back at them as they advance, we suddenly see at the
sides of the screen that they are emerging into—and indeed thus realize that,
watching them, we are already standing in—a problematic space: "*the edge of
the woods, where several trees have been cut.*" Immediately as I see this I am put
on guard and confounded, because even though the forest thicket was an obstacle as from behind I raced after them through it (the trees reaching out ag-
gressively, as in *The Wizard of Oz*, and one even succeeding in grasping that

scarf), it was also, and principally, a haven of sanctity and security, a hiding place from pursuit by the very worst of men (and, as such, another version of the cornfield). But now, without warning—and shockingly—the nestling trees are gone. The forest—obstacle, but also haven—is suddenly at an end. I am somewhere else, somewhere I may very well not want to be. And what I feel at the apex of 1223, moving backward, is just this queasiness and uncertainty, a loss of a world—accomplished deftly in one quick shot because of what is peripherally apparent to the eye.

However, in shot 1224, and suddenly looking from Roger and Eve's point of view, I see that the awkwardness of my placement is ineffably greater than I supposed a fraction of a moment before. With a start—and the music at this instant has a desperately sharp and nauseating dissonant *tutti* chord resolving edgily into a brazen minor one—I see exactly where I am, which is to say, where I have somehow *already*, and quite unknowingly, been in train of going, in a vision accessible through a screen construction that has discrete elements. Night is falling, the last light dissolving away so that it is barely possible to discern topography with the eyes. Ahead, where there was formerly a skein of trees, there is vast openness, charged air, horrifying freedom. The ground beneath has ended. This is the edge of the world. As Roger and Eve have reached a precipice, continuity of action at this moment is itself a threat to continuity of life. But the small patch of ground ahead now appears neither sharp, nor straight, nor utterly cut off. There are huge rolling forms, petrified waves. It is just in the instant before the cut to shot 1225 [14] that they recognize their predicament by finding themselves, and at the same time they make their discovery I make mine, too. Therefore, as Roger speaks, his is nothing but the voice of my own self-awareness now making openly the horrifying pronouncement that has already been on the tip of my tongue.

We are on top of the monument! (Of course, had the scene been set earlier in the day, there would have been enough light to reveal the topography more readily, and the shock would have been diminished.) The shock is in my realization that in following Roger from the hospital, watching him crawl up the outside of Vandamm's house, and being engaged in his attempt to rescue Eve, I have been mounted to an unexpected and unobserved height by Hitchcock; that in fact no information was given at all about the topography of the area in which, with Roger, I moved. Then, at this moment I enter a direct relation with the filmmaker and know him to have been manipulating me throughout the narrative, not merely in terms of what I know but in terms of where I have been placed "physically" to know it. Finding myself at the top of Mt. Rushmore, I am aware in a fresh and chilling way of my incapacity as a viewer of this film to control my own movement.

Further, monuments are generally to be looked at, and one must typically be in front of and somewhat beneath them to do the looking. Monuments thus raise to thought the issue of organized perception, of audiences. To be at the top of the monument is perceptually to be in absolutely the wrong vantage from an audience's point of view. My identity as viewer is thus thoroughly, swiftly, shockingly compromised, because I am part of the thing that viewers line up to look at, even as I am caught looking. (I am not only high in the air; I am onstage.) Hitchcock was fascinated with the power arrogated to viewers by their complacent and commanding positions of view and we can consider this moment in *North by Northwest* as a reflection of earlier moments in his work: say, our sudden presence on the torch-bearing hand of the Statue of Liberty in *Saboteur* or behind the eyepiece of Jeff's binoculars at the instant that Lars Thorwald suddenly turns and sees him in *Rear Window*.

What Hitchcock designs is the sudden placement of his characters in positions that could not have been anticipated fully. With Roger and Eve, we have been positioned for a view we desired, even envied (the stone presidents themselves constitute a "viewing audience" with a spectacular panorama to "enjoy") but would never have chosen, safe down on the ground and staring eagerly through a viewing machine at the aerie from which it can be had. Equivalent in a significant way is Roger Thornhill's introduction to George Kaplan: he meets the man for the first time from an awkward and chilling point of view—within George Kaplan's body, at the instant that body is being kidnapped.

HIGH SOCIETY

You have to use a setting in its depth. It's not enough to say, "This is a background."

Hitchcock to Peter Bogdanovich

Shot 1224 is far from an isolated exploration of height in *North by Northwest*. Height seems to be everywhere in this film once we begin looking for it, even though the pretext of the narrative is a chase story across America in the direction of the new West.

In the opening shots, Thornhill is caught descending from a great height that represents his status and his narcissism, his control over (advertising) imagery and therefore his ability to manipulate knowledge and belief. The aerie from which he is taking a break invests him with a mask he dare not wear with his mother—at least, not when she is on the ground. By Mrs. Thornhill at the Glen Cove police court, and again at Lester Townsend's residence, he is henpecked and controlled, adolescent, subject to moral review—in short, lowered—and in the lobby of the Plaza he must be coy in order to gain her cooperation, the coyness betraying his elemental powerlessness. Yet when he is with her up in Room 796, he becomes an expert, leads action, casts off her frail attempt at controlling humor (when she is certain the invisible Mr. Kaplan has his suits mended by invisible weavers). Riding down with her in the Plaza elevator, however, as the kidnappers and other patrons flank him, Roger becomes the more a butt of Mrs. Thornhill's humor and the more her patsy the nearer the elevator comes to the ground. It is not just the antipathy of Licht (Robert Ellenstein) and Valerian that Roger escapes as he runs across the lobby, but also the old lady's reach.[15]

Much of the aggression and humiliation suffered by Roger is expressed vertically: Vandamm's henchmen descend with him out of the Oak Bar of the Plaza and into the limousine that bears them to Long Island. In Townsend's study, they force him down onto a chair so that Leonard can pour bourbon down his throat. In the vehicle intended to carry him to his death, Roger narrowly escapes the catastrophe of falling down into the surf as the wheels careen off the road and partly over the North Shore precipice. In the conclusion of this episode, asked by the medical examiner to walk a straight line, Roger decides instead to lie down on the court stenographer's table. Nor is the staging of Roger's experience at the UN a strictly lateral affair: though the Members' Lounge of the General Assembly is not on ground level, it is not, either, at the top of the Secretariat building, a point of view from which we stare directly down as Roger flees the scene after being photographed as the apparent killer of Lester Townsend. Therefore, it is not the intrinsic dramatic imperative of the setting that lifts us to a height, so much as the openness of the setting to the dramatic need of the filmmaker. Our perch outside the Secretariat is high enough that Roger seems little more than an insect crawling across a geometrical pattern on the ground. From this moral perspective the business of the murder of Townsend is little more than a graphic doodle to busy the eye momentarily—a clear enough signal, I think, that the film is about something quite beyond—quite above—the world of Townsends and Vandamms. Indeed, all the stage business of the killing is verticalized: the knifing is made apparent to us as Townsend, like a tree, careens forward into Thornhill's arms; then Thornhill crouches on the ground with the body, grasping the knife, while bystander-witnesses stare down at him. While Roger takes flight from the UN, our view of him from high above reduces the dramatic magnitude of that flight, and at the same time his persona, so that we are well prepared for the ensuing scene in Washington where Thornhill is discussed by distanced bureaucrats (higher-ups) as though his life is of no practical significance.

On the Twentieth-Century Limited, verticality is eroticized through embodiment as we focus on Roger's and Eve's relative height, a quality made overt by the cinematography of their embrace. A vertical relation between Roger and Eve is also evident in his standing while she sits in the dining car, and in the vertical play whereby she secretes him in the upper berth while lying casually on the seat beneath to withstand the interrogation of the visiting police. He will come to dominate her. At Union Station, Chicago, the mise-en-scène gives play to the vertical descent from the train, with the disrobed porter lingering on the railway car steps so he can look down at Roger exiting in his clothing. Roger is debased, a criminal in flight, grounded. Once an executive, he "is" now a menial, uniformed laborer carrying someone else's bags and, indeed, one small figure in a virtual army of such men, visible in a stunning shot from the ceiling of the main hall where redcaps seem suddenly, deliriously, to be everywhere.

I will discuss the celebrated cornfield scene, in which Roger is grounded quite literally, later. Here let me establish only that although the narration is set in a perfectly flat environment it is characterized by vertical presumption. That threat might descend in this scene is signaled at its outset, where we see in a high crane shot the entire expanse of territory in which action will take place. Finally Thornhill is crop-dusted like one of the insects he seemed to be as we watched from the top of the UN Secretariat. In Rapid City, all the cinematic action is vertically established, from the respectful gaze up toward the Mt. Rushmore monument by means of the telescope at the visitors' center, through the fake killing in which Roger drops to the floor, through his being knocked down by the Professor's park ranger assistant in the pine forest and his precarious escape upon the window ledge of the Rapid City hospital, his climb to Vandamm's veranda, his view of the (Frank Lloyd Wright–style) living room from the balcony above and his casting the matches down toward Eve's feet,[16] his overhearing Vandamm's plan to dispense of Eve "from a great height, over water," another of Vandamm's (lethal) airplanes descending for nefarious purposes, the pursuit downward over the faces on Mt. Rushmore, Leonard's final vertical threat (photographed from shoe level looking upward), the forest rangers' production of vertical salvation, and Roger's double vertical redemption of Eve.

I have avoided mentioning the most obvious verticality, which is our general journey from sea level in Manhattan to the relatively higher ground of South Dakota, in parallel with the increasingly exciting action in the plot. We go up with the story, in short, and descend rapidly to earth in the final moments, just as Eve is elevated into what we are to presume is bliss. And that is a fascinating final moment: if in fact elevation is a symptom of problematization—it surely was for us throughout the film—troubles may just be beginning for the new Mrs. Thornhill, who is now in a very good position for a healthy fall.[17]

A particularly delicious invocation of verticality and also a scene central in the turning of the action of the film that has received shockingly little serious consideration and, to my knowledge, no analysis in depth, is the auction at the Shaw & Oppenheim Galleries in Chicago. The auction is a steep one, in which various members of the *haute monde* wish to outbid one another— which is to say, ascend the economic ladder—for objects of great apparent value (appurtenances of high status). The very slight physical verticality— that the stage upon which the objects to be sold are first displayed is elevated; that the activity is generally organized around the objects elevated upon that stage—is a persistent visual code for the profound social verticality implicit in the action. "The essential point," said Hitchcock, "is that he is in an auction room and you must use the auction room."[18] Indeed, he is in the auction room because Hitchcock, who has ways of using an auction room, has sent him there.

Shortly after arriving on the scene, Roger is vituperative with Vandamm. Discussing Eve (and standing while she sits) he puts her down, though she is down already, and the residual warmth of our sympathy for her may well lead us to feel that, though he looms over her, he lowers himself with every negative sentiment he expresses. His heroism later, both in the pine grove and at Vandamm's, will thus seem a delightful surprise since—reversing completely the dramatic strategy George Bernard Shaw's sphinx announces in the prologue to *Caesar and Cleopatra:* raise a man very high before hurling him into the dust—Hitchcock here prepares the strength of an elevation by producing a declension that is, at least tonally, apparently shameful. Vandamm, for his part—though sensibly the villain—is elevated by his social acumen, his fine language, his chivalry on Eve's behalf, his bonhomie, to a status measurably above Roger's: he is the one prepared for a fall later. The treatment of Vandamm (a reflection of the development of the character of Tobin [Otto Kruger] in *Saboteur*) is interesting for its irony: Vandamm is an unknown socially, and so his "real" class and whether Roger's is above or below it are speculations we must make.

We will soon see that the lowering of Thornhill is also strategically vital, since if he is to save himself he must become the sort of rude social imbecile capable of misbidding egregiously in a setting such as this. Our acceptance of the vertical rhetoric, then, leads us to the belief that when he disrupts the auction, Roger, desperate and at the end of his rope, is actually descending into the vulgar, saying anything that comes to his unformed mind in order to get the attention of the auctioneer. Grant's comic performance is delicate and delicious here, as he leads us to go along with him in a kind of play version of the moment in a classic Hollywood swordfight (a play upon a play) when the hero's weapon is malevolently flicked out of his hand. We see him as culture-less, powerless because of his jealousy, unable to behave properly. His etiquette has flown off, or been lifted, and he remains the untutored claqueur we can deeply fear ourselves to be in the face of the sophisticated posture and masquerade visible in this room.

A careful view of the particular tactics utilized by Roger for gaining the upper hand at the auction house will reveal his actual power. In order to be able to move along the plane of the auction room floor—that is, to escape Vandamm's trap alive—he must first warmly antagonize, then ignite, and finally fan the displeasure of a crowd of meticulous socialites devoted to keeping up appearances and thus to never showing anger—or any other heat—in public. His misbidding can therefore never be haphazard (and simply dismissable), but must always as it escalates operate through a provocative process of acknowledging the social scene he is violating even as he violates it. Roger has just realized that he has a much better chance of survival if he goes to the police, but Licht and Leonard are covering his exits and there is no egress for him unless he can manage to produce social disarray.[19] The next item up for bidding is a canvas the auctioneer touts as likely to "enhance any collection of fine art." Two thousand two hundred and fifty dollars has been bid when Roger lurches into the fray: "Fifteen hundred!"

Hitchcock carefully prefaces Roger's gaffe for us by setting up three preparatory actions: first, Eve's departure with Vandamm and Roger's subsequent need to take action at all costs here and now; then, Roger's imprisonment in the social scene, this accentuated by the hushed and respectful tones of the crowd and the perfectly silent decorum of Licht's and Leonard's threats; and finally, a circumstantial context, the auction of a painting suitable for anyone's collection, in which we hear subtly invoked by the estimable auctioneer not only the august character of a "knowledgeable collector" of delicate refinement and limitless means (such as, in fact, Vandamm has appeared so far to be) but also, by implication, the comic antitype, an "ignorant Philistine" who will put anything in a frame and has no discernment, no cash, no breeding, no style—in short, the Roger who is here about to present himself. One more little issue: since both the auctioneer and the bidders are speaking from offscreen, neither we nor Roger can pinpoint where, or who, they are, and so we can neither focus on them nor be certain what they are saying.[20]

We are displaced topographically and dramatically, then, and can share some of Roger's alienation from the scene (even though, presumably, he is positioned to see and hear the players hidden from us). Indeed, the last bid we hear before the auctioneer calls twenty-two fifty is actually two thousand, so bids can be signaled silently outside our range of vision. The purpose of this artful construction is to make our "bumpkin Philistine" slightly more justified to us in his Philistinism, so hopelessly replete is his surround with indecipherable meanings. Otherwise, it could be slightly more difficult for us to sustain engagement with him. Further, even a hypothetical "knowledgeable collector" is justified in a misbid; Roger may be such a person. Roger's perfectly staged incompetence will appear as such only by degrees, then, and develop as such with only a tiny dramatic current of its own. All this architecture, I would emphasize, for one simple strategic purpose: so that when Roger makes this first "mistake," it is taken by both the auctioneer and the crowd, and by the viewing audience watching that crowd watching, to be an innocent one. We sympathize with him in his charming goofiness, because he is lost in this sea of sociability just as we, too (with the very best intentions that every viewer claims for his present reading), would be lost. The auctioneer's indulgent (and smiling) response? "The bid is already up to twenty-two fifty, sir."

What has happened is as far from a social rupture as one can get while behaving incorrectly. It is a mild acoustical dysfunction, an anomaly, not even half the size of a *faux pas*, because not even a genuine *pas*. Roger is still "sir." His next move takes him one step up the ladder of deviance,[21] as he becomes a little willful, a little insistent, perhaps even eccentric, a man in need of special treatment and one calling attention to himself as such in this effete domain where invisibility is *de rigeur*: "I . . . I still say fifteen hundred." What a glance he gives Leonard! It says, to my eye, "You cannot without disgracing yourself make a move upon me." He is seated, after all, in officially sanctioned conversation, an auction being little other than a dialogue with a stamp of approval upon it. Žižek has written zestfully on the centrality of the defense against self-disgrace in this and other Hitchcock.[22] Roger's cue also reminds Leonard the actor who is performing Leonard the interested bystander, "Your persona is socially beneath mine (i.e., you are no bidder) so you do not hold the position from which you can give the public impression of presuming to look down your nose at the idiosyncrasy of my comment."

The power to define (label) Roger now passes to the prevailing agent of social order, the auctioneer (Les Tremayne), who treats him, gently, as a mild nuisance to be ignored if at all possible: the man repeats that he has twenty-two fifty, and beckons the crowd to offer him twenty-five. After the auctioneer's second call, and just before his third—thus with aplomb in timing that perfectly illustrates a deep and true familiarity with the auction scene he is expertly otherwise hiding—Roger makes another noise: "Twelve hundred!" This time, inability to gauge the script of the proceedings can no longer be proffered by anyone as Roger's excuse. Nor is he merely an eccentric who wishes to be funny. He is persisting in the face of disattention, a child who will not take a polite reproof and who must be overtly chuffed. There is a murmur and the crowd turns to look at Roger, focusing him, if only briefly, with their sharpest and most punitive gaze. Here is a beautiful expression of a common tactic in social control. After attempting and failing at a polite disregard in hopes that the offender might notice himself not being noticed and give appropriate self-correction (since being socially noticed, particularly as film would have it, is being), moral docents proceed to the employment of their capacity-to-gaze as isolation, appellation, and censure. *Peek-a-boo, I don't quite see you,* followed closely by *You there!* (as the song goes, "You and nobody else but you!"), leading soon enough, if necessity is felt, to *Stop!* Stratificationally the gaze is from above, embodying power to correct and deny. In this scene, the auctioneer is above, and he directs this activity from his pulpit.

But the isolating gaze, however reproachful or sincere its intent, is precisely the treasure Roger the artful dodger most fervently desires to filch from the pockets of the earnest Brownlows who constitute this crowd! Absent this gaze, Roger can be eradicated by Vandamm's men without anyone paying heed. Now, however, he is on a little stage-before-the-stage, a forestage, and the crowd's upright (and uptight) stares illuminate him boldly. As the auctioneer announces that the painting has been sold for twenty-two fifty, and prepares to move on to the next item, Roger is positioned for an even bolder move, a bravura *ritard,* stalling on the painting just when the auctioneer wants to escape it for another triumph. "Twenty-two fifty?" he opines, "for that chromo?"[23] A long shot epitomizes the social distance that the immaculate and sanctimonious crowd—and the immaculate and sanctimonious viewing audience identifying with this crowd's penchant for order—would love to establish from this clochard. In fact, of course, the painting really is a "chromo"—any colored artifact (and especially one shot in Technicolor®) could be called that—yet the term seems derogatory in the refined air that has been lent it by the stuffy sententiousness of the proceedings and the bidders' eagerness to inflate themselves in their purchasing. Roger O. Thornhill is a creature of profound social skill, however; from Townsend's house to the Plaza, from his behavior on the train to his grace on the prairie we have seen that. He has no trouble distinguishing a real art lover from a pretentious (Chicagoan) socialite trading money for social standing in an elite sanctum such as this. (There is a rendering of *The Great Gatsby* just beneath the surface here.) And given what he knows, his comment about the "chromo" is especially well turned, the minimum quantity of fissionable material precisely placed to create the surest destruction.

The audience buzzes and the auctioneer looks shocked, thrown off his stride, though he has done this routine a thousand times. Vandamm's thugs are getting edgy. When the auctioneer suggests an opening bid of seven hundred and fifty for "A Louis Quinze carved and gilded . . ."—Roger interrupts with a *coup de grâce*, a pronouncement of the one question this and all other manifestations of the art world are built upon cloistering, the one question that blows the keystone in any auction house arch: "How do we know it's not a fake? It looks like a fake." Well, indeed, how *do* buyers know that what they're buying in auction houses aren't fakes? The items do precisely look like fakes, in the sense that fakes designed for such circumstances are made to look authentic. It is in the very nature of fakery that things should look like fakes, exactly as fakes look like the things they are faking.

But at this instant in the film I take Roger to be speaking about the whole construction, not just this item and not just this auction. He himself looked like George Kaplan, and was a fake—of this he is ineffably certain. Kaplan is also a fake, though Roger does not know it yet. Both Vandamm-as-Townsend and Townsend himself look pretty much like fakes, wooden, scripted, mechanical. All these actors, indeed, look just a little bit like fakes—an artifice, not a failing, of Hitchcock's. The paintings in Townsend's study looked like fakes, all done literally from the same palette. An interesting point about Eve, and one that has not yet occurred to Vandamm—who left the proceedings before this edifying little query of Roger's—is that she, too, looks like a fake, just a little too prim and nicely behaved. This is perhaps most evident as we look at her reclining in her sleeper on the train and looking up to the fat detective who is interrogating her. She is like a doll configured to take a reclining posture, every hair in place. Roger's earlier clue, that Vandamm, Eve, and Leonard made "a picture only Charles Addams could draw," was apparently lost on Vandamm (who doesn't stoop from *Country Life* to the *New Yorker*): perhaps, also, on us.

The art world—at least the classical art world represented in this scene— depends on authenticity and provenance, on pedigree. And the issue of hereditary purity, it turns out, is invoked from the beginning of this film in Roger's relations with his mother and her crowd (reflected even at the Townsend mansion in Glen Cove); in the use of the Plaza of all possible hotels; in the awkward play of social class on the prairie (the conglomeration of costumes after the crash of the crop-duster). By suggesting even obliquely that Shaw & Oppenheim would auction fakes, and that the members of this sophisticated audience could be sufficiently ignorant as to be duped by them, and therefore that the basis of the buyers' current investments may in fact be unstable and their bought prestige thus tinny and nothing but a manipulation of surfaces, Roger has struck a central nerve, but also reflected obliquely some overriding concerns of the film. He has committed, too, a masterpiece of social manipulation, motivating at least one particular total stranger, a matron who has every good reason in a situation like this to maintain at all expense a bloated masque of effeteness and dignified reserve in the face of any noxiousness, to erupt: "Well, one thing we know. *You're* no fake. You're a genuine idiot!" This eruption, of course, is the first real tactical component of his defense, and so in rejoining, "Thank you," Roger is being nothing but genuine. Indeed, as he has been demonstrating for some minutes that he is in fact a genuine genius, the matron's comment (and it must come, in this film, from a matron, in order that the director's view of the other "matron" who criticizes and belittles Roger on a regular basis should be perfectly clear) is a revelation of her blindness, a testament that she really has come to this place tonight not to discern but to be in the company of hollow, esteemed, imperceptive people, highly praised objects, and large sums of money. When he thanks her, there is no intended irony, since she is making a terrible sacrifice in providing the little explosion that will save his life: after all, the masque she is wearing is that of an Estimable Citizen and Social Pillar. When she opens her mouth to block his tactical advance, her reserve of *hauteur*, all built of composure, is (perhaps forever) lost.

On the other hand—and the point I would drive home here is, Roger knows this—one offended matron is hardly, on her own, sufficient infantry to mobilize the good gentry of Chicago. The gentry, sexist as they are, will disown her reaction as overabundant, feelingful, frivolous, impecunious, feminine. She has become enthused, but Roger must take further, and much more explicit, action to cause a band to form around her as its core. He becomes a terrorist.

The first step is a dutiful and acquiescent entry into the social contract he is about to smash. If he cannot yet be impounded for aggression upon the state of order, action will surely be taken when he breaks his word, if he is indeed the "gentleman" he is pretending to be:

AUCTIONEER (*to Roger*): I wonder if I could—respectfully—ask the gentleman to get into the spirit of the proceedings here?
ROGER: All right. I'll start it at eight.
AUCTIONEER (*smiling in relief*): Eight hundred. Thank you.

This is an important dialogue. "Getting into the spirit of the proceedings," we must admit, is a far cry from adhering to the legal obligations of the engagement to trade. It is an entirely voluntary commitment, and not even one of intelligence, that the auctioneer is seeking from Roger. And the desperation of the moment—the "respectfulness" of the asking—can lead us to see that this request is in fact a limiting one, a last-ditch attempt to secure the very minimum commitment the auction house is in a position to require from its itching guests, that they at least play as if they are bidding (which is, of course, what all Hitchcock's extras are perforce here doing). Auctions of this sort are not formal structures of obligation and control but loose affiliations of like-minded and like-feeling individuals willing to play with one another at competing for valuables no one of them is supposed, in truth, very painfully to want. One should be able to lose an item, in other words, without going psychotic. Vandamm's earlier, and suaver, behavior during the auction sale of a figurine can now be seen in retrospect as a preparation for this, since he never showed outwardly how desperate he must have been in truth to get his hands on that object. And others in the room, bidding against him, might have been either innocent dupes caught in the belief they were just having fun at an evening of competitive shopping, or, indeed, serious competitive shoppers: by which I mean, spies working for other governments and trying casually to outbid him for whatever was contained on the film we will much later see is hidden inside this instrument.[24] However purposeful and serious the shopping, nevertheless, shopping is clearly seen by the forces of control (the auctioneer and his assistant) as a matter for the willful engagement of spirit, not the apparently cynical interplay of status and power. Join in nicely. Have a good time. Shopping is thus a type of innocent play here, not an economic mechanism for the rational (orderly) distribution of scarce goods to a competitive market.[25]

If Roger is asked to play nicely, however, he is only too happy to comply, since he really does intend to play—indeed, with the very structure of this event in order to turn it to his purposes. And when he says he will start at eight—"eight," not "eight hundred" or "eight thousand"—he is being as precise in his language as at every other moment in this film, the perfect advertiser. In reading "eight" as "eight hundred," the auctioneer is merely continuing to make use of a sophisticated signal system for encoding intent—we have seen it in play in some bidders' choreographic gestures and now hear its aural aspects as well. Of course "eight" means "eight hundred"—could only mean "eight hundred" and could never be imagined to mean anything but "eight hundred," although "eight" is always, also, "eight." It is the auctioneer's game the auctioneer believes Roger is nicely playing, a game that is a context for resolving the ambiguity of speech.

The scenic movement is now doubled, as from the auctioneer's highly interpretive point of view everything Roger says for the next several moments can imply a slightly fractious but thoroughly respectful "war-playing" according to the "rules" of the "game." Taking Roger at face value, we understand a bidding gap of a wholly different order to have been opened, one that is so very huge the auctioneer's complete failure to take note of it can only be seen as utterly laughable. I put the implied readings in square brackets:

> AUCTIONEER (*offscreen*): Nine hundred. One thousand is bid. Go twelve? [Will someone offer twelve hundred?]
>
> ROGER: Eleven. [I said eight dollars. I now offer eleven dollars.]
>
> AUCTIONEER: Eleven [hundred] is bid. Thank you [for complying with my suggestion (and being so well-behaved)]. Go twelve [hundred dollars]. I have eleven [hundred dollars]. (*offscreen*): Go twelve [hundred dollars]. Who'll say twelve [hundred dollars]? Eleven [hundred dollars] once. Who'll say twelve [hundred dollars]? Eleven [hundred dollars] twice. . . .
>
> *Roger looks over his shoulder at the back of the room. A man in the last row raises his hand.*
>
> AUCTIONEER (*offscreen*): Twelve [hundred dollars], thank you. Twelve [hundred dollars] is bid. I have twelve [hundred dollars]. Go thirteen [hundred dollars]. Who'll say thirteen [hundred dollars]?
>
> ROGER [*breaking the spell*]: Thirteen dollars!
>
> *The audience bursts into laughter.*

The audience may well seem to be slow on the uptake laughing at this juncture, since we have been laughing ever since Roger started the bidding, fully aware that his mounting bids are not meant in the "spirit" in which the auctioneer is taking them. But the tables in that room have been completely turned, and now it is the auctioneer and his assistant who are at odds with the general spirit—the spirit having suddenly, thanks to Roger, become one of hilarity and revolution. "You mean thirteen *hundred*, sir," he is forced to frown, spoiling the fun in the name of business—a taboo. Roger is about to become the enemy, the imputed cause of aggressive intrusion, so Roger must again seize the day. He throws a javelin: "No, I . . . I mean thirteen dollars. That's more than it's worth!" This last comment is a direct insult to all the decent burghers sitting around him, who have been acting as though they recognize value when they see it (even without expertise, for what is wealth but presumption?) and now find themselves confronted with the suggestion that they have been stupidly and hugely overbidding. They are happy to throw money away, but they do not wish to appear foolish while doing so. Blood, as it were, has been drawn. As the auctioneer goes about his business of regaining the floor, we see his assistant whisper to his stenographer, who picks up a telephone.

The telephone is the sacred, or lethal, instrumentality—we can think back to the phone at Union Station, from which Roger's escapade to the cornfield was arranged, and the phone in Room 796 of the Plaza, on which a nefarious voice murmurs, "You answer his telephone and you live in his hotel room, and yet you are not Mr. Kaplan." Roger seems saved for an instant, but perhaps not swiftly enough. He needs a climactic move. When the auctioneer gives a last call at twelve hundred, the hero pounces: "Two thousand!" If he is as wildly unpredictable as this (that is, to the crowd, innocent of his abysmal predicament)—he is out of control. The contrarian revolutionary mode is one thing, and can be rationalized as clowning, but this is rank tempestuousness, a dire threat to any centripetality and any pattern. Questioned, Roger ups it to twenty-one hundred. Balked at, he suggests twenty-five. The audience is getting noisy. "Would the gentleman *please* cooperate?" begs the auctioneer, desperately clinging to the epithet that is his only raft. The assistant auctioneer (Olan Soule) now lights the fuse by obstreperously announcing that the last bid was twelve hundred—in short, that nothing that comes out of Roger's mouth need be recognized at all. "Twenty-five hundred!" the "madman" proclaims. "My money is as good as anybody's." And in fact it would be, most certainly, even though the crowd has begun to think otherwise, if Roger had any money in his pocket. He doesn't, and rarely does in this film—I will come to this later—because he's no real spender. He is establishing the bona fides of his dignity, at any rate, and the auctioneer is moving on to disregard him when, after another final call at twelve hundred, Roger offers "Three thousand!" and the auctioneer, deaf to his voice, brazenly sells off at twelve hundred.

This is a precipitous juncture, because now the auctioneer has been pressured to arbitrarily disconnect from the action an engaged bidder who is operating in the "spirit" of the event. He is destroying his own auction. Because he has openly set a posture, on behalf of the auction house, of gaining the highest possible sale price (even appearing greedy in doing so); because Roger has never once lied; because Roger has complied utterly with the auctioneer's request that he get into the spirit of the entertainment; and because now Roger has in fact offered more than twice the current bid for the item; Roger is entirely within his rights—and also perfectly comprehensible (to us and any other observer) as being so—when he takes offense at the auctioneer's

move and its open, even vulgar, insulting import (while in truth, it is a move
he helped engineer). "Now, I'm not going to let you get away with that!" cries
he. "That's not fair!" A large, well-dressed man starts to move toward Roger,
indeed, since even this comment cannot socially be registered from such an
"incompetent," and the camera pans to follow him into the confrontation. "I
think you'd better leave, sir," the man says, taking Roger's sleeve. Roger now
snaps: "You take your hands off me, or——"

He has been counting on the presence of men such as this self-nominated
hero, slavish in their obedience to the authority of the gallery and as insensi-
tive of dignity, fairness, honesty, and gentlemanliness as they are devoted to
an image of themselves as artistic, cultured, urbane, sophisticated, and privileged. Defense of the auctioneer by thugs like these is the light at the end of
Roger's tunnel. Roger will punch the man just as the police enter to observe,
providing the perfect reason for them to haul him away (to safety). A vertical
structure—this time social, not spatial—has been put in place to gain our attention and set us up for deception. Roger is manipulating the stratification
system to cause a toppling. He is no bumbler, but an architect. So again, he
is not what he seems. What he has done to the genteel normativity of an auction room in this "scene" that he has had Roger "make," Alfred Hitchcock
does with all the situations depicted in his films.

A Perverse Consumer

The class order invoked openly in the auction sequence, and implied
throughout the film, was a central feature of America by the late 1950s and
lingered through all Hitchcock's American work as a predominant—if
subtle—intellectually charged concern. In the first week of March 1939,
Hitchcock had crossed the Atlantic,[26] changing artistic horses, as it were, in
midstream. Whereas the suspense and architecture of his English films had
been firmly set upon a foundation of traditional authority, distinct class structure, and the etiquette and linguistic grace requisite in a small island society,[27]
his American films would open themselves expansively to a frontier of possibility represented ultimately by existential crisis, dramaturgical confounding,
and the cash nexus where desires meet things: as Karal Ann Marling puts it,
describing a central film of the 1950s, "In the form of Cadillacs, oil wells, private planes, mink stoles, twin beds, and dresses from Neiman-Marcus, civilization has clearly tamed the frontier."[28]

There are no American Hitchcock films in which the consumer society is
not pointedly reflected or thematically central. *Rebecca*, the transitional work,

conceived in England but shot in the United States, is, finally, about a headstrong girl gaining material advantage by swapping one employer for another. In *Foreign Correspondent* Johnny Jones is in Europe to flog a story in the popular press. *Mr. and Mrs. Smith* is about the marriageable woman as product. Johnnie Aysgarth in *Suspicion* is a penniless roué with consumption troubles. Barry Kane in *Saboteur* is trying to prevent malevolent traitors from selling out the United States and in the climax triumphs over a villain who didn't spend enough money on his tailoring. The roué returns in *Shadow of a Doubt*, where Uncle Charlie murders wealthy widows he has seduced for their fortunes; he is ultimately exposed because instead of buying his niece a gift he passes her a used—and engraved—emerald ring. The consumer society is mocked up in miniature in *Lifeboat*, where symbols pass for the objects they represent, and trade in suspicion and information flourishes in an atmosphere of covetousness. Central to the diegesis—if invisible—in *Spellbound* is a lunch at Twenty-One, in the 1940s a gastronomic heaven for high consumers. High consumption is typically the prerogative of financiers and spies, or spies dressed as financiers, the central figures in *Notorious*. In *The Paradine Case*, a narratively central love affair instances romantic theft, a shadow of consumption. In *Rope*, the cowardly but wealthy killers celebrate with conspicuous consumption—a chicken banquet. In *Under Capricorn* Charles Adare meets Sam Flusky because he wants to know how to get rich. The climactic interaction of *Stage Fright* centers around a star offering her maid a healthy gratuity. *Strangers on a Train* is about an exchange of services. Father Michael Logan of *I Confess* is forced to own knowledge he does not want—involuntary consumption. A cupidinous man in *Dial M for Murder* cravenly fingers money before thinking, and is thus trapped in a murder scheme. *Rear Window* is about the consumption of images, and also Jeff Jefferies's squeamishness about marrying a shopper; the hero of *To Catch a Thief* steals the heart of a girl who could buy anything; *The Trouble with Harry* positions a corpse as an object of trade; *The Man Who Knew Too Much* puts consumer tourists in a position where all the money in the world won't help them; *The Wrong Man* is about a misperceived theft; *Vertigo* centers on the reconstitution of the dead through middle-class shopping; *Psycho* is about inadvertent consumption, because Marion Crane slides imperceptibly from guarding $40,000 to stealing it. We find bird-shopping at the architectural center of *The Birds*; identity-shopping and safecracking in *Marnie*; shopping for mathematical secrets at the center of *Torn Curtain*; the Communist rejection of consumerism at the center of *Topaz*; the Covent Garden market at the center of *Frenzy*; and at the center of *Family Plot* both a bishop held for ransom and a pesky inheritance. In *North by Northwest*, as William Rothman points out, a great deal, even a character, is reduced "to the status of a commodity bought and sold."[29]

It is easy to mistake *North by Northwest* for a featherweight picaresque, a thriller that is essentially comic, full of "outlandish adventures,"[30] and many of its admirers have done so.[31] Peter Bogdanovich, indeed, deems it "pure entertainment."[32] The central motor element of the forced journey northwestward has been lauded—credibly—as an adventure.[33] Roger O. Thornhill has been obsessively studied for his roguish charm (one of Cary Grant's trademarks, of course: James Naremore calls him the "ideal male fashion model" and points to his "unpretentious casualness" and "lack of vanity"),[34] as though he is a Candide at play in the Metropolis, Vandamm his parodic Pangloss. But following Roger as an innocent or fawning over him as a lover involves commitments of attention that blind us to one of his central preoccupations, which happens as well to have been a favorite focus of the man who made him: money. A fan of his adventure may forget that Roger is not merely a New York executive in a gray silk suit, a man as at home in the mansions of Long Island as in the Oak Bar of the Plaza, and a holder of tickets to a rave Broadway show, which is to say, a paragon of middle-class virtue, but a high-class salesman.

As such, he is the butt of a particularly tasty joke and the agonized sufferer of a special torment. In the consumer paradise that was America of the late 1950s, advertising had become the epitome of language, with the effect that billboards and magazine ads were both poetry and art while remaining the cash nexus. Soon later, Rauschenberg and Warhol would reflect this. Advertising genii were fabulously wealthy and they controlled the cash flow of the society at large, since consumption was the piety of the age. As a supreme Madison Avenue ad man, Roger typifies this glorious potency of financial fluidity. But because he makes the slogans that sell us the merchandise, he sees through the things and persuasions of the marketplace and there is no product true enough to rouse his desire. As he is himself a siren, he can be lured by no siren song. He is therefore cast (in terms compatible with a strictly economic and consumerist logic) as a man cut off from meaning, since he is impotent to shop.[35] Without the violence of resentment and the rage that produces it, Roger experiences the world as a sea of fragmentation. He sees objective, desirable, material, frangible reality even *a priori* as a maelstrom of shards, sales angles, demographics, come-ons, exaggerations, appealing luminescences, provocations, and shadows. Having sold everything and anything, Roger is having a crisis of conviction, and one could argue that George Kaplan comes along just at the right moment—a perfect entity to entice, solidify, and frame his belief before, at the end of its tether, it expires altogether.

We may begin an examination of Roger's perversity with a moment when, searching for George Kaplan, he cavalierly declines to take sound—but free, and thus, in his logic, unacceptable because valueless—advice.[36] The reference is to the celebrated cornfield encounter at Prairie Stop/Highway 41, a scene in which our protagonist fails to board a bus (green, like the one Hitchcock himself attempts to board at the beginning of the film, and thus a token of his redeeming, teasing presence).[37] There he encounters a man who, while noting a plane "dustin' crops where there ain't no crops,"[38] invites him to enter the bus and ride back the way he came. As the door closes behind him, indeed, this man (Malcolm Atterbury) turns to give Roger a regretful look. The observation about the plane is an overt warning from a local expert, delivered just in time for Roger to escape. But as the man's name is not George Kaplan,[39] he and his conversation have no transactional value. Hitchcock takes care to point out to us both Roger's complete disattention to this man and the man's civil good nature and plain honesty.

The fictional locale for this sequence and this uninspired failure on Roger's part—it was photographed in fact near Bakersfield, California—would have been at or near the Greyhound flagstop at St. John, Indiana,[40] a vast but uninspiring locale. The lack of inspiration—by which I mean, wind—is notable, and technically relevant to Roger's immediate future. The windlessness of the place is inscribed for us when a fourteen-wheeler labeled "Zephyr" blows past Roger from the north. It symbolizes wind, of course, but here—both in the diegetic vastness of the monumental tranquillity and emptiness and in the domain of film—the symbol is all we have. Almost instantly, in a whoosh, it is gone. So it is that when Roger flees from the attacking plane into a waiting cornfield (in a reprise of the finale of Robert Aldrich's *Apache* [1954]) and the pilot, making a pass overhead, releases insecticide upon him, the poisonous cloud merely drops among the stalks: there is no wind to carry it aside. As a result, to avoid asphyxiation Roger must make a run for it. He encounters a second large truck (green again), this time stepping onto the road so that lurching to a halt it almost flattens him (although, a screen type, he is already flat).[41] The plane crashes into the truck ("awkwardly," says Brill),[42] there is an explosion, and Roger is forced to steal a vehicle to escape the scene. He has become a thief and has narrowly escaped death by strafing, by poisoning, by collision, and by fire, all in the press of only a few moments in a war zone in the middle of nowhere, and because he would not take free advice.

What if he had, however? Borne into nowhere by a bus from Chicago by way of Gary, Indiana, discovering no one at the appointed rendezvous, he might have followed the stranger's hinted advice, climbed aboard the bus on the other side of the road, and ridden back to Chicago. He comes to the Ambassador East Hotel and seeks out Eve Kendall, quite oblivious that an attempt was planned on his life and has now been aborted. Eve is evasive, shocked to see him—because in fact she helped set up the ambush (in order to elaborate the cover identity created for her by the Professor). She waits until she has trapped him pantless in the bathroom, then escapes to the auction at Shaw & Oppenheim. Roger eventually follows, having read her destination from the bedside telephone pad in her hotel room. He walks into the auction, sees her, approaches, and discovers . . . Vandamm and Leonard. He is shocked at this grouping, to be sure, but can still muster the sanctimony to make deprecating comments about Eve and insult the dignity of Vandamm. Vandamm threatens him, makes a bid for the sculpture, and strides out.

The reader familiar with *North by Northwest* will already be murmuring, "Yes, all of this is exactly what does happen in the film." In short, nothing in the ultimate configuration of Hitchcock's plot needs to change if Roger does *not* confront the plane in the cornfield, except two elements that can now be seen as vital, since a principal intent of the cornfield sequence is to place them in the film.

First, the wisdom of a stranger, a vitally important product. Roger displays a haughty disregard for it, though it is offered openly and freely with no price tag, a pure manifestation, therefore, of neighborly civility. Here the civility is dramaturgically modest; one must find oneself in the open, with no distractions at all, to catch its subtlety. The importance of the wisdom is established in retrospect, by the magnitude, elaborateness, malevolence, and general dramatic flair of the flamboyant strafing sequence, emphatic in order to reveal to us that the simple line uttered by the man we have never seen before— "That's funny . . . That plane's dustin' crops where there ain't no crops"—is in fact hugely pregnant with importance and forewarning. Indeed—lest it be thought I am aggrandizing the man's contribution to the story, since in fact his "offer" is taciturn and entirely an implication, he need say very little if anything beyond refuting that he is the Kaplan Roger has come to the lonely place to meet. If he fails to mention the oddity of the cropduster "where there ain't no crops," nevertheless, once he has boarded his bus and departed, Roger will be shocked by the sudden approach of the plane on a trajectory to strafe him—just as he is. The man's comment can function only to warn the sort of person attentive enough to take warning. The cornfield scene makes it pos-

sible for Roger to meet this kind of man (a denizen of this territory), then disattend him and the wisdom he gives freely.

The cost to Roger of this disattention is the second principal element of
the scene: demotion. He is no longer a man above the economy—a con-
troller, a manipulator, a power so aloof that getting and spending will never
vitiate him. Until now he has been accused of a crime he did not commit, and
so his flight is comic. But in this scene he detaches himself from the hegemony of the economy by taking somebody else's pick-up truck: an event the
importance of which is emphasized for us choreographically, as the cowboy
who owns it runs down the road after him, doing a strange frustrated little
dance as the exhaust trail vanishes. Roger is in the world now, running for his
life, his interactions no longer diversions for pleasure and his attitudes no
longer poses to entertain someone else.

Back to "Zephyr." That massive truck, when it is not doubling in a movie
scene as a symbolic element, is in real life the mainstay of the economy Roger
Thornhill touts for money. Tractor-trailers were developed for the trans-
portation of manufactured goods across broad distances—interstate com-
merce. But Roger, vital as is his connection with the commercial world, is un-
moved by its momentum, untouched by the flash of its progress down the
road beyond getting a little dust in his eye that he can quickly wipe away. Both
information and goods on the move fail to attract him because he is not a
transactor, he is a man for whom transaction is itself a product. We may have
seen that his perverse distance from the consumer business was touched upon
directly at the origin of the film, in the very cerebellum of consumer culture.
As consumerism is inseparable from advertising, I mean, of course, Madison
Avenue.

Let's move (at last) to that origin. At the beginning of *North by Northwest*
Roger is emerging from the C.I.T. Financial Building[43]—the brand new
C.I.T. Financial Building, I might add, built by Harrison and Abramovitz and
completed just before shooting began—at 650 Madison Avenue between
59th and 60th Streets,[44] around the corner from those pleasure dens of the
magnate and commercial class, respectively, the Metropolitan Club and the
Copacabana.[45] Directly, and with profound significance for his fate in our
narrative, we apprehend a potentially disturbing fact about him. Although to
all appearances he has his secretary Maggie in tow, he does not really control
her; Maggie, indeed, controls him. It is true that without his physical guidance, because she is taking his dictation, it is somewhat difficult for her to
navigate forward on the sidewalk through the dense crowd of pedestrians[46]—
to proceed through the diegesis, that is, since at this time we are dollying

backward in their path as she walks with him. But all of Roger's business ap-
pointments—say, his future—are in her calendar, not his. Roger's situation
at this moment therefore anticipates Godard's *Le Mépris* (1964), in which the
Lumières will remind us, "Il cinema è un invenzione senza avvenire."[47] If
Maggie is Roger's future, and if he is to be thoroughly cinematic as the Lumières would have it, he must lose her. Presto: the Oak Bar of the Plaza, a
male preserve (at least in Roger's company). But losing Maggie is not as safe
as it seems. Without her, we learn on the sidewalk outside the 59th Street entrance to the hotel, he cannot even contact his mother (whom we may with
some justification call his past). Lacking both these women, Roger is trapped
quite wonderfully (like the viewer) in the present. Having spent his days
hawking experiences (and the material goods by means of which to attain
them), he is now trapped inside one. His capacity (again like a viewer's) is myopia: to see clearly what is directly before him, but without an overall vision
of where things lead. Roger's local vision is especially acute. He notices
things, draws them to our attention. But he remains lost in the existential forest and often cannot take from others, in a civilian exchange, information that
could point him the way. If conventional experience is something we buy and
sell in negotiation with other social beings, Roger is outside this social market as much as any other.

Roger's freedom from the conventional economy, the alienation from motive and exchange implicit in the fact that he spends almost no money, distances him from the burden and treasure of value, since he has no grounds on
which to discriminate between what is cheap and what is priceless. His perverse incapacity to be informed (to gain a purchase on information) is an economic riddle at least as much as an intellectual one, a manifestation of his
stubborn need to dominate the informational exchange of others (which is
what advertisers do as a matter of course), but also evidence that other
people's points of view aren't yet worth much to him. This is in part an occupational hazard for Roger. In a society fully shaped by advertising—which is
to say, by the powers of advertising executives—the very objectivity of our
world of reference is an artifice, a mask. Talking about our world, we refer not
to things but to products. We take our language, our news, our sense of the
real, our very dream from consumption designers. In this way, our talk is only
the package called "dialogue." Roger, a maker of that package, can hardly also
regard it as experiential bedrock, and so when characters offer him a helpful
word he perceives it only as one more hype.

More than hype, advertising is an ideal form of theft, in the limited sense
that it falsely promises to exchange for the shopper's cash an artifact of in-

tense value and utility, of completeness, of pure and satisfying character. The product in mundane fact does not satisfy, and boasts only a limited utility, else further and repeated sales, a central requirement of consumerist mass production, are not guaranteed. In consumerism, the present must predict the future absolutely; and can do so only by being a failure. Personified by Cary Grant, Thornhill seems far too genteel to sink to theft maliciously and so he performs it with dignified panache,[48] typifying himself as a charmer who could never transact as he urges everyone else to, at market. What a catalogue of thievery he authors! He begins by scheming to lift the absent Gretchen Sabinson's confidence, as he dictates a completely insincere card to go along with gold-wrapped chocolates: "Just say to her, 'Darling, I count the days, the hours, the minutes. . . .'" Then he pilfers rights to a taxicab from a well-behaved—that is to say, naive—gentleman, on the grounds that Maggie is ill, at the corner of Madison and 60th Street.[49] (The sick-and-helpless-woman ploy is as artificial a tag as gold wrapping or "Darling, I count the days.") At the Oak Bar of the Plaza he attaches to himself—virtually by contagious magic, or an amnesiac kleptomania—an identity that is not his own, and that he is not even aware he has taken, triggering the plot within the plot that might be called the George Kaplan Story. In Lester Townsend's study in Glen Cove, Roger snatches an illicit read of material on another man's desk, a cadge that will ultimately lead to an innocent stranger's murder since it is only through his reading the address label on this newspaper that the name of Lester Townsend is invoked for him. He "borrows" Laura Babson's Mercedes (just as "Mrs. Townsend" claims to the police), albeit under the influence of others naughtier than he. All this acquisition is accomplished by Roger without a state-sanctioned economic transaction in which he displays appropriate piety by parting with funds. The genius of Hitchcock is that he leads us to applaud the pilfering wholeheartedly, because all this action is legitimated in terms of action that rationalizes it harmoniously with Roger's potential for survival.[50] Threatened in the elevator of the Plaza by Vandamm's henchmen, he escapes from the building and steals another taxi, this time from a couple of tourists, playing the typical New Yorker taking advantage of civilized outsiders who haven't yet learned the arcane art of snagging a cab in rush hour in the city. At the United Nations he steals admission to the Members' Lounge. A berth on the Twentieth-Century Limited all the way to Chicago is no cheap ride, but Roger travels blithely without a ticket.[51] In the prairie cornfield he not only disregards the stranger's astute advice but also fails to recognize it as such, pay for it, or even offer thanks. We can say, indeed, in the case of a priest of the consumer temple like Roger, that the fact the advice comes without a price tag accounts for its not being heeded. Call this squandering, not theft; but it is as irresponsible socially, and it leads to at least one death.

Roger's denigration into the marketplace is the moral lesson of the film — that, originating above consumption, he finds himself needing to scramble in order to save his life. Scrambling, he learns to meet others, to care. Caring, he is forced to scramble further in order to save them. By the time he comes to South Dakota, Roger is a trader in the marketplace, as hopeful and serious as any other. If he operates outside conventional bounds he has learned to be deviant, not superior, and there is hope. But something must happen to Roger in this film to transform him. He must begin to wonder about himself.

LOOK WHO'S HERE

As we see with a visit to Room 796 at the Plaza, George Kaplan has amassed a bevy of identical suits [52] and also hotel rooms across America, the services of maids and valets, photographic memories, and livery brushes (all, we must wait to know, fabricated in order to give him a substance that can match his name). The theme of the hotel room scene, first prepared in the hallway outside as Roger and his mother encounter Elsie the chambermaid (Maudie Prickett), and then uttered plainly by Roger soon after entering the room, is "Who is it that is in this place?" (though that isn't exactly how he puts it), in other words, the intermapping of identity and meaning. We will certainly come around to Roger in light of this theme, but let us begin with Elsie, precisely because that is how Hitchcock handles it. As in so many of his films, a deeply revealing and thoroughly subtle moment is here prefaced by a calculated, but seemingly disconnected, chill.

With his wily mother who has naughtily purloined the key for him, Roger is trying to sneak into a private room in the plushest and most exclusive hotel in New York. A shrill and utterly peremptory voice interrupts him, from offscreen—which is to say, and in every sense of the phrase, from beyond: [53] "Just a minute, please!" (The tone and edge of this establish for us what has already been established for Roger, namely, that he is in train of trespassing. If the edge of the voice is detected by Roger, I also feel it, and I am made a trespasser, too.) A hotel maid now walks forward from a nearby room. She is a uniformed personage and therefore represents local authority. Social control is taking place. Roger is in trouble. But the maid has only perfunctory business to transact: "Will you be wantin' me to change your bedding, sir?" This is at once—and most deliciously—a very public and a very private question, and Roger's guilty suspicions about the appropriateness of his behavior draw us to read the private side. Bedding is an intimate arrangement of surfaces, yet the hotel employee who sees to the bedding of a client is acting according to a delicate, but thoroughly public, script: the bedding is the property of the hotel, and therefore within the authority of the maid, a role defined, in fact, partly according to its responsibility for such materials. Changing someone's bedding, on the other hand, is an action involving connections about as intimate as can be found, and if Roger is not the client his presence makes a claim for, the maid's question becomes a probing, even potentially erotic, one. We see in the response, and in Cary Grant's exquisitely stammering execution, "Yes, well, uh, but not right now," a full expression of the duality of the situation. The maid, for her part, is "wonderin'" about "changin' the linens."

Linens are private garments of all sorts, close to the bone. The point of this little scene, dramatic for a moment and then routinized into something archly (and deceptively) banal, may well be lost on us as we experience it:[54] the intimacy in the innuendo of the conversation, the vague suggestion that the maid is much closer to Roger than even he would suppose. It is an intimacy of some kind, professional or not, and its ambiguity is placed in order to focus and narrow our concentration so that at the next moment we are ready to accept as fully, even urgently, significant something Roger says rather blithely (as is his wont) about this woman, whom he and we might ordinarily disattend, and an intimacy most profound: "She seemed to think I'm Kaplan." Then, in a double take, which is more touching still, something occurs to Roger for the very first time that may well have struck viewers much earlier (though I suspect it hasn't): "I wonder if I *look* like Kaplan?"

It is intriguing to realize that this is the first moment a physical resemblance has offered itself to Roger as explanation for his odd position. When they kidnap him, for instance, he treats Licht and Valerian as though they are daft, obsessive, stubborn, misinformed, and optically challenged, but not for a moment as though they have made the kind of honest mistake anybody could make about two men who look remarkably alike. Even we can fail to have suspected, who watched the gossamer and articulate misperceptions through which the kidnapping was propelled and know very well that Roger gave some direct, if unintended, clue to bolster the kidnappers' calculations. Like him, we think, "These are merely willful men." He does not see himself as a product, one of those packaged items the external appearance and signal capacity of which is constructed by advertisers such as he. Here we have one of Hitchcock's excellent jokes, the man who spends his life making and touting products for avid consumers himself turned into a product and raptly consumed but, of course, against his will (and beyond his belief). The noble Professor and his team, after all, are ultimately packagers. Though in his own (limited) view, Roger has always been a natural man, beyond construction and beyond manners, he at this moment, and for the first time, looks to the possibility that he may be giving off appearances. And the appearances are those of Kaplan.

Retrieving a scrap of paper from the blotter of the desk and archly sighing, "Look who's here!" as he regards it ("Who? Where?" his mother replies), he gives a plain show of belonging in this place, belonging perfectly. And indeed, every move he makes in the room gives sufficient motive for such a reading of him. The way he opened the door, the way he touched the doorknob, the way he moved upon the carpet, opened the closet, negotiated with the valet, picked up this piece of paper and now answers the telephone, leave no doubt for us that, however doubtful he may be himself, Roger is as at home as any "gentleman in room seven-nine-six" (as the maid puts it) could expect, or be expected, to be.

He is at home psychologically, too—settled cozily before the hearth of his own worldview. When he says, "Look who's here!" he is referring by the word "here" to the photograph in front of his eyes, to the space of his own deeply felt presence, but only he (and we, who watch his every move) can know this. His mother—now, and in general, oblivious, and with her back to him—thinks "here" is the more general space of the room, and in rejoining, "Who? Where?" she wonders, startled, whether suddenly someone is with them. But who *is* here?

The elaborateness of this scene, with Elsie the maid being invited to come in and attest to the fact that she has never seen Mr. Kaplan before; and the valet delivering a suit that doesn't quite fit Roger, then making the same claim Elsie made; is more than a mere transitional device. Room 796 is an existential crisis for Roger because here, and only here, he comes fully and desperately to question whether he is the man he thinks he is or the man others think him to be. And now he, too, comes close to entertaining the supposition that he is George Kaplan, a consideration that puts him in a position to estimate Kaplan openly for the first time. And it is his wily mother who gives the most powerful clue. When Roger thinks aloud that it is "the damnedest thing" that "no one in the hotel has actually seen Kaplan," she quips, "Maybe he has his suits mended by invisible weavers"—exactly and perfectly the sort of stale joke this dowdy but canny oddball of a woman might tell, and yet: truth in jest. What is she doing but riding high at the expense of her butt (as all jokesters do): tailors. Here, then, a certain haughty disregard is expressed

for the class of skilled wage laborers. It is a class joke, affirming class affiliation even as it puts Roger sufficiently at his ease to grimace. But this is the
woman who has been changing Roger's linen for a great number of years. We
learn about his class identity through mother, and perhaps see more clearly
the chumminess in the Oak Bar, the social comfort (even in a state of imprisonment) at Townsend's in Glen Cove, the high-style inebriation in the Glen
Cove police court, and much more. Though George Kaplan is accustomed to
purchasing the services of hoteliers, chambermaids, valets, tailors, and
weavers invisible and otherwise, Roger O. Thornhill, we can now see, is not.
He commands the world, but will not demean himself through the friction
of purchasing; he is a figure who is waited upon, by Maggie, by the bellboy,
by the valet, by the chambermaid, by the train porter, by his lawyer, by his
mother. He is not certain he is the man who belongs in this room—which is
to say, Kaplan, a rank consumer—because he is above him. As if to visualize
mother's point, he examines Kaplan's suit and finds the jacket too tight, the
trousers several inches too short. Kaplan is diminished.

Kaplan, Mrs. Thornhill is smirking, is nothing but a man who would have
his suits mended. A wonderful irony of this scene is something we will only
later in the film be in a position to appreciate. If, as we will learn, Kaplan is
nothing but a role, he has the same status in reality—for us, bent on admiring Roger's elevation—as Thornhill. As any actor within certain limitations
could have played Thornhill, though the contract went to Cary Grant,[55] any
actor can play Kaplan, and the "contract" has gone to Roger Thornhill. The
chambermaid's conviction that it is Kaplan she is speaking to in Room 796,
therefore, is utterly realistic, indeed true, though not real. Or at least it is as
true as our conviction that we saw Roger Thornhill pretending to be George
Kaplan in order to get into that place. Since there is no Kaplan, the issue of
whether Roger is him or not falls entirely by the wayside when we come to
think of the film as a whole, because there is also no Roger Thornhill. After
we eliminate the obstructive riddle of who-is-who, what is left is the opportunity for Roger to define himself as being beyond the enterprise of consumption, as being above the sort of man who would buy and wear suits like
these or who could lack a New York townhouse with his own valet.

Kaplan may be a shopper but Roger is not. One of the vital and central features of shopping as organized activity is a shopper's capacity to detect and
read the surround, to decide not only what is threat and what is not but what
can be acquired and through what mechanism. Shoppers read the world as a
comprehensible terrain—a text, and the reading of the social environment as
cultural text is a form of intellectual shopping. But *North by Northwest* is in
part an essay on Roger's capacity to detect his surround without troubling to

comprehend it, his class-based illiteracy—a favorite Hitchcockian theme. Roger is playing with Kaplan's stuff, not thinking of acquiring it, just as in all of the thefts I mentioned above he was playing with consumables, not really taking them. It is his playfulness that endears him to our hearts and permits that he should go unpunished at the resolution of the tale. Embedded in the text-within-the-text of the film—namely, the letter Roger is dictating to somebody named "Sam" and that Maggie is copying furiously as first we see her—is a subtle indication that Roger lives outside the world of consumption altogether:

> Even if you accept the belief that the high Trendex automatically means a rise in the sales curve, which, incidentally, I don't, my recommendation is still the same. Dash. Spread the good word in as many small time segments as we can grab, and let the opposition have their high ratings while we cry about it all the way to the bank.

This text openly suggests that although he makes his money in advertising, and is indeed addicted to its stun, Roger does not philosophically subscribe to the naive consumerist rhetoric he twists to create sales not only of products but also of advertisements for products: to wit, that seeing a seductive commercial makes a television viewer hop out to buy a product.[56] Roger, a maker of such inducements, knows better. He is outside, and in a sense above, the lexical machine his attentions drive and therefore positioned to see all the world—even the sacred temple of advertising itself—as a contrived pitch, to regard human interactions of all kinds with a jaded cognoscenti's eye. Such a portrait of the advertiser as cynical consumer was far from ordinary in the 1950s. An economy desperate for consumption favored advertisers who could make buyers think their statements were truths, their products realities, their claims facts of nature, people's manipulated sense of deficit cosmic pathos itself. But because Roger directs consumption he is above it. In a similar way, because he has made this film, Alfred Hitchcock is no believer in its assertions and developments; nor is he interested in the fate of Roger Thornhill, getting on a crosstown bus at the earliest possible moment to head east, which is to say, away from us and the trajectory of the story. Roger's life has the potential to be independent of the media he influences, and this will be his redemption because it will make possible that he escape from himself in a crisis—himself as seller of the world—and begin an act of recognition and sharing.

If Roger is above the consumer economy, above the ravenous, aspiring middle-class gentlemen who sup on jellied grapefruit and avocado bisque, calf's brains with black butter and crêpes Suzette, and chat with women who drink mint frappés,[57] it is because his aims are transcendental and consumer exchange is too cumbersome for him. The plot ploy of "George Kaplan" is a mechanism for providing him with an ongoing pretext for escaping yet another economic matrix, that of the transacted, exchanged construction of self that we build by negotiating on the street corners of life with other people's estimations of us. Thanks to the Kaplan motif, Roger is constantly in a position to deny others the opportunity to tell him who he is—all this in a society where keeping up with the Joneses, being popular, is the definition of morally proper middle-class behavior and a principal gear in the economy driven by advertising.

Yet if Roger is outside consumer life, he has been pretending not to be. On the surface, he has been wearing an antic disposition,[58] long masquerading as nothing if not the epitome of bourgeois sensibilities utterly *au courant* with, if a little aloof from, consumer habits of the times. He knows the rules intimately. If he is not signaling romance by getting Gretchen Sabinson candies, he is at least getting the most lascivious ones money can buy: Blum's almondettes, each one wrapped in gold, and four pounds of them to boot— nothing more fattening or less innocent.[59] He is properly sentimental—says so himself in the curtain line, "But I'm sentimental," meaning not only, "I am a man full of sentiments and sentimentality" but also "I'm a figment made all of sentiment, not flesh." (Our sentiment, of course, who else's?) It's an admission designed to relieve us of the obligation to care by showing us that our care is all there is to him, all, in fact, there has ever been. He's apparently got middle-class taste, humming "I've Grown Accustomed to Her Face," drunk, in his cliffside drive, to show that on some transcendent, thus authentic, level he likes Broadway. And the show he is missing while he sleeps off his stupor at the Glen Cove police station[60] is the only one that was playing at the Winter Garden in 1957, when this film was made in current time: *West Side Story*. Of this, the most popular production number was "America," a frenetic fandango (apotheosized throughout this film in the celebrated 6/8 fandango motif by Bernard Herrmann) that said about the United States what Alfred Hitchcock might have thought as a relatively new immigrant (he had been naturalized in 1955):

> I like to be in A-mer-i-ca!
> O.K. by me in A-mer-i-ca!
> Ev'rything free in A-mer-i-ca
> For a small fee in A-mer-i-ca![61]

Like Leonard Bernstein's on Broadway, Herrmann's here is tropical music, becoming ever more frenetic and bizarre, ever more southerly, as we head further north-northwest along the vector of our voyage.

The sanity that is the counterpoint to Roger's mask, the ability to tell the hawk(er) from the handsaw when the wind blows southerly, is neither a false democratic attitude, such as the one he has been sporting; nor an aloof snobbery that has pretense to escaping the demands of civil society. And it is a lecture delivered on the tarmac at Chicago Midway, jet aircraft screaming all round, that shows him this. Only here does Roger really listen to another person, open himself to being affected by the trade of meaning. The Professor—the C.I.A. agent we have no reason at all to believe professes anything in real life—reveals to him that George Kaplan, the man who acts for loyalty and not for money, does not exist. Yet Eve is a secret agent, her life a desperate performance; and she is in danger. To save her, Roger must accept staging as his fate and become Kaplan, must make live a performance that until this moment has been nothing but a hollow rehearsal and a game.

BEYOND SINCERITY

Les films avancent comme un train, tu sais. Comme un train dans la nuit.
    François Truffaut, La Nuit Américaine

But having come this long analytical way by care of indirection and musing, I must halt. We need not fear—Roger will certainly seize the tender Eve out of the clutches of the evil Vandamm, and live with her, presumably happy, ever after. Yet what should trouble any viewer of this film about what I have written so far is just this: the gracile Vandamm must be thought a moron. It is obvious to us, after all, that most of the rhetoric of the motion picture is an argument about Roger Thornhill being George Kaplan, yet we are quite certain Roger Thornhill is Roger Thornhill—indeed, just to leave no doubt, Roger *O.* Thornhill. Vandamm, clearly intelligent, is therefore mistaken, and also low, since even if he is suave he is not so suave as to be able to admit his mistake. This is preposterous, even unbelievable, and certainly indecorous of him. He is unworthy of our attentions, even with the screen of the elegant performance of James Mason. Vandamm being trivial, however, Roger's triumph over him is debased. The film is a waste of time.

Throughout this analysis, indeed, I have been alluding to—indeed, sometimes playing off—a frequently recited, conventional reading of *North by Northwest*. According to it, Roger Thornhill, incorrectly but inescapably taken for another man, is spirited to a hideaway in Long Island for interrogation; made the object of an attempt at murder; set up, when this fails, as a murderer himself; and thus set in motion on a flight across America where he meets a beautiful woman, falls in love, narrowly escapes her secret associates' attempts to kill him once again, learns that she is in fact a secret government agent herself, saves her from being killed by the people who were earlier trying to kill him, and finally marries her.[62] This reading needs some correction.

The kidnappers are manifestly certain of the propriety—from their own point of view—of the kidnapping they have perpetrated, and this certainty includes a "knowledge" of Thornhill as Kaplan:

ROGER: My name is Thornhill. Roger Thornhill. It's never been anything else!
STRANGER: Of course.
ROGER: So obviously your friends picked up the wrong package when they bundled me out here in the car.
STRANGER: Do sit down, Mr. Kaplan.

The conventional view claims, echoing no one but Roger himself, that Thornhill is not Kaplan; that he is Thornhill; and therefore that the kidnappers are errant. Given that they are looking for Kaplan, the kidnapping is an utter mistake, is intended for someone else, has caught up an innocent man in an undertaking to which he does not properly belong.

The kidnappers have indeed made a crucial error, but it consists not in believing the man they are seeking, George Kaplan, is our Roger Thornhill; but in believing George Kaplan, the object of their search, is indeed a man. The George Kaplan of their belief is at least something of an arbitrary construct, moving around the country—

STRANGER: On June the sixteenth, you checked into the Sherwyn Hotel in Pittsburgh as Mr. George Kaplan of Berkeley, California. A week later you registered at the Benjamin Franklin Hotel in Philadelphia as Mr. George Kaplan of Pittsburgh. On August the eleventh you stayed at the Statler in Boston. On August the twenty-ninth George Kaplan of Boston registered at the Whittier in Detroit. At present, you are registered in room seven ninety-six at the Plaza Hotel in New York as Mr. George Kaplan of Detroit.

—like some kind of wraith; is indeed a wholly artificial construction:

> PROFESSOR: We didn't invent our nonexistent man, and give him the name
> of George Kaplan, and establish elaborate behavior patterns for him, and
> move his prop belongings in and out of hotel rooms for our own private
> amusement.

and as such he is susceptible of performance by any qualified actor, Roger
Thornhill included. In whatever sense any actor on earth "is" the role he is
playing, then, Roger "is" George Kaplan. At least during a performance, it
makes little sense to think of actors in relation to their characters in any other
way. In his very affecting analysis, Stanley Cavell walks almost far enough
down this road to catch the bizarre import of this:

> The theme of theatricality is generalized by the fact that the part Thornhill
> is asked and forced to play is that of someone named Goerge Kaplan, who
> doesn't exist; but to play the part of a fictional character is just what actors
> normally do. It happens that in the fiction of this film the new fictional iden-
> tity is imposed by reality, thus generalizing the theme further into the nature
> of identity and the theatricality of everyday life.[63]

But Cavell does not go so far as to say the kidnappers have not caught up the
wrong man, and that Roger's great challenge in this film is to realize this.

Hitchcock goes far beyond thematizing theatricality. For him theatricality
is a central existential riddle, even a primordial setting, and its concerns are
personal, conceptual, philosophical, aesthetic, and moral. Further, there is
some reason to doubt how "real" (fictionally speaking; Cavell's term) the circumstances are in which Kaplan is invoked and overlaid, both "Vandamm"
and "the Professor" taking on masques at will and having no reason, throughout, for using any real identity whatsoever.[64] Most important, however, as I
will argue below, the fictional quality of Kaplan is not universally apparent.

Roger's "being" George Kaplan involves not only casting, the attachment
of an actor to a role, but secret casting, since while being thus attached Roger
is not aware either that he is himself an actor playing a role or that Kaplan is
a role to be played. To the same extent that he must use anticipatory following in actually collaborating on the Kaplan routine, he experiences secret
teaching in being put onstage in the first place since what he believes to be
happening (while we happily watch)—at least until he begins, in Room 796,
to have serious, by which I mean phenomenological, doubts—is a simple case

of mistaken identity. This film is not only about the theatricality of everyday life, then. It is a view of everyday life as unwitting theatricality, as being an organization of experience open to an upending of the common and conventional sense of what theater is, where its boundaries are, where and to what extent it is artificial. While believing ourselves to be offstage, we can be blindly entrenched in a performance, performance consisting not in our intentions to give a show but in the capacity of others to read us as giving one. The challenge is to achieve a perspective in which we can see what we are seen to be doing, instead of being locked in the mere acknowledgment of what we look like to ourselves. To gain such a perspective, we have to have some view of the control system that is directing our scenes. Social class, the access to control, is therefore a vital issue in the structure of our perception of what is real and what is artificial.

It is important to consider that Roger's innocence does not lie solely in his ignorance that he is playing the role of Kaplan. It includes his ignorance that Kaplan is a role at all; and also his ignorance that he is engaged in any kind of role play. The first is of course the result of careful design by the Professor and his cronies; and Roger is not the only dupe to be taken in. That Roger takes himself seriously in general, however, and cannot imagine others taking him otherwise, owes to his sincerity. We may understand sincerity, following Goffman,[65] as a belief in one's own performance, a concomitant acceptance of the outcomes of that performance as actualities—which is tantamount to a belief that one isn't acting at all. The sincere person believes himself to be the individual associated with the name printed on the birth certificate he claims for his own. He believes himself to be expressing what he believes himself to be feeling, because expression is taken to be inwardly guided and authentic. Roger's sincerity is evidenced not only by the fact that he wants to avoid calling himself George Kaplan; but also by the fact that he presumes himself to be morally right, not just situationally tactical, in this avoidance. So perfect is the fit between the actor and the role that the role seems not to be there.[66] And the act seeming like reality, the actor does not see either that he is acting or that acting is being done at all.

In his sincerity Roger is unwavering in the first part of the picture. Maggie gives him clear suggestions that his behavior (embodied in his dictation) will cause him to appear coy in the eyes of Gretchen Sabinson, but he does not see himself this way and is not guided by her. At the Glen Cove courtroom, his mother informs him that respectable others will see him as preposterous, yet he clings sincerely to a story they are bound to find incredible. That, loyal viewers, we have followed his account and could verify every word of it is an immaterial circumstance here; we are not known in this court and its officers were no company for us in our observations. Roger does not believe in wearing masks, and so he denies that he is wearing one. He sees himself a natural man.

If in his existential escapade Roger's first step is a naive and selfish blindness—*because he is quite wrong about not being George Kaplan*—he will certainly move to other positions. At the Plaza with his mother, snooping around Room 796, he begins to see that if he is not Kaplan himself, nevertheless he is at least the sort of person who could easily be mistaken for Kaplan by everybody else in the hotel: he is Kaplanesque. His mother is convinced, however, with a sincerity that is of course wholly historical, that he can only be Roger, son of Thornhill. Roger, the genuine thing. The tentative and slightly disturbing uncertainty Roger experiences at the Plaza—without it he would never ask his mother if he should answer that phone—resolves into a dazzling clarity at the UN. As shocking as Lester Townsend's sudden death there is to Roger, and as touching as the moment must be, since Townsend falls into his arms, it is the presence of the photographer and Roger's awareness that he is now to be represented as a killer in the press that jar him for the first time from his sincere convictions that he is thoroughly, naturally, spontaneously, wholly, and only the innocent he believes himself to be. Henceforward he must be concerned for his appearance in other people's eyes, an appearance now about to be embodied as such in a mediated form analogous to this film in which we are watching all this. And *we* are certainly obliged to take appearances seriously.

In this light, we can understand his self-consciousness with Eve—"The moment I meet an attractive woman I have to start pretending I have no desire to make love to her"—and the attention paid in the mise-en-scène to his self-lathering in the men's room of Union Station. The cornfield scene is the cinematic development of a conflict between Roger's self-assured curiosity (about meeting Kaplan in this strange place) and the naked vulnerability of his position (from the point of view of the pilot of the cropduster). As the scene progresses, Roger becomes more and more conscious that the pilot's reality and his own are indistinguishable. His situation, then, is framed in someone else's view, and in his being pinpointed in someone else's viewfinder. And he *is* meeting Kaplan! The auction scene is a testament to Roger's gaining full control of his identity as a role directed by others, because in it he manipulates not so much the self he feels but the self the auction crowd (read, audience) expects him to display and reads him displaying.

North by Northwest can therefore be seen to be a journey in which, by stages, the central figure becomes a person capable of direct and complex experience. It is not in the sleeping car of the eastbound train in the finale that Roger expresses his devotion to Eve but in the midst of the most intense vertical anxiety, as he is most intensely caught up in the physical action of survival. Nor is it cerebral parrying or artful disguise or mere horizontal flight for his life across a prairie or across a continent that catches Roger up as he recognizes Eve, but rather the potentiality that confronts every mortal in every frame of mortality, a great fall, which is to say, a tumble not out of being but out of character:

> ROGER (*holding Eve who dangles from the monument*): Well, if we ever get out of this alive, let's go back to New York on the train together. All right?
> EVE: Is that a proposition?
> ROGER: It's a proposal, sweetie.

For what is the climb but the prospect of the fall?

A final word about the final shot. Persistent has been the eagerness of critics to notice the phallicism of the train entering the tunnel, but in his profound wit it was Hitchcock, no one else, who led them. In an interview with Jean Domarchi and Jean Douchet,[67] he affirmed, indeed,

> There's nothing symbolic in *North by Northwest*. Oh yes! One thing. The last shot. The train that goes into the tunnel after the love scene between Grant and Eva-Marie Saint. It's a phallic symbol. But don't tell anybody.[68]

They told everybody. But everything in Hitchcock is presence long before it is symbol. The train at the end of this film is a train before it is a phallus—a user of space, a mover, a vector, a flight; a harbinger, silver bright, running from a mercantile jungle to an unseen future, from a world of character roles being exchanged in a relentless marketplace and desperate consumers gaining purchase on the shards of civilization, to something beneath, more ineffable, out of the spotlight. The dark, T. S. Eliot called it. "All go into the dark."

A Bromide for Ballantine:

Spellbound, Psychoanalysis, Light

Nobody knew exactly what was on the way.
Robert Musil

EDUCATED CONVERSATIONS

Alfred Hitchcock is not reported by his most popular biographer to have un-
dergone psychoanalysis. Certainly one has the suspicion (a little more than
occasionally) reading *The Dark Side of Genius* that Donald Spoto might have
advised him to. On page 249, for instance, Hitchcock's presentation in *Psycho*
of a flushed toilet is described as pushing "iconoclastic, schoolboy perversity
to its bathroom limit." On page 305 he is ascribed a "juvenile and sometimes
pathological association between matters of bedroom and matters of toilet."
On page 456, the allusions to bodily functions in his films are said to "mark a
recurrent, obsessive motif." On page 274, during a discussion of *Shadow of a
Doubt,* we learn that Hitchcock's "confused feelings, his guilt, the clash of love
and resentment, were unleashed by [his mother's] death."[1] Hitchcock sometimes ate strangely, as we learn on page 412:

> "He always said he hated the idea of swallowing food or drink, and in fact
> everything seemed to be taken in one huge gulp," Herbert Coleman re-
> called.[2] Others witnessed the odd habits of a man who perhaps loved the idea
> of being sated more than the act of ingestion, which somehow seemed to him

indelicate and reminded him of nausea and sexual activity—connections he
frequently made to dining companions at inappropriate moments.

And he was more than eccentric, apparently. Spoto quotes a second-unit cameraman on *The 39 Steps* labeling him a sadist in his personal relations;[3] and
describes him as hypochondriac, sexually repressed, and obsessed with privacy and solitude. A reporter commenting on *Rebecca* is revealed to have
deemed Hitchcock "never happier than when seeing someone writhe."[4] Perhaps the most compromising of symptoms (and one which placed him in
prestigious company), gender ambiguity, is attributed to him on pages
432–433:

Hitchcock's temperament was very like that of Henry James, who also par-
took of Victorian puritanism in its American and English variants. As Leon
Edel wrote of Henry James, so it was with Alfred Hitchcock: a "spiritual
transvestism"—which fascinated the director in its literal and figurative
senses—protected a sense of masculine integrity. It was thus true of Hitchcock, as Edel wrote of James, that all his life he harbored "within the house of

the [artist's] inner world the spirit of a young adult female, worldy-wise and curious, possessing a treasure of unassailable virginity and innocence and able to yield to the masculine active world-searching side. . . ."

Henry James died in 1916, a year before Freud published the first volume of his *Introductory Lectures on Psychoanalysis;* and so, regardless of how ideal a subject for Freudian study his virgin innocence might have been, he was far less likely than Hitchcock (born in 1899) to form at least intellectual associations with Freud.[5] Indeed, I think there is clear enough evidence in *Spellbound* that if Freudian analysis was not part of Hitchcock's life experience per se, we hardly need follow Spoto's recurrent *ad hominem* diagnoses to affiliate Hitchcock with Freud. Freudian thought was well understood by—and significant to—Hitchcock's creative mind, as it was to all other serious thinkers of his generation.[6] By "Freudian thought," though many (and some conflicting) interpretations are possible, I mean to suggest a certain creative regard for darkness.[7]

As late as 1938 Freud had written, and then in 1941 published—only about three years before work on *Spellbound* commenced—the summative essay, "Some Elementary Lessons in Psycho-Analysis." Appearing in London in *Schriften aus dem Nachlass,* it would almost certainly have been known to May E. Romm, "one of Los Angeles's top psychiatrists,"[8] and the practitioner whom David Selznick, producer of *Spellbound,*[9] had been consulting since late 1943. According to Leonard Leff, indeed, Romm went beyond mere medical consultation with Selznick; it was she who inspired him with ideas, "less about himself or his depression, perhaps, than about psychiatry as the subject of a potentially important film, one that would renew his association with his principal contract director."[10]

If this report is true in laying the genesis of *Spellbound* in the Selznick-Romm dialogue, it certainly omits some of the feverish egotism ascribed to Selznick in Otto Friedrich's description of that psychoanalytic relationship:

David Selznick enjoyed pouring out his thoughts to Dr. Romm, and that outpouring apparently helped him to get back to work. Then, of course, he began treating Dr. Romm as one of his employees. "He became too busy for Romm," Mrs. Selznick recalled. "He was forty minutes late, if he showed up at all. When he arrived on time, he was often unwakable through the entire session. He recounted these antics as though they were amusing. . . . He misinterpreted her patience as enchantment with him; in fact, he was afraid she was falling in love with him. He rang her doorbell at midnight and, standing

outside, demanded to be heard. He found it unreasonable of her to refuse."
After nearly a year of this, Dr. Romm decided to cancel Selznick as a patient.
Selznick didn't seem to mind. He told his wife that he now "knew more than
she did; *he* could analyze *her.*" [11]

This was the Selznick who epitomized the active world-searching male to
whom Hitchcock's "virginity and innocence" would have to yield: and he was,
at least in lay terms, a Freudian, or certainly a man capable of comprehend-
ing Freudian thought. But Hitchcock was an intellectual confidant of
Selznick's. As Jay Presson Allen would much later say about him, "Hitch was
certainly literate. He had no education but he had read a lot. People like that
are sponges and learn a lot from educated conversations." [12]

What Sigmund Freud reiterated in "Some Elementary Lessons," what, indeed, he had been teaching since at least 1892,[13] was a central psychological
chiaroscuro:

> Everyone—or almost everyone—was agreed that what is mental really *has* a
> common quality in which its essence is expressed: namely the quality *of being
> conscious*—unique, indescribable, but needing no description.
>
> . . . No; being conscious cannot be the essence of what is mental. It is only
> a *quality* of what is mental, and an unstable quality at that—one that is far of-
> tener absent than present. The mental, whatever its nature may be, is in itself
> unconscious and probably similar in kind to all the other natural processes of
> which we have obtained knowledge.[14]

Consciousness is *part of* mentality, a kind of highlighted zone in a surrounding ocean of obscurity. In according it so central a position in the architecture
of his theory Freud also gives emphasis to the unconscious darkness, which
lies outside the illumination of our awareness, as a vital plasma of creative
spirit itself. At the same time he questions our insistence on favoring consciousness as thought, knowledge as intelligence, perception as realization. As
Shakespeare had suggested long before, having Hamlet lecture his buddy
Horatio, there is more to reality than we see, more to intellect than we know,
more to mental life than we are cognizant of feeling, intuiting, suspecting,
willing, and remembering. Darkness, in short, is itself a form of luminosity.
The hidden is real. The undiscovered is a source of thought, a material with
which creativity can work.

Readers who are familiar with the surface plot of *Spellbound*[15] will realize
that in synopsizing Freud (in this admittedly clumsy fashion) I am in many

ways also summarizing the action of the film, since the convolutions—in present and past time—of the story are centered by the truths that the putative Dr. Edwardes (Gregory Peck), our lead character, *categorically refuses* to remember or openly know. He is a man afloat upon the surface of his own unconscious. But I hope to show that the film's debt and homage to Freud transcend this surface treatment. Whether or not it "integrated all previous cinematic lore" on psychiatry, as Alexander Doty suggested,[16] *Spellbound* deals with a passage downward, to the disorganized and obscure psychic depths, and then back up again, to the civilized and luminous—but ultimately artificial—social surface.

AUS WIEN
'Ooooh' and 'aaaah'

Darkness, as we may call it, is conventionally thought a quality of buried impulses and memories: of the repressed, of pain, of jealousy, of vigorous passion, of loathing, of malevolence and distrust and all that we call "evil."[17] To the extent that we would like to believe our civilization is a triumph over darkness, an Enlightenment,[18] we find ourselves apt, as we explore social structure in the "light of day," to discover order and pleasure, moderation, delicacy of sensibility, trust, loving-kindness, and all that we call "good." The balanced and restrained "good society" has not been more thoroughly or more clearly iconized in modern times than in fin-de-siècle Vienna, where the glimmering architecture of Otto Wagner and Josef Hoffmann and Adolf Loos, the optimistic design of Josef Maria Olbrich, the libertarian painting of Gustav Klimt and Egon Schiele and Oskar Kokoschka, the vaporous writing of Stefan Zweig and Robert Musil, Hugo von Hofmannsthal and Arthur Schnitzler, the crystalline philosophy of Ludwig Wittgenstein, and the fabulous music of Gustav Mahler and Alban Berg, Anton von Webern, Arnold Schoenberg, and Hugo Wolf all began or flourished; and where at Berggasse 19—until he moved to London and wrote the "Elementary Lessons"—Sigmund Freud lived.

Vienna of the early twentieth century has been undervalued, according to Kirk Varnedoe:

Histories of modern art and architecture conceived before the late 1960s made Paris the master center, with satellites in Berlin and Munich. The Vienna of Gustav Klimt's and Egon Schiele's paintings, or of Otto Wagner's and

Josef Hoffmann's architecture, was relegated to the margins, as the pretty but unserious provincial domain of what would politely be referred to as specialized tastes. But in recent years serious studies of all these artists have appeared, coincident with a ground swell of appreciation that has dramatically increased the auction prices for artists such as Klimt and Schiele. Independently and as advertisement for the Vienna vogue, this school of painting has come by now to seem an essential part of the modern tradition.[19]

Our admiration here, suggests Varnedoe, is for a world of serious devotion to composition, carefully controlled illumination, and intensified use of materials—all qualities we can find in the underlying principles of Freudian psychoanalytic science and therapeutic endeavor, but also in the filmmaking practices of Alfred Hitchcock. With Freud, the analysis of dreams, for example, is an intensification of the use of materials; the focus on control of illumination shows up in the analysis of wit; and the theory of repression depends upon understanding mental organization in compositional terms. With Hitchcock, we can consider the flat lateral elegance of compositional design in the train sequences of *The Lady Vanishes* where the motion of the train *is* the motion of the film—the frame construction is Hoffmannesque. Or we can regard the subtlety of illumination in the visitation to the crofters in *The 39 Steps*—the evocation of the lighting is Klimtian. Or we can esteem the compositional use of depth-of-field and lens in the mountain murder of *Secret Agent*—the regard for lenses and settings, for the distant as the proximal, for the enormous contained in the momentary, smacks of Mahlerian orchestration. And always, Hitchcock's twisting, provocative, often hilarious, yet always serious mode of thought is like Wittgenstein's.

The Paris-Vienna axis that Varnedoe invokes was alive for Sigmund Freud because of his hero, a man who was not among his Viennese contemporaries but who had lectured in neuropathology at the Hôtel de la Salpêtrière in Paris until his death in 1893. There was an engraved reproduction of a painting, indeed, of Jean-Martin Charcot, "*Le Leçon clinique*," by Pierre-Albert Brouillet, to the right of the entrance to Freud's consulting room. In it, Charcot is introducing to the Salpêtrière staff a female hysteric (a prototype, one could certainly argue, for Mary Carmichael [Rhonda Fleming] in *Spellbound*). Just as sunlight streamed optimistically into Freud's window beside this framed print, it streamed metaphorically into Charcot's lecturing room within the image itself. It is true that briefly but directly, between the end of 1885 and the beginning of 1886, Freud had studied at Charcot's side and there formed a staunch affiliation for the man's careful science[20] and method.[21] But in an obituary, written in 1893 for the *Wiener Medizinische Wochenschrift*, the younger man might well have been describing a rotund British filmmaker as yet unborn when he said of his teacher,

> He was not much given to cogitation, was not of the reflective type, but he had an artistically gifted temperament—as he said himself, he was a '*visuel*,' a seer. He himself told us the following about his method of working: he was accustomed to look again and again at things that were incomprehensible to him, to deepen his impression of them day by day, until suddenly understanding of them dawned upon him. Before his mind's eye, order then came into the chaos apparently presented by the constant repetition of the same symptoms.[22]

One is easily reminded of Hitchcock the *visuel* (his meticulous, even obsessive, attention to the optical configuration of his screen and to the visual outplay of characterological symptoms) or of Hitchcock "looking again and again" (the correlation he established and developed, in a cinematic grammar, between audience sympathy and focal length) or of order coming to Hitchcock's mind's eye (the many discretely visual features of his filmmaking such as precise details of setting and social tone and his economy of camera movement). The fondness for observation that Charcot evidently possessed and Freud learned to imitate, and Hitchcock's, were of a piece.

It is hardly necessary to establish a case that Alfred Hitchcock was directly and personally influenced at Freud's side in order to experience wonder and fascination at the profound inspiration he, and therefore filmmaking in general, must have felt in the wake of psychoanalytic theory and practice. In psychoanalytic theory, the need for psychoanalytic light, after all, was everywhere because outside therapeutic clarification all was inscrutable—so unnarratable—shadow. Hitchcock's analytical light functions in a similar way to escort us across the boundary between knowledge and suspicion. Indeed, in Hitchcock the greatest spiritual darkness is very often represented as a world in which everything can be seen very well (we may think of Lars Thorwald, the wife-slayer, looming too visibly in the hot flashbulb glare in *Rear Window*, or the too visible downhill car ride in *Family Plot*, or Harry, the Trouble with whom is that he won't be hidden), and this is because Hitchcock operates as a filmmaker exclusively from the perspective of sanity. Nothing dramatic need be alluded to in shadow when the vulnerable lens can lend it clarity. In Hitchcock material darkness, a palpable visible thing that has retained a potency to disturb, becomes brilliant with evocation.

Hitchcock's work, I think, bears more than casual affinity to psychoanalytic theory, notwithstanding his 1946 comment that psychoanalytical films could be "dismissed as a passing phase." [23] First, the history of its reception. In considering the widespread resistance to the deeper and philosophically abstruse and charming aspects of Hitchcock's films, a resistance clear enough in early criticism and persistent today (that it is always, for instance, the slightly self-conscious *Vertigo* that critics admire as predominantly ideational, never *The Trouble with Harry* or *The Man Who Knew Too Much* or *Torn Curtain*, which are resisted as blithe), we may recall that psychoanalytic theory had precisely the same affronting, even alienating, effect when, in the optimistic empire diffused from lambent Vienna, it was first offered. The birth of psychoanalytic theory must have made it seem that a dazzling, scotomizing cloud had been released over the world. Darkness, after all, had been pronounced. "It was true," says Peter Gay,

> that no one had yet permitted himself more than a brief, shocked look at the fundamental realities [Freud] had been the first to lay bare; such conduct was only a vast collective piece of resistance, proof not that his disagreeable truths were false, but that they were disagreeable. After all, in suitably disguised form—in myths, fairy tales, and tragedies, in the aphorisms of moralists and the folk wisdom of nursemaids—they had sometimes risen to the surface of man's consciousness, only to be rapidly repressed once more. [24]

The Freud who "could understand the resistance, and explain it, along with the facts it resisted," [25] was like the Alfred Hitchcock who could say wisely to François Truffaut one day in August 1962, "You know that the public always likes to be one jump ahead of the story; they like to feel they know what's coming next. So you deliberately play upon this fact to control their thoughts." [26] Nor would Freud have failed to acknowledge as brother the Hitchcock who knew that in 1943 his public was rejecting *Saboteur* because in its finale they were being asked to sympathize with the plight of an abject murderer, thereby affiliating with moral and emotional darkness.

In his comprehension of the barriers people would erect to his theories, indeed, Freud foreshadowed Hitchcock's astute, precise sensitivity to his audience—that entity, Hitch told Ernest Lehman, "like a giant organ that you and I are playing":

> At one moment we play *this* note on them and get *this* reaction, and then we play *that* chord and they react *that* way. And someday we won't even have to

make a movie—there'll be electrodes implanted in their brains, and we'll just press different buttons and they'll go 'ooooh' and 'aaaah' and we'll frighten them, and make them laugh. Won't that be wonderful?[27]

Moreover, at each narrative instant, like Gay's Freud, Hitch "could see without difficulty why his listeners might hesitate and object: had he not gone their way before them, experienced the same hesitations, offered the same objections?"[28] And it was to dissipate those objections that was Hitchcock's greatest joy:

> I don't care about the subject matter; I don't care about the acting; but I do care about the pieces of film and the photography and the sound track and all of the technical ingredients that make the audience scream. I feel it's tremendously satisfying for us to be able to use the cinematic art to achieve something of a mass emotion.[29]

In the articulation of their technically quite different schemata, Freud and Hitchcock also shared a fondness for the utile metaphor, the one blueprinting an architecture of the mind and laying out a process for therapeutic rationality and the other designing an optical-narrative instrument for inducing suspenseful catharsis.

At least in Freud's case, as Gay suggests—but I would insist, also in Hitchcock's—metaphors were important because modern man's "resistance to wounding truths was so diversified that it invited . . . analogies from the most varied of human occupations: warfare, politics, cookery, travel, family life, the arts."[30] It is true that all of Hitchcock's films are metaphorical, but, intriguingly, his metaphors are the same as Freud's: war, politics, cooking, traveling, family life, art. The motive energy of *Foreign Correspondent*, for example, is war. War is also the compacting and containing frame of *Lifeboat*. And the "MacGuffin" of *Topaz*, like that of *Notorious*, is ultimately a nation's capacity to go to war. The social intrigue of *Under Capricorn* is based in politics; and a central wellspring of action in *Secret Agent* and again in *The Lady Vanishes*, yet again in *The 39 Steps*, yet again in *Saboteur*, still again in *The Man Who Knew Too Much*, again in *North by Northwest*, and again in *Topaz*, is an actual or portended political assassination. In *Frenzy* we oscillate between cooking on one hand and the Covent Garden produce market on the other; and there is central importance to cookery and dining in *The Paradine Case* (especially the idea that a story is being cooked up to sway the court), in *The Man Who Knew Too Much* (1956),[31] and in *Rope*. Although all films are voyages, some explicitly draw our attention to this fact—*Vertigo* and *North by Northwest* to name two. Without looking at travel it would be impossible to penetrate *The Man Who Knew Too Much*, *Torn Curtain*, *Foreign Correspondent*, *The Lady Vanishes*, *Notorious*, *To Catch a Thief*, *Rebecca*, or *Shadow of a Doubt*. Family life organizes *Rope*, *Shadow of a Doubt*, and *Stage Fright*, not to mention *Young and Innocent*, *The Wrong Man*, and *The Trouble with Harry*. Ersatz sibling rivalry connects Guy and Bruno in *Strangers on a Train*. An ersatz father-son relation, mediated institutionally through the Church, centers *I Confess*. A macabre multiple take on family life frames *Rear Window*. The suspicion in *Suspicion* is a family affair to begin with, as is the notoriety in *Notorious*. And to *Rear Window*, *Vertigo*, *The Wrong Man*, *The Trouble with Harry*, *Stage Fright*, and *The Man Who Knew Too Much* (1956), layers of meaning are added by open reference to the arts: photography, painting, jazz, painting again, acting, and song, respectively.

Freud's major contribution to civilized Vienna at the turn of the century was to demonstrate its precariousness, and the richness of the shadows upon which it was founded. Hitchcock's civilization is revealed to be no less artificial, no more enduring. Judge Harnfield's haughty civility in *The Paradine Case* is built upon a miasm of peckish barbarism. "Jeff" Jefferies in *Rear Window* uses his lens, with plenty of art, as a way of surreptitiously fondling from a distance. The etiquette of Rupert Cadell in *Rope*, of Bruno Anthony in *Strangers on a Train*, of Charles Oakley in *Shadow of a Doubt*, of Tobin in *Saboteur*, of Heinrich Gerhard in *Torn Curtain*, of Vandamm in *North by Northwest*, and of so many other Hitchcockian characters is a mockery. Psychoanalysis made exactly such a mockery of Viennese culture at the fin de siècle, positing that its shining towers stood upon a rude secret life. And *Spellbound* is an explicit treatment of psychoanalysis. Necessarily, as much as couch lingo and interactional technique, it shows the psychoanalytic frame of mind, the dissecting point of view. It confronts the viewer with the notion of man as impulsive vault and civilization as denial of man.

But what is buried is not as dark as the burial, and what is denied is not as problematic as the denial. The most central postulate of all Freud's thought is that the buried store within us, as hidden as we may think it and as dark as its form appears, is potentially a source of immeasurable light. The obscure vapors Freud was liberating into the "civilization" of Vienna from the dark Satanic mills of Viennese man's most secret inner vaults were not besmirching the horizon at all; or scudding across the skies in obfuscating clouds; or polluting flesh toward an inexorable and horrific death. What had been buried and was now released could lead to benison, to reason, to health, to

what Barthes would later call a "jouissance."[32] What had been secret could be
made public without damaging the environment. But *the fact that it had been
hidden* could not, and was the problem.

Further, and horrifyingly, if the darkness was truly light, if the greatest of
truths were lurking there, then it was possible to be usefully, happily, even
beatifically confounded "in the dark" and what had been esteemed as brilliant
logic might be only a questionably shady, if not nefarious, dullness of mind
and spirit. Implicit in the program of psychoanalysis was a pervasive social
critique according to which the artifice that had hitherto been called Enlightenment, the quest for knowledge and release, could seem a journey to
the heart of darkness. Or, to penetrate Conrad's famous metaphor, those who
voyaged to the dark center might find the territory curiously bright and the
murkiest form not a jungle ritual but a "munificent civilization," propelling
the voyage. The real search for the light of meaning had to reject false pathways, what Thoreau came to call the "ruts of tradition," and head toward what
had not yet been seen. Or, better: toward what had once been too powerfully
seen, and was repressed. It was only through forgetting, then, that we could
come genuinely to remember. This was the message of Freud. And in *Spellbound*, a truly spellbinding film, this was the message of Hitchcock.

LIGHTNING STRIKES

In the upstairs bedroom-study of the director of the charming little asylum,
Green Manors, the hero and heroine of *Spellbound*,[33] Dr. Edwardes and
Dr. Constance Peterson (Gregory Peck and Ingrid Bergman), having fallen
swiftly and deeply in love, are locked in an embrace. While this screen moment has a conventional form, it is also a knot and a puzzle to be undone. Let
us use the embrace as a point of vantage (for embraces are surely also that)
from which to see elements of the film.

Green Manors does seem very much like an insane asylum when at the beginning of the film we meet some of the patients: self-destructive Garmes
(Norman Lloyd) or hysterical nymphomaniacal Mary Carmichael.[34] But
soon later we are in the company of the medical staff,[35] and there is a chummy
academic clubbishness in the banter, a soupçon of amicable competition in
their regard for one another. (Of course, the amity of the competitiveness
may be no more than a mask of civility, which these doctors would know far
better than we.) Here, intellectual rigor and academic striving are invoked, as
is the play of wit and the potency of the mind. Relentless in verbal sparring,
some of these professional thinkers are higher than others in what Thomas

Scheff, for quite other purposes, called a "ladder of awareness."[36] Every character in the film can be positioned upon this "ladder," with the effect that the characterological structure is a vertical one. An inverse relationship has been established between our moral approbation of characters and the extent of their information, so that knowledge, of the sort we see displayed at Green Manors, is both not good and not attractive. "Edwardes," for whom we feel the most profound warmth and protectiveness, in fact knows nothing.

Constance does fall in love with this newcomer, but her affection is first mustered at a distinct physical remove, in fact before the two set eyes upon one another. As the author of a book that Constance has already read, *Labyrinth of the Guilt Complex*, an authorial embodiment of Edwardes's persona has preceded him to Green Manors and Constance, as astute a student of the invisible Edwardes as Freud ever was of Charcot, attached herself to this embodiment by devouring the writing—"I've read all his books—a very keen unorthodox mind"—and preparing herself to find her author-hero intellectually stimulating even before the beginning of the film. This "crush," which is foiled explicitly for us by both Garmes's crude treatment of her and the unbridled Carmichael's undisciplined advances to the self-possessed Dr. Fleurot (John Emery)—is one of the ostensible motives of Dr. Murchison's early tone of ironic, but affectionate, teasing as he talks with Constance about his august replacement: "I shall hover around for awhile, like an old mother hen, at least until Dr. Edwardes is firmly on the nest."

Dr. Peterson's *preparation* to love Dr. Edwardes the author has much importance (not least because she never meets him). In origin, and in quality, her admiration from a distance may remind viewers of their own preparations for, and attitudes during, a film like *Spellbound*, where, thanks to publicity, they can have been ready to admire Ingrid Bergman and Gregory Peck entirely in advance of contact.[37] This preparation is, of course, the essence of what stardom is all about, or at least what it is touted to be by publicity departments, agents, gossip columnists, and the like. Anticipatory adoration is generally a characteristic of filmgoing audiences since the advent of the star system (well in place by the end of the 1920s). Adoring Dr. Edwardes, then, Constance is one more of Hitchcock's many audience (or viewer) surrogates.[38]

There is also something self-deprecating, or at least self-questioning, in Constance's early devotion to a man who cannot at this point see her. A seductive text—in this case, *Labyrinth of the Guilt Complex*—may certainly function to mask writer from reader; but it also functions to do the reverse, and only a reader seriously attached to masquerade takes pleasure in forming admiration for a writer who cannot imagine or touch her. Her safety from that contact, indeed, is one of the attractions of the activity that produces it. Avid reading is thus always in part about hiding. As Constance "meets" this author through his book (the "meeting" will be more intense, indeed, because it is a "marvelous book"), the author is an 'Edwardes' distinct from the fleshly "Edwardes" who comes to be present for her in physical fact and at the same time utterly removed from the true, real Edwardes (now dead), who actually wrote the words out of which the authorial persona 'Edwardes' is formed and against which the visiting "Edwardes" is measured—and whom we never meet. Even as the real, unknown Edwardes becomes the authorial 'Edwardes' in the event of Constance's reading, meeting becomes "meeting"; in exactly the same sense you are now "meeting" 'me.' And if it is possible that 'you' are enjoying yourself immensely—'I' may seem to hope you are, and I really do—perhaps it is true that you are not. But surely in encountering 'me' through reading you are masking off the possibility of encountering me in some other way. Because you are willing, even eager, to do this—that is, to become the 'you' who reads—and because I am willing to help make it possible by becoming the 'I' who has written, the act of reading can occur.

But if the story of *Spellbound* is a reading (I mean not merely that one gives it a read, as one does any film, but that it is about what one does when one masks off a text in this way), the film also reveals the development of a woman's particular potency as reader, because in ultimately giving over her admiration for the author of this landmark book in favor of love for a man who has written absolutely nothing, a very ordinary kind of man, she becomes a woman who can touch openly, who is willing in her love both to see and to be seen. She transcends reading and text.

Another implication that has profound significance for the narrative and our involvement with it has been hinted at already here. Constance Peterson's willingness to admire this particular author through his text makes it necessary for us, later, to acknowledge that her own personality is doubled, and that ours must be, too, if we are to sympathize fully with her. Doubled? Although the Dr. Edwardes she admires is *not* the man Constance is embracing in the study (and is also totally absent from the film in a physical sense), he certainly *is* the author of *Labyrinth of the Guilt Complex* and has a "very keen, unorthodox mind." As he is both here and not here, she is with two men, the one holding her in his arms and an absent one. That she does not know this at the time does not make it untrue. Initially she is innocent of this duality, to be sure, but not for long, and when she knows that her friend is not Edwardes in fact, her admiration for the book does not evaporate. As she is both with and not with 'Edwardes' the author, she is both with and not with this present man who is visible to us. If she is with this "Edwardes" and not with him, too, at least in retrospect we will have to understand that we are both with her and not with her as she stands there kissing him. To make this more explicit: for the viewer watching silently in Dr. Edwardes's upstairs study-bedroom, it is clearly *not* Edwardes that Peterson is falling in love with, though she tells herself it is Edwardes. We have every reason to know this as does Constance, in fact, as she wanders upstairs in the middle of the night with his book clutched at her breast. The signature on the note he sent to her before their picnic, earlier in the day, a note asking her for help in his study with the unruly patient, Garmes, and the inscription in the limited edition of *Labyrinth* that she is clutching, do not match. Having seen the light streaming from beneath the dark door of his room, having stared at her dark shadow upon his door, she lets herself into his quarters without knocking—hardly the deference due a newly arrived superior. Her close-kept façade begins to unravel as the man wakes from dozing in his reading chair and smiles at her. "I—I—I—was going to read your new book again, I would like to discuss it," she stammers; "I have never discussed an author's work with him."[39] But then she reverses: "I thought I wanted to discuss your book with you. I am amazed at the subterfuge. . . ."

"You're very lovely," he breaks through. He is speaking, of course, from a great depth, since he does not (as we will soon learn) know who, or exactly where, he is and therefore lacks sensibility of the context in which it might or might not be appropriate to say such things. He speaks, as it were, from the heart, the darkest depth, with no keen navigational fix on propriety.

"Please don't talk that way," she defends herself. "You'll think I came in to hear that."

"I know why you came in, because something's happened to us. I felt it this afternoon. It was like lightning striking. It strikes rarely." The music (by Miklós Rózsa) swells and we cut back and forth between close-ups of his eyes and hers. As her eyes close and thus open upon her inner life, she "falls" inward for "Edwardes," who is somehow now, for her and for us, yet in a trace, Edwardes. At once she knows, but does not know, him. She has learned from him, yet he is a mystery. He is her mentor; he is an alien. And watching her two-ness, understanding each half of it, we are divided, too.

The twin domains of rationality and emotion are thus harmonized in Constance Peterson, intellectual student and feelingful woman. She is certainly more than, as Gabbard and Gabbard suggest, a "sexually repressed automaton."[40] If in this study scene we are given a first glimpse of her capacities for passion and passivity, it is a view framed by an earlier, and well-detailed, exposition of her inward life as rhetorical, didactic, reflective, analytic, and metaphorical. "It's rather like embracing a textbook," her randy colleague Fleurot said, trying to grab her while she sat at her desk making notes. She is linguistic and grammatical. Indeed, if she resembles the Viennese spirit, we may find it apt that Hitchcock opted for an actress with a Germanic accent, and that he allows the accent to play a figurative role. In her, we face European knowledge and reflection, but also American passion and abandon. She goes with the new director for a Romantic *déjeuner sur l'herbe* but eats a down-to-earth liverwurst sandwich (traditional but also practical and kinetic). Whether as European seer or American virago, however, or as both, Peterson is now embracing Edwardes/"Edwardes" and enjoying what we can only regard as a classical Hollywood kiss.

"The Kiss"—the Viennese Klimt also, and notably, depicted it—is the moment when first she opens herself to a universe that waits beyond the arcane but precise lacings of her dear psychoanalytical theory.[41] "I don't understand how this happened." It is the moment when the full possibility of her partner's otherness (as "Edwardes") is fully manifest for us. And Hitchcock reveals the passage inward that is implied by this kiss—quite, indeed, as though he had been studying the Klimt canvas as a sketch for it, though we have no particular reason for believing he had[42]—by means of a staged effects shot in which, after her eyes close but before we discover the lovers in one another's arms, as music lifts, and as their barriers apparently progressively dissolve, doors are seen opening to doors that open to doors that open to doors that yet open. There is something vaguely labial about this set-up, perhaps the silence of the openings, which suggests a nexus between sexuality and mind dear to Freud. The musical phrase, the fluidity and automatic freedom with which the doors swing, the brief hiatus—to entertain the audience's aspiration—before each door begins to swing, the fact of Constance having closed her eyes in preparation, all conspire to suggest that our passage is inward (though, of course, doors lead both ways).[43] Perhaps, indeed, it is our desire for intimacy that clinches the reading. But we seem to be progressing toward a core, and the fact that the scene has been moved, from its inception, by Constance and not by "Edwardes" leads us to read Constance as the principal diegetic "space," or placement, being made accessible by the openings. Here film, with its capacity to "cling to the surface of things,"[44] transcends itself by suggesting another dimension. And the point of the shot that I wish to emphasize is that the innermost interior space, the sanctum sanctorum, as shown on Hitchcock's screen, is not a dark abysm at all, but a flooding radiance of pure light. Not moral light, which "plays some of its most beautiful rays over the somber facets of Evil"[45]—which is to say, nature allegorized—but pure light, light in itself, cinematic light, light that clears the darkness, light that heals. If it is a labyrinth we are looking at, and the minotaur is in its heart, he snoozes in a reading chair with a very bright light upon him.

Whether it is Edwardes's study at the top of the stairs or J.B.'s hidden memory, the deepest closet in the corridor of opening "doors,"[46] or the top right drawer of Murchison's desk at the conclusion of this film, nevertheless the closer we come to the secret chamber the more brilliance we find there, the more we can understand, the more intelligibility and possibility for knowledge we find, and the more plainly we can see riddles unriddled. The brilliance is the capturing illumination of dream and *cauchemar* together. Hitchcock's films are like dreams, too, in that they are dynamically structured with both condensation and displacement and in that they are manifested in visions. If it could be said of Charcot, who used his eyes[47] but wrote with his hand, that he was a *visuel*, what epithet, indeed, must we attribute to Hitchcock, who inscribed, in such precision, with a lens?

In Dreams Awake

The warm, strong autumnal sun lit up the statue and the front of the church. I then had the strange impression of looking at those things for the first time.
    Giorgio de Chirico (1912)

There is a dream sequence in *Spellbound*, designed, we may be pleased to know, by Salvador Dali.[48] This sequence is—in every conceivable way—central to the business at hand. J.B., the amnesiac who thinks he is Edwardes, must recount a dream to a psychoanalyst in order to find out who he really is, why he has had amnesia, and what has become of Edwardes, who was, it seems, his own psychoanalyst. Without the dream, none of the action of the surface "plot" can resolve. No identity can be clarified. No happening can be fully witnessed. That structurally films were dreams, Hitchcock was aware. And so there was no need for a structurally realized dream sequence inside this film: any filmic narrative would have been sufficiently dreamlike to suggest the world of dreams. As one simple example of film's affinity to dream condensation, let me quote Hitchcock's little speech to Peter Bogdanovich about the construction of filmic space. It nicely establishes that he had no

illusions of representing reality onscreen, indeed, no hope of picturing anything but a purely constructed and condensed world:

> When I'm on the set, I'm not on the set. If I'm looking at acting or looking
> at a scene—the way it's played, or where they are—I am looking at a screen,
> I am not confused by the set and the movement of the people across the set.
> In other words, I do not follow the geography of a set, I follow the geography
> of the screen. Most directors say, "Well, he's got to come in that door so he's
> got to walk from there to there." Which is as dull as hell. And not only that,
> it makes the shot itself so empty and so loose that I say, "Well, if he's still in a
> mood—whatever mood he's in—take him across in a close-up, but keep the
> mood on the screen." We are not interested in distance. I don't care how he
> got across the room. What's the state of mind? You can only think of the
> screen. You cannot think of the set or where you are in the studio—nothing
> of that sort.[49]

If Hitchcock is fixed within the screen, so are we, and generally. But the inclusion of the dream sequence *as such* gives us access to a specialized, stylized
depiction of a mental zone separated from the conscious (which is the conventional locus of filmic narrative, however dreamlike it is for us as we watch
it). If the narrative conscious, when made filmic, is a dream of consciousness,
then the "dream sequence" is a kind of dreamed dream.

The filmic technique most typically used for dream-rendering in conventional cinema involves three phases: an optically printed transition mechanism (perhaps a three-second blur or waviness in the image, often produced
prior to the era of computer effects through using Vaseline on the lens) leads
to an unmodulated statement of the dream content shot in "normal" film
speed with a lens that is either 50mm or just slightly wide-angle and articulated through conventionally continuous screenwriting. The "dream" concludes with a reprise of the transition mechanism to bring us back to "waking
reality." The effect of using the transition mechanism of specialized bracket-
ing is to facilitate reproduction of the "dream content" in ordinary cinematic
terms consistent with a redefinition of it as "unordinary." While this effect
does felicitously imply that films themselves are but scarcely removed from
dreams—since the "dream" content (the "dream") and the surrounding "reality" content (the story that contains the "dream") are shown in the same
way, separated by relatively simplistic transitions—there are severe limitations in what it can express about mental architecture, that structural arrangement by means of which—indeed, *in* which—dream transformation occurs.

Since the standard convention for viewing filmic action, however "real" it may be, is as conscious perception—either that of the narrator or that of some central character—filmic dreams seem as "real" as filmic waking life once we are embedded in them. While it is true that when we dream, our dreams seem real while we are dreaming them, it is also true that when we regard our dreams, and think of them against the grounding of "reality" that anchors them (to use Goffman's term),[50] they seem built of a different stuff, subject to foreign laws. In sleep we travel across borders without knowing it, and therefore in sleep borders do not exist. That is a major difference from waking reality, where the world is constructed as a set and series of delimitations, boundings, exclusions, and permeations. Reflecting upon our sleep we can see that we have been tourists, and the lands we have visited seem bizarre. As the psychoanalytical dream analysis (by Dr. Brulov [Michael Chekhov]) set forth in *Spellbound* would be instigated from without the dream territory, but would need to make precise exegetical reference to the dream itself, Hitchcock, following Freud, required a means of showing the dream world as a different place, subject to different natural laws and in which language and emotion could be built into new configurations. J.B.'s dream could not, therefore, simply be recounted for the audience, or set out to be experienced; but needed to be quoted, entered, and departed, approached and avoided. In ways that would be instantly recognizable by the viewer, the deep territory being pointed to by Peterson and Brulov (in their analysis) had to be topographically distinct from the surface territory in which the pointers were doing that pointing, since no less than the thing-being-pointed-to the pointing itself was the subject of the narrative.

In order to depict the unconscious as a discrete zone of experience for an audience that tends to take filmic reality as consciousness, it is necessary to use technical means of transformation that are explicit, and recognizable to the conscious minds of viewers—because it is the conscious mind that apprehends a depiction no matter what that depiction claims to represent. Robert Benton's *The Still of the Night* (1982), deeply affected by *Spellbound*, makes use in its dream sequence of altered film speed, green lighting, and subjective point of view;[51] but the effect is only an exaggeration, albeit startling, of the straightforward dream convention described above. In *Spellbound*, by contrast, Hitchcock makes use of a design framework conceived by an artist who had been openly interested in Freudian thinking, and whose canvases simulated precisely the sorts of condensations and displacements Freud posited as central to dream work. The Dali constructions were themselves transformations that rendered the material of the shots distinctly unordinary, and thus

they made it conceivable for Hitchcock to use a relatively conventional filming style and obtain very bizarre results. But it is important to note that Dali's
surrealist set designs notwithstanding, the director arranged for shooting the
sequence (on a soundstage) with especially high-key lighting that would ex-
aggerate and expand the contrast between bright and dark areas. In fact it had
been his earnest desire to do something more:

> I felt that if I was going to have dream sequences, they should be vivid. I
> didn't think we should resort to the old-fashioned blurry effect they got by
> putting vaseline around the lens. *What I really wanted to do, and they wouldn't*
> *do it because of the expense, was to have the dream sequences shot on the back lot in*
> *the bright sunshine.* . . . . But I used Dali for his draftsmanship. I wanted to con-
> vey the dreams with great visual sharpness and clarity, sharper than the film
> itself. . . . Chirico has the same quality.[52]

Hitchcock's intent was that "the cameraman would be forced to what we
call stop it out and get a very hard image. This was again the avoidance of the
cliché. All dreams in movies are blurred. It isn't true."[53] But the dream was
shot using miniatures and sets, inside a studio, a procedure that produced disappointment for more than Hitchcock. "In one of the scenes of my sequence," wrote Dali,

> it was necessary to create the impression of a nightmare. Heavy weight and
> uneasiness are hanging over the guests in a ballroom. I said to FeFe [Dali's
> friend and agent Felix Ferry]: "In order to create this impression, I will have
> to hang 15 of the heaviest and most lavishly sculpted pianos possible from the
> ceiling of the ballroom, swinging very low over the heads of the dancers.
> These would be in exalted dances poses [*sic*], but would not move at all, they
> would only be diminishing silhouettes in very accelerated perspective, losing
> themselves in infinite darkness." FeFe communicated the idea which was ac-
> cepted with enthusiasm by Hitchcock. They passed the idea along to the ex-
> perts, because in Hollywood there are many, many experts to perfect every-
> thing. Some days after I went to the Selznick studios to film the scene with
> the pianos. And I was stupefied at seeing neither the pianos nor the cut sil-
> houettes which must represent the dancers. But right then someone pointed
> out to me some tiny pianos in miniature hanging from the ceiling and about
> 40 live dwarfs who according to the experts would give perfectly the effect of
> perspective that I desire. I thought I was dreaming.[54]

In the surface plot what is important about the dream is its exegesis by Dr. Brulov with his former pupil Constance Peterson's help. But even more telling than the dream analysis is the fact that the dream sequence is the second explicit reference in the film to the innermost (deepest) locus of mental processes, the unconscious, and that here, as in the earlier "corridor of doors," that locus is depicted as being structured by brilliances, not obscurities. As with the theme of the opening doors, for example, a dream theme of scissors cutting away vast swaths of drapery printed with eyes reveals an innermost, furthest space, behind the last curtain, which is all brilliance. The "proprietor" of the dream club where J.B. is "playing cards with a man with a beard" has a light stocking pulled over his face, so that his head is radiant. This "proprietor" watches from behind a chimney as the man with the beard plunges from a sloping rooftop. The victim drops a distorted Daliesque wheel, which cascades down the roof into a close-up. It is brilliant white. Finally, in a high contrast shot, J.B. races down a slope in brilliant sunshine, while a great, dark, winged form flutters above his head. Meanwhile, all the while J.B. recounts this dream, more and more light floods him in the chair in Brulov's study. We move closer and closer to the interior, and the illumination is blinding.

But what is brilliance, what obscurity? In both Freudian language and Hitchcockian rendition, obscuration is the action taken to send experiential clarity away, to bury it. J.B.'s neurotic fear of parallel lines, for example, buries an event of his youth. Apparently, the "natural" essence of buried experience is that if it were not buried it would be plain and visible—problematically so. Obscurity is thus not real in itself, but only a process for masking the real, which is light. But masks (that obscure) must themselves be seen—must block us *ostensibly* from what we cannot get at.[55] So the essence of obscuration, like the essence of what it hides away, rests in its capacity to be luminous itself, to reflect and transmit light, not in its capacity to absorb and contain it. Everything high and low, good and vile, is for the eye. Throughout the critical literature on Hitchcock, and in his own writings about himself as well as his interviews with others, the point is made again and again that he believed all the details of narrated experience had to be shown carefully upon the screen. This characteristic of the filmmaker is far more relevant to his work, I would argue, than any dark personal mysteries he cloaked in fantasies however arcane. The screen was a kind of consciousness for him, and what was unsatisfactory and unclear in experience (because of pain, guilt, or social impossibility) had to be brought clearly into its space: "Space should not be wasted, because it can be used for dramatic effect."[56] *Space should not be wasted.* Or: where unconscious was, there shall conscious be. There is nothing available for filmic discourse (or, it can be suggested, for psychoanalysis) but light and more light. Darkness, indeed, is but a potential for light. The more we see, the later it gets. Darkness is before, primordial. Illumination is ultimate, what we fall through experience to find.

Because of Hitchcock's predisposition in *Spellbound* to express rather than repress or suggest, because of his emphasis on clear structure and didactic illumination, it may be difficult to see how the film has much in common with mainstream works of this period rife with *films noir.*[57] Certainly, in the dream sequence we find characteristics Schatz has emphasized as central to noir: "impressionistic lighting, an environment rendered surreal through set design and camerawork, the general feeling of the character's inadequacy and alienation."[58] Schrader suggests a social-critical dimension of classical noir, a focus on an "honest and harsh view" of society,[59] and indeed we can detect it here, both offscreen and by implication, if we consider that a major consequence of the presentation of Hitchcock's deepest inner space as bright, as a source of illumination, is that darkness must be expelled into the surround. The self is luminous; the world in which the self must struggle is obscure.[60] By systematically diffusing the self into the world, the psychoanalytical process and Hitchcock's filmmaking both strive to produce a general enlightenment.[61]

Instead of posing the dark and repressed personality as a localized source of anxiety and withdrawal in the context of a nicely ordered social world, Hitchcock inverts the formula, jeopardizing within an altogether shadowy context the radiant struggle of a decent human being to survive. Even his villains tend to be decent human beings who failed to uphold their decency against overwhelming social forces that wore them down, what William Rothman calls "Wrong Ones":[62] educated and often advantaged by class, they are moral if twisted, owning couth if little determination to display it in the face of persistent criticism and degradation. To stress his inherent decency finally pushed past its limit, for example, the malevolent Thorwald in *Rear Window* is shown being subjected to demeaning harangues. In *Family Plot*, Arthur Anderson kidnaps a bishop who abused him as a child (a plot twist uncannily prescient for a film made in 1975!). Alexander Sebastian in *Notorious* is a gentleman who has a domineering harridan mother and a weak resolve. The assassin in *The Man Who Knew Too Much* (1956) has self-doubts that render him vulnerable to middle-class British deprecation. And generally in

Hitchcock films the noble protagonist represents a light, even a dim light, urging forward in a sea of darkness, repression, and difficulty. In *Spellbound*, Constance Peterson wakes in the dark of night, robes herself, steps out of her room, climbs the stairs, enters the library, retrieves Edwardes's book, and stands outside his door, this entire long sequence being rampant with shadow and signal illumination. Her room has a glowing door as she proceeds to leave on a course of investigation and discovery. Seen from outside in the hall as she passes onward to the stairway, the aperture of her past, representing nothing but relative ignorance, is a swatch of darkness. The stairwell is cut with compromising bars of darkness, as is the upstairs landing. There is forbidding darkness on Edwardes's face and in his hair, yet a radiant invitation in his eyes. Green Manors, the socially structured, sane, civilized holding tank for the mentally disturbed, is darkness; but Constance, striving toward understanding there, travels in and toward the light. But as we shall see, prizing and approaching illumination are no guarantee that darkness will be transmogrified or banished.

IMPOTENCE

If the Reality Principle is scotomizing, and the pleasure dome of the id a way station toward utopia, we must expect to find the world that represses our instincts a potential source of not only pain and discomfort but also organization, since it is the pressure of organization that vitiates the polymorphous energy of impulsive play. Boundary, government, grammar, form, class interest—all these are attributes of the reasonable world recognized and adapted to by the ego. In *Spellbound*, the love between Peterson and "John Brown" is the core of the surface story, and for most observers it has constituted the received meaning of the film. Any analysis that sees *Spellbound* as essentially about Constance and the recovered memory of her patient/lover, however, must fail to account for much else that is to be seen.

An especially fascinating lacuna—which has nothing whatever to do with love or amnesia but much to do with the organized world in which this love and this amnesia have happened—is the sequence set at the Rochester home of Dr. Alexei Brulov, Peterson's psychiatrist, mentor, and friend. It is Brulov, indeed, and not "Edwardes," who with his arrival in the filmic frame nudges aside Dr. Murchison (Leo G. Carroll) as Constance's guide through the wonderland of psychoanalytic theory. In this very important group of scenes— the arrival at Brulov's house; the nocturnal shaving escapade; the breakfast

psychoanalysis and dream revelation—we learn not only about psychoanalytic technique in general but also the true relation between the patient's amnesia and his obsessive, recurring fears.

"Edwardes" is in flight from the police, who share his conviction that he is
the murderer of the real Dr. Edwardes. Constance finds him and guides him
to her old professor, who will analyze and, she hopes, cure him. But when
they arrive at Brulov's house, the professor happens not to be in. This opens
the way for what is generally taken as a passage of "comic relief." Constance
and her "fiancé" John Brown (as the amnesiac has now permitted her to name
him) have been directed by a grumpy and disaffected housekeeper into the
professor's study to wait for his return home. There they encounter a pair of
gentlemen who are also waiting for the professor, and here is the dialogue
"John" and Constance are permitted to overhear—and we with them—in
this play-within-a-play:

> MAN ON LEFT: H-how's your mother been lately?
> MAN ON RIGHT: Oh, she's still complaining about rheumatism. She figures I
> oughta get transferred down to Florida. I said, uh, do you expect me t'sacrifice
> all chance of promotion just because you've got rheumatism?
> MAN ON LEFT: Did you take the subject up with Hennessy?
> MAN ON RIGHT: Yeah. He said a transfer could be arranged but I'd probably
> have to start all over again as a sergeant, and I said personally, I think that's
> unfair, after all the work I did on that narcotics case.
> MAN ON LEFT: What did Hennessy say to that?
> MAN ON RIGHT: Oh, a lot of things. He made some crack about me being a
> *momma's* boy.

It is at the mention of a narcotics case, in the seventh shot after the four
characters are settled comfortably with one another, that J.B. realizes for the
first time—and we with him—that he and Constance are in the company of
policemen. If Hitchcock had intended this scene to be only about Constance
and J.B. being confronted by the police just when they have begun their
flight, he could have managed the ironic set-up without six full shots of purely
extraneous material. *Space should not be wasted.* We must examine this scene,
with a view to finding in the "nonsense" a meaning that is clear and coherent:
this was also Freud's technique in listening to dreams.

Our early information is that these two gentlemen, who do not yet have
names, are clearly engaged together in some sort of work under the supervi-
sion of a man named Hennessy. One of them has an ill but nagging mother

whose demands that he seek transfer to Florida have put him in conflict with this boss.[63] He is struggling, then, in simultaneous relation to two separate, yet intertwined, powers—his mother and Hennessy. The mother apparently fails to understand how her rheumatism can be insufficient reason for him to want to move south (refuses to accept that he may be subject to a system of control in which she is not herself paramount). At the same time, although this man was successful on a narcotics case earlier, Hennessy saw no reason to elevate him in the chain of command. In Hennessy's eyes, if the man is more concerned with pleasing his mother than gaining the approbation of his superior, he is a momma's boy—this conclusion implicit in the man's resentfully stressing the epithet when he pronounces it. Keeping him down is for Hennessy a means of educating the officer into manhood, a process made all the more humiliating for the subject because he is in pronounced middle age. The speaker is therefore suffering pressure due to the fact that he is a "servant of two masters."

These humiliating circumstances are not at all funny. They are problematic, although we may laugh in discomfort because of the age of the victim or because the exact nature of the situation is also socially unspeakable in a domestic setting like this one where mothers are to be worshipped. (Brulov has a charming and well-tended little house.) More importantly for a reading of the film, however, the man's very explicit analysis of the power relations between Hennessy and himself can draw our memory—if we have not become as amnesiac as J.B.—to the Peterson-Murchison-Edwardes triangle. We can recollect that there was something not quite satisfied or accepting in Murchison's resignation from the directorship of Green Manors—"The old must make way for the new, particularly when the old is suspect of a touch of senility"—and intuit that whoever contracted for the employment of Edwardes as Murchison's replacement also produced Murchison's resignation in the first place—

CONSTANCE: I should think the Board of Directors would realize you're feeling much better—you've been like a new man since your vacation.
MURCHISON: *The Board's as fair and all-knowing as a hospital Board can be . . .* [italics mine]

—and in doing so sat upon him, indeed, much as the unseen Hennessy does over the gentleman in the drawing room. That the identity of these two chatters is unknown at this point, that until the middle of the scene we do not even recognize their means of employment, generalizes the power relationship they are discussing, applying it to any mature adults who have not succeeded in gaining access to power in a post-war capitalist state that extends adolescence in order to produce a servile, politically impotent labor market. Impotence is the theme here, not comic relief. It is shown in its dark social form, a set of conditions that obtain in structured situations and not just in private sentiments of helplessness.

But is not impotence everywhere in *Spellbound?* At Green Manors Harry the orderly (Donald Curtis) cannot stop the catty Carmichael from scratching his hand. Peterson is similarly helpless: she cannot find the key to unlock Carmichael or, for that matter, her hapless colleague Fleurot, who is himself so impotent in his attempt to make love to her he must abort their conversation in mid-thought when Murchison arrives. Murchison, we then discover, is impotent in the hands of the Board of Directors. And the new head, "Dr. Edwardes," is terrorized and made powerless by the vaguest parallel fork marks on a tablecloth. Peterson is impotent to help herself from being swept away by "Dr. Edwardes" but he is himself impotent in another way (since he is no doctor at all): in dealing with the guilt of Mr. Garmes he must seek Peterson's help. His hopeless lack of memory is a diffuse and disturbing general impotence. We will learn that in his childhood this man suffered a truly paralyzing instance of impotence, when his brother died; and that on the ski slopes of Eagle Valley, at the moment of the real Dr. Edwardes's death, that childhood impotence was powerfully reborn. Our present hapless subject in Brulov's study, Lt. Cooley (Art Baker) as he turns out to be, is impotent in the face of his mother and again in the face of his boss, Hennessy; and then a third time in the face of his colleague Sgt. Gillespie (Regis Toomey); and, of course, in the face of Constance and J.B. as well, since they are patently overhearing his private tale of woe. The patient Garmes has a peculiar impotence: unable to persuade anyone that in fact he killed his father, he must settle for their commiseration with his "hallucination." Dr. Brulov, a man not noted for his impotence, did not find a way to shake the police from dogging his life in Europe and cannot find a way here; and he is pathetically inept at brewing the cup of coffee that could wake him to the quotidian world. So he is frozen in a philosophical dream, a doddering professor, until Constance chances on the scene to relieve him.

But we also see displayed, when Brulov and Peterson decode J.B.'s dream together, and emphasized with snazzy inserts of the dream itself, a contrapuntal potency, the power to discover, to imagine, to amalgamate, to interpret: Joseph's power. If the vertical antinomies of power and powerlessness, impotence and potency, can be physical and economic (as in the case of the policemen in the study), they can also be intellectual. That thought and mental processes can be a root of power is an idea dear and absolutely necessary to Freud (and also, of course, to the Frankfurt School that followed);[64] and a central piece in the narrative puzzle of this film. The psychoanalytic technique is aimed to open new powers to the patient through unravelings, clearings, illuminations, recollections, views. But when a patient does not know his own identity, enlightenment is without perspective, surreal. For his own part, the unseen Dr. Edwardes who is the glyph at the heart of this film has created a radically new psychoanalytical technique: rather than just conversing with his patients, or just hearing them, he takes them bowling, goes skiing with them down mountaintops. This is a less literary and more cinematic technique, producing a refreshing and healing view through movement—for the patient without perspective, a view that is cubist, but for any of his patients clearly a view that is progressive.

The Edwardes technique is adjudicated by both Brulov and Peterson, the former disparaging from above and the latter admiring from beneath. A vertical intellectual dimension is thus struck between dismissal and respect, between Brulov and Constance. In giving consideration to Edwardes's active, participatory technique (as a possible aid to helping J.B., who had been "wearing" him), Constance involves herself in a kind of ladder of awareness at one moment, in the Empire Hotel, by using (and outwitting) the house detective (Bill Goodwin): this points to a vertical hierarchy of mental power. And if we examine the final psychiatric consultation between Peterson and Murchison, we find not just a search for a proper psychiatric statement or the solution of a murder mystery, but a contest of philosophical positions to determine mental superiority. The language of the encounter is diagnostic, but the form is a struggle for power between Peterson, mentally "young in the profession," and Murchison, the mentally "broken-down old horse." Dr. Edwardes, Murchison's threatening successor, has conveniently disappeared from the equation.

Dr. Brulov is the center of mental potency in the film, at least for Constance, with whom we identify. Constance, who will save J.B. from perdition with the powers of her mind and the conviction of her heart, builds her strength upon her thinking and her thinking upon Brulov's, just as J.B. ultimately builds his own upon hers. Immediately on his entrance to the house, Brulov takes command using powers of mind:

COOLEY: Uh, Dr. Brulov, I'm Lieutenant Cooley of Central Station. This is Sergeant Gillespie.

BRULOV: What for?

COOLEY: We thought you might give us some data on Dr. Edwardes?

BRULOV: Data? What is this kind of persecution?
COOLEY: But yesterday you had some kind of theory.

An argument and power struggle has been invoked over the extent of Brulov's intelligence regarding the Edwardes case, and over the propriety of the police attempting to appropriate that intelligence. "If Edwardes," suggests Brulov, "took along with him on a vacation a paranoid patient, he was a bigger fool than I ever knew he was. It is the same as playing with a loaded gun." As the police are always presumably playing with a loaded gun, they are here being reproached for their quotidian capacity for violence by this student of civilization. The comment about Edwardes is intended to put the police off the scent. I take Brulov to be saying, "If I have such a biased opinion of a colleague's professional practice, I cannot reasonably be challenged as a source of information." But the deep tenor of Brulov's comment is especially significant: he can appear to realize (by suggesting that his colleague Edwardes did not) the gravity and power of the mental process. To compare a paranoiac to a loaded gun is to suggest that mental configurations can have physical outcomes, and negative ones. But if the mind is a serious topography, the well-ordered mind (i.e., Brulov's) is a sublime vista, a "super-optical, transcendental self-absorption" seen from the top of a mountain.[65]

Every note sounded in this discussion is about power and hierarchy, which is to say, about the scale of impotence: Brulov has just come in from lecturing at an army hospital (speaking, that is to say, from "above" to an audience that listens, intellectually if not geographically, from "below"). It is by ranking that the chatting men introduce themselves to Brulov, senior on the premises—yet not to Constance or J.B.—as Lieutenant Cooley and Sergeant Gillespie. Brulov invokes police inquisitions. The men want to be given data on Edwardes, and one who solicits data is inferior to one who possesses and dispenses it. Then the power of the police suggests to Brulov persecution. Further, the magnitude of Edwardes's foolishness is being estimated by Brulov—the bigger a fool Edwardes was, the less respectable. Brulov informs Cooley that he does not think on command, that he is not a bloodhound, and thus defends his honor, claiming more status than should be accorded either a dog or a police inspector (a bloodhound). The suggestion that Brulov and Edwardes were friends—equals in status—is disputed by Brulov, who claims superiority in professional terms but seems to wish it more generally as well—he seems to come from Vienna, after all, the fount of psychoanalysis and culture, while Edwardes is an unruly upstart from the West. Brulov admits he had a spat with Edwardes at the psychiatry convention in Boston, but in a way that makes it evident they were not on equal footing when they argued. Further, the "quarrel" was an episode about which the police can be shown to have incorrect—and thus inferior—information. Further, Brulov questions Edwardes's psychoanalytic technique, mostly in terms of its misguided focus upon equity: "taking people skating, or to a bowling alley" means, in stratificational terms, playing alongside them and relinquishing power. Brulov thinks such a maneuver preposterous. Indeed, the fatal downhill ski run we will learn Edwardes made with J.B. at Eagle Valley is an ecstatic epitome of shared, equalized experience in which status differences are absorbed in the rush of uncalculated adventure. To cap this brilliant cadenza on power and powerlessness, status, vertical position, and honor, the exiting Cooley gives a neutral "Good-bye, ma'am" to Constance but a deferent "Good night, sir" to J.B., and then Brulov sardonically predicts he will be subjected (by these power-hungry authoritarians) to brutality.

"What do you suppose they are snooping around me for?" he wonders aloud to Constance, "The next they will give me is the third degree."[66] In his estimation of the level of interrogation to which he has just been subjected (that it was all but the third degree), Brulov can easily be taken, by viewers uninterested in power and control, to be exaggerating in his typically charming, idiosyncratic way. But Brulov is a recent immigrant from Eastern Europe, a sort of expert on dominance and submission—certainly on dominance of the politically freighted kind. We have the slight impression, indeed, that Constance, not quite mindful (for a moment) of his past, takes him too lightly. But J.B. knows what it is to have the police breathing down one's neck, and he doesn't find Brulov's comment frivolous at all.

If potency and impotence—especially the mental sort—are key themes in this film, we should expect to see struggles for power. Indeed, Mary Carmichael struggles to climb upon Peterson's judgments; Fleurot and the other doctors jostle to evaluate her romanticism and femininity; Murchison is at war with his condition of forced retirement; "Edwardes" is conflicted against the hold of his blurry past. And Constance herself, at least in the scene of "The Kiss," is engaged in a quest for power, since falling in love with her superior will have profound political implications for her professional status. If she is not thinking of vertical stratification and its relation to professional life, her male colleagues at Green Manors surely are and know that she is pulling strings. But looking at *Spellbound* in terms of power, prestige, social climbing, and control—in short, seeing the ladder of awareness as something the zealous mind can climb—allows us to note as well one more strange and illuminating fact. . . .

Autumn Leaves

At the beginning of this study of the powers of the mind, Hitchcock chose to plant an epigraph from (of all works) *Julius Caesar*. What we are looking at as the credit cards pass is a tree in an autumn wind, its dead leaves blowing away to leave it bare. The suggestion is of outworn and lifeless matter being thrown off by a vigorous force. If the tree is the mind and the dead leaves are obstructive repressed feelings, the wind represents the vigor of psychoanalytic insight. But the autumnal dispersal of the leaves (Hitchcock would come back to explore it in *The Trouble with Harry*) is also a brutal act of power. Cooley and Gillespie are dying leaves on a branch of the police department. Murchison is a dead leaf at Green Manors. In psychiatry, however it tends toward rationality and light, there is also domination, and only some of those played upon by the force of a therapeutic institution are patients.

As a key to the framing of power and powerlessness in *Spellbound* we find this epigraph:

> The fault . . . is not in our stars.
> But in ourselves . . . ,

pointing neatly to psychoanalytic practice and implying that we ourselves control our destinies, not the world we live in with its brute forces or the caprices of fortune. But the Jesuit English schoolboy who was Hitchcock knew his Shakespeare and this passage, from *Julius Caesar*, is not fully quoted. The authentic lines, relating to power and its abuse, come from a discussion between Cassius and Brutus about the ability of a weak man to rise to power. Cassius states:

> Ye gods, it doth amaze me
> A man of such a feeble temper should
> So get the start of the majestic world
> And bear the palm alone.
>
> .   .   .
>
> Why, man, he doth bestride the narrow world
> Like a Colossus, and we petty men
> Walk under his huge legs and peep about
> To find ourselves dishonourable graves.
> Men at some time are masters of their fates:
> The fault, dear Brutus, is not in our stars,
> But in ourselves, that we are underlings.[67]

Not without resentment, Cassius is speaking of the Caesar who had once been afraid to swim a river with him, now become Emperor. It is the human desire for passivity, for self-degradation, he argues, rather than divine ordinance, which seems to have the effect of raising one (even undeserving) man by artfully lowering many others. Some of us wish, and choose, to be low. We could say, some decline resistance. Yet also: powerlessness is belittling.

Being underlings is the central existential and psychoanalytical problem of *Spellbound*, and underlings are everywhere, not always voluntarily. Cooley has not come to terms with Hennessy, or with the offscreen Mrs. Cooley. Gillespie, in his turn, has not adapted to his superior, Cooley, though he has shown by discreetly and politely asking after Mrs. Cooley's health that he is attempting to do so. Mary Carmichael has not submitted the twisted force of her sexual impulse to Dr. Peterson nor, in his way, has Dr. Fleurot. The philandering stranger in the hotel (Wallace Ford) must submit to the constraints of the house detective as, presumably, must the desk manager who supplies the registration cards that make it possible for Constance to locate "John Brown." And the detective places himself in her power because he is constrained by his own lust; as a house employee he is not obliged to help a strange woman sitting in the lobby locate a registered guest. Knowing himself to be in no way associated with a crime, Brulov can openly refuse to submit to the power of the police; who, needing information he is closely guarding, must bow as underlings to his superiority. Murchison is an underling whose retirement was mandated by the Board of Directors, even though, by his claim, after his vacation he is a "new man."

Further, acquiescing to power knowingly and rationally and understanding its operation are both tasks that require a state of mental balance. Being an underling is something one must be able to handle in a hierarchical society, however genuine is one's striving for equality for oneself and others. The culminating scene of Constance Peterson "undergoing analysis" in Dr. Murchison's office attests to the fallibility of an imbalanced mind, Murchison's, when faced with the problem of its own powerlessness. By arranging a filmic setting in which an ultimate confrontation between moral opposites can take place in a therapeutic scene, and in therapeutic terms, Hitchcock shows how in medicine and thought, as in politics and society, it is power that structures and dominates. Narratively, the conversation between Peterson and Murchison is a kind of old-fashioned showdown, after all, but rhetorically it is a competition of diagnoses.

I wish to examine two signal implications for both the structure of *Spellbound* and the theory of psychoanalysis. First, as I have already suggested, superiority can be seen in mental as well as in physical terms. Hitchcock suggests physical power by J.B.'s placement above his brother in the childhood reminiscence; by the strategic placement of the man with the wheel in the dream; by Murchison watching from his aerie as Edwardes arrives at Green Manors; by J.B. hovering over sleeping Constance, razor in hand, after the shaving escapade at Brulov's; by Fleurot attempting to embrace Constance from above as she makes notes at her desk. But mental dominance is no less important. Murchison has directed Green Manors from a relatively arrogant stance; "Edwardes" is noticeably humbler. Peterson and Brulov amicably joust to see which derives the more stringent psychoanalytical decoding of J.B.'s secret communications. Cooley deferentially gives Brulov every reason to note that he does not intend to presume any powers of intelligence in the face of the elder, and more learned, man. And the prime cause of the real Dr. Edwardes's death, as we learn at the climax, is a case of one man finding himself unable to come to terms with his own intellectual inferiority to another. Just at the moment that John Ballantine, coming in frenzy to his memory and his emotions, knows that he did not push his brother, in childhood, to his death—that he did not assume a position of power—he gives Constance the tools to discover that the murder of Dr. Edwardes *was* a killing of exactly that sort.

But a corollary to the notion that mental power counts is that the doctor-patient relation is itself a locus of power and powerlessness. The powers of the world torment us, but even in the therapeutic relationship we may find that "we are underlings." If powers can be mental, the process of psychoanalytic therapy involves a patient willingly deferring to the analytic powers and language of the discipline, as embodied by the person of the analyst. One submits to analysis before working out a transference and coming to a new perception. That audiences might be unaccustomed to the potential brutality in the undertaking that would form the heart of his film Hitchcock was well aware, placing just after the title sequence an "introduction" to psychoanalytic practice that functions, with its rather moralistic punchline, as a kind of disclaimer.

Our story deals with psychoanalysis, the method by which modern science treats the emotional problems of the sane.

The analyst seeks only to induce the patient to talk about his hidden problems, to open the locked doors of his mind.

Once the complexes that have been disturbing the patient are uncovered and interpreted, the illness and confusion disappear . . . and the devils of unreason are driven from the human soul.

Brulov is a kind of exorcist, then. Though his charming house is a shelter, there is no dearth of power—even gendered power—there: Constance is a welcome guest as long as she agrees to make a good cup of coffee in the morning. And, blessing her "engagement" to J.B., Brulov enjoins them to have babies and not phobias.

As though following through on his order, Constance and J.B. climb the stairs to the bedroom and go to sleep. In the middle of the night he awakes with anxiety and walks into the bathroom. He mixes shaving soap and prepares his razor (he must cut away the mask from the man in the mirror), but then stumbles out into the bedroom in a trance, the open razor still in his hand. He is alarmed to see, in the play of moonlight upon the jacquard bedspread, exactly the pattern of parallel lines that provoked him in the play of her fork on the tablecloth when first he met Constance at Green Manors. With that razor open in his hand he gazes at her sleeping, and then, ominously, he descends the stairs to find the old doctor. We are certain he has violence in mind and that Brulov, having been up late reading, is to be slaughtered (shaved). But the doctor has a glass of milk for J.B. and for us—the milk is consumed by being poured into the camera[68]—and upon drinking, J.B. and we along with him black out.

The milk, it is later revealed, contained a bromide;[69] wily protective Brulov stayed awake in preparation for what he expected would be an attempt at violence by J.B. upon Constance. But a bromide is both a sedative and a platitude meant to comfort by making reference to the tried and true. When J.B. awakes to the reassuring ceremonial of Constance's morning coffee, and the abbreviated psychoanalysis that will unlock his dream, we may be led by the warmth and romantic aptness of this "morning-after routine"—the therapy session is treated like a read of the morning paper—to forget that this particular patient enters the extremely vulnerable therapeutic relation with two analysts, not one—hence, outnumbered—and under the residual influence of drugs. This culminating scene is thus a brutal portrait of a therapeutic assault by an artist whose intense sensitivity to the language and intellectual modeling of Freud did not extend to a fondness for the institutionalization of his ideas in the psychoanalytic establishment. That establishment, represented here by Brulov more than by Peterson, I think, is for Hitchcock the institutionalized studio system, Selznick International in particular, where, even with a love of the language and technique of film that has probably never been matched, Hitchcock found himself essentially solitary, uncomfortable, and outnumbered in the face of David Selznick's incessant, unyielding, and manipulative oversight.[70]

That for all its avidity in penetrating psychoanalysis as a hierarchy

Spellbound should rest upon the foundation of a love story is the bromide Hitchcock has prepared—and hidden in the milky white preparation of the film—for *us*. The formulaic is a platform from which we are shown the unanticipated. The oddity of this *film blanc*, indeed, as *film noir*, is just that not only release and freedom but also the most problematic and abrasive realities inhere in what is luminous and brilliant: the innermost mind as depicted in the door sequence, the linen tablecloth, the snow at Eagle Valley, the bedspread, Constance's complexion, and the whites of J.B.'s eyes, Murchison's pallor, the orderly's white shirt and Green Manors which it symbolizes. Brulov's glass of milk is a token of all that is in need of tranquillity but not tranquil itself.

The psychoanalytic dream-decoding is the most explicit attempt in the film to make direct use of Freudian language and consulting technique as overt subject matter. If Selznick, caught up in his own psychoanalysis, was devoted to the technique and suggestions of May Romm for the construction of material like this, we know, too, that Hitchcock was hardly as devoted to Selznick; and that this artful scene in Brulov's consulting room—where hangs no portrait of Charcot or even Charlie Chaplin—a scene that is a puzzle and a power struggle at once, sets us just far enough from the psychoanalytic establishment Selznick had embraced to see the decoding process as both a liberating and dominating act, clarifying and containing at once. On the set, Hitchcock, Leff informs us, took pains to avoid Romm:

> Perhaps Hitchcock feared that Romm's logic would impede his intuition. Perhaps he regarded psychoanalysis as just one more gimmick peripheral to the real work of telling a story on film. Or perhaps, a very private person, he did not wish to reveal even so much as his professional life to a professional analyst.[71]

But he could not avoid the implications of Freud's exploration of the mind, as they bore on his plot. Without the explanation of J.B.'s dream there could be no hope of J.B. remembering, and therefore no past for him, and therefore no future. But the explanation Brulov and Peterson fashion for J.B. is derived in a particular, and powered, social context. Though the patient's mind is a horde of secrets, the doctor always knows more; and it is through releasing his secrets to the sanction and comprehension of the analyst that the patient can gain illumination. This particular brightness, therefore, is an attribute of power, conferred at a moment of what must finally be obedience. If J.B. can tell Peterson and Brulov what he is dreaming, they can show him what he has been trying to say to himself. In laboring for David O. Selznick, of course,

Hitchcock had learned that the same bromide applied to him. In submission to the rigors of the studio production process—and no producer was as controlling as David O. Selznick—lay any hope of release (and self-knowledge) through finishing and distributing a film. It was Hitchcock who had learned the lesson of being an underling.

For a finale he had Constance take J.B. skiing, just as J.B.'s original psychoanalyst, Edwardes, might well have done. As they near a precipice together he suddenly remembers that he *had* gone skiing with Edwardes, and that Edwardes had slipped into the precipice right before his eyes, before he could do anything to save him. Hitchcock with this scene fully exploits the paralytic horror of seeing with clarity in the precise moment of one's impotence, an experience that may have threatened him, working for Selznick, just as much as it did the fictional J.B.[72]

With *Spellbound* Hitchcock seems to have felt the planting of a seed, however: to free himself from Selznick, to produce his own films, to replace the dominant superego of the Hollywood establishment with his own creative force. He would continue the collaboration for *Notorious* (which he would produce but release through Selznick) and *The Paradine Case*, in both of which the brutality of power would play centrally; but now, just days after the wrap party at Romanoff's on October 13, 1944,[73] Hitch went off to his friend Sidney Bernstein in England, thinking of a more independent cinematic life. In 1948, free of David O. Selznick Productions, and fresh as a genius child, he would make the unparalleled *Rope*.

The Tear in the Curtain:

I forbid you to leave this room

If I were to talk to myself out loud in a language not understood
by those present my thoughts would be hidden from them.
Ludwig Wittgenstein, Philosophical Investigations

Where the test is real the powers are real.
Norman O. Brown, Apocalypse

TIME'S FOOLS

Many are they who have made two decisions about *Torn Curtain:* it is a film
about espionage, and it is virtually crazed with flaws, far from what any serious viewer could call a serious Hitchcock work. "Unsatisfactory," Robin
Wood dubbed it, "episodic, lacking the really strong center we have come to
expect."[1] Donald Spoto trumps by calling it "a disappointment for just about
everyone, and none more than Hitchcock himself, who agreed that it lacks
the interest, wit and style of his recent works. . . . It's a good example of a picture with some intellectual substance and a great deal of polish and dignity
but little emotional power. . . . *Torn Curtain* has to be judged a minor achievement."[2] More recently, in an utterly popular venue but holding to the old refrain, Kathleen Kaska labels it a "bloated espionage suspense film."[3]

I would like to attempt a riddling of conclusions such as these, by offering

reason for suspecting there is more to this film than has met the critical or popular eye. Specifically, I would like to suggest it is not a spy film at all, but a film set in the context (and written to some degree in the language) of spying. Abstract endeavors require concrete circumstances. Rather than being trivial or minor, it is a very important film, a work of real magnitude about a vital and disturbing issue, the ability to believe. No Hitchcock film—not even *Topaz* or *Rope*—has so energetically been disparaged by the critical and popular establishment. Yet *Torn Curtain* is a work filled with the most endearing and provocative nostalgia, a film in which the human mind is a central protagonist against the human heart. Where else in Hitchcock, after all, can we find a killer chiding the hero for being insufficiently respectful in an art museum; or a daffy old man happy to reminisce about charming Vienna, where his sister was run over by a tram? Where else can a hero be found with whom it is so sensible, and yet so painful, to identify?

Espionage is, however, the *punctum* apparently most salient and provocative in *Torn Curtain*. As it cannot be denied that, on the surface at least, Michael Armstrong (Paul Newman) is engaged in the business of spying, some dogged attention must be paid to that aspect of the film's structure—

its laterality—the aspect most responsible for leading viewers to see espionage as everything. But the viewer is warned in the opening sequence that
it is academic life, not spying, that is the focus of attention here. Or, more accurately, academic life as clandestine intelligence. The business of spying is
education, plain and simple.

The ostensible story here, as in some other Hitchcock films, involves a pair
of optimistic Americans traveling in Europe.[4] Armstrong is an American
physicist and Sarah Sherman (Julie Andrews) at once his academic assistant
and fiancée. While attending an International Congress in Copenhagen,
Armstrong receives a strange first edition from an antiquarian book dealer
and, signaled by a code printed inside, furtively flies across the Iron Curtain.
Her curiosity intensely aroused (though only engaged to Michael, she may already be said to share with him a "marriage of true minds"), Sherman follows
him to East Berlin, where she learns that he made prior arrangements *to defect*. Her bitter chagrin at his moral cowardice first leads her to reject him, but
is itself reversed when she comes to learn his inner secret: that he is an American agent on a mission to Leipzig to "steal" an arcane atomic theory from a
physicist with whom no one but he is mentally equipped to converse. He succeeds. Her love blossoms again and the two soon find themselves trying to escape back to the West through an obstacle course put up by secret police and
innocent German civilians alike. There is an apparent lateral quality to the
movement of the story, then, back and forth from West to East to West again.
I will spend some time with this movement, in order ultimately to juxtapose
against it an analysis of something else. "Sometimes you have to go a long way
out of your way in order to come back a short distance correctly," Edward Al-
bee wrote, almost, but not quite, about this film.

The lateral journey, the West-East plot—*Torn Curtain* as spy film—requires the presence of borders and thresholds and the drama of traversing
them. Although in this film the development of narrative suspense is clearly
pinned to the capacity to read—neither a linear nor a lateral issue: the physicists read papers at their conference; Armstrong obtains a book and reads
what other readers will not (the secret message); the airline ticket agent reads
out Armstrong's itinerary to Sarah, who follows him to East Germany; Armstrong reads prepared remarks at the East Berlin Airport; German Chief Inspector Gerhard reads from his notebook about Sarah Sherman when the issue of her staying with Michael is raised; Gromek the nosey bodyguard reads
the π symbol in the sand before trying to arrest Armstrong; Prof. Lindt attempts to read Armstrong's mind as they discuss their Gamma-5 research and
is, indeed, a cipher only Armstrong can read; the German highway police are

in a position to read the movements of the Leipzig-Berlin bus on which Michael and Sarah are escaping; the Countess Kuchinska reads the streets of Berlin to offer help; Michael reads the scenery in the theater as the dancers dance and as the prima ballerina, pirouetting, reads him with her eyes—nevertheless, the sense of the Iron Curtain as a border illicitly crossed and then crossed again, and the fact that characters migrate and then find themselves in dangerous territory, capture viewers powerfully. Why is this so?

Apparently central in the topography and lateral movement of this complex action is a package of experiential bifurcations—a set of narratological spaces arranged, as it were, side by side. The Western world is separated from the Eastern world; and the Western bloc from the Eastern; West Berlin from East Berlin; operatives of the capitalists from operatives of the Communists. (From the end of the Second World War until the official razing of the Berlin Wall in 1992, this particular division was a staple of western spy fiction, both printed and filmic. John Le Carré in *The Spy Who Came in From the Cold* and Len Deighton in *Funeral in Berlin* established careers on the basis of fictions that fiddled with it.) Further: because they are separated in spatial placement, American physics is separated from Communist physics. Too, more crucially for the deeper meaning of *Torn Curtain*, the kind of mind that can produce physics is shown to be radically different in the two worlds, so that East is distanced from West not merely as a locus of productions but as a mode of consciousness and desire. I say this because we are drawn to the radical difference in Sarah Sherman's attitudes toward Michael Armstrong, as it becomes apparent to her that his loyalties have shifted longitude: he becomes, it seems, a different sort of morsel. Her view suggests a perspective from which it can easily be believed that the sort of person who calculates a trajectory in Moscow differs radically from his colleague in Washington; the difference in loyalty implicit in the two versions of theoretical analysis implying, too, a moral antagonism.

But this contemporary Babel Hitchcock will show to be myth. Were it real, the sort of conference we see depicted at the beginning of *Torn Curtain* would be icy indeed, with academics from each side of the "curtain" refusing utterly to communicate with one another and, indeed, being incapable of making sense of each other's utterances. Not only political alignment but also thought itself, even poetry, would be divided. However, founded on the presumption that American physicists can indeed speak plainly and directly across the arbitrary divide is the Communists' apparent inducement of Michael to defect. Presumably for them, in defecting his professionalism will be constant. If, then, we are to account for Sarah's personal anxiety about

Michael's character and inner thought "going over to the other side," we must try to fathom what she can possibly think may be altered in him, given that his mastery of the stuff of theoretical physics will indeed remain untrammeled as he "moves" from West to East and proceeds to imagine and formulate in the name of another hegemony. That the new hegemony will be physically repulsive for Sarah—not just morally problematic—is a proposition we must grasp and believe deeply in order to make sense of *Torn Curtain* as a lateral film: in other words, we must grasp that Michael's voyage alone is a basis for her disturbance.

Yet this proposition is hard to accept. It's too heady. It's too abstruse. And indeed, if such a proposition is indicative of the real content of this film, no wonder so many viewers look down their noses. Is any of the lateral action, I must ask, so very central? What if the disturbance for Sarah is *not* produced by Michael's crossing the Iron Curtain? What if the Iron Curtain is not so important in this film at all? Perhaps in order for me to see what Hitchcock has achieved in *Torn Curtain* it is necessary to navigate around and through such lateral plot arrangements as have been laid in my path—I call them, in a proper German manner, gavottes and imagine myself trying to cross the dance floor while they are busily in progress.[5] These traps have to do with spying: probing and withdrawing from a Communist world, enduring danger and surviving. But what if they are laid to enrich and inform, to embellish *but not to establish*, the real central tale?

The lateral stories are intricately built and, I believe, designed to be unsatisfactory. At first Michael Armstrong is a lover and defector, for example, faced against Sarah Sherman and then against the charming and lovable East bloc security-agent-cum-tourist-guide, Hermann Gromek (Wolfgang Kieling). Later, he sheds his mask to become an intelligence operative, at which point Gromek disappears as Michael's counterpart in favor of a second H.G., this time the chief of State Security (read: counter-intelligence), Heinrich Gerhard (Hansjoerg Felmy). The Armstrong-Gerhard antipathy, too, dissolves when Armstrong and Sherman make their way to Leipzig University in order to find, and "debrief," Professor Gustav Lindt (Ludwig Donath). Here, in a third liaison, Lindt-as-physicist becomes a central protagonist, and it is Armstrong-as-physicist who faces him. Armstrong is thus, in narrative order, lover/romantic, intelligence agent, and intellectual and he experiences three critical dramatic encounters, one in each of these personæ: the murderous love scene (as Truffaut puts it)[6] with Gromek; the physical seclusion from Gerhard and his forces in the furrows of the academy; and the metalinguistic conversation with Lindt, as he prises from him the secret of

Gamma-5. Matching Michael's transitions, Sarah is first lover, then detective, then navigator; and if Michael's antagonists are Gromek, Gerhard, and Lindt, Sarah's own are Prof. Karl Manfred (Günter Strack), the woman in the farmhouse kitchen (Carolyn Conwell), and Dr. Koska (Gisela Fischer). The three acts, or gavottes, that compose this ostensible tale of spying (a tale, once again, I plan to bypass) involve domesticity, deceit, and reflection in that order as, first, Michael contends with his relationships with Sarah, Gromek, and Manfred; secondly, as he contends with Gerhard's inquisition and his own need to mask himself in a lie; and thirdly, as he wrestles with Lindt to learn the atomic secret. I will elaborate the three gavottes in some detail, in order that it may be very clear what attachment to them causes us to lose or neglect.

I: THE GAVOTTE OF DOMESTICITY

All three gavottes involve narrative movement from "West" to "East." In the "Gavotte of Domesticity," Armstrong and Sherman, cozying in bed under several layers of blanketing, hide from the physical brutality of a civilization gone awry. Aboard the M/S *Meteor* in the Norwegian Osterfjørd, the heating system has failed and what should be a pleasant intellectual holiday (read: aggressive intellectual competition) has become a frigid nightmare. Alone of all the physicists of both genders that we meet, Armstrong and Sherman have the presence of mind—or the moral openness—to experiment with the thermodynamic possibilities of body heat. But the closeness of the cinematography and the witty charm of their dialogue, as Michael proposes they "call this lunch" and Sarah ripostes that he has "a very unscientific mind," suggest another, hidden, narrative field in which lateral migration of a sort is possible. Masculinity and femininity are here posed as opposite experiential polarities: a convention, to be sure, in Western film of the 1960s but one that prevents Sherman's moralism ("Stop, this is supposed to be a serious congress of physicists") from fully anticipating Armstrong's double entendre ("Tell me, Miss Sherman, what is your position . . . on anti-deuterons?"). The overt play with gender during this lovemaking signals not only the explicit relation between these two principal characters but also their impenetrability to one another, the magnitude of the conceptual and linguistic "voyage" each must make to empathize with the experience—read: "get" the deep meaning—of the other. This rather scenic essay on mental and experiential distinction springing from body difference is preparation for Sarah's later, rather noteworthy, failure to comprehend Michael's deep motives as he "defects."[7]

It is possible to think the table has been set, as it were, for two parallel mystifications and pursuits, each involving a (lateral) doubling of territory and a journey as metaphorical unification and involvement: Armstrong receiving communications that lead him off his scheduled itinerary; and Armstrong ceasing to be the person Sherman thinks she knows. The viewer as interpreter, to some extent using Sarah as model, needs to know where Michael is going and who he is, *really*. For her part, and to assist the viewer, Sarah must both follow him geographically and find a way to the center of his thought. Seen and understood in this (typical) way, this first "movement" of the film continues with the Elmo Bookshop episode in Copenhagen where a secret instruction is passed to Armstrong inside a book; his decoding of the glyph— "π"—as the name of an underground group he must locate; his hastily arranged flight to East Berlin; and the genteel but exceedingly awkward ceremony of welcome from the authorities in Germany, shown in a bizarre and intoxicating scene where every statement is made in German and translated into English, the better to beguile us with the workings of state bureaucratic protocol (and the better to reflect through a bold linguistic metaphor the "travel" from one "world" to another). In all this, just as Michael journeys to his new homeland, Sarah journeys to find the "new Michael."

The story of the little film-within-a-film that is the "Gavotte of Domesticity," adventurous, perhaps, if seen from Armstrong's perspective—he is breaking away from entrapment by a girl who persists in talking of wedlock ("Marriage should come before a honeymoon cruise") and from a dead-end job that represents "an unparalleled appointment in the history of Western science"—is a bleak essay on loneliness, frustration, helplessness, and courage when examined with Sarah Sherman in focus. For years she has labored as Armstrong's unheralded assistant, has given him not only her help but her affection, and her body, hoping that if in return he does not offer the conventional promises that could legally oblige him to her, he will become at least a friend she can trust and comprehend. But now he is engaged in an activity of which she has no understanding, which has inspired him to fly across the Iron Curtain in order to sell out the government and society she believed held his loyalty and certainly holds hers. If he can leave America for another love, of course, he can also leave her; and so she is undecided in East Berlin not only as to whether she should stay with him in his new life but also as to who he is beneath the newly visible facade she has all along been taking for his real self. This "romantic" story, photographed for sadness through gray gauze,[8] is the *Torn Curtain* most viewers and writers are familiar with.

If the content of this first ostensible lateral tale is domestic discord, disillusion, the futility of trying to know another person—in short, a deep chill where one had looked for convivial warmth, then the form through which it is realized is secrecy and affiliation, thus, social etiquette:

> The sociologist Simmel sees showing and hiding, secrecy and publicity, as two poles, like yin and yang, between which societies oscillate in their historical development. I sometimes think I see that civilizations originate in the disclosure of some mystery, some secret; and expand with the progressive publication of their secret; and end in exhaustion when there is no longer any secret, when the mystery has been divulged, that is to say, profaned.[9]

Hence the inclusion of the lunch scene at the Tivoli Gardens, a scene that is too rarely discussed, in which Michael's break from Sarah is cast in terms of very bad etiquette. Around them, rather distinctly in rear projection and thus metaphorically separated in another focal domain, diners are exquisitely appropriate with one another. This scene is prepared by the brief confabulation in the lobby of the Hotel d'Angleterre, where Michael is flawlessly proper in his etiquette to Prof. Hengstrom as he gracefully begs off a lunch date set up long in advance.[10] Etiquette can be seen as a secret face, an invisible mask through which facts are silently and efficiently sifted, key relevances hidden, and other relevances apparently given play, but which at the same time, because it is invisible, does not manifest itself as a filter. Donald Spoto prepares us for this reading of *Torn Curtain* as a masquerade of etiquette with his comment on a session at the American Film Institute in February 1970: "[Hitchcock's] entire career, both in the content of his work and in the gradual refinement of his technique, was devoted to tearing apart the English canonization of manners."[11]

II: THE GAVOTTE OF POLITICAL INTIMACY

In the second gavotte, the second narrative construction that can be read as a horizontal passage by readers committed to, and seeking, horizontality in this film, we are introduced to Armstrong's capacities for deceit and manipulation. The story begins with his consultation at the airport with Gerhard, his formal agreement to engage in high-level theoretical physics for East Germany, and his acceptance of a teaching appointment at the University of Leipzig. It proceeds with his journey to Leipzig and his collegial relationship,

such as it is, with Lindt. But Armstrong makes an unannounced side-trip (a
second one; the first was his flight to Berlin in the first place), an adventure
Sherman seems less fit to accompany than do we, who have not yet committed ourselves to denying Armstrong and are thus morally entitled to follow.
Pursued by Gromek (with a certain insouciant skill) he moves furtively
through the Berliner Kunstmuseum[12] (using it as a forest [of symbols] in
which to lose his pursuer) and then takes a taxi to a remote farm, where he
meets in secret with a man who is clearly working for the American Government (Mort Mills). Because our attachment to Armstrong, being cinematic in
origin, is stronger than hers, we are morally entitled to know before Sarah
that he is a double agent, deceiving (alienating) Gerhard even as he pretends
to cooperate (affiliate), and, of course, deceiving Sarah as well, both in order
to prevent her from giving him away and in order to guard against putting her
in the invidious position of appearing self-conscious under enemy scrutiny,
since, unlike him, she is not trained to give performances.[13] Sarah's naïveté is
thus one of the constructs of Michael's sly routine, a routine we can see self-
reflexively noting its own double structure as both self-protective and protective. Further, Armstrong's tactical need to keep a mask up to Gerhard is
what forces him to murder the busybody Gromek—and to murder him
silently, given that the taxi driver (Peter Barone), a potential witness, is sitting
in the car outside the farmhouse where the action takes place. Masquerade is
also the root of Michael's double-tiered performance with the inquisitive
Lindt in Leipzig, and of the need he shares with Sarah for assistance from the
underground and for disguise, as he tries to move back to the West.

So if the first "story" was about Armstrong's deception of Sherman the
second is about his deception of Gerhard; if the first is played with moral the
second is played with political strokes. And the code of the second plot is not
secrecy as an emotional weapon, but secrecy as both a tactical (read: economic) information preserve and the manneristic organization that sustains
it—thus, intimacy: closeness and understanding on the one hand; distance
and mystery on the other. This is why Hitchcock presents Michael's conversation with the "farmer" by jumping from a very distant to a very close shot.
It is why Gerhard and Armstrong must seem to bond as gentlemen who "understand women"—the intimacy of their friendship, cold as it is, renders
Michael's betrayal more acidic. Consider, too, that in the balletic murder of
Gromek, an intense evocation of an abbatoir sensibility is evident in the death
embrace of the man's fingers upon Armstrong's shoulders (and near Armstrong's neck) as he is being gassed—this is intimacy at its height. Consider
the chase of Armstrong by Gromek in the Kunstmuseum—all performed

with only the American prey visible on the screen and the America-loving hunter manifested through the clicking, echoing sounds of his footsteps in nearby rooms. As Simmel, Chion, and others have pointed out, hearing is the intimate sense. There is a tangible, physical *touch* of those steps, a play on the functioning of the eardrum beset by the touch of sound waves. The Kunst-museum, indeed, is a gigantic inner ear, the walls of its chambers laid over with feasts for the unhearing eye. And hearing is produced through direct vi-bration, not chemical transformation as in sight; so the sequence is pro-foundly intimate, percussive, emotional in quality even though it is chemical in its reference—the tiled stone floors, the vast arrays of calming painted landscapes.[14]

Etiquette is also the sheath of feeling, and in Gromek's casualness of man-ner is a great and signal warmth. While Sarah is a charming companion for Armstrong—efficient, attractive, intelligent, creative, loyal, reliable, and di-rect—it is also true that there is something new, unsentimental, and histori-cally limited about her relation to him. She is in love, shall we say, but she is not fond. She is prepared to become fond. But Gromek is fond already. His fondness for America and, by extension, Armstrong as the visiting American are patent; his fondness for his life in New York, at "88th and 8th,"[15] touches us with sadness, since he was clearly happier there than he is here. The killing of Gromek is the saddest killing in all Hitchcock because Gromek wants so much for Armstrong (us) to like him, to recognize him as a fellow, specifically a fellow New Yorker. But Armstrong is not a New Yorker (like, say, the "farmer"), and his relation to Gromek puts business before reminiscence. What is charming, *Europisch*, about Gromek is that he puts reminiscence be-fore business.

So our journey in this second plot of the film involves the transcendence of all that Gromek stands for, and his murder is the mechanism through which that transcendence is achieved. The Europe that is fond of New York, that remembers the glories of life on 88th Street, goes into the oven like a cake.

Since the charm of Hermann Gromek was an infectious one, after his murder we are rendered especially vulnerable to two contaminations that are particularly undesirable for Hitchcock the storyteller. First, we might view Michael Armstrong in negative light, given that now he is a cold-hearted killer, and to whatever extent we cherish a memory of *Der Zauberer* Gromek, this tendency toward a judgmental chill will be aggravated. The hero will lose our commitment. Even worse is the possibility that the amicable Gromek might himself take over the film emotionally, invade its center and diminish any potentially significant affiliation the audience could later make with other characters. Gromek, then, must be abandoned. And it was in view of doing exactly this that Hitchcock abandoned on the cutting room floor a lengthy and fascinating sequence in which Armstrong, Sherman, and Manfred take lunch together, on their way to Leipzig, in the refectory of a steel plant managed by an old friend of Manfred. A good deal of screen time is given for reminiscence, character development, and a ceremony involving a lengthy speech in German, praising Armstrong for leaving the capitalist warmongers and coming to work for the peace-loving democracies (and which must be partially translated by Manfred). But across the table Armstrong suddenly sees a ghost, the figure of Gromek smiling benignly into his face. This man, bald but otherwise identical to the security agent, comes up and introduces himself as the brother of Armstrong's guide, shows him an upsetting photograph of Gromek with his children, and asks Armstrong to bring a gift to his brother. He walks to the cafeteria line and with a knife identical to the one the farm woman had used to attack his brother, slices a huge piece of sausage and wraps it. The scene ends with a close-up of the sausage in Armstrong's hands:

GROMEK'S BROTHER: *Blutwurst! Ist meinem Bruder seine Lieblingswurst. Vielleicht sind Sie so lieb und geben Sie sie ihm, wenn Sie ihn sehen.*
(Blutwurst! It is my brother's favorite sausage. Perhaps you will give it to him when you see him.)[16]

The scene had to go, Hitchcock told Bogdanovich, "because the brother was so sympathetic. He was played by the same actor who played Gromek. He shaved his head and did a totally different character."[17] Gromek could not be reinvoked with charm.

What I would call the third gavotte, the third conceivable lateral voyage or interior plot, involves, but is not about, secrecy and intimacy. It brings up the issue of language.

III: GAVOTTE OF THE VIEWER'S DESIRE

Armstrong's relation with Lindt is neither independent nor spontaneous. It is conditioned by a number of other relations established with and for him beyond the boundaries of the narrative. First, that he is an operative of the United States government—officially or unofficially—makes the connection with Lindt obligatory for Armstrong, not merely desirable.[18] But secondly, because his motives are ulterior, Armstrong must perforce give Lindt the impression he is attempting the friendship purely out of personal whim and scientific curiosity, the impression that he is befriending Lindt out of a desire, not a need, to do so. Thirdly, and most important for the plot, from the viewpoint of the audience it is Armstrong who wishes to meet Lindt in this film; not Lindt who wishes to meet Armstrong. But Lindt in fact *does* wish to meet, and use, Armstrong at least as much as Armstrong wishes to meet, and use, Lindt. He must wish this, or Armstrong has no hope at all of gaining access to his presence. Lindt's designs upon Armstrong are known to Armstrong. They are the foundation upon which he can build his structure of deceit. But if these designs were given too much illumination by the filmmaker, we would care so much about Lindt that he would become a protagonist of the film. Armstrong's handling of Gromek, in that event, would seem positively benign compared to what we would feel he had done to the sympathetic Lindt we had been following. In order that we may appreciate Armstrong's motive instead of Lindt's, it is essential that Lindt's passion to attract Armstrong be played down, and Armstrong's passion to attract Lindt be played up. Yet Armstrong must, to some degree, be the apple of Lindt's eye, at least temporarily.

But the narrative problem is this: in fact Armstrong as he is has no attractions for Lindt. He is too uninformed (and that is the source of his mission), too unsophisticated (like the rest of the New World), too malicious (a baker if not a butcher), and even too rude. If Lindt gets a straightforward glimpse of the real Armstrong, he will hardly invite him to Room 29. This is why it is necessary for so much of the interaction between Armstrong and Lindt to be interrupted—principally by the agents of Gerhard tracking Armstrong. As long as every encounter with Armstrong is abortive for Lindt, he will eagerly look forward to one more encounter. Just as Armstrong is looking forward to a chance to get into Lindt's mind about Gamma-5, Lindt will be similarly hungry, and there is a real chance that the crucial meeting will take place.

For some time, too, Armstrong can be played with by Lindt as a mouse is by a cat. On the strength of the allegation that he is a willing defector who wishes to study with the esteemed Dr. Lindt, Armstrong is brought to Leipzig and subjected to the sort of interview that obsequious graduate students must put up with at the hands of professors with whom they would like to write their dissertations. For a full professor of theoretical physics at an American university, this seance is derogating enough, to be sure; but the deference required of Armstrong, and the slight to his honor, are aggravated by Lindt's coy introductory game of remaining incognito in the large theater-classroom where a handful of inquisitive academics sit. From the back, he plays the heckler. As Armstrong has been given no formal introduction, he is in no position to recognize or openly address his irreverent adversary by name, lest he reveal that he has already, elsewhere, been briefed. (He must pretend, in fact, to be what we, who have *not* been briefed, really are: ignorant about that obstreperous man in the back row.) The authorities' brusque interruption and cancellation of the interrogation (which has been staged as a "seminar presentation") removes us from the potential dramatic complications of the scene—that one of these geniuses is bound to ask Michael a question he cannot handle and explode his game—and allows the business of the development of the relationship to be carried on more directly. (The reader may imagine how tedious that scene would have been without the interruption, with Armstrong prating on in mathematical jargon and distinguished German academics probing him with questions far too arcane for us to appreciate. Indeed, it would have been like real academic life, which is rarely suitably engaging as a subject for film.)

If the hero must overcome his own forced innocence, coupled with the blatant brutality of the academic structure, in order to come close to Lindt, a second obstacle is of an altogether different brand and can bring a delightful comedic respite. Lindt has agreed to see Armstrong face to face as an accepted equal—in short, he will allow him into the inner sanctum of his academic territory—*but he doesn't want to talk shop.* He wants to talk women, wine, travel, philosophy, news. In short, Armstrong's trip from America to Denmark, from Denmark to Berlin, from Berlin to Leipzig, increasingly perilous, increasingly bleak in all its aspects, has produced as its apotheosis an opportunity to sit with the greatest mind of the Eastern bloc and engage in small talk. While we chuckle at Hitchcock's architectural mastery in establishing this buoyant moment, however, we may miss the more scathing narrative effect Lindt's casualness produces. There is now, thanks to Lindt's unbearable (and unbearably *gemütlich*) playfulness, a division in *our* loyalty and desire. We adore him. So if Armstrong presses him, he is a rank bully. More: for Armstrong to press in any way against Lindt's thoroughgoing backstage professional chumminess is for him to abrogate the identity he must wear to retain any hope of later penetrating Lindt's secret, because in academic circles, a colleague who keeps wanting to get the conversation off the soccer scores and onto one's research findings is certainly not simply a colleague. On the other hand, if Armstrong is satisfied to follow Lindt's limp lead, we will never find out if he finds out what he needs to know before himself being found out.

Called up in this twisting formula are both the business of spying, which is something Lindt pays considerable attention to in this closely guarded environment; and the business of academic research, where even with the most negligible connections to State and Security Affairs, to espionage, or to war nevertheless work and work-related information is closely guarded. One's reputation, career, esteem, and ability to survive are all dependent upon "originality," after all. The fact that both spying and academic research can be in play there together is, of course, one of the many reasons the academy is the quintessential setting for espionage: academic research is by nature top secret, and so who would look among a bunch of egotistical and secretive intellectuals for a genuine military spy? To put it more bluntly: if secrecy is everywhere, how can we see secrecy? How, at least, would defensive secrecy for espionage purposes be distinguished from defensive secrecy aimed at securing tenure?

That Armstrong is stymied means he cannot press Lindt. But he also cannot hesitate, because, with Gerhard in Berlin having found the body of Gromek and having set battalions upon his trail, Armstrong has only a matter of hours to fathom Lindt and escape to safety. (The entire episode with Gromek, indeed, is in the film to elaborate an assiduity and devotion that will necessitate a murder; that will produce a body; that will produce the hiding of that body; that will produce an absence; that will produce a search; that will produce Armstrong's desperate need for haste exactly in a circumstance where haste will be cause for suspicion.) The need for Michael to press forward is extended to me as I watch, so that I bridle with its urgency: partly because Lindt's secret is the "MacGuffin" at the heart of the film, a treasure I would possess (a treasure that I want, indeed [as Hitchcock said again and again], more than any character wants it), and partly because I must have Michael escape the cold and overcivilized—the extraordinarily purposive— Gerhard, and not empty-handed and pathetic either, lest he lose his worthiness to be my hero. But because of Hitchcock's design, my need for his swift action automatically produces a corollary need *that Armstrong not press at all,* that he engage in small talk, because in the face of Lindt's fastidious—but, to my eager mind, silly—chattering, any other tactic than scathing patience will give him away as an usurious hack and thus precipitate a catastrophe. He must ferret out the key information so that he may find success now; and yet refrain from ferreting, in order that he may be successful later. It is a conundrum. "Jam is not jam unless it is a case of jam to-morrow and never jam to-day. Thus by pushing his jam always forward into the future, he strives to secure for his act of boiling it an immortality," John Maynard Keynes wrote of the "purposive" man; and that is the man I must become—that Hitchcock certainly had become—in order to appreciate purposive Armstrong's condition.[19] So, "Be the spy," barks my first conscience; while, "Wait—be the poseur," barks my second.

Since if he pushes forward to do his business now Armstrong brings the narrative to its end, yet if he waits he puts the narrative on hold and prolongs our pleasure, two matching conflicting desires arise as well. At once, I wish the film to be over; and also to go on forever.

But even as narrative progress demands a penetration of surface realities— a movement from Lindt and Armstrong conversing as mannered colleagues to Lindt and Armstrong trading vital information in a key dramatic moment that will resolve the deep construction—it also invokes a certain telltale self-consciousness. After all, the polite chit-chat cannot with safe speed be modulated into a narratively significant conversation without my being made aware, at the same speed, of *narrative significance itself*—that is, depth of promise and implication entirely uncharacteristic of the trivial chit-chat— and, then, of myself hotly requiring it, hungering for the precise interview that brings connection. I must know, and with urgency, that so far the Lindt-Armstrong liaison has been only an absorbing construction against which I would struggle for those depths. Otherwise, there is no option but that I satisfy myself with bobbing in the surface gab, not only taking it seriously as filmic content but also interpreting it as a revelation of the characters at their truest and thereby establishing for myself a secure, even comfy, relation with the garrulous Lindt and the gamey Armstrong as real persons. Armstrong as I really do apprehend him, however, pressing against the clock for information, not only forces Lindt to confide in him but also forces *me* to see Lindt, Armstrong himself, Sherman, everybody, as merely part of the mechanism of a plot, first governmental and then Hitchcockian.

Yet it is Hitchcock who has established the chit-chat that puts me quiveringly on the wire. And so this third movement of the film can be said to be about our own status as viewers, and our building desire to terminate that status in a climax that resolves the tensions of the plot. If the narrative escapade requires a mask or curtain, a separating membrane to divide actors from characters and those who walk into the theater from the onlookers they become,[20] then the action of the Armstrong-Lindt tactical ballet is itself a vital tearing of it. What is it, after all, that is awakened when Lindt plays hard to get, but our own eagerness to put the Michael Armstrong we know at risk in order to capture him? End the movie but get the formula! The blackboard exchange initiated by Armstrong later on is, in this light, his own tearing of a narrative curtain—the curtain of Lindt's postures to begin with, but by the climax of the scene, as Lindt awakens, also the curtain of his own.

But *this* torn curtain is not yet the curtain that holds us from the screen; it is only an *onscreen curtain*, separating characters from other characters, and its rending is part of a play-within-a-play. All the film is curtained off from us, precisely as Armstrong and Lindt are curtained off from one another. In daily life we are all presenting aspects of ourselves from behind "curtains" of posture, affect, and potential. When our "curtains" are torn, we may suddenly be prone to revealing more—or other—than we intend; and our identity open to being reconstructed, to our peril.[21] Armstrong the loyal citizen and lover is revealed to be a traitor; who is revealed to be a double agent—a loyal citizen and lover—only posing as a defector/traitor. But seen from Lindt's point of view, Armstrong the honest defector and collaborator is revealed to be an agent, then a mere lover. Indeed, when he is plainly visible to us as a lover and not a colleague, as we shall see, Armstrong becomes a doomed Paolo to Lindt's vengeful Malatesta.

Indeed, for a moment it seems that in Lindt's eyes Michael has diminished into a randy undergraduate, too preoccupied scouting girls to learn how to discourse upon advanced theoretical physics. While many disaffected critics of the film saw it as a rather slim essay on the Cold War, the "torn curtain" being in fact the Iron Curtain represented by the Berlin Wall, *Torn Curtain* is for me about a different kind of curtain altogether, and the Cold War is nothing but a counter—elaborate but hollow—utilized by Hitchcock as a game-piece around which to set the action. He is never, in his film work, as interested in the drama of high politics and nationalistic intrigue as he is obsessed with the mechanism of intelligence, the framework of belief, and the way identity can be held hostage to both.

FALSE TRAILS

Wherever they are laid, false trails will certainly appear quite genuine. They will be complex, they will be involved, they will be delicate and dramatic and coherent and in all other ways "real." But the appearance of reality does not make things real. What the reader should find troubling about the "lateral" analysis I have given so far, the three "gavottes"—echoing in some ways Spoto's analysis that terms the film "travel/espionage" and Wood's analysis that labels Armstrong's voyage a "quest"[22]—is, first, that like a very great deal of what has been written about Hitchcock, it is so literary, depending for the most part on dialogue and plot rather than on what we can see—optical, physical, topographical, and aesthetic relations. For literary analysis, films are essentially illustrated dialogues (what Hitchcock disparagingly called "photographs of people talking"),[23] the imagery a sop and aid to the viewer's crippled imagination. So many interesting scenes and moments in *Torn Curtain* must be disregarded, or treated as mere embellishment, if we take the reading I have given so far very seriously as a pointer to the deep content of the film, if we insist on assigning the "voyage" tale a central place. So much of what we experience cannot be fitted to the "espionage" frame and must be seen as either superfluity, or unnecessary decoration, or a director's nervous twitch. If this is a film about Armstrong journeying across the Iron Curtain, it is surely a fatuous, overelaborated, even baroque piece of work (not to mention a film of little but historical interest now that the Curtain is gone).

Let me briefly review some of what is utterly unnecessary to that Cold War espionage theme, but notably present in *Torn Curtain* anyway. In setting these items out, I would like to produce only the minimal necessary perturbation in the reader's easy acceptance of the received version of this film—secret agent crosses Iron Curtain on dirty business, while simultaneously being in love—so as to make it somewhat probable that it will be seen not as a spy story at all, but as a story that could be told most fittingly and most urgently if it was set in the context of spying. What, then, is very obviously present to our senses while at the same time being basically irrelevant to the espionage theme?

There is, first, the look and usage of the peculiar classroom—a traditional middle-European *Vorlesungssaal*—in which Lindt and his associates interrogate Armstrong in Leipzig: dark, wooden, tall, theatrical, so perfectly drawn that one can virtually smell the wax on the wood. Sitting way up near the back of this room, a student listening to what is being spoken from below could experience vertigo.[24] The room is photographed to give a very clear picture of its quality, but even in its stunning physical form this lecture theater is not about spying. Why not use a professor's office, a grassy space under a beautiful linden tree or a seminar room with a nice round table, all perfectly realistic and suggestive of "University Life"? The logical conclusion is that Hitch has simply sought verisimilitude, an attribute for which he has demonstrably and consistently shown fondness.[25] But Hitchcock's penchant for verisimilitude does not account for the interrogation scene being set in a *Vorlesungssaal* or anywhere else in a university. Except that he was interested in the academic setting per se, such a scene need not have been set on a campus at all. And why, indeed, *is* the filmmaker interested in the academic setting? Why is

Armstrong a professor of physics in the first place? Many creditable spies are not. And given all that, why this particular sort of room in this particular sort of place used in exactly this way? Scene precedes action in Hitchcock only in the sense of a specific location conditioning specific dramatic possibilities— note Hitchcock's oft-quoted comments about how the Dutch windmills in *Foreign Correspondent* or the Niçois *marché aux fleurs* on the Cours Saleya in *To Catch a Thief* functioned. Here, having been given the academy, we certainly have the possibilities of the lecture theater. *Yet why are we given the academy?*

Also immaterial to a spy narrative is the elaborate opening sequence on a cruise ship whose heating system has gone off. Anyone can be freezing in a fjørd: why a congress of physicists? And yet, why must anybody be freezing? The sequence is certainly a little reminiscent of the honeymoon ship in *Marnie*, and yet I believe we will see there is plenty of material in *Torn Curtain* without any scene requiring interpretation in terms of another film. Could the M. S. *Meteor* be a ship of fools, its passengers caught in a trance of madness? [26] Even if it is, what has this film to do with thermodynamics? Why are the passengers frozen? In shot after shot, we see the ice-white deck, or an icy pale blue wall, or people huddling against the chill, or instruments reading off the low temperature, not to mention the drinking water solidified in the goblets. There is much in this film to do with thermodynamics: Gromek's faulty lighter, Lindt's cigar as broadsword, the fiery hellish scene onstage in the theater, Michael's crying "Fire!" to abet the escape, the stage manager's fiery hair, the fire by which the lovers warm themselves at the end—but to do a spy story about crossing the Iron Curtain one does not have to fiddle with the temperature or bring flame into the picture. Is it all for decoration?

A "lateral" curtain-crossing espionage tale also does not require to show, very clearly, and more than once, the presence of a sharp-beaked ballerina (Tamara Toumanova, star of Arthur Freed's production *Invitation to the Dance*). Nor does such a story require a ballet at all, let alone a dedicated choreography of Tchaikovsky's *Francesca da Rimini*,[27] or a ballet company, a stage manager, or a mise-en-scène that very astutely reflects upon Michael Powell and Emeric Pressburger's *The Red Shoes* (1948).[28] (Hitchcock uses Michael Powell's art director from *The Red Shoes*, Hein Heckroth, in this film.) The scene Hitchcock has remodeled from *The Red Shoes*, in fact, shows a ballerina's stage performance as an audition for the benevolent attention of an older and extremely puissant man, who is always on the lookout both for talent and for imposters trying to get his attention. The Lindt-Armstrong classroom scene and the ballet scene in *Torn Curtain*, conflated together, would produce a version of this earlier scene. But *Francesca da Rimini* and *The Red Shoes* are not about espionage and the Cold War.

If a reading of *Torn Curtain* as spy film does not account for some of the scenes we find in it, and especially for how they are elaborated, it certainly also fails to explain—other than as frippery—some particular characterizations to which the filmmaker gives very devoted attention. I am thinking of Hermann Gromek's pretensions at social class, his sense of dismay that Armstrong might look down on him, his nostalgia for Pete's Pizza; and also of the potato-fingered earthiness and practicality of the woman who kills Gromek. Her competence and Gromek's nostalgia have nothing whatever to do with the story of an Iron Curtain adventure, yet they do evidence the presence of class and class boundaries, as does the sudden materialization of Countess Kuchinska (Lila Kedrova), a pathetic being with a flair for self-promotion and an air of loss. She is no mere European *grande dame* desperate to flee to America. She is a countess, and a fallen one at that. Her presence is a signal of the flattening of class hierarchies that was the American dream, and an open questioning—particularly when we see Armstrong balking at the idea of sponsoring her—of America's public claim to classlessness and democracy. Does the countess want to come to America because she can be free there? Or is it because she can be a countess again, in what she suspects is an *echt* aristocratic state? In the end her motive illuminates the object of Armstrong's loyalty: in that his possible defection can be seen as an abandonment of the territory that lures the countess so powerfully, his acceptance of her, brief as it must be, is a testament to his faith. Yet she is pathetic. So, therefore, may be the America that she desires and he stands for. But what, we are left to wonder, is all this characterization about and for, if this film is a spy story? The otentatious blue feather in the countess's hat, Gromek's attempt to put on a Brooklyn accent, the farmer's wife's skill with a shovel—all these shrink into bric-a-brac.

Is all of this to be disregarded? Disregarding is problematic in Hitchcock, but especially in the face of Kieling's charming performance as Gromek, or the oddness and sharpness of the opening ship sequence, or Toumanova's austere grace. And whatever is to be made of our hero's apparent failure to rise in his career, a noteworthy fly in the ointment of any viewer's easy affiliation with his clandestine adventure? When we see him defect, reflecting upon this fact can help us understand his motives—he is disaffected and resentful about American society's failure to reward and honor him—and so it can be argued that Hitchcock has inserted Armstrong's weakness just in order to enhance his audience's credulity in the face of the defection, given that it is, after all, the congenial Paul Newman they are watching cross the line.[29] Appreciating his resentment, we will be as surprised as Sarah to learn later that his betrayal was staged—we will be surprised and relieved and exhilarated in our attachment to him, that, treated as shabbily as he was there, he is still willing to risk his life for America. Our knowing that Armstrong is a failure does work in this direction. But when he admits he is an agent, he does *not* suggest that his career trouble was a fiction to help him cover himself. The career trouble was real, and is still real, and will remain real, so that no matter how successful Armstrong is in his spying it will nevertheless be the case that he is, was, and will be no star professor. And Lindt is. We need to try for an understanding of the film that will address this discrepancy. This film, after all, asks us to identify with a man who doesn't do what he does very well; by contrast, in *The Wrong Man*, Manny Balestrero plays bass with extreme capability; Dr. Ben McKenna in *The Man Who Knew Too Much* is a fine doctor; Roger O. Thornhill is very successful advertising executive; Guy Haines in *Strangers on a Train* is a tennis champion, not a duffer.

And there is more. Sarah and Michael's escape to freedom turns out to require a ride on the Leipzig-Berlin bus; but an *ersatz* bus, part of the π underground movement, not the real one that drives the route every day. While the real bus creeps up from behind, threatening to give away the dummy bus to the road police, we are given opportunity to see direct evidence of two different—yet identical-looking—vehicles on the same road, undertaking the same route in the same way but for different ends. One bus is superior to the other, more authentic, but does not represent nobility; and the artificial underdog must struggle to avoid being crushed by its own lack of authenticity. The two buses are not unlike the two Michael Armstrongs, the patriot and the defector; but they are also not unlike the *other* two Michael Armstrongs who present themselves to Lindt: the authentic student and the fake, but prominent, teacher. It is not the horizontal route between Leipzig and Berlin that is the locus of the dramatic tension in this scene, then, but the vertical hierarchy which provides one bus more legitimacy than the other in the eyes of the state: a hierarchy that also lends more credibility to Armstrong as a teacher than to Armstrong as the student he really is. And as it is the fake bus for which we are cheering, it is also the fake Armstrong, since only he has any hope of achieving triumph. In this vital sequence, authenticity trumps legitimacy, in true cinematic fashion; but the issue of authenticity also trumps the issue of lateral movement in the narrative. The movement back across the Iron Curtain, then, is just the pretext. In order merely to have spies escape to their home country, a filmmaker does not need to invoke the problem of hiding the artificiality of a fake bus; nor does he need to populate this bus with fake passengers who may interact with the protagonists, except as a means of hiding that fakery. To deal with fakery, a story need not wander to Eastern Europe.

Are we to neglect as pure decoration these fascinating elements that are so ostensibly *not* linked to the "central" spy plot, thereby discovering in Hitchcock a director obsessed with fillip and embellishment? Or can our knowledge of him as a prudent and devoted designer lead us to recognize that everything in the film, the spy tale included, is part of the architecture? It seems to me that to really understand *Torn Curtain* one must see beyond the horizontal narratives of the "three gavottes" to a vital series of arrangements in which highness and lowness are—at least metaphorically—invoked as significant dramatic positions. Central among these arrangements is a strand of conversations between Armstrong and Lindt, in which the relation between teachers and students is struck as a theme and played out to some fascinating conclusions.

Each of the pungent visual elements I have mentioned above mobilizes a particular exposition of that teacher-student relation. The *Vorlesungssaal* sets up the action in Lindt's private classroom later, and reminds us that it is professorial business—the profession of professing—that has brought Michael to East Germany. The interrogations in Gerhard's private room at the airport and later in his office are but preparations for the more serious interrogation in the film, which is professorial, the questioner being above the candidate in status, power, and the ability to exercise threat.

If we look again at the frozen cruise ship we find a package containing frozen academics at the International Congress of Physicists—Dr. Walter Keller of Princeton University, Isaac Wiseman of the Hebrew University, and others. These are the competitive forces who gather annually to "yak yak yak," as Lindt would put it, but whose capacity for action is frozen not only by the sort of discursive lethargy Marx complained of in the *Theses on Feuerbach* but also by their occupational need for intellectual defense, as we shall soon see. To teach is to reveal, and thus to make oneself vulnerable; to sit in chilly silence is to preserve the opportunity to dominate. Meanwhile, the professional antagonism implicit in the situated practice of philosophy is cued for us by the announcement on a large poster that "Neutrino Collisions" will be the topic of an upcoming lecture.

As to the ballerina, she invokes not just the enemy regime but also the didactic and the hierarchical. She is too lofty to be taught because as an epitome of perfect form she has clearly already learned everything her masters had to teach. She is a paragon of the dance, even—and at the same moment—as she is a paragon of vigilance, all of this learned quite formally in a "school for ballet" founded upon the slavish devotion of the student to the teacher. To contrast the ballet performance, we are shown a scene in a university club, Manfred clomping back and forth with Sarah on the dance floor as Armstrong slides Dr. Koska around in a clandestine conversation. All this filmic dance is about a greater "dance," the liberal social arrangement where any and all movement is said to be possible and classist European didacticism is out—otherwise billed as American democracy. We can discover throughout *Torn Curtain* references to the America that Michael's voyage is a plot to strengthen and defend: it is the new Eden that Countess Kuchinska, an icon of hopelessness, so fervently desires to visit; the focus of Gromek's nostalgic remembrance, where if you don't like an Art Museum you are likely to say it's "Strickly for the birds. . . . They still say that? We used to say it all the time. *'Ah, dats strickly for de boids!'* "

The ballet, too, is "high" art. If classical ballet speaks of the body, it speaks grammatically, but America is the nexus of idiomatic, not grammatical, speech. Gromek is a perfect Everyman, Armstrong's antitype, the newworlder Armstrong is not. Armstrong, long a nerd, was never so hip, wouldn't be caught dead in black leather or dining at Pete's Pizza. Through academic endeavor he has managed to climb, while in the world of footnotes and slide rules Gromek is clearly a loser. Kuchinska, too, has fallen and now explicates a need for a "sponsor" so that she can go to "The United States of America." She has found no reward in the East of the present, all her glories lingering in her yesterdays, and so she is something like Gromek, but hardly so cool with lingo. In her supplication is the most overt depiction of groveling desperation in any Hitchcock film. (Even as he was being put to the oven, pretentious Gromek never made supplication like this.) Though she has retained her title and has nobility, she is so low that a simple nod from two American commoners has the power to change her life. In the sense that her needs are so overwhelming and so profound, she is beneath education, yet to Michael and Sarah, who have in a sense been taking their freedom for granted, she *is* an education. I wonder when I watch her whether she is in this film to reveal just this hunger and poverty, the fact that she is a countess only exaggerating her condition so it may be perceptible. For a moment she is the means for Sarah and Michael to know, and we through them, what the quest for knowledge is really *for*. Michael, after all, quests for Lindt's secret to help America, and America is the place to which such outcasts as the countess wish to flee. She is what his search is really all about, but he has this to learn.

Education also characterizes Michael and Sarah's ride on the Leipzig-Berlin bus, where they learn of the preparedness, courage, and good-natured fraternity of Germans who, by and large, collaborate to free them. Michael and Sarah's emphatic helplessness during this bus ride makes clear to us that this journey is not just an escape but a moral lesson for them: about kindness, about the human condition of power and powerlessness beneath the *fort-da* sham of lateral political antagonism, about cooperation as an antidote to dominance. The single uncooperative—indeed, panicking and paranoid—fake passenger, who demands to be let off the bus, nicely throws into relief the kindly cooperative stance of all the others.

But the tortured relation of Lindt and Armstrong is also visible as an essay on the eclipse of dominance by cooperation, so that the lessons of the bus ride are stresses and summaries of this principal theme rather than divagations from it.

TEACHERS AND STUDENTS

Everybody who is incapable of learning has taken to teaching.
   Oscar Wilde, The Decay of Lying

Pedagogy is precisely as *Europisch* an endeavor, as classical a form, for the (northern) Prussian Lindt as was *Weltschmerz* for the (southern) Berliner Gromek. If it is not natural, it is certainly automatic. Seen in this frame, teachers are in possession of knowledge and students beg for a share. Therefore teachers have status and students labor deferentially to attain it. Teachers are clever and polished but students are raw. As teachers and students, so writers and readers:

> The idea persists that writing is an activity of thoughtful, idealistic, moral people called authors and that they are committed to protecting certain values vital to a well-ordered society. Books mold character, enforce patriotism, and provide a healthy way to pass the leisurely hour. To this assumption there has been added in our day the image of the author as a celebrity, someone worth hearing at a reading or lecture even if you have no intention of parting with a dime for one of the author's books.[30]

Even the especially bright and much accomplished student has yet a thing or two to learn from the "wise old man."[31] If there is a kinetic energy that flows from the lecturer's podium (down) to the classroom, it is taken to constitute a kind of nourishment the student's appetite should at once crave and discipline itself to receive. Yet the most delectable grains of it are reserved for the most deserving—which is to say, the most deferent (i.e., the most ostensibly hungering)—students.[32] Michael Armstrong's climactic conversation with Gustav Lindt—the pupil-teacher interaction he has made his long journey to experience—takes place in a room that for some time seems to have no altitude at all, principally because the dialogue between the two men, framed on the blackboard in terms of mathematical equations, must invoke all the "altitude" there is in the encounter. The room itself, No. 29, is named although not set geographically for us. By the decor of the hallway outside we are led to presume it shares the lower depths of the main building with the lecture theater we saw earlier. Our passage to it is unremarkable: as Lindt informs Armstrong, leading him along after they have escaped together from the offscreen Kaminsky's barbershop, "It's probably the most secret room in the country, but, see—no guards." It is here that Lindt has spread his most valuable—and also most arcane—theories openly for all to see (but none to comprehend) in mathematical formulae on the blackboards: to be precise, on the lower panels of two-tiered boards, which can easily be covered by drawing down the upper panels like curtains. It is presumably here, too, that Lindt teaches his students, the relative inferiority of whose intellectual powers is indexed by the openness with which he can parade his thoughts in front of them with complete secrecy. If the upper blackboards are the curtain he *could* use to hide his thoughts—but at the moment does not—an analogue to them is the innocence of the students, their imperceptiveness in the face of what he blatantly shows. Intelligence, then, would disturb the tranquility of this working space were it presented by anyone other than Lindt. The intelligence of the student is a tear in the curtain of secrecy, because it penetrates the secrets on the blackboard, ciphers for the secrets in the professor's mind.

The sort of game Armstrong plays with Lindt—one could say, plays *upon* Lindt—has been artfully described by Harold Garfinkel as "secret apprenticeship."[33] It is one individual's purposeful treatment of another as teacher while guising the fact that such treatment is going on. While there are numerous circumstances that could support the playing out of such a relation, what is always at stake is the "true"—which is to say substantial—identity of someone cloaked in a deceptive performance;[34] in our case, the incriminating fact that Michael Armstrong is no defector (fully knowledgeable about Gamma-5) but instead a U.S. government agent (who wants to find out). Secret apprenticeship, for Garfinkel and for Michael Armstrong, can be one of the principal features of passing, which is the ongoing activity of pretending to be other than one "really" is in circumstances where disclosure or discovery can lead to precipitous ruin.[35] Armstrong is Lindt's pupil, *but Lindt must not know it*. Especially Lindt, I might add, who knows so many things and is so charmingly astute.

In many—but especially in two—ways Armstrong does not qualify to take information openly from Lindt (a very exclusive man). First, he is politically problematic, capable of exporting any data he picks up for use in the wrong quarters. (It is true that I use "wrong" from Lindt's point of view, but we must remember that by the time Armstrong is engaged with him we rather like Lindt and are therefore prone to seeing the world as he does.) Secondly, the elementary fact of his political disaffiliation is negated for Lindt by an egalitarian, democratic attitude toward learning that is the antithesis of everything Lindt stands for. Lindt is patrician, old school. He takes it perfectly for granted that the teacher inevitably informs the student; indeed, he has nothing to learn from his inferiors and is vulnerable to being at first uncomprehending, then stupefied, when he sees that Armstrong has one-upped him. Armstrong, on the other hand, has traveled from, symbolically stands for, and behaves as though he incarnates a contradictory and democratic spirit of cooperation in which teachers learn as much from their students as students learn from them. To have had an egalitarian relationship with Miss Sherman, as Michael has—or with any woman young enough to be his student—is for Herr Prof. Lindt unthinkable.

Technically, Armstrong's fakery will require a bravura denial of his own relative ignorance, this accomplished through a perfect simulation of what Lindt would call professorial mastery and what the Yankee Armstrong would call immodest performance.[36] The viewer of the film is aware throughout the confrontation scene in Room 29 that Armstrong is not in fact the expert he shows himself off to be, but watching him bluster requires that we see his activity at once from two sides—he is being audacious (something Lindt would condemn in his students and expect of himself) and he is being the arrogant lecturer (something Lindt would—does—admire and Armstrong would otherwise critique).

Lindt's protectiveness about his informational treasure, the so-called secret of Gamma-5, is itself not merely a neurotic fixation on his part, but a carefully structured endeavor. In the province of academe, philosophy is common labor and the worker's success and survival depend upon the production, with some predictable regularity, of that fiendishly mercurial substrate, thought. But regardless of the avidity of one's concentrations, the passion of one's elaborations, or the strenuousness of one's exertions at refinement and clarification, thought nevertheless remains, in all its glorious abstraction, a thing that must be demonstrated in order for others to benefit and feel thankful enough to pay. Thus, more important than what we consider important to say is what we say in fact; and more weighty than what we imagine is what we publish. To be a full professor at the University of Leipzig or any other in the world (there is no Iron Curtain in academic bureaucracy) one must give displays of one's mental activity: thought, calculation, preparation, conclusion. One must speak some sort of language in the pages of reputable journals or books, accessible at once to one's students in the lecture theater, one's colleagues in the faculty lounge, and one's peers around the world. But this kind of open speech renders one's position structurally vulnerable in a number of interesting ways.

Since it is not possible to publish—and thus officially register—everything one says, when one makes a statement there is nothing to prevent others from publishing it in their own name (if they can see that you have not), with the claim that they thought it before you did. To openly question others with a view to accusing them of plagiarism is a routine that cannot be enacted too much, before one's own reputation comes under inspection. Thus, there is nothing at all strange in Lindt not being particularly open about his discoveries or theories, whatever they may have been—and, indeed, far more germane to this film than Lindt's work on Gamma-5 is Lindt's attitude toward that work. While all academics wish to share their work with their fellows, thus contributing toward the establishment of a more reasonable state of knowledge for all mankind, it is also a fact of academic life that one's paycheck and likelihood of qualifying for tenure can depend on attaching one's own name to the characteristic expression of a particular thought—and preventing other people from being able to do so in one's place. In other words, in his secretiveness Lindt is being a full professor of theoretical physics much more than a Communist agent, and his apparently eccentric behavior is perfectly typical of university life.

But in developing his experiments with Gamma-5, Lindt has not been working in a community of scholars, abstracted from the general community, for the joy of brotherhood, learning, and noble study. The Medieval Academy is long gone. Further, he is not working merely for the elucidation of truths to those students whose parents can afford to pay—the classical university. He is a faculty member in a large, bureaucratically controlled institution (one with a public address system), in this particular case funded less by private grant than by government subsidy. His work must be handed over to the government, not merely because he is living in a totalitarian regime where the government controls everything but also—and principally, for this plot—because he is an employee in a state university and the state is paying his salary and supplying his chalk. Let us remember that Michael Armstrong, too, works with a certain amount of state control. The secrecy surrounding Gamma-5, then, is also just good business practice for the university; and in a way, deep down, Armstrong is ultimately a potential industrial spy, as is every other student who wants to make Lindt's acquaintance to talk about this project.

There is plenty of evidence of these two structural determinants of Lindt's secretiveness—academic secrecy and state defense—in the film. That the state controls the scene is clear from Herr Haupt's (Harald Dyrenforth) power to interrupt the inquiry of Armstrong, a somber academic ritual, and from Gerhard's ability, even at a distance, to declare Armstrong *persona non grata* until Gromek's disappearance is tidied up. As well, in his own response to the team of professors for whom Armstrong is supposed to be performing, Lindt is quite explicit in defining his social position. He is condescending and openly irritated, now that he has in Armstrong the sort of foreign audience to whom such disaffection can be played out. It is like one of those family moments when, in front of a guest, a constrained child will suddenly and revealingly chide the parents who have been keeping him on too tight a leash until the visitation. Happy and relaxed with the direction from his government, Lindt would hardly wave off the clucking professors and the burly security man so dismissively.

A little later, as he joins Sarah, Michael, and Manfred at their table in a supper club, Lindt repeats exactly this piqued dismissiveness—"Yuk yuk yuk yuk! Let us have some intelligent conversation"—when Manfred tries to extricate him from the company of the sociable Americans with the suggestion that "the Vice-Direktor is waiting." While the dismissal of Manfred is essential to the plot, providing Lindt and Armstrong a moment alone to arrange for a meeting the next morning, Lindt's having a second chance to show the extent of the bureaucratic control under which he must work is hardly the only way of arranging it. Indeed, in order actually to give the order that will send Manfred away for a bit, "Now go. Go, get on. Dance!," Lindt is forced to temporarily leave his employee relation to Manfred[37] and put on the mask of the older male in a display of *gemütlich* gentility. When Sarah asks Manfred to dance and he demurs, Lindt "coaches" him: "Rubbish! You cannot refuse such a charming young lady!" Lindt is a minion of the bureaucracy, and that he is clever enough to skip into the persona of an elderly, suave, European gentleman who always has a wink in reserve for a pretty girl is not as significant as the fact that he knows when, and with what style, to do the skipping.

Many viewers of *Torn Curtain* have miscalculated that the use of the academic setting is merely one of many possible convenient ploys to lead our attention to the central concern, which is the fight between American and Communist governments. In short, this is apparently a film about the Cold War *that happens* to be set in academic life, as, in some way, are other Hitchcock films set as they are by happenstance. All of Lindt's obedience to Gerhard's directives and his irritation with Manfred, seen in this rather harsh light, are merely mechanisms for forcing the East-West confrontation as the main motor of the plot. But in fact Hitchcock has done the reverse. He has used the East-West chiaroscuro in order to highlight, to dramatize, and to render more clarified the kind of secretiveness one will find only in the academy. It is the academy he is showing us in this film, not world politics. Michael Armstrong, after all, need not have been a physicist—he could have been an army major. And he need certainly not have found, once across the Iron Curtain, a hallowed university the ascetic corridors of which to haunt.[38]

In order to see evidence of Lindt's secretiveness as a manifestation of his career position (and not merely a marker for the spy genre), it helps to take note of the many instances of his intellectual snobbery: his allusion to the intellectual poverty of Manfred's whining; his arrogant superciliousness in the face of his colleagues in the lecture theater; his particular way of adopting Michael Armstrong into his confidence—"You're a brilliant young man. . . . You know, there aren't many of us, Armstrong." In short, Lindt sees himself as being a member of a very small club—indeed, rather a Platonic one at that: "Here [he points to his head]—there is where the work is done. The rest is all mechanics."[39] His colleagues, then, are only technicians, hacks. He is the artist, and Armstrong is conceivably worthy of sharing his limelight (or at least having a favored seat from which to admire him in it).

But not if Michael's moral bona fides cannot be established; not if he is a plagiarist. When Armstrong makes a claim that he has solved the theoretical problem of Gamma-5, almost immediately Lindt pronounces the Publication Formula: "*Solved?* If you've solved it why didn't you publish the results?" Armstrong is quick on the tongue, and also well briefed: "You mean like you did last year in the *East German Journal of Physics?*" But Lindt is pressing ownership: "Then, you know that this thing you're talking about *I* happen to have discovered, too." And Lindt *has* published it; Armstrong has not. The statements—and the thoughts that can be claimed to underpin them—therefore "belong" to him.

There is another, even commanding, reason for Lindt's retentiveness in the structure of academic activity itself. As a professor he is paid to profess,

the implication being that he must have an audience to profess to. In this respect he bears a distinct affinity to Hitchcock and other filmmakers, whose
brilliance of inspiration is never more dictatorial than their urgent need for a
houseful of paying customers. To attract the audience that will sit in front of
his podium, Lindt has long ago developed a persona of the unfathomable, incomparable genius who understands everything but is also difficult to understand. Students flock to him not merely to bask in his light, but to challenge
themselves against his sharp mind. Can they grasp the full extent of what he
is saying? Can they, indeed, master him by going one step further? To provide for students this sort of engagement is an essential task in the economy
of teaching since bright graduate students do not travel from far and wide to
work at the side of a person who holds no secrets from them. But the moment
a particularly astute student does manage to take a step the professor has not
taken, the old man ceases to possess value. In order for him to extend his career, then, he must not only mystify students but elude them. There must be
continuing promise of his everlasting opacity, not so firm a promise as to vitiate students' hopes of someday overstepping the master, nor one so evanescent that it offers them no challenge as they pit their strengths eagerly against
his. So the relationship between professor and student is a kind of hide-
and-seek game, in which success—and pleasure—for both parties resides
specifically in the maintenance of a tissue of mystery between them. More
than just a mystery, too, the tissue is an architectural element that maintains
the structures it differentiates in vertical relation to one another, one below
and one above, one full of the capacity to hold and to give and the other desperate to receive. It is a tissue of the greatest social and political valence, le-
gitimating a certain form of privilege and domination over other possible
ones, safeguarding knowledge and also maintaining a degree of ignorance, re-
energizing power and obstructing the will of the powerless to gain power
even as it opens a pathway for the movement of power from generation to
generation.

This tissue is the *Curtain* of *Torn Curtain*, and its treatment and rending is
the theme of the confrontational scene between Lindt and Armstrong in
Room 29, to which I now turn in very close focus.

HANDWRITING ON THE WALL

The language-game of reporting can be given such a turn that a report is not
meant to inform the hearer about its subject matter but about the person making

the report. It is so when, for instance, a teacher examines a pupil. (You can measure to test the ruler.)

   Wittgenstein, Philosophical Investigations

As they enter the professorial sanctum, Lindt is prepared to welcome Armstrong as a brother intellectual, even as he is acting as an agent in an elaborate state machine for capturing information from the younger man and passing it on to the USSR. Armstrong, on the other hand, knows that he has accomplished nothing as regards Gamma-5 and that Lindt, who believes himself to be playing the role of student, is in fact teaching him. But in order to get Lindt to teach he must pretend to teach Lindt, because Lindt does not altruistically pass on what he knows to his real students. Again, that Armstrong is working for the U.S. government, that his "enemy" status might account for Lindt's taciturnity, is of only surface interest here, because it doesn't invoke the setting. As any querulous student keeps the professor mum, what would produce taciturnity in a senior professor like Lindt is exactly that Armstrong might reveal himself as an eager student, as a "young man" who is not quite "brilliant"; in Lindt's words, "You're not gonna work with me, Professor, if that is the extent of your knowledge." What this amounts to is, "If you don't know, I am not going to teach you."

Central to the play of knowledge and innocence here is the arcane mathematical language spelled out on the blackboards as we enter the room, and by means of which the ultimate conversation between Lindt and Armstrong is framed so that we will be students, too. It is in these glyphs, the decor of the territory Michael finds "nice and familiar," that we are to discover the innermost workings of Lindt's mind. Indeed, to the extent that thought cannot exist until it has revealed itself, we may read the boards for Lindt's thought *itself.* Both symbolically and substantially they are his brain and subsequently Michael's, as he steps forward to write upon them. The process of teaching, in which the instructor's mind works upon the student's, is thus nicely externalized and objectivized for us by Hitchcock's direction of the scene, with Lindt brusquely erasing Armstrong's equations and impatiently replacing them with his own. It is mind working upon mind, erasing and replacing content, effected for us through an interplay of chalk inscriptions.

But the hidden point of the scene is the complete inability of the viewer to decode the writing that Armstrong can easily read.[40] If I have had a twinge of anxiety on his behalf that Michael is in danger because he may not be the physicist he pretends to be—he has, after all, been fooling people throughout the film in one way or another—I am relieved to note that he does not gawk at the blackboards as I feared he would and as I do myself. Here, Hitchcock gives a lovely *double entendre* to the open gaping Newman actually does perform, since on the one hand Armstrong is both shocked and galvanized to be in the presence of the actual formulae, and on the other, now that the treasures are in front of him he must optically swallow as much as possible in the shortest possible time. But as the hero of the film, he must also, and inevitably, act out my response in one scene after another; and my response in the face of these arcane formulae is bald incomprehension. For a moment I am led to feel he is affiliating completely with my incomprehension, but suddenly I realize he knows much more than I do and that, therefore, I will have to listen very carefully if I am to follow the interaction.

Yet a considerable portion of the dialogue between Armstrong and Lindt is in an English that is at best unconventional: "Omega x plus drei omega y epsilon" is really an esoteric argot of Greek, Latin, and German. I am forced to read the faces in order to read the minds, and thus to occupy precisely the fool's seat of the student who can't quite keep up with the lecture (but wants to); who, further, is willing to believe a face reveals what a man is thinking because he does not suppose a face can be a cover. (At the beginning of the film, of course, Michael's student Sarah unwittingly occupied that same position.)

But Michael is a secret apprentice. Trying to learn everything in just a few moments, he must nevertheless mask his true purpose and status by pretending to be a colleague. (The luxury of being the fool is not his.) Part of his performance is a display of comfort and familiarity on initially entering the room. At that point, not grasping what is on the boards (Lindt is the one who knows, and his superciliousness in the face of the blackboard scribblings is impenetrable), Michael must fake understanding sufficiently to converse, and his ability to convince us seems ample evidence of his ability to convince Lindt. The "understanding," the *verstehen*, that Michael feigns is so well played (not by Paul Newman, mark, but by the Michael Armstrong that Paul Newman is playing in this exceptional performance) that we are lulled into relaxation, into trust, and into forgetting that we were quite right to fear for him in the first place. He is in murky waters, and he is far beyond his depth. If he knew what Lindt is talking about, he would not have had to come here. The board is a mystery and he must immediately labor to resolve it. But Lindt's view is that Armstrong finds all of this "nice and familiar"; that Armstrong can dialogue with him, can "offer" him something.

We, too, feel—or at least desperately hope—that Armstrong can tell

Lindt something, partly, I suspect, because no other move will promise success and partly because he will deserve our respect only if he can outreach us even a little in understanding. So we want to hear what he will say. And in this, we are like Lindt. Therefore, at this crucial moment in the film, Lindt's point of view, not Armstrong's, is our own because it is to identify with Lindt that Hitchcock has led us through his structure; the seduced Merlin, not the seductive Vivian. The more frustrated Lindt becomes with Armstrong's hopeless theoretical forays on the blackboard—

LINDT: I'm afraid, Professor, you have very little to offer.
MICHAEL: You know, Professor, I came here because the . . . people who allocate money in my country . . . were not intelligent enough to pursue a . . . wholly original concept. (*Indicates what he has written on the board.*) *That works.*
LINDT: (*He changes some units in Armstrong's formula.*) So!
MICHAEL: No no no no *no* no!
LINDT: Pfft! It will blow up!

—the more personable he seems to us, and the warmer grows our sympathy for him. The quirky, paternalistic, even atavistic, performance by Ludwig Donath is just what is called for to lure our good feeling: "The Russians thought I was crazy. They didn't know I'm Lindt!"[41]

Consider, for example, the enchanting childishness with which, chewing his cigar, he waits in profound impatience for the imbecilic Armstrong to spell out his inanities on the board; then the cartoon-style "dictatorship" in which he makes his corrections. If he is an intellectual tyrant, still we cannot but love him for his eagerness, his spontaneity, his uncompromising honesty that requires him to flinch—literally—at every error Armstrong makes. There is charm, too, in the coupling of his brilliance with what seems a goofy naïveté: "They're asking all the students of this section to search for you. Why, what have you done?" And we cannot but fall for his schmaltzy extremity of certainty: "I don't care if you come from the moon! I tell you what you say is rubbish!" The "adorable old gentleman," however, is only Lindt's pose, as we can see when he has been brought to the limits of his patience by Armstrong's ineptness and tactlessness:

MICHAEL: Well, what if you took it *this* way? (*Scribbling on the board*) . . . *This* way . . .
LINDT: Oh, no no no *no nooo.* [*He throws away his cigar.*] *LEARN!*

The winning whine is now a menacing growl; and the Grouchoesque cigar a silly prop to be thrown away upon a—upon *the*—hysterical command, "Learn!" Lindt is dead serious now because if Armstrong is wrong about the formula, he is nothing but an untutored bumpkin unworthy of a great man's time. If, on the other hand, Armstrong is right, Lindt's career is *kaput.*

The darkening tone prepares us for Lindt's final explosion to Armstrong, prefaced only moments before by his mimicking an explosion as he predicts one: "Pfft! It will blow up!!!" Watching Armstrong reading his blackboards Lindt suddenly and in an instant catches the truth, like Balzac's *artiste* referred to by Benjamin.[42] "You have told me nothing!" he begins to sing. "You *know* nothing!" He yanks the upper board down with an explosive crash as, counterweighted by Hitchcock's technique, our viewing position is hoisted swiftly to the ceiling. "*I forbid you to leave this room!*"

Armstrong, of course, is not listening to Lindt's commands and has left Room 29 behind him. But what is contained in that dictum of the old professor's, shrieked in the most Teutonic of voices and echoing—now that we are near the ceiling to hear it—with the shrillest implication? The most obvious reading is that Lindt is commanding the criminal Armstrong to hold his position until the authorities arrive to incarcerate him. If we understand the scene this way, Lindt is little more than a police agent himself; and his earlier self-labelings as a genius theoretical physicist are nothing but hollow pretense. The scrawls on the blackboard are his mere cover, not his thought, and his position in the University is an elaborate set-up to keep hidden his real identity as an unthinking military weapon intended for secret use. His dismissive and derisively pompous negation of the authoritarian Haupt and the forces of Gerhard that Haupt represents are sham, then, intended to mask the fact that he is himself little more than one of Gerhard's local henchmen himself. While this reading may satisfy our need to position Lindt relative to the escaping Armstrong, it in no way accounts for the tremendous investment that would have to have been made by local authorities to establish Lindt— again, not really a physicist but just a scheming cop—as a clandestine police agent at a university where there was no particular reason, before the action of this film, to suspect espionage. Nor would such a reading account for our own investment in the brilliance of Lindt, an investment that is a source of considerable humor and pleasure in the film, or for the long scenes in which Hitchcock establishes Lindt as a genius. Furthermore, Armstrong recognizes the blackboard writing as legitimate scientific theorizing, and we must take his behavior at face value because he has far too much to lose by being wrong. Lindt, therefore, is a physicist, not a police agent. To the argument that perhaps Lindt is an agent of both the police and the academic establishment, I suggest two answers: first, metaphorically he may be. Perhaps the academic establishment and the police state are not so different, given the importance of hierarchy, order, control, secrecy, and punishment in both. But as an element in Hitchcock's story, Lindt must be clear. Hitchcock eschewed structural vagueness and would never have wanted his viewers, at this climactic moment, to be confused by an ambiguity about Lindt that could lead them in opposite directions. If he is with police, after all, he is Gerhard's associate, both a fearsome threat and unsympathetic. In Lindt's cry must be only impotence, so that in a flash of transference it is Armstrong we side with, the capable thief, now racing away. What we race away from is, at once, great harshness and philosophical genius, that is to say, the pain of thought. Lindt's cry is not a triumphant shriek because he has netted a mere spy, but something else.

I forbid you to leave this room!

I can hear in the music of this utterance the dictatorial yet mannered formalism of the old *Schulmeister;* not the police but the academy speaking, the hierarchical structure of pristine and precise intellectual power commanding its own inferiority. Not "Stay where you are!" or "Don't move!" or "Don't leave this room!" but "*I forbid you.*" Donath gives a telling gesture of rigidly pointing and slicing with his forefinger in the obedient air. If Armstrong has won the battle of defenses, prising the secret information from Lindt and proving that Lindt lacks the capacity successfully to retain it, still he could only have needed to do so if his knowledge was minimal. Therefore, "You know nothing" is a very telling line spoken from the lips of a German intellectual High Academic. What it betrays is Lindt's conviction that he remains the supreme and unchallenged intellectual champion—the man worth stealing from—and yet also his ineffable sadness that Michael is not the intellectual companion he supposed. "I forbid you" implies that he claims status and superiority, and that he labels Armstrong as beneath him, and that there is a certain cold irrepressible logic in his thinking of things this way.

But a final unfolding awaits.

CAN'T BUY ME LOVE

If Lindt is announcing himself as the reigning mental monarch and if he is defining Armstrong as his intellectual inferior, still, we hear echoed in his forbidding tone the pungent disappointment such a paragon feels when a "brilliant young man" turns out to be not as brilliant as supposed. Lindt must see in an instant that he is growing old; his powers of discernment are fading; he has come to be the sort of old fool young students take advantage of in general; his whole system of thought and mode of approach to theoretical problems is becoming an atavism; and therefore after this escapade his career will never be quite the same. What such a man can hope to look forward to, given that he lacks the Countess's rather barmy anticipation of moving to the United States of America, is, at the very least, the company of a student he can still take pleasure in teaching; some shining and quizzical eyes to look into; some questions to frown upon with a gentle smile. And from his eager animation during Armstrong's presentation at the blackboard, from his good-natured mental wrestling, we can suppose Lindt to have hoped that Armstrong would be *the student of his dreams.* That the American is an upstart who knows nothing turns out, from this point of view, to provide room for boundless optimism in Lindt. If Armstrong knows nothing, he has a lot to learn and this can be the beginning of a beautiful friendship.

Lindt's plea is therefore a last gasp to secure for himself a pupil—someone to pass his knowledge on to. He wants what he does not in fact have; what Sarah Sherman is to Michael Armstrong, a loving heir. But if Sherman wants Armstrong as lover and husband, Lindt is in a crucial respect her competition, since both of them require from Michael a cocoon of intimacy in which to bond. And the pathos of the blackboard scene is that its culmination is the rejection of an old man by a young one. If we move back for a moment to the look of adoration on Armstrong's face when he recognizes the intellectual step Lindt had taken to achieve the Gamma-5 formula—

> MICHAEL: Surely there's something missing?
> LINDT: But it works!!! In Russia we built it, it works!!!! (*He paces.*)
> MICHAEL: My God! (*We zoom in.*) It's brilliant, you jumped a step, didn't you!
> LINDT: Of course it's brilliant. It's *genius!*

—a look, by the way, Hitchcock, who almost never zooms, zooms in to ensure our noting—we discover the love of the young mind for the older, the Platonic love that Michael does not, and cannot, have for Sarah as long as officially she is only his assistant (though on many occasions we can see that, as an assistant, she has such a love for him). In forbidding Michael to leave his room, Lindt is attempting to bind him as a mind-mate. We have seen already that he is unconcerned with the prattle of the military-bureaucratic authorities on the public address, and that his fascination for Armstrong is an overwhelming one. The Armstrong who committed the thievery is of relatively little importance. But Armstrong the man, who staged Armstrong the thief, is a lure. Both Armstrongs have skipped out of the sacred chamber, however, booty in tow.

That Armstrong succeeds while Lindt fails is not a result of the fact that one operates in America and the other in Germany, since both Armstrong's moment of success and Lindt's moment of failure take place in Leipzig. In the climax of *Torn Curtain* the divided world is unified again, at the blackboard. It is not a result of the fact that Armstrong is a better teacher: first, he is a better student than he is a teacher, and secondly, he is a worse teacher (though a better academic) than Lindt—he has less to teach (Sarah would do better for her career to be working with Lindt). But Michael sacrificed intellectual rigor for the potential of heterosexual romance and Lindt did not: that is the capital investment central to this film, an investment western society favors. That is why the film must begin (and end) with a love scene between Sarah and Michael. It is a Michael Armstrong affianced to Sarah Sherman who needs thievery to gain a formula Lindt possesses by pure dedication and thought. Note the fire of passion burning in the old man's fingertips as he chalks his formulae on the blackboard oblivious to the rest of the world. This is surely a holy, a transcendental, fire compared with the baser frictional warmth being experienced by the protagonists as first we meet them.[43]

But the western system, as Hitchcock shows it, won't ultimately work as education. Sarah will be generous to dislocated countesses. And she will help Michael with his work, collecting parcels for him in bookshops; but her marital involvement and the living out of her romantic dreams will block her from becoming the kind of student for Michael that Michael could have been for Lindt. Michael will never be quite brilliant enough to deserve Lindt's compliment. He will never benefit from the conversation that could have ensued when Lindt fully appreciated the extent of Michael's skills at seduction.

This film, then, is hardly about East-West relations at its heart. It is about the marriage of true minds to which these purely political, territorial relations—whether symbolized in a film such as this or actualized in everyday world affairs—constitute an impediment, the "marriage" never quite forged between Armstrong and Lindt or between Armstrong's bureaucratic cage and Lindt's academic demesne. For Michael—it is far too evident in Room 29— adores Lindt, just as we do. Repressed by his dedication to intelligence gathering, for him thought has become a product to be appropriated and exploited. For Lindt, thought is a system of human relations, a vertical system, to be sure, in which there is domination and strictness, obedience and hunger, but always, too, revivifying fire.

"Let me succumb for a moment to the fascination of the mysterious East and tell you of the examination procedure for the course in internal heat," Norman O. Brown wrote, discussing the University of Tibet:

> Candidates assemble naked, in midwinter, at night, on a frozen Himalayan lake. Beside each one is placed a pile of wet frozen undershirts: the assignment is to wear, until they are dry, as many as possible of these undershirts before dawn. Where the power is real, the test is real, and the grading system dumbfoundingly objective.[44]

Neither Michael nor Sarah glows with internal fire by the time they are safely in Sweden. Wet to the bone, they huddle before a hearth in one another's comforting arms. Press photographers do not quite succeed in getting pictures of them. But we do, and see that once again, as at the beginning of this circular tale, they are wrapped in a blanket that keeps them hidden from the working—the quotidian—world. Perhaps Michael here recalls, too late, what Gromek wondered with affection, and only a little ironic detachment, before dying: "What's the matter, you don't like our art museum?" Or, in plainer language, "Let go. Admire the beauty, as long as you're here." But more likely he has abandoned Gromek to history. Caught up in the point of business, Armstrong lacks a relation between himself and his surround—a π—but moves instead in a bubble of fixation that, as viewers adequate to him, we share.

In the art museum, where Armstrong is too pressed to take a look at anything, we are never permitted to stop to look at anything, either. The footsteps of Gromek—rushing to catch him, we imagine, not eagerly approaching art—carry us forward and out. European culture as represented by the museum—the world of Gromek and Lindt—is overwhelmed by the new technological *realpolitik* represented by Gerhard and Armstrong. The admiration of beauty is supplanted by the chase.[45] Ballet, too, is transformed from art to business, with the perfidious ballerina, a citizen of Gerhard's world, not Gromek's, using her pirouettes as platform for an intelligence operation. That she is utterly chilling as a character may remind us that all of the really warm folk in this film are of Gromek's world, not Gerhard's; Lindt's world, not Armstrong's: direct people, simple people, people with memories and feeling. On the steamship to Stockholm, it is the clownish red-headed baggage master Hugo (Frank Alter) who ultimately gets the Americans out alive, arranging a stagy routine whereby they can elude authorities. Sarah and

Michael are hiding in the ballet company's costume baskets; that is, they have become "costumes" to be worn in somebody else's dance.

Though he is certainly adept managing baggage, Hugo has no use, it turns out, for the baggage of ideology as, sadly, our protagonists (and Hitchcock's audiences) do. While they confabulate smugly about their adventure to the East and back, about good guys and bad guys and winning and losing and lessons painfully learned, he goes off happy, silent, and down-to-earth, counting his money, along the quai. Hugo is the trader who profits by exchanging goods, not ideas, baskets and not words—a figure anticipating a central character in Antonioni's *The Passenger* a decade later. His maneuver of switching the costume baskets to fool the malevolent ballerina and the soldiers she cues is reflex, a happy conjuror's trick, not a triumph of wit. Appropriately for the ending of such an intellectual story, and one in which the baggage of thought plays such a central role as ballast upon the characters' backs, he, of all the characters we meet, is the only one who is beyond thought, knows nothing, and has nothing to learn.

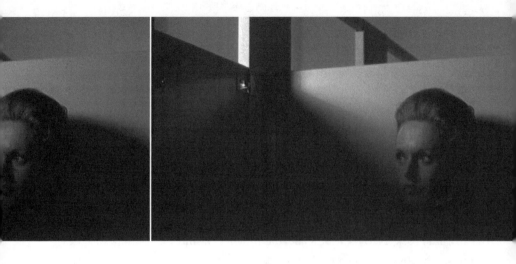

Once in Love with *Marnie*

It's quite remarkable to discover that one isn't what one thought one was.
Spellbound

STAKEOUTS

The old, sad story—promising youth blighted, dragged down by money, position, noblesse oblige.

Mr. Mark Rutland has tamed a jaguarundi. There is a framed color photograph of her, token and reminder, with a great pink mouth and green, eager, all-seeing eyes, nearby a cabinet containing some pre-Columbian artifacts (that are all he has that belonged to his deceased wife), in his large, high-ceilinged, leather-upholstered office at Rutland and Co., 213 Arley Street, Philadelphia. It is a Saturday afternoon in 1963. Outside the building, over the almost empty parking lot, a thunderstorm is brewing. Jaguarundis, Mark tells Mrs. Mary Taylor, a young widow recently employed by him as secretary (and who has volunteered to do some typing for him after hours), are notoriously loath to trust. As she begins to work on his manuscript, which is about arboreal predators of the Amazonian rain forest, the storm breaks. She is caught in a paroxysm of terror by the lightning and Mark suggests turning on the overhead light, the switch for which is by the door. She gets up and races across the room, gelid with fear. Moving to her side, he tells her to re-

lax, "the building is grounded" and she's quite safe. But the flashes of lightning, which to her appear red, blood red, have her paralyzed. She screams, "The colors!" "What colors?" asks Rutland. Now with a stunning crash a heavy branch falls through his tall window, smashing into the antique cabinet and shattering the pre-Columbian artifacts to smithereens. Rutland kisses Mrs. Taylor's temple, and we zoom into their faces as his lips slide down to her mouth. They kiss. She bends down and picks up a shard of pottery: "We all have to go sometime," says Mark, tossing it down again. He offers to drive her home. In the car she says she is sorry about the cabinet, which was everything he had of his wife. "I said it was all I had left that had *belonged* to my wife," he replies.

This strange and exquisite scene—one that needs no place in a melodramatic tale of a pathetic kleptomaniac's sordid love life, as *Marnie* is very typically interpreted to be[1]—is a wild and complex knot of motive, theme, and innuendo, in which we take pleasure in some of the very deftest writing and most carefully modulated acting in all of Hitchcock. It has for me the quality of a cloistered garden, in which paths lead off in many directions, so let me follow some, to trace their lines of preparation and development outside the scene.

Mark Rutland (Sean Connery) is attracted to "Mrs. Taylor" ('Tippi' Hedren), not just employing her, as is evident from the quality of their kiss and from the innuendo in his calming reassurance to her, "You're quite safe." She is not in his office, then, only to do after-hours typing. We may recollect how "Mrs. Taylor" was hired in the first place, noting what was explicitly revealed in the setting of that action. For example: Rutland made no show she could see—being preoccupied, as she was, in devotion to the petit bureaucrat Mr. Ward (S. John Launer), who was interviewing her for a job—but considerably freer at that moment than "Mrs. Taylor" (i.e., watching a movie, not seeking patronage), *we* were placed to know that Rutland was secretly directing Ward to hire her—giving the nod (literally)—at least because he found her sexually appealing.[2] Now she races into his arms this stormy Saturday, not party to this information. But watching the scene and taking a special pleasure in the connections between the protagonists (some early arrangements for which we witnessed), we are. She is apparently experiencing an emotional moment; he is staging. We enjoy this discrepancy, though it disempowers her, and the link between such disempowerment and such enjoyment, as we will see, is central in this film.

Secrecy riddles this scene. Although in her application interview "Mrs. Taylor" played widowhood upon Ward, the sympathy it could have inspired (though we have no reason to think it did, Ward being notable for his detachment) had nothing whatever to do with her getting this job. Further, "Mrs. Taylor" was no widow and did not merit, on such a basis, the kind attentions of anyone. Further, if the Saturday typing session was arranged to make a liaison possible—one kept secret from the other employees and even from "Mrs. Taylor" herself—Rutland's eagerness in the moment is a fact he certainly shares, expressly and with a remarkable honesty: "You're quite safe." That is, "You're quite safe now, because the storm has interrupted me." She, however, is so obsessed with the weather she does not read his deeper message and cannot imagine his deeper intent. Even though he has placed it squarely before her, the sexual passion that moves him—and titillates us—is a complete secret to her. "Mrs. Taylor" is the purest innocent.

Yet "Mrs. Taylor" is not really "Mrs. Taylor" and so she is at a far remove from innocence. And Rutland knows this, but only we know that. Later, when he reveals to her that he knew all along she was performing, the script calls for "shock piled upon shock." We were shown the moment of Mark's recognition behind "Mrs. Taylor's" back, just as she was begging Ward for a job; we also saw Mark hide his awareness. In his capacious office, now, as he continues to call her "Mrs. Taylor" and we see her smug conviction that she is deceiving him, in fact we can suspect it is he who is deceiving her, playing along and not just playing about. Mark's reasons for being so cagey, however, are a secret from us. I might add that he is himself in very large measure a secret on the shallowest surface level in this film.[3] I hope to show that to understand the logic of his actions one must pay very close attention to small matters, aware that Hitchcock composed all his work with the keenest eye for the smallest and most revealing detail: more about Mark Rutland soon.

However, now that what Goffman called "fabrication"[4] has entered our conception of the structure of the scene, and of the film, we may see, too, that "Mrs. Taylor," for her own part, may have had subterranean reasons for making herself available to type on Saturday, reasons incompatible with Mark's reasons for asking her. If so, this fact is her secret. We may wonder what her reasons can have been, if she is not—as she very well seems not—interested in coming closer to the boss. There is still more:

Much later, Rutland will show that he did have a very clear idea that Saturday what "Mrs. Taylor's" subterranean motives could have been, that he knew she had been engaged in thievery in many places and was very likely planning a theft at Rutland's now. But today, to us and to "Mrs. Taylor," he gives no hint of being suspicious and so his suspicion of her is itself a secret.[5] Even before she walks into his lair proper, it is warmly, though formally, that he welcomes her in a resonant voice that wafts through the door. His formality, exactly balancing the deferential "Mr. Rutland" she uses for him, carries much more ironic weight than may at first appear since, in a masquerade of his own, he is playing to her masquerade—yet to us he seems perfectly uncontrived. To generalize: a great deal is going on in front of our eyes that we do not presently grasp.

From Mark's point of view, as a person who knows he has admitted a criminal to his precincts, there is irony and play in the fact that the first thing "Mrs. Taylor's" eyes light upon, and that he politely labels for her, is a (fabulously valuable) collection of pre-Columbian art assembled by his late wife. But if the art is a potential target of theft when she eyes it, the storm redefines it quickly enough. It is a curious question, indeed—and we may certainly later realize that Mark may have been wondering—what troubles "Mrs. Taylor" most in that brief storm: the lightning flashes themselves or the fact that because of them all these thievable goodies are demolished before her eyes?

Secrets form one screen through which we can watch this office scene.

Control forms another. The bough that crashes into Mark's office, destroying the art collection, is, predictably enough, empty of arboreal predators—indeed, it is utterly bare, a dead limb, rather like the wife Mark Rutland is still carrying around in his vocabulary. Though Sophie the jaguarundi would once have nestled in a tree like this one, she is now in a frame, tamed, located, reduced to two dimensions, frozen in place (rather like "Mrs. Taylor" at the light switch). She is made an artifact of civilization, in a process Mark began by teaching her the wholly social attitude called "trust." Later, having found out who she really is, Mark will try to control "Mrs. Taylor." But the frozen posture of the cat is our second clue to the creature's affinity with "Mrs. Taylor." Earlier, when the young woman looked over at the photograph, and we cut to the photograph she was looking at, we saw that Sophie was posed in her picture precisely the same way "Mrs. Taylor" had been in the frame (her picture), the cat felinizing the typist just as the typist criminalizes—re-naturalizes—the cat. If, as Mark suggests, trust is a great deal for a jaguarundi, trusting him will also be a great deal for "Mrs. Taylor," a matter, in fact, of losing control. If it is also a little problematic for us to trust Mark completely—in casting Connery Hitchcock may have had precisely this difficulty in mind for us[6]—we may be able to sympathize with "Mrs. Taylor" and experience her world. Mark is certainly a sympathetic man, and attractive, and stylish—even, at moments, heroic—yet there must also be something sufficiently questionable about him to make the heroine's doubt plausible. Otherwise she is not only a criminal, and a neurotic, but also a fool. His control must be just a little too astute, enough to put the viewer on edge.

The ability to cause creatures, cats or women, to trust him is an even greater deal for Mark than for them. Rather than seeing here a depiction of a solitary, manipulative, domineering male character or a symbolic allusion to the isolation, manipulativeness, and structural domination of American men in general at this time (this scene was written just before, and revised on the day of, the assassination of John F. Kennedy), we should attempt to understand Mark Rutland as a signal case of the upper-middle-class gentleman with vested class interests. Hitchcock was no professional sociologist, but he understood the intricacies of class systems, British and American, and there are no Hitchcock films in which some contribution to a class analysis is not present.[7] Hitchcock was intending this, though a little disconcerted about the difficulty of representing class consciousness in an America where the tapestry of social stratification was becoming invisible to the audience's attentions.

"Today," he told Truffaut in August 1962, "a princess can marry a photographer and no one lifts an eyebrow." Indeed, the purported openness of the class structure of late capitalism might make a class-based reading of this film seem archaic, but Hitchcock's serious intent here was "the story of the prince and the beggar girl,"[8] a saga of breeding.[9] *Marnie*, I will argue, is all about class, and this accounts for much of the information we are quite systematically given that has nothing to do with the spurious tale of Marnie Edgar as a psychologically warped petty thief who changes identities every time she pulls a job. The thief tale is the setting, not the deep meaning of the film, and we shall see why. In this important typing scene, Mark is identified as an aristocrat—not only as a tamer of jaguarundis, but more basically as a man who acquires them for taming. He either voyages on expeditions, or purchases from those who do. He makes collections. He marries people who make collections, or supports the habit of collecting in people he marries. Teaching the wild beast to trust him is a sympathetic maneuver from our point of view (the middle-class sensibility values emotional warmth), yet it displays his superiority, the ability to elevate his humanity above rank animalism. In the comparison of "Mary Taylor" and Sophie, indeed, we have a basis for discriminating her fine expressive sensitivity from the cat's lither, more original, yet grosser one; but also, of course, for seeing her as yet one more base item to be caged, organized, catalogued, kept in place.

Taming and teaching are possible where there is stratification. We saw this theme explored in *Torn Curtain* and we see it explored all through the present film, as Mark makes it his responsibility to lead Marnie out of the depths of her pain and history to a health that is both progressive and high. It is from an intellectual height that, as she moves forward into his office, he poses behind an opulent rosewood desk to welcome her (in a delicious forward dolly) and asks blithely whether she is interested in pre-Columbian art. It was from desperation of one kind or another—but in any event, relative powerlessness—that in her interview she pled to work anytime, and as much as possible, thus setting up the invitation for this Saturday afternoon. It is from a privileged (and masculine) pinnacle of social experience unassailable by her coy sarcasm that he speaks of himself, a scion, as having been "drafted into Rutlands," and that he delivers an erudite, if minuscule, lecture on zoology: "It includes all the animal ancestors from whom man's instincts derive."[10] To which "Mrs. Taylor" replies, with a "mocking smile," "Ladies' instincts too?"

Soon after these words, the verticality of trust and fulfillment are emphasized in the fascinating macro close-up of Mark's and "Mrs. Taylor's" mouths as they kiss. By zooming in for so intimate a view, we escape the ravages of the thunderstorm (that is, we pull away from its presence as a narrative element) and thus empathize with "Mrs. Taylor's" fear and her need to be protected. But the screen protagonists in this remarkable shot—Hitchcock never elsewhere made a zoom into so short a perspective—are mouths, not characters who possess them; and the play of mouth upon mouth as the storm crashes,[11] a play that takes over the entire screen and that we must involve ourselves with thoroughly, is vertical, emphasized as such by the opening gambit of Mark kissing Marnie on the temple and then slowly moving down the side of her face as we slide in to the viewpoint of maximal intimacy. What is above is mouthing what is below—training for trust—and being mouthed are bodies more than persons, body parts, openings to great tunnels. One could speak of the appropriation of territory, the possession of the right of way for movement. And if the jaguarundi has come down out of her tree for Mark, it is in the service of literature: he is writing a manuscript on just such creatures as she in his capacity as the presiding officer of a publishing house (empowered to put out that book when he has finished it). All the discussion of animals in this scene, then, and of manuscripts, of zoology (part of a manuscript), and of instincts (part of zoology), is about Mark's dominance in class terms. Mark's comment about lady animals figuring very largely as predators is meant to throw informed light on the origins of gender and class structure, giving us reason for reading Marnie's motives in terms of status and stratification rather than psychology: structured powerlessness, not psychosexual neurosis, make her the masquerader she is. That the coy banter about men's and women's instincts is directly linked to coy banter about the "criminal class of the animal world" suggests that for Mark gender differentiation is about class experience, not personality.

I go on about this scene at such length partly in order to introduce central themes of *Marnie* while showing how they are embodied materially in action that is visible on the screen—all the scenes in this stunning film are as informative as this one—but also, and mostly, in order to show how very densely packed a Hitchcock scene can be. If we read all the scenes in this way—and I urge that viewers should—the narrative expands and unfurls into a vivid, even symphonic structure and the filmmaker's concerns appear broader than the rather localized kleptomaniac frigidity or sexual discomfort many reviewers and critics seem happy here to see.[12] Not that Hitchcock's films will not work on a superficial level. They will—*Marnie* is also about romance and theft. But in watching we may dig and find that the surface story is a wrapping put in place only to keep the bugs off.

RUTLAND

In taking a closer look at *Marnie*,[13] we might begin with the stratificational rut that Mark and his father (Alan Napier) have fallen into. It is the central rut of rut-land, that topos of fixity and determinism, of power and tradition, from which Marnie's fey movement from identity to identity and her stallion Forio's leap from hurdle to hurdle cannot quite help her escape. "Static, even stagnant,"[14] the Rutlands' rut, metonymized by the capacious Wykwyn, is a comfortable country estate from which the traditional "lord," the *seigneur*, need never trouble himself to move. There is narrative testimony to this august, this senior, position. Wykwyn seems less a point of departure for exploring the world than a seat of wealth and consciousness the world visits, and so I expect to find a guest book there, something fancy and established, on the pages of which I can read a kind of history by perusing the list of names. This guest book is the opening title background for *Marnie*, and the rhythmic turning of the identical, thick, creamy pages suggests stability and consolidation through the passage of time.[15] With extreme stability comes the inwardness of majesty. If it is not quite inbred (from too much casual rutting), nevertheless the Rutland family—drawn with Jamesian precision by a director who thought he "didn't know these people"[16]—is a structure the values of which are congruent with inbreeding. Lil Mainwaring (Diane Baker), for instance, Mark's sister-in-law, is described utterly without cattiness by Ward's secretary Susan Clabon (Mariette Hartley) as having "lived with them and old Mr. Rutland out at Wykwyn. And I get the feeling little old Lil plans to stay on . . . *permanently*." Prepared by this tacit *dramatis personae*, we are hardly shocked later in the film to find Lil exuding something more than sisterly possessiveness toward Mark in the presence of Marnie, at the tea party, at the soirée, or in the corridors of the great house.[17] She is, indeed, for Joe McElhaney, "a crucial third element in the chain of desire in the Mark/Marnie marriage."[18] If it is her presumption to take up the place vacated by her unfortunate sister at Mark's side, nothing in old Mr. Rutland's bearing or the Rutland employees' attitude is an obstacle to her progress, and Lil has come to take her freedoms in this territory for granted. Marnie's presence, then, and Mark's too-open affection for her constitute an audacious challenge.

With inbreeding comes lassitude. As Mark himself puts it, "Nothing *ever* happens to a family that traditionally marries at least one heiress every other generation." Old Mr. Rutland is in such a rut that his day is utterly configured upon "good Horn & Hardart cake at tea." He will hear nothing of a woman who doesn't smell like a horse—in short, he likes people who are near the barn, which, as we see, is straight outside the main house. Landed aristocracy is immobilized by its own capability, paralyzed by the fact of its emplacement. In fact, if we watch the way characters move in this house, we see a kind of leisurely and leaden strolling. And the house in which they move, and which we can presume they observe languidly as they glide through it, is configured for us as a rigid and purely pictorial space. By contrast, when she is emotionally overwrought and riding Forio, Marnie's world is a jumble of fragments, intensities, luminous flashes.

Frequently in Hitchcock there are scenes that seem utterly incomprehensible as contributions to the story—even if they entertain—and which cannot neatly be accounted for in a conventional analysis that takes the surface plot seriously. In this film, the pecan pie scene qualifies, to be sure, but another is a scene, carefully scripted, that was revised before final shooting. A brief office escapade with Artie Nelson (Linden Chiles) has its diegetic root in a post-Victorian fillip of "cultured" gender behavior, prominently articulated in middle-class culture of the 1950s and early 1960s and referenced earlier in this film:[19] the express inappropriateness of males putting their sexual arousal on plain display. To the extent that one can find men in conditions of extreme stimulation contriving through posture, language, or dramaturgic choreography to give the impression that they are acting out of innocent, nonsexual motives, one can claim the operation of something the Victorian culture (out of which old Mr. Rutland emerged) would have called "civilization." The same "civilization" motivates and organizes the reduction of pre-Columbian social organization to an art collection, the presentation of a proper tea party, the presence and behavior of a butler at the door during a fabulous soirée. (Ding-dong.)

Here is the scene: Artie Nelson is plainly turned on by Mary Taylor (very like Mark Rutland), and has a friendly routine[20] of playing turned-on by Susan Clabon. Sexuality, not doughnuts, draws him hither,[21] and in the October 29, 1963, version of the shooting script this angle is given explicit play:

SUSAN (*noticing Artie*): *You.* I wondered how long before you'd come sniffing around. Mary Taylor . . . Artie Nelson . . . Sales Department.

ARTIE: *Ward* hired *her*? Wha' hoppen? He slip up and eat a piece of meat or *what*?

SUSAN: I doubt it. It looked more like orders from higher-up to me.

ARTIE: Rutland! You mean I'm up against whatdy-call-it? . . . *Droit de seigneur*? Know what I mean? Like has Rutland got you all staked out, honey, or is there any chance for us rabble?

MARNIE: To answer all of your questions, Mr. Nelson . . . I have never met Mr. Rutland. He does not know me. He does not have me 'staked out.' And no. There is no chance for the rabble.

SUSAN: Well Artie, looks like you just got yourself filed under 'C' . . . for 'cool it.'

The sexual motive is present in Artie in this scene for the same reason this scene was intended (although in the final edit not included) in the film: to make bold for the viewer Mark Rutland's seniority, his *seigneur*-ity. These social arrangements reveal a feudal class structure, with the landholder holding conjugal *droits*. Mary Taylor's disaffection notwithstanding, Artie gives a fine display (by reflection) of the system he believes to be in operation to guide and control the sexual passions (that is, power sources) of various men. Ward is gelded by virtue of his reputed vegetarianism; Mark is in power to "stake out" women as territories; and even Marnie/Mary, refusing to be staked out, is certain without doubt that there is a rabble, and that Artie Nelson is properly in it.

That Mark is personally hesitant to treat Marnie in a superior fashion makes him a fascinating character, if not quite a feminist ahead of his time. But the social system in which he occupies his role is described better by Artie's presumption and old Mr. Rutland's rutting behavior, by the hunt, by the barn, by the smell of horses, by the loyal though uncomprehending obedience of Cousin Bob the banker (Bob Sweeney). The old man has to approve of Marnie before she can come into the family; and as soon as we see his towering benevolence we feel comfortable he will. That social class and a vertical hierarchy of power underlie the visible relations in the film is made even more explicit when we learn that old Rutland does not stoop to visit the publishing company he owns; admits, in fact, that he is bewildered anyone can find anything to do there. Says Clabon, "They say he's never even been *inside* this place! And the company was really headed into the ground." To be savior, Mark has had to take drastic steps, but he has put a sociable face on every brutal (that is, physical) move. As Susan tells it, in his first week he "retired . . . *retired*! . . three board members, the acting president, the president's secretary, and the secretary's secretary." We shall see all through *Marnie* the dainty social face of brutality.

But back to the Saturday afternoon thunderstorm for a last small detail. Why of all conceivable good things did the elder Miss Mainwaring, who married Mark Rutland and "died of some kind of heart thing" (in Clabon's words) when she was only twenty-nine, collect pre-Columbian art? She needn't, for this scene or any other, have been a collector: the storm is terrifying enough, and the tree can come crashing through the window without destroying a cabinet full of anything. The Saturday tryst-got-up-as-work session, which Mark Rutland has arranged with "Mary Taylor" and during which there is a signal discussion about animals and humans and trust and predation, does not require for the development of its themes about gender and fidelity a cabinet of pre-Columbian sculpture, but that sculpture does in fact contribute much. First, it is exceptionally fragile, as fragile, perhaps, as any artifact known to man. For suggesting the ease with which a magnificent work can be destroyed—for preparing us for Forio, for the sad decline of Mrs. Edgar (Louise Latham), for Marnie's ultimate collapse—there is no simpler analogy. Too, the pre-Columbian age is the oldest source of artistic materials in the New World and therefore represents at once art (to which Hitchcock is devoted), antiquity, and the non- or at least post-European West. The theme of the West is important in *Marnie* and throughout the American Hitchcock in particular because it is in the New World that social classes encounter one another in direct relations that had been technically impossible in feudal Europe. Virginia, Maryland, Pennsylvania—the settings of this film—were the center of the original American colonial establishment. Here is where the New World was founded, where the old European aristocracy first butted directly against the "rabble" in a connection that lingers in traces at the heart of the class relation between Mark and Marnie. Most important of all, however, and because it is so very old, pre-Columbian art signifies the elemental, the essential, the human condition reduced from all appurtenance and distraction. It is time and trust (the time it takes to trust, and the trust we must have in time), feeling, and death and long memory—long and clinging memory, indeed, that sooner or later has to go; the past that must be lost, the pattern that must be undone, the self that must be yielded in order for the creature to survive.

Without the shattered pre-Columbian sculpture as its configuration, Marnie's condition is a neurotic excrescence of her childhood—individual in focus, twenty or twenty-five years old and thus relatively small, idiosyncratic, particular. But with the sculpture, it is a thing not of the psyche or the individual family but of age-old conditions and circumstances, a form that must be excavated from entrenched and settled relations of class and habit, stratified privilege, the petrifications of post-feudal experience. If social class as we experience and know it is not exactly pre-Columbian (it is post-feudal), still the ancient and fragile artifacts symbolize something far greater than the individual biography and psychology, something that envelops us. If in this film characters will offer psychological explanations for Marnie, we need remember that they do so in the context of the destruction of this pre-Columbian art; the psychologizing (a way of contemporizing through biography) is not to be taken so very seriously at face value.

It is the jaguarundi's tree that has fallen through the window, its crash suggesting spatial boundary and dislocation. The topography setting this action is not merely a realistic Philadelphia but a vast canvas of historically based social structure leading not only back through generations of jaguarundis to pre-Columbian times but also outward from this managerial suite to vertical social hierarchies more broadly conceived. Structures of obedience and organization are of the essence here, not the parking lots, photographs, office furniture, and manuscripts through which they are manifested. The trust that has been shattered on the floor is any person's trust in a powerful superior who controls the means of survival. And, as we all have to go sometime, trust is vital as both obedience and an element of social form. Mouths that could have gnawed and torn at each other now taste a finely shaped tenderness instead.

The organization of mouths, however, like that of the rest of our physicality, is the stuff of toiletry . . .

SOMEONE'S IN THE BATHROOM WITH MARNIE

The face is everything. If the face doesn't fit, change the character.
   Hitchcock

Four times in this film, Marnie uses a bathroom in our company.[22] In a bit of conversation originally written for her to overhear on her third visit, while she is secreted in a toilet stall until the other workers have gone home for the weekend so that in leisure she can ransack the Rutland safe, an unseen worker named Shirley is complaining about a girlfriend's attempts to set her up with a man: "'Oh, you'll *love* him, Shirley! He's your *type*. He's real executive material.' *Executive Material*! You should have seen the executive way he shoved those nickels in the automat!" Although this offscreen dialogue is replaced in the final print by another set of comments (about the perils of waiting for a man to telephone), that Hitchcock was very approving about this script and that he intended to use it make it interesting as a reflection of his concerns in this scene. As we will see, other references to Horn & Hardart's automat show up in the film, making this moment worth some patient attention as an indication of Hitchcock's scenic structuring, of how the writer and filmmaker were thinking though the sociological implications of their story.[23]

This scene is a beautiful illustration of Hitchcock's meticulous dramatic preparation of his viewer. We may begin with the observation that there is no need for a woman planning a heist from the company safe to spend time in a toilet stall beforehand; she need only arrange to have sufficient overtime work at her desk to keep her busy until everyone else has left, and overtime work, we learned from that special Saturday typing session, is not strange at Rutland's. It is secrecy and privacy that Marnie wants as a preface to robbery, however, and this scene is about privacy, not thieving; proximity, not money; intimacy, not crime. Or, when Hitchcock treats the subjects of privacy, proximity, and intimacy he uses criminality and cash as a pretext. As "Mrs. Taylor," Marnie collects her handbag as she prepares to leave at day's end, then furtively withdraws a second bag that has been secreted in her desk (introducing the idea of the bag as pouch—hiding place—and the desk as pouch-around-a-pouch). When she comes to the Ladies' Room she stops outside the door. This hesitation is for us: we are about to enter a sacred territory, a pouch around pouches (toilet stalls). Our movement after her as she goes through the door (the movement is a jump to a pick-up shot inside the lavatory) is a prelude to her own imminent movement past the threshold and into the sacred precincts of the Rutland safe.

The pouch symbolizes Marnie herself to some extent. As she places herself silently in one of the stalls, she is a pouch inside a pouch inside a pouch. First audacious as we stepped into the washroom with her, we are now brazen enough to enter her stall. The space within is cut with shadows, like Father Logan's confessional in *I Confess*. We are overtaken by the density of color: the teal of the stall, the red of Marnie's lips, her amber hair and dark searching eyes. The excitement and much of the meaning of the moment is provided by a conjunction of two oddly related facts, that the chattering salesgirls do not know she is there, but also that since we are with her they do not know we are there either. Characters in films never know of our presence, it is true; but by being placed with Marnie in this particular secret place, we come into the "back" precinct of what can be known by characters in films, into the *characters'* dressing room, and our invisibility is felt as a wholly new kind of experience. What approximates us to Marnie here is not a direct relation but an indirect one: that both she and we are overhearing these women who are oblivious to us; that Marnie is as out of place as we are, though for different reasons. Marnie is out of place because of what she is doing, because of what she is not doing, and because of what she is intending to do. We are out of place merely because we are here: that is, because we would not let Marnie out of our sight. She, then, is not the normal clerical worker she pretended to be. And so her crime is that she is a fraud. Our crime is being film viewers caught upon a central character to such an extent that our etiquette dissolves.

Now, the point of being in a secret place is to learn a secret, and the intriguing secret Hitchcock was prepared to have us learn as we waited in this stall, coming out of Shirley's rather established working-class perceptions by way of her unhesitating working-class mouth, and masquerading as a gender anecdote, is a moral prescription about social status. "You should have seen the executive way he shoved those nickels in the automat!" In the wise Shirley's observation, the otherwise unidentified "he" of her tale is definitively not executive material, because he committed the gaffe of eating at so indecorous a place as the automat. He is a habitué of the vulgar world. The automat for Shirley—though we do not meet her, nevertheless she is our tutor in this cache—is a cafeteria for merely the likes of working folk like her, and any man who shoved his nickels there[24] could not possibly be sensibly mistaken for an executive type. Executives, we may presume—Shirley makes such a presumption—would eat *pots de crème* at Helen Sigel Wilson's at 1523 Walnut Street. In the shooting script, as we heard this little tale we were to be focused on Marnie's attentive face as she listened, too. Her eyes at this moment look upward, lambent, receptive, symbolizing for an audience beset by opticality her susceptibility in the always invisible process of listening. Cued by her rapt fascination and wariness, we are meant to hear every syllable of this conversation, detecting it not merely as a story Hitchcock has arranged for us to overhear while we are waiting patiently in the bathroom stall but as a story Hitchcock has placed us in a bathroom stall in order to overhear. It will do to remember this mini-saga of the automat, mundane and tangential as it seems to be.

Horn & Hardart, purveyors of the automat experience, had been invoked a little earlier at a tea party at Wykwyn. At a critical moment for the success of the friendship of Mark and Marnie and thus of the plot of the film, charming and down-to-earth old Mr. Rutland, having established himself as an adorable recluse—"It bewilders me what any of you can find to *do* at Rutland's. I want my tea"—makes a very queer little speech. The moment is one in which, through an artifice, Mark's catty and jealous sister-in-law has forced a staging—"Oh, dear . . . I think I rather sprained my wrist this afternoon"—that leaves Marnie to pour (and thereby reveal her social class background).

At this, old Rutland, symbol of affluence, power, and class, announces, "The meals in this house are shocking bad but I do insist on good Horn & Hardart cake at tea."

Horn & Hardart cake? But since the thrust of this scene is to give Mark and Marnie an opportunity to evacuate the house for the privacy of the stables, no cake at all is required here. The scene is written fundamentally to introduce Marnie—and us—to Mark's father, and Hitchcock is pleased to set it in such a way as to facilitate this alluring old man making an adulatory comment about exactly the sort of Horn & Hardart product that, in a deft reflection, will be disparaged by an unseen secretary in a scene shortly to follow. What, then, is the old man saying, in his decorous British accent, that viewers might need to hear? I take his message, and the viewer's expected reading, to be something like this: that America is not English, which is to say, following William Carlos Williams,[25] that America is American. American culture is founded on a principled rejection of the class distinctions that are the beams of the British structure. Though old Rutland is a man clearly raised in the United Kingdom, though in fond nostalgia he has named his retreat "Wykwyn," which is Old English for "abode of domestic friendship,"[26] though he retains his interest in old country customs—a preference for horses over women, a strict adherence to afternoon tea rituals, an aristocratic deprecation of work—yet he typifies now, for the typical viewer, the American self-made baron of democracy, cherishing as a private and newfound pleasure something to be obtained not from a private *pâtissier*, nor from some weathered retainer of a cook utilizing an old and inherited domestic recipe book bound in faded leather, nor from a posh restaurant, but from the automat. Now, if in the quirky performance by Alan Napier[27] Rutland seems populist to Hitchcock's audiences because of this affection for ordinary cooking, he may nevertheless be reflecting the real world of American wealth and privilege, the rich, after all, being quite as likely to prefer Horn & Hardart as anything else. But Hitchcock knew that his viewers would have expected to see quite a different, more refined, type of aristocrat;[28] that a Rutland who doted on Horn & Hardart would appear modern, appealing, and quintessentially American, which is to say, modest.

The automat at once symbolized and embodied all the elements of straightforward Anglo-Saxon American modernism of the mid-twentieth century:[29] an egalitarian do-it-yourself ethic,[30] a utilitarian sense of grand design,[31] mass production nicely balanced with the illusion of catered service,[32] a technological thrust made emphatic by the structural presence of polished chrome, a motor logic implicit in the ceaseless movement of customers through the space of the system and of food through the space of the cus-tomers, a dramaturgically exploited efficiency culminating in a kind of "mag-ical" replenishment[33] of food items from behind the high, surrounding stage wall of glass-fronted cabinets that had held them.[34] Horn & Hardart was not the Savoy, Fortnum & Mason, the Ritz, or the Cafe Royal. But Mr. Rutland treasures "good Horn & Hardart cake at tea." This is an explicit statement about the egalitarian, technically impelled, anti-aristocratic values of the American class structure, seen from the point of view of a man who has experienced the British one for comparison—and first. Rutland may have reminded Hitchcock of himself. Horn & Hardart was so esteemed by Old Mr. Rutland, in fact, that he made the company a kind of centerpiece of his son's wedding: "Really *splendid* cake, you know. Tended to *that* myself. I've made the acquaintance of one of those excellent Horn & Hardart executives."

Mark has inherited the liberal style of his father, but presumably born in America he romanticizes the England that Old Rutland has rejected and is thus able openly to display his class power—training the jaguarundi or deal-ing with Strutt, he is a businessman who can be presumed to be "in the busi-ness of doing business." If the baronial old man who likes the food from the automat would abjure lording it over people, or applying the principles of the hunt to human prey (the sort of crass middle-class "business" Hitchcock could have witnessed daily in his travails in Hollywood), his son is different: "I've caught something *really* wild this time, haven't I? I've tracked you and caught you, and by God, I'm going to keep you." We could be listening to Jack Warner gloating at Olivia de Havilland.

An earlier filmic voyage to the bathroom is less organized than the one I have been discussing. A little flustered, perhaps, by the obnoxious attention of Artie the office boy, Marnie has been careless with a bottle of red ink so that a blob has spilled on the white blouse she is wearing. "THE SCREEN IS ONCE AGAIN SUFFUSED WITH A RED GLOW," reads the shooting script of October 29. "For a moment Marnie stares dumbly at the red stain on her blouse. Then, without a word to Susan, she moves rapidly out of the office." Virtually running, she traverses the office compound, her eyes fixed on the stain. Mark approaches her but she moves forward, not seeing him as he asks, "Are you all right, Mrs. Taylor?" As she pushes into the washroom he turns to stare in concern. Inside, standing in her camisole, Marnie is washing the sleeve under "a gushing faucet" of water, her face "a mask of concentration as she scrubs ferociously at the stain."

But we have already, and quite formidably, been introduced to Marnie

Edgar's panic at the sight of red. This scene, therefore—and the *macula* upon her shirt that is its point—is less a reminder that red is a problem than an invocation of the theme of stains and a linking opportunity for Marnie to place herself in a washroom. The washroom invokes moral and sexual propriety; it is a place Mark would stain by his presence even as the ink stains the pristine garment. Here, Marnie's presence in the lavatory is a way of drawing boundary lines and suggesting Mark's presence just outside as sexual, since legally the washroom is a room he owns and can enter at will before it is a sanctum devoted to the female presence. We are invited to wonder about the relation between physical and bodily "property" and "ownership," and thus conjugal contracts—those gender-based arrangements according to which people's "private" functions become other people's business, which is to say, in some measure less private. Surely prefigured here in theme if not in form is the honeymoon experience to follow, what Robin Wood calls "one of the purest treatments of sexual intercourse the cinema has given us."[35] The narrative frame of the filmmaking, however, stands above and outside even Mark Rutland's patriarchy, since if he cannot enter that washroom, we can. We are shown here, as well, something of the vital relationship between gender status and social power, since "women's trouble" of some sort is sufficient warrant for Marnie to treat her employer's question—"Are you all right, Mrs. Taylor?"—as though it were not being asked, and her employer as though he were not there to be asking it. A subtle supportive function of the interplay earlier with Artie can now be detected: it prepared us for women's disregard of men—as such—in the workplace (Artie was acting not as an employee but as a male), a tactic Marnie will soon use on Mark Rutland and which might seem incongruous to an audience of the early 1960s not already thoroughly briefed on the political manifesto of gender equality. When she disregards Mark in the hallway, she is openly viewing him not as an employer but as a man masquerading as one.

Indeed, it may be that in all of what Mark does he functions as a man in masquerade: a man masquerading as a host, as a signer of deals, as old Rutland's child, and so on. It may be, but we shall have to voyage further into *Marnie* to round out an approach to this theme—that Mark must learn to be in life without the agency of masculinity, and that this is one of the director's profound, and astonishingly prescient, messages.

At any rate, the hierarchical alignment of power between men and women hinted at in the scene as described so far is made quite explicit as Susan Clabon, entering the washroom to assist, blurts, "Well, the way you rushed out of the office! *Mr. Rutland's* standing out there!" This generally imperious male can be imagined to be "standing out there" imperiously; and his thought that Mrs. Taylor is hurt is a male attempt to define the situation, to transform her into a damsel in distress. Again, this is preparation, because Marnie will turn out to be in a great deal of distress but not distress of the psychological sort Mark is imagining. (I am here in conflict with many readers of this film, who are convinced Marnie's conflicts are essentially psychological in nature.) Mark's swift reading of her as hysterical is erroneous, and her tone as she talks with Susan gives us to suspect he is presumptuous in making it. If we learn on this voyage to the bathroom that Marnie is a little neurotic[36] about immaculateness, we discover, too—squatting in this exclusively female territory— that women are not inevitably to be seen as powerless in the face of men.[37]

The issue of immaculateness is worth a brief detour. The central conundrum of the Immaculate Virgin, a mystery well pondered by Hitchcock and others interested in the symbolism of religion, is Mary's ability to mother without first having been stained (by contact with men). Here lie fascinating and important political questions of identity and power, to be sure. But narratively in *Marnie*,[38] the young woman's inability to be touched by a man—

MARNIE: The only way you can help me is to *let me alone*. Can't you understand? Isn't it plain enough? I *cannot bear to be . . . handled*.
MARK: By anybody, or just me?
MARNIE: *You. Men!*

—a handicap constantly reemphasized through lighting, design, and dramaturgical set-ups, is produced by a history of her having touched one all too much—but not sexually. The stain Marnie incurred as a child evidenced her having taken action to put a man's malevolent sexual touching to an end. Her withdrawal is then a kind of self-inflicted punishment for, or correction of, a crucial, early, and problematic approach that was centrally about gender, power, and class—the economic arrangement whereby men come into actual (some would say temporary) ownership of women's bodies. Marnie's first stain was a battle wound inflicted by her against this economic system, and in the context of a prostitute's occupational hazard. If she spends a good portion of her young life in trauma as a result, it is Mark Rutland's saving grace that he does, at the end, escape his own masculinity—his need to be male in all things before being human—to become her true friend, bringing her to realize her action was brave and right. Ultimately, male contact in Marnie's case is not staining but cleansing, and her early "traumatic" experience was of rendering immaculate (or no longer maculate) a significant member of the gender class for whom society reserves its harshest stains. In short, Marnie was a revolutionary who redeemed her own mother, and has forgotten.

From this point of view, for us to insist on reading Marnie as needing to make herself into a reincarnation of the Immaculate Virgin—needing to cleanse that dirty sleeve before the stain sets, and using the washroom to achieve this—is to reduce her to political naïveté and denial. In her relations with Mark Rutland, Marnie Edgar is not necessarily frigid, terrified of sex, withdrawn and innocent, or cowardly. It is Mark who suspects her of this, but he is not yet aware of Marnie's early sexual experience, which is to say, her early experience with the boundless sexual willfulness of the deviant sailor. Nor is she herself aware, because it has slipped her mind. The reading of Marnie as a "hesitant woman," then, is simply premature, simplistic, and insufficient. She is a woman on the edge of very dangerous territory, having acted against male privilege as a little girl and acting against male privilege again now, at the sink haven with Mark trapped outside.

Just antecedent to the honeymoon struggle of Mark and Marnie on the cruise ship, a scene that brings the sexual tension between them to a peak as her withdrawal and his domination come face to face—"What we see is virtually a rape. To the man it is an expression of tenderness, solicitude, responsibility; to the woman, an experience so desolating that after it she attempts suicide"[39]—is her final intriguing voyage to a bathroom in the film. We have come aboard to find ourselves in the honeymoon suite, its niches garlanded with healthy yellow and bronze congratulatory chrysanthemum bouquets, as Mark is fixing himself a drink. "Booze?" he offers Marnie, who is in the adjoining room. But when he hears no answer and steps forward to take a look, he discovers (preparing us for what will come later on this voyage, and then most disturbingly) that she is not there. He crosses the room and taps, with suave reticence, on the bathroom door, this time keeping his distance not as an employer but as a newly appointed groom carefully managing the emotional state of a "nervous bride." "The battle ground of marriage is not, contrary to the movies and *The Ladies' Home Journal* . . . I repeat, is *not* the bedroom. The real field of battle is the *bath*. It is in the bath and for the bath that the lines are drawn and no quarter given. Now it seems to me that we are getting off to a dangerously poor start, darling. You have been in the bathroom . . . (*consults his watch*) . . . exactly forty-seven minutes." Although we may be presumed to come to this fascinating speech with socially organized presuppositions about the function of the bathroom—that it is the locus of a fundamental accounting of caterings to our own embodiment: cleaning, pruning, evacuating, inspecting, trimming, masking, and so on; and thus a temple to ultimate privacies of the person—in the present scene this function is not the central focus of Hitchcock's interest. Here are not pimples and wrinkles, not eroticism of texture and anatomy, but power and powerlessness in relation to one another. Toilet secrecy and privacy are not, for Hitchcock, about eros, cleanliness, and unmentionable humiliations as much as they form a nexus of social status and power. As we have seen so far, in *Marnie* the bathroom is the place where basic riddles and revelations of social class have been expressed. And if it is inescapable, for us and for Hitchcock, that this place is also the setting for urinations and afflatus, for toenail painting and for the relief of cramps, we must see that these activities have form in relation to power, not outside it in some mythos of the uncultured body. The dramatic social play that happens in bathrooms is signally and universally human—is the stuff and substance that lie underneath the class-ridden social drama according to whose script we play out our situated scenes. The battle for the bath, then, is not a cute game of who gets to hog the toilet or the tub for personal care but a genuine struggle over an ultimate, crucially important power to mask and deny commonality, to elevate the self on a ladder of status, to gain ascendancy over others.

In everyday life, our calculations and effacements in that private chamber effect our ability to play on the playing field. But in *Marnie* the bath is the place where power is discussed so that the viewer can hear about it. As they come off and the brutality of class emerges from beneath them, the faces we wear can be known as manufactures. And so the bath is where we are nothing but mortal (what everyone else is), where we can see how social life is our pretense to be more or less than this with promise of reward or under threat of loss. Social class can be invoked, teased up as a construct, in the toilet because in the toilet there is no social class.[40] The society and social construction "out there" can be seen plainly as a tissue of performance because in the toilet there is, at least for a moment (or for forty-seven minutes), nothing but biology.

If bathrooms are utilized in *Marnie* for stating the idea that we construct power and social arrangement over a basic physical potentiality, we can hardly be shocked to see that in its very first iteration in the story, the bathroom as thematic setting is the temple of disguise, performance, masquerade, refacement, and artifice. This is the entrancing scene early in the film where the unnamed black-haired woman from the railway platform and the hotel room lifts herself up from the bathroom sink and sees in the mirror, as we look on and the music explodes, a bright-eyed blonde. This scene takes place in a hotel, and just before it takes place we were warned to pay attention by a nattily groomed Alfred Hitchcock stepping out of another room in the same corridor. "Watching carefully?" he seems to say to me.

If the bath is a factory for the maintenance of class, this film is an opportunity for us to bathe in power and stature and in the consideration of them. It could be argued that many of the anecdotes about Hitchcock's toilet naughtiness and obsessiveness could be decoded as class statements as well, and it is certainly the case that his particular interest in disguising from the perceptions of unknown others the simple fact that he made actual use of toilets, that he possessed a digestive system that produced excretory requirements like any other human being, exemplified, if it did not in fact grow from, a keen sense of civilization as a vertical hierarchy, in which one removed oneself from the plateau of the animal by first ritualizing, then decorating, then theatrically staging and camouflaging one's toilet use as dramatic social behavior.[41] For Alfred Hitchcock, then, as for the rest of us, the lavatory is a locus of elevation, distinction, division, and identification. Given that *Marnie* is a tale about the perils of social class, it is hardly surprising that we should be brought there so many times for signal moments. The toilet is the appropriate, indeed perfect, setting for this pungent theme, and so here once again, as he had with windmills in Holland, mountains in Switzerland, the casbah in Marrakech, the Statue of Liberty in Manhattan, the West End in London, the flower market in Nice, or the autumnal forests in Vermont, Hitchcock deftly married action to place, idea to image, filmic meaning to mise-en-scène.

But for all her time at the lavabo, will Marnie ever manage to save that face?

RUNNING ON

As with most Hitchcock films, there exists for this one a conventional critical reading that has by now become virtually canonized. Even though Hitchcock himself spoke of Marnie's frigidity and kleptomania as cause and effect, "or effect and cause,"[42] avid but credulous critics were apparently not led to surmise anything could be more central to *Marnie* than the sexual malaise of an unfortunate girl and her subsequent and uncontrollable passion for theft. Marnie's stealing is again and again seen as a substitute for "normal" sexuality; and the most frequently proposed formula is that, unable to secure the love of her mother in earliest childhood she proceeded in adult life to substitute for it the cash in other people's safes.

Even as progressive (and contemporary) a critique as the inspiring Robin Wood's, which begins by defending Hitchcock's visual expressivism and cinematic artifice, cannot long desist from the conclusion that money is "Marnie's way both of taking and of trying to buy love."[43] What is wrong with this proposition is only that it gives yet another, but sincere, voicing of the emblematic phrase from Ecclesiastes that Marnie quotes sarcastically: "Money answereth all things." It suggests the film is about the acquisition of love. That so craven an epithet should emerge from Marnie's lips is hardly testament to Hitchcock himself believing it anymore than she does, or to his belief that Marnie steals love; or reason for our believing that the characters in his films are agents for expressing Hitchcock's meaning for him; or basis for us to suppose that he structured this film upon thievery (regardless of what he may have said for public relations purposes).[44] Indeed, much of the film is inexplicable if we try to imagine it as a statement about getting and spending as substitutes for love, about buying passage into the emotional life. Further, we do not see or celebrate Marnie actually acquiring.

If in this film Hitchcock was interested only, or even principally, in the *purchase of affection*, then Mark Rutland's capacity for genuine love, for example, and his purchase of a horse that someone else could adore; old Mr. Rutland's self-deprecating good humor; Marnie's deep and true love of horses that far surpasses the pari-mutuel window; Strutt's unbearable concupiscence; Bernice Edgar's touching lameness and her elegiac memory of Billy, the boy with the sweater, are all become nothing but pointless decorative riddles. If Marnie is to have trouble in her lovemaking to Mark, and if she is to be a robber, why need we see her ride a horse? If we are interested in Marnie's "frigidity," why need we meet, and be captivated by, old Mr. Rutland? Possession of a sort may indeed be central in *Marnie*, but hardly as a form of, or substitute for, sex. Sex, rather, is often shown as a form of, a substitute for, possession— male sex, at any rate, not female, in every case but one, as we shall see. In this film it is not that the protagonist cannot have sex and therefore obsessively acquires through theft; it is that the protagonist is fundamentally disempowered from acquiring, and is therefore forced to use her sexuality as a crutch toward status.

The first statement of this theme is lascivious Strutt's (Martin Gabel) interview with the foul-minded police detectives about a woman who has robbed him and disappeared, a scene evidencing male collaboration over and against other social class formations and thus establishing an overarching gender hierarchy; here, Strutt and the detectives, all relatively ignorant fellows, together outrank a female secretary who, although cannier than

Strutt, must generally keep silent because of her subservient position. Gender and sexual innuendo, then, are framed in and as social hierarchy. Lust belongs to the ones in control, who do not, by virtue of their position, necessarily achieve understanding. Recapitulation of this theme is provided by the scene between Mark and Ward, as Mark's phallic interest is explicitly shown to override bureaucratic prudence in the hiring of "Mrs. Taylor." Social status as the relative ability to possess is what is central. We are soon afterward treated to Lil Mainwaring's arrival and glib departure, flashing the family wealth she has gleefully lifted from the safe; then to Artie's youthful escapade at seduction—but he is no *seigneur;* then to Mark's rather subtle steering of "Mrs. Taylor's" panic in the Saturday work session to produce an opportunity for a beneficent kiss—this is sex in a setting of employment (ownership), not romance. At the race track a disreputable man (Milton Selzer) who thinks Marnie is a girl named Peggy Nicholson has a stimulated leer in his eye, yet we never doubt he has fiscal motives for wondering who the attractive blonde is; a money problem has led him to an erotic imagination. At Wykwyn, prudent and prudish Cousin Bob displays a version of male sexual jealousy, in this case converted thoroughly to numerical form, as he whispers to Lil about Mark's expenditures at the wedding. And there is the domineering sailor (Bruce Dern), himself an occasion for the baldest expression of male sexuality in the film: the setting of his rape is a clear-cut depiction of a form of slave labor.

Marnie's "sexual deprivation" is a political expression, an acknowledgment that sex had become, by the early 1960s, an entrenched male domain, which is to say, the prerogative of the monied class. For a woman, sex was a central locus of powerlessness, a state of affairs subtly alluded to in the floor-cleaner scene where, creeping away from the safe she has just robbed, Marnie's shoe drops:

> *The Watchman comes through the corridor, into the main office. We swing the camera with him to the Cleaning Woman. He shouts at her in the manner of a man who knows she is deaf.*
> WATCHMAN: You're sure making time tonight, Rita. What's the big rush?
> RITA (*scarcely looks up*): I wanta get to bed, that's what's the big rush.

Even if Rita is clearly the tired old worker, not the bedroom delinquent the double entendre suggests, the double entendre remains to tickle us. But the scene in which Marnie's troubles begin—though it is at the end of the film—portrays a similarly tired old working female, a woman comparable in many ways to deaf Rita, and whose specific job is not half as important—for Marnie or for us—as the conditions in which she is forced to perform it.

The sailor rape scene is interesting if only because it did not provoke screenwriter Evan Hunter to issue complaint as he did regarding the shipboard honeymoon.[45] Given that here we are shown a rape quite blatantly, what can be so especially offensive about the idea that in the honeymoon scene the new husband might be seen to aggress upon his wife, as some critics see him do? I think, this: in a society where the *droit du seigneur* was still largely unquestioned, forced sexual attention within a marriage was viewed by the middle-class mind not as rape, but as male desperation; Hitchcock was showing a male spectacularly failing to rely on his privilege. I suspect Hunter's middle-classness could not bear to write the officially sanctioned husband as a rapist, yet he had no problem countenancing Bernice Edgar's violation (since, unmarried to her attacker, she was fair game). She had often committed the sin of sex outside of marriage, and so was not *protégée*. Hitchcock's vision of the shipboard honeymoon scene, which cost him a male screenwriter and earned him a female one, prepares us to see the inherent dominance in socially defined masculinity and to interpret the later sailor flashback not merely as (similar) manly violence, not merely as (similar) trauma for a woman, but as the explicit abuse of femininity and humanity that it is. As a customer, the sailor is purchasing sex; as a male he is brutally dominating the woman who is selling it to him.

Let me begin a discussion of the sailor flashback with what may seem an obtuse comment. Even as much as the scene conveys details of plot, it also stands as clear evidence that Hitchcock could certainly have made use of casting substitutions if he had wanted to. The actress who plays "Marnie" in the flashback (Melody Thomas Scott) is herself a little girl; and so the actress who plays "Bernice" could have been a very young woman. It is important to the continuity of the story, and to the deep statement of this scene, that between the Bernice who sits with her cane in her little house recollecting all this *now*, and the Bernice in her nightgown who was living it then, there should be seen and felt to be more continuity than between the Marnie remembering now and the Marnie experiencing then. This is for technical reasons: in the construction of the recounting of the dream, which is Marnie's recounting, we find a film-within-the-film, and Bernice is the "stage audience" absorbed in watching the inner performance. (Indeed, all of this is yet another interior film, being watched by Mark.) That Bernice is both *in* the inner performance and watching it could be confounding to a viewer, unless there were a clear line of attachment between the inner "character" and the outer "viewer," both of whom are her. Therefore, she must seem distinctively younger in the memory than she is now, yet not so very much younger that we lose the link.

However, Marnie's condition, as we shall see, is detachment. The Marnie who "narrates," "configures," and "establishes" the film-within-the-film is unable as she narrates to feel an easy and complete bond with the Marnie who is acting in her narrative. Indeed, the purpose of the narration—the reason Mark encouraged it—is to summon up that bond if at all possible. And thus the very little girl who is palpably *not Marnie*, but speaks *with Marnie's voice*.

Interestingly, while we have no trouble mentally grasping that the Marnie we have been watching throughout and the little girl are one and the same character regardless of the radical difference in their appearances, nevertheless the two Bernices, visually somewhat similar, strike us as being separate and different, if only because the flashback "Bernice" is so much more mobile and expressive than her older "twin." Further, the weariness of the younger Bernice and her abject conditions are exaggerated through the use of make-up, costume, and set design. As we journey back for this memory, then, we find a woman who works very hard; who is ill paid; and who is incapable of preventing her financial powerlessness from making her physically grotesque. While there is suggestion here that she may be morally grotesque as well, what assaults us as viewers is the collection of finite and material details that sum to her poverty and exhaustion: details of personal hygiene, indeed toilet, over which the abjectly poor can have very little control.

Bernice is whoring because she is poor, not because she is morally lax. By contrast, consummate moral probity is a luxury of the powerful. This is a theme viewers saw Hitchcock develop in *I Confess*, as we shall see in the chapter that follows. One could go further and suggest that "moral probity" is itself socially defined so as to emphasize the vested interests of the class in power. The film is a journey from stuffy Strutt to abject Bernice.

The daughter of the flashback—who, I must repeat, for all her relative youth seems very much the same as our present Marnie—is essentially loving and devoted, puissante, and also dislocated. Now for the first time we learn how the dislocation works and is possible, the deeply frightening meaning of Marnie's repeated nightmare, the knocking, the mother's voice calling, "Marnie, get up!"; and we can begin to understand our own earlier frisson of dislocation and terror as at Marnie's side, first seeing it as she napped in her mother's upstairs room, we were confronted with a looming shadow in the doorway demanding that we wake up and come away. That after such a moment Hitchcock leaves the camera in place until that figure slowly, thunderingly, descends the staircase and passes completely out of our sight is no lapse. He is stretching, and thus demarcating, not the incident but the feeling of portentousness, of doom, of vulnerability, that it produces in us. Thus, even for a viewer seeing the film for the first time, the sailor flashback scene is underpinned by echoes of haunting, troubling, displacing, and portentous recent images in this house and is affixed in the very recent past. Louise Latham is quoted by Tony Lee Moral as recalling that the set was closed while this sequence was filmed: "It was like a graveyard."[46]

Our initial approach to the sailor flashback is immediately earlier, in a brief scene in Mark's car (as they approach Baltimore on the highway) in which geographical confusion is set out as a central theme:

MARK: We'll be in Baltimore in another half hour. Is Van Buren on the north side of town?
She does not answer.
MARK: I said is Van Buren on the north side of town?
MARNIE (*expressionless*): South.

The flashback is thus our moment for approximating Marnie's position as spatially unstable, as directed toward the within and the before; our moment for understanding what it is to be cast out with no warning from a place in which we are warm and safe. But if Marnie is placeless, she is unlike everyone else we meet in this film: Strutt, owner of a company, possessor of an office in which to complain to the police (police who have badges, departmental assignments, positions of authority vis-à-vis one another and other people); Strutt's secretary, who has a clearcut and stable—a yawn-producing—position in his company; Mr. Garrod, who owns and runs a stable, with the help of numerous visible employees all of whom have fixed positions of employment with him; Bernice Edgar, who either owns or rents her house, at 112 Van Buren Street, Baltimore, with a front stoop on which local children play; Jessie Cotton, the little girl who has "usurped" Marnie's place with Bernice, but who has a mother of her own (who is out of work) and a father (who is gone) and who is very much at home in Bernice's house; Mark and all the employees we meet at Rutland's—Susan, Ward, Artie, Rita, the night watchman, even the unseen Shirley—each with a relatively secure position in the company, as has Cousin Bob at his bank, old Mr. Rutland at Wykwyn, and Lil Mainwaring as a hanger-on to the family; the man at the race track, who is a friend of Frank Abernathy from Detroit, not a free-floating personality; the farmer's wife, who provides Marnie with the gun after the hunt accident, and who gains an identity by attachment to the farmer as does Mrs. Strutt, a personage who gains obvious benefit by remaining attached to her husband; and even the waitress at Howard Johnson's, whose comfortable position is indicated by the extreme casualness of her tone as she asks for an order from two people who have no interest at all in eating.

To see the film from a conventional perspective we need only ask over and over again what must be wrong with Marnie, that she cannot "fit" as these complacent others so snugly do. But an unconventional approach is more illuminating, like the recurring lightning in this film. Not "What has Marnie done so that she fails to fit?" but "What have these 'normals' done so that they do not fail?" What resources do they bring to bear? What is the weight of position that they can use? All our social activity requires the mobilization of resources and thus, presumably, the possession of or access to resources that can be mobilized. But to possess or access a thing is to occupy a place. To be without location—to be dislocated—is to lack social standing (indeed, to lack a substance, a space beneath standing and in which to stand),[47] and to lack standing is to lack the means for making possession possible.

The entire sailor flashback is played for ambiguity and confusion in Marnie's state of mind. Her adult voice is transformed to a child's, so that she is present in the scene simultaneously at two points in historical time. In order to provoke Marnie into remembering the vital tale, Mark simulates the knocking in her recurring nightmare by rapping three times on the wall of the stairwell, near her head. But as he does so the camera frames his hand in a macro-close shot, so that even for us the sense of place is blurred and shifted. Before switching to Marnie's point of view for visualizing the tale-within-the-tale, we jump to a very close view of her face, again isolating her expression from the physical placement of that expression in social and geographical space. Other effects are employed to depose us: an extension of perspective, using a long lens; a wash of the coloration in the painted set; a change of lighting in the inner frame to very high key. In the foreground we see objects from the room of the present, while in the background we see a tableau from the past—a repetition of the technique Hitchcock had used in the rotating hotel room/stable shot of *Vertigo* and indeed used earlier here, as Marnie suffered a nightmare at Wykwyn in a room that hybridized her posh marital bedchamber with her old sleeping quarters in her mother's house. As the flashback progresses we become as confused about location as Marnie is and we perhaps relive that painful moment near the beginning of the film when, knocking on her mother's door to the sound of the children singing,

Mother, mother, I am ill
Send for the doctor over the hill
Call for the doctor
Call for the nurse
Call for the lady
with the alligator purse[48]

Marnie is met, suddenly, with a vision of her own early self, Jessie (Kimberly Beck), staring distrustfully from the threshold that is in fact the boundary of Marnie's own past.

As she remembers it in the flashback, this was a past in which Marnie's placement was determined by the whims of the men who employed her mother—"Hurry up, Bernice . . . get the kid outta the bed." And it is possession, the proprietary claim, that produces the explosion and the trauma, since as the drunken sailor tries to befriend the displaced little girl her mother says brusquely, "Get your damn hands off my kid!" Gender power and gender rights having been invoked by the female employee confronting her male employer—the employment is constituted by gender itself, one might say— the sailor contests by refusing indignantly to remove his hands from the child, and this leads directly to the attack by Bernice, his aggressive parry, then his falling upon her, "hitting, biting, scratching, kicking," and the child's eventual, lethal, participation. "Make him go, Mama! Please! I don't like him to kiss me! Make him go!" the little girl squealed, yet now she is a puppet in the hands of the present Marnie who is ventriloquizing.

It is not, however, sexuality or masculinity that Marnie once was, and still is, rejecting. And in order to grasp this point, which is the most central constructive element of the film, we must now enter fully into Marnie's apparent consciousness, leaving our position as viewers aware that she is sitting on a staircase in her mother's house caught up in a memory, and fully adopting as our own thought the content of her memory. It is for the purpose of assisting us with this adoption that Hitchcock leads us with a macro close-up of Marnie and then takes us wholly to her vision, without cutting back to her again; and it is for this purpose that he has the adult Marnie mimicking (successfully) the voice of the child. If we enter the play-within-a-play we forget that it is just that, and suddenly Bernice's garish make-up becomes normal, the caricature of the sailor merely a portrait. And though Wood has persuasively enough argued that the point of the obvious matte painting of the ship at the end of Van Buren Street is to articulate Marnie's locked-in state, I would suggest that perhaps it is more useful in preparing us for this entry to an obviously staged reconstruction: is there any other way to present memory accurately? Like Marnie in the taxicab on the street and the ship berthed at the end of the block, present experience and the memory of the past head toward one another but cannot penetrate each other's territory, cannot meet.

When we enter Marnie's consciousness we realize that the sailor is many people to her, none of whom primarily represents masculinity as potential sexual appeal. First, he is the boss, the person paying her mother, the person with the power to demand that she be moved from her secure establishment so that he can occupy it, the person who can extend his control of the mother to include a helpless person under her protection. But he also presumes expressive rights—attempts to soothe the child after displacing and attempting to possess her. In a sense, then, he attempts to replace the father she has never met. Again, we will see none of this if we take the grown woman's point of view, because from her canny point of view now, what is problematic about this male is that he is a sexual predator. We must sympathize with the child's less tutored point of view—all of Hitch's work is about sympathy—as she lies sleeping in the bed from which her world extends outward: that the sailor is a being who dispossesses, a being for whom she is not a person but an object taking up desirable space. And so her primary experience of him, long before she is forced to bash out his brains, is as a creature who disconnects her from her self and her world. He—and surely he is one of many such men—works in a routine "arrangement" with Bernice, reconstructing Marnie by replacing her. And the replacement is doubly signaled in this film, first by the early scene with Jessie Cotton, and later by the vocal doubling in the flashback.

Replaced early in life, Marnie has no personality and no territory of her own. So, replaced she is displaced. And with no sense of place, she cannot benefit from the social identities that might immediately establish her—as Frank Abernathy's "friend," as Strutt's secretary, as Ward's assistant, as Mark's fiancée and wife. If it is social identity that makes possible the engagements in which "normal" people can work for their living—even the Bernice Edgar of the diegetic present has such a platform from which to act—Marnie is without some very basic equipment. She is an itinerant performer, forced to cadge what sustenance she can by any available means. We can imagine that after her first crime, cover-ups become part of the business of her daily life, so that even as her past is inutile as a social resource her future is a continuingly unfolding improbability, or suspense. Marnie is a character whose life is like a film.

"What interests me," said Hitchcock to Jacques Bontemps and Jean

Douchet in discussion of this film, "is emotion in relation to movement."[49] Marnie Edgar is a metaphor, therefore, for his interest, and for film itself: always becoming instead of being, always running on instead of standing in place, never showing how things will turn out before they do.

HAD YOU, LOVE

Grammar lords it over kings.

  Molière

As I have already suggested, I think it is improbable that Hitchcock himself, certainly committed to a pleasant lifestyle in Bel Air, believed what he gives Marnie to paraphrase: "A feast is made for laughter, and wine maketh merry: but money answereth all things"[50]—although he presided over many feasts made for laughter, and suffered merriment at the taste of only the best wines. He was not committed to the ultimate moral superiority of cash. As lucrative and commercial as his films were, and were constructed to be, they never ceased to intrigue philosophically and morally, linguistically, dramaturgically, and aesthetically. They are too rich, not with luxuries but with complexities; not with rewards but with riddles, to be mere exploitations. He valued wit and repartee, philosophical consideration, architectural construction, what Jacques Rivette called a "perilous enterprise."[51] Though he knew how to manipulate and benefit from the middle-class ethic of Hollywood studio production—when, after working on location, he departed with his company he paid all his bills on time, and left lavish tips behind for the many persons who had helped—his care in his work was always that of an artist, not a magnate. And he was a visual composer before he was an extravagant spender; though he surely never hesitated to spend where spending was necessary.[52] So Marnie's affair with the rich prince is meant to appeal to *our* middle-class sensibility; to our tendency to predict that he will cure her, for surely we do predict it. Hitchcock's "money," however, is bet on another horse—form. Old Rutland has plenty of form, if young Rutland has only some, and form, in the end, will bring Marnie the clarity she needs. This is because her neurotic problem has sprung from an abuse of form, someone throwing her out of her bed and her world; and in the end it is Mark's capacity to see the fair way out of the puzzle, not his money, that will guide Marnie out of her storm.

But Mark's guidance is a gift, and therefore something Marnie will have trouble accepting, having as she does a need to possess unconventionally and to obtain without having been given. If Marnie merely filched things for her own pleasure, we would find her ultimately predictable and uninteresting. What helps us develop sustained interest in her is an odd twist. She not only takes what is not hers, thus committing a sin of addition; she rejects what she has not taken. The taking is thus more important to her than what is taken. In a society devoted to the religion of capitalism, Marnie Edgar is too devout. Roger Thornhill, another character who has trouble with free gifts, saw everything as a sales pitch in *North by Northwest*. Marnie sees everything as loot. When these two step outside the conventional market, it is in flight, not love.

Mark Rutland, like the horse he gives her, will be unacceptable to Marnie in the end—unacceptable or unretainable. But to show her rejecting him, in the face of his generosity, Hitchcock devises an elegant scheme for setting her rejection as a grammatical act. In order to appreciate this elegant and interesting piece of architecture we must attend to Mark Rutland as a man who is not simply an heir, a doer, a lover, and a bit of a roué, but also a single-minded and utterly conventional grammarian—a moralist. This is a matter of learning and concentration on his part, not nature. For all his charm, we will remember, old Mr. Rutland had been a wastrel, since in his hands Rutland and Co. was falling apart.[53] Mark must see the world for what it is and address it with propriety; so his ability at enunciation, as an index of subtler and broader grammatical strength, is a vital center to his being. The climactic fugue in Bernice's house is made possible because of his forthright and direct honesty. He is, first, the one to know that the time has come for a certain revelation, and to take steps so that the revelation can be made; then, a person who can very clearly see his own motives in this affair, and with them his intentions as a director of other people's behavior. Further, it is his ability to distinguish his role in the climactic scene—we may note that it is more narrator than son-in-law—that leads him to escort Marnie away before the sad command, "Get up, Marnie, you're aching my leg," can mobilize any further unpleasant feeling on her part.

Mark's competence in speaking, both linguistic and semantic, gives him advantages that are narratively required in order for his character to be balanced against the impetuous, defensive, alluring, brazen Marnie who would otherwise dominate every scene. He can use it to keep her at length, such as when he escorts her through the Wykwyn lobby to the front door on their first morning back after the honeymoon, or when he notifies her he has no intention of being sought by the police: "Perhaps *you*, Madam. But not *me*!" He can use bravura eloquence to stage-manage a performance he will give with Marnie, pointing out to her *in media res* the importance of vocality—

MARK: We can go together and make private calls on all of the places you robbed. You express deep sorrow and repentance . . . sincere and *vocal* contrition. And while you sob, I show my cheque for the amount stolen, press it into hot little hands and ask as a special favor to a distraught husband to withdraw the charge.

—and soon later to disabuse himself of the noxious Strutt: "You *can* see, Mr. Strutt, how very *dis*advantageous any action on your part would be . . . for *everyone*. For me, certainly, for a sick girl, and for *you*." And, as language is so efficacious a utensil for Mark's need to detach himself from others, he can use speech and speechifying to unload the catty and adhesive Lil, who won't give him five minutes alone with "Mrs. Taylor":

MARK: Lil, I'm sure your sturdy young wrist has recovered enough to slice Dad another piece of cake.
MR. RUTLAND: Yes, I think I *will* have another slice, m'dear. Not too thin, please, and more tea if you will.
Lil, as she understands that the wily Mark is ruthlessly abandoning her, protests piteously, holding up for exhibit her limp wrist.
LIL: I *can't*!
MARK (*mocking*): 'When duty whispers low,
> *Thou must,*
> Then youth replies,
> *I can!*'

No slouch with a tongue herself, but hit, Lil fires back: "Rat-fink! And you *misquoted*!" Ralph Waldo Emerson's "Voluntaries," written upon Civil War themes and published originally in the *Atlantic Monthly* for 1863, would perhaps have been standard parlor knowledge of the East Coast landed gentry. It was liberally dosed liberal philosophy, sentimentally maudlin stuff, and Mark's misquotation is certainly not one he is unaware of. The text he is quoting,

> So nigh is grandeur to our dust,
> So near is God to man,

When Duty whispers low, *Thou must,*
The youth replies, *I can.*

refers to *the* youth, a generic, but quite definitive, character and also a set of
duties that Lil is perfectly aware she is distancing herself from. She attempts
to free herself, at least syntactically, from an obligation to remain chained to
the teapot while Mark runs off with Marnie. He has changed the "the" to
"then," as a way of converting these lines into a moral prescription apposite
to her particular circumstance at this moment—she is younger than he is; and
by doing so has pinioned her. She detects his verbal power, and signals it directly to us. Having been cued here and elsewhere, then, to what Mark can
accomplish with language, we are ready for a conclusion in which the whole
tenor of the film and all its action are swept into a single evocative verbal moment and made incandescent.

Much attention has been paid Hitchcock's signal opening sequences, but
he was, after all, a classical artist and his finales are more important, still.
Mark and Marnie are moving away from Bernice's house. The children are
outside again, because the storm is gone and the sun beaming. They are still
chanting their provocative rhyme but as Mark and Marnie pass, the chant and
the children's actions freeze. "I don't want to go to jail. I'd rather stay with
you," Marnie says. And now, Mark Rutland says something to make any attentive member of Hitchcock's audience sit up.

(*With a short, happy laugh:*) Had you, love?

For the romantic viewer convinced her marriage will now bring an eter-
nity of daylight, Marnie's "I'd rather" is a clear contraction of "I would
rather." But Mark owns a grammatical fluency akin to Hitchcock's—who was
educated in Britain. His response is a clue that she meant—or that he took
her to mean—an "I'd" that is past tense. Not "I would rather" tomorrow and
forever; but "I had rather" yesterday. That is why, questioning her for clarification, he says, "*Had* you, love?" She is saying bluntly that previously it had
been her desire to remain with him. The pure romance of that earlier attraction, Mark knows, has been mitigated by the fact, now very evident indeed
since he is the one who will keep her out of jail—

MARNIE (*her voice very low*): Will I go to jail?
MARK (*in his answer, the authority and assurance she is looking for*): Not if *I* can
help it.[54]

—that for Marnie he represents only the better of two alternatives, the other being quite unthinkable. He will bear her away from the past, to be sure, but he must wonder, does she truly desire to go anywhere *with him*?

If jail were not one of the presiding possibilities, would Marnie be wanting to stay at Mark's side? This is an eternal question for men, to be sure, and one that reveals the tactical motives of their quest for perduring power.[55] But it is hardly a question artists, particularly male ones, were asking openly in 1963. That *Marnie* might be about psychopathological femininity is the merest gloss. It is a very sad tale of unrequited love, a woman needing a man in spite of herself and a man happy to be at her side, regardless of the reason.

IN THE LAND OF COTTON

She is always in danger of expulsion from the temple.

Jay Presson Allen, on "Bernice Edgar"

But hold. In some ways we have been listening to *Marnie*, not looking at it. When after a viewing we look back from a tranquillity to our earlier emotion on seeing the film, we can remember moments of astonishing vividness that are but vaguely connected with the official story—either the conventional story of pathological thievery most critics use as the grounding of analysis or the more complex story of social status to which I have been pointing. We touch upon moments, visual and acoustic, that seem very well to belong to another space, even another world, moments that, configured very differently, would in no significant sense have altered the meaning of the apparent basic plot and action; or that, absent altogether, would still have left the apparent essence of *Marnie* whole.

Yet this latent structure—for the moments seem related intrinsically, as I shall try to show—is very much not absent, while yet residing outside the ostensible main action. Here are some of its components: first, Bernice Edgar's devotion to baking a pecan pie. This is not just any pie for Miz Cotton and her hungry little daughter, and it is not merely a part of a decorative background. The pecans are scattered all over the kitchen floor, and it is Bernice's duty, though she is arthritic, to pick them up. As the pie, the baker: a certain sucrosity, a use of "honey," an affectation and a deliverance. And, of course, the South.

Secondly, Mark Rutland's quotation of Ralph Waldo Emerson. Next, Bernice Edgar's lascivious drawl, particularly as she recounts the tale of Billy and his "magical" sweater: "Bil'-uh," she calls him, and as I hear her I can still see her jaw slide. Next, Lil Mainwaring's curious hesitation to approach Marnie's bedside and make contact with her after Marnie's terrible nightmare at Wykwyn, quite as though Marnie is an untouchable, a member of an ostracized caste, a fighter in an enemy army. In a scene ultimately excised, indeed, she says, "I'm going to get rid of you, one way or the other," as though prim, businesslike, northern Lil and Marnie are two women at war. Further, the fact that Bernice Edgar's neighbors on Van Buren Street are, of all possible creatures, Miz Cotton and her daughter Jessie—Hitchcock was never frivolous with names.[56] Next, Marnie's keeping her horse stabled near Middleburg, Virginia, rather than in Maryland; coupled with the soft lush beauty of Garrod's farm, and the distinctive note of hospitable warmth Marnie finds at the Red Fox Inn. Next, the fact that although Marnie's vocal pitch changes when she has flashback memories of her childhood, there is a notable change in her pronunciation and rhythm as well. "Mama" becomes "Mom'-ma," for instance. Next, the exact cities where Marnie has pulled her criminal escapades: New York, Philadelphia, Buffalo, Elizabeth, Detroit.[57] Next, Mark Rutland's fascinating, and outrageous, little tale of a curious African flower: "But if you reach out to touch it you will discover that the flower is not a flower at all. It's a design made up of hundreds of tiny insects called Fattid bugs. They escape the eyes of hungry birds by living and dying in the shape of a flower."

In yet another projection of this film as the tale of psychological and emotional disability, this "brief monologue (almost tossed away by the film)" has been seen as "crucial for understanding the relationship between touching and looking which structures much of *Marnie*. The desire to touch another human being who does not want to be touched animates the system of looking and perceiving which always determined Hitchcock's cinema."[58] But this is also a tale about strategic camouflage, and ultimately about the way a particular creature might have need of camouflage in a warm climate, camouflage, indeed, that makes the creature seem an object of sultry beauty.

Next, Bernice Edgar's grotesquerie as a prostitute in the flashback; and the grotesque self-parody implicit in her modeling the mink stole Marnie brings as a gift. Next, our strange and subtle sense that wherever she goes, Marnie is giving a little performance: not merely pretending to be a woman with a bona fide identity and background when she lacks both, a woman possessing a biography out of which she can muster the material to establish herself in situations; but also, and perhaps foremost, feigning the sort of woman who could put on such characters one after another, the type who is a substrate beneath many surfaces:

Beginning with the first compulsive fantasy of her young childhood—i.e., that the night of trauma never happened—she has loved only in fantasy. One result is that she has evolved into an excellent actress, able to improvise quite brilliantly in almost any situation. She has assumed, perfected and discarded so many roles, that to act (to *lie*) is as natural to her as putting one foot before the other.[59]

Finally, we may have an odd and unnerving sense that just on the margins of the diegetic frame in many of the scenes we see, somebody is whistling.

Whistling, indeed, is as good a place as any to begin. Let me state again that I am trying to conjure a second, hidden structure of meaning in *Marnie*—one that is not explicitly represented on the screen but that can be felt to be undeniably present because of what is represented in fact. We do not explicitly hear wolf whistles to accompany Marnie's entrances, but very often those entrances are choreographed (by her) to be appropriate for wolf whistles. Marnie certainly fantasizes them (her posturing suggests), and has done so for years. The wolf whistle is a signal of presumptive possessive superiority in he who gives it. Sailors use whistles, wolf whistles and mechanical ones, though the particular sailor we meet does not have a moment to—perhaps the woman he is with does not merit wolfing, and since he is off duty he has no need for the sailor's pipe, actual or substitute. And it was Bernice, at any rate, who whistled for him. The prostitute is the whistling woman, "neither fit for God nor men," as the English proverb (Hitchcock may well have known) puts it. People whistle for other people to come and serve them, and we can imagine that if she knew better how to whistle, little Jessie Cotton might whistle for Bernice. She is the demanding, and dominating, kind. Mark certainly whistles for Cousin Bob to bring him money at the wedding. Strutt is emphatically a man who whistled for the police, and who wants to blow the whistle on Marnie, from the moment we meet him. Indeed, his opening scene is a case of whistle-blowing, and the close shot of him going off at the mouth, "Robbed!" is like a close shot of a police whistle. Mark "mucking up" his "spinster's" tea with a shot of rum is wetting his whistle, rendering it inutile for the graver purpose of signaling disorder and giving command. Indeed, rather than simply blowing the whistle on Marnie and having her arrested, he wets his whistle after having given a wolf whistle and having whistled for Ward to hire her.

All these whistles and whistlings are nuances unseen onscreen, and unheard, and yet directly implicit there. Perhaps even more implicit is that peculiar form of fakery and impotence known universally as whistling Dixie.

One "ain't just" whistlin' Dixie when one is authentic, has the goods, is in on the right and verified information, is substantially endowed. But Marnie, whose identity is fake, *is* whistlin' Dixie—and therefore is a whistling woman herself. Of Marnie's proximity to prostitution her mother has much to say, notably—though at the time we are unaware of this fact—because she herself is something of an expert, with insider knowledge and learnèd concerns. She begins with the characteristic that Hitchcock has been celebrated for bringing to our attention, blondness:

> BERNICE: You've lighted up your hair.
> MARNIE: A little. Why? Don't you like it?
> BERNICE: No. Too blonde hair always looks like a woman's trying to attract the men. Men and a good name don't go together.

Bernice's understanding of the relation between good women and men is a down-to-earth and practical one:

> MARNIE: Do you really like the scarf, Mama? It's real mink. There! You look like an old man's darling!
> BERNICE (*snorts*): No *man* ever give me anything so good.
> MARNIE: We don't need men, Mama. We can do very well for ourselves . . . you and me.
> BERNICE: A decent woman don't have need for any man. Look at *you*, Marnie. I tell Miz Cotton . . . look at my girl, Marnie. She's too smart to go getting herself mixed up with men . . . *none* of 'em!

The need for men is institutional and economic, not personal.

We must ask, however, why it should be that of all the whistlin' one could do, whistlin' the particular tune called "Dixie" calls one's authenticity into question, because the hidden nexus in this film involves not just the whistlin' we do not quite hear but the Deep South we barely see. "Dixie" is an anthem of the South, and of the Lost Cause. The true Southerner would never have lacked the words,

> I wish I was in the land of cotton,
> Old times there are not forgotten [60]

and so have needed to be whistling—whistlin'—in place of them, with some lack of authenticity. *Whistlin'* Dixie, that is, not singing it, is disloyalty. In this context let us turn to Miss Jessie Cotton and say of her that there is more to her presence in the film than the fact that she lives nearby Bernice Edgar; the fact that she is fatherless and that her mother works until six; the fact that she and her mother could "use" gladioli; the fact that she is intellectually precocious; and the fact that Bernice has been "thinking serious about asking Miz Cotton and Jessie to move in." Jessie is also cold and reflective, one could say calculating—perhaps for the same reason Marnie is, and perhaps because she senses herself to be above. With Marnie she is possessive and imperious, as though Marnie's territory is by rights her own. Bernice is Jessie's babysitter and social inferior; and Marnie's embarrassment is that if she has climbed above her mother she has not yet been able to command the position of respect on Bernice's knee that seems naturally to belong to Jessie. We may imagine that the South has been re-created in this little house in Baltimore, and that Hitchcock's choreography makes the suggestion it is in fact Jessie's place. Bernice Edgar's house is the Land of Cotton. And, of course (all the plot of the film revolves around this), "Old times there are not forgotten."

It is therefore necessary that it be a pecan pie, and no other, Bernice is baking for her young mistress. In order to show that he comes from the very furthest social remove, it is necessary that Mark Rutland quote—and, for emphasis, misquote—Ralph Waldo Emerson's meditation on the courage of young (northern) men about to go to war. Mark Rutland—even more, his father—represents the reason the South is subjugated; the reason Jessie Cotton and other southern belles like her must be bitter even if they are privileged; the reason "white trash" like Bernice must be so passionate in their lumpen craving for the objects of desire to which they hold no rightful claim, being displaced utterly from the system of production. She has been forced by economic necessity to become a moneychanger in the temple, then, if the home is the temple; and so she has every reason to fear being expelled, and to devote herself excessively to pristine domestic pursuits. This fear of expulsion is one of the motive forces of Bernice's proud declamatory defense of the temple in rejoinder to her daughter's casual epigrammatic use of the text from Ecclesiastes: "We don't talk smart about the Bible in this house, Missie." But also at play here is a southern critique of what Bernice surely perceives to be Marnie's newfound northern moral laxity; "this house," then, is a southern house, and Marnie has imported foreign pieties to its precincts.

The South is our secret scripture here.[61] When we see Bernice's appropriation of the stole, and hear her drawl that Marnie is "the only thing [pron. *theen*] I ever did love"; when we note Bernice's dutiful housekeeping—"She is a compulsive housekeeper. An unwashed dish, an unmade bed, an untidy table top are *frightening* to her," Jay Presson Allen writes in a character note, and her description of the house is even more explicit:

> The living room, indeed all of the rooms of this house, are marked by the diligence of the housekeeping. The rooms are ugly and stiff and utterly parochial, their principal aura one of relentless respectability. In the living room there are doilies and meager but carefully nurtured pot-plants of the African violet variety. The mantel and cupboard shelves are repositories for pridefully displayed bits of bad china . . . cups, plates, figurines. . . . Wherever in the room a bit of metal shows, it is polished to a regimental sheen.[62]

—and when we recollect the soft fields around Garrod's farm and the sweeping territories around Wykwyn, which has the look of a plantation; when we observe Marnie's struggle to camouflage herself like the Fattid bug, to become, not just Mary Taylor and the other simulacra but a respectable woman of undeniable class whose maternal connection must at all costs be suppressed;[63] when we sense, with discomfort, that Bernice's young performance with the sailor is a grotesquerie—that its setting is something of a grotto; and when we consider the war between Lil and Marnie, based at least to some degree on Lil's perception of Marnie as a flower from a different growing zone now spreading like a weed in her own territory, it becomes clear that beneath the surface tale of the film lies a subtle recounting of the domination of the South. If Marnie and Mark can be together, their parents could not: Bernice has now an unshakeable grasp on the good name together with which men do not go, and as the screenwriter herself says of old Rutland:

> He is not at all stupid, but he is simple. He has in almost seventy years probably dealt with nothing more complicated or bewildering than the politics of Franklin D. Roosevelt, and the death of Mark's mother. He has probably come to accept Roosevelt's defection as, essentially, New Yorkiness . . . a geographical weakness. As to his wife's death, who can say about a sixty-nine-year-old man who is so obviously happy and contented in his single state?

Thus it is that at the film's conclusion, Marnie accompanies Mark as an avenger from below the Mason-Dixon line, redeeming the South against its losses by single-handedly and with the greatest of dignity pilfering the vaults of the great northern cities and businessmen. Lil Mainwaring, an equally manipulative, remorseless, and adventurous woman, had a very different presence, northern, urbanized, technical before Marnie dispossessed her.

Popular film plots in the 1960s were still obsessed with rationalizing idealized heterosexual unions. But Hitchcock turned the romance genre on its head. As they drive away from the camera we understand that Marnie is the girl for Mark because he will never quite succeed in taming her, and because the war he will have to fight against this rebel, in the bathroom, the boardroom, and the boudoir, will never altogether be won.

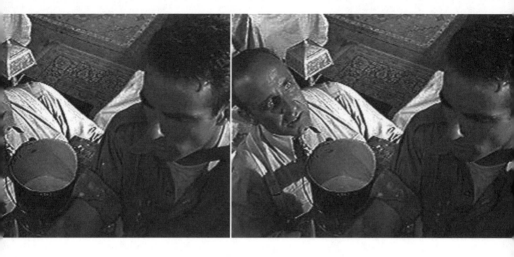

I Confess and the Men Inside

We don't talk smart about the Bible in this house.
Marnie

OVERTURE

Riddle: (1) A murder is confessed by a suspicious-looking man, while we calmly observe (calmly but improperly, because he is in a confessional). But (2) though we have seen the body the murder has produced, and seen the man fleeing the scene where the murder was done, we did not see him actually do the killing and so we do not know that as he confesses he is telling the truth. Would a man lie in a confessional? Well, why not, if he is a man willing to commit a murder? But regardless of our knowledge we believe him, not because of what we have seen but because of the way he confesses and the way his listener listens. We may presume he is telling the truth, but (3) the man soon gives very clear evidence he is notably capable of not telling truths, indeed, of constructing elaborate fabrications. What, then, are we to think? But now, (4) accused by the police (people who expect to be believed when they speak) of this same murder is the priest who confessed that confesser. We admire this priest and our admiration relies on stories we hear about him from others who may not know him as well as we do. If we did not see the confesser perform the murder, we also did not see the priest confessor who is accused of the murder not perform it—did not see him doing something else at the

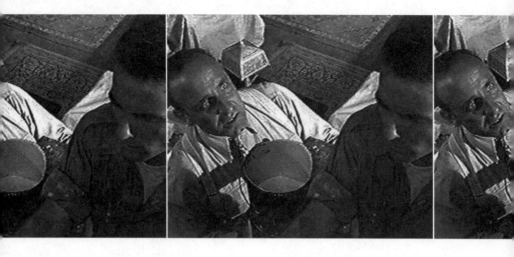

same time, though it goes without saying we take him to be innocent. But why should it go without saying, since the police—officially respectable sorts—are apparently not willing to take this innocent to be innocent? We must feel we know something about this priest the police do not know, yet so early in the film how could we possibly know it? Nor is our intense belief in the priest shattered when, learning he has been camouflaging an illicit love affair, we are made privy to a motive he could very well have had for killing the unpleasant man who is dead.

There is more: we never meet the victim of the murder except as a character in a story told by people who had a great deal to lose were he to stay alive and much to gain by artfully constructing a story; or else as the object in the murderer's confessional; yet we are offered, from a charming kind of distance, a glimpse of him. And even with only a glimpse, we loathe him the moment we see him. Yet the priest has our ready affection, even though the police, the Crown Prosecutor, the judge, and all the citizens of the city seem to think him an immoral cad.

The more we watch *I Confess* the more we are led into a territory where everything can only be watched. This is the great conundrum of cinema, that everything must be seen but at the same time everything can only be looked at. Knowledge, therefore, is of a tenuous kind. Although not looking is conceivable, and perhaps morally valuable, it is cinematically impossible. Film posits a morality in which vision—and therefore performance—dominates. Jean Starobinski notes that "sight is asked to lead the mind beyond the realm of vision into that of meaning."[1] This morality is more excitingly at the center of *I Confess* than the facts of who did or did not kill the ugly lawyer, Villette (Ovila Legare): indeed, we are given to know swiftly who the killer is, but this knowledge proves insufficient to take us through.

Meanwhile, everywhere is the Church. Everywhere is darkness. Everywhere is the gaze. (Sanctity. Security. Sight.) Of Hitchcock's films this one is perplexing because although what happens in it is very clearly told, seeing the film we are left to wonder what the story is about—and it is a glorious, almost sanctified wonder, not a disappointment or dissatisfaction. There are great gleaming gazes, swooping patches of delicate brilliance, lambent surfaces, soft sadnesses, gentilities of spirit, hushes of the multitude, lyrical lost pasts, silent orderly sentient façades, youthful innocences, perspiring hungers, struggles of the mouth, and over all of it a great mystery. This is a work to which one can make approach only by crossing a river.

Indeed, gliding by ferry across the Fleuve Saint-Laurent during the opening credits, in the crepuscule, perhaps after a rain because the clouds of an overcast sky have broken away to reveal some light, one may well ask, "What is this place? What this river? Who this ferryman?"

TRUE CONFESSIONS

What use to confess our faults at
the moment the vessel is sinking?
    Claudius Claudianus

Admirers of *I Confess*[2] might be helped in understanding the world in which its action is set by knowing that in 1953, when it was released, this and other motion pictures were still under State control in the Province de Québec; a control predominantly influenced by the Catholic Church. For example, to see films, children under the age of sixteen typically went not to a theater but to the church basement; and this even for titles that were twenty years old. Québec Province was the last stronghold in Canada—indeed, the last in North America—to preserve well into the twentieth century that dark feudal social form in which, not yet overstepped by a secular and mercantile state and also ramified through all of the enterprises of organized social life, the Holy Church cherished quotidian control over the prospects of men. French Canada was still, in the mid-régime of Premier Maurice Duplessis around the time of the filming of *I Confess*, a nation within a nation, where the clergy shaped, measured, and marshaled not only the moral, but also the educational and commercial life of the people. As Gérard Pelletier put it:

> The Quebec episcopate and the clergy . . . were still in charge of a great many of the normal functions of a modern State. They dominated education, from primary school to university. Through the religious orders they owned or managed almost all the hospitals. Their good works took the place of social security and public welfare for orphans, young delinquents, vagrants, the handicapped, the blind, the deaf and dumb, and many more I could mention. The clergy were into everything, and everywhere powerful.[3]

It is no accident of setting, then, or quirk of plot, that this film set in La Ville de Québec takes root in and around the Church, and is so heavily populated by priests and those who pay them strict homage or by outsiders struggling to arrogate to themselves the powers still invested at the altar.

The social and moral tensions imported to Québecois society by the ascendancy of Duplessis to power in 1944, and highlighted by his longstanding dispute with clerical dominion and his express intention of having the bishops "eating out of his hand," as he liked to say, continued into the contemporary age a philosophical and economic struggle that had its roots in feudal Europe.[4] Was it holy science or secular science that would organize, focus, enervate, conceptualize, and philosophically ground human inquiry? Was it holy study or secular study that would strive to fulfill the highest purposes of learning? Was it holy ordinance or secular statute that would establish and frame relations between the sexes, between good men and bad, between crime and normality? In the sixteenth century, it was still a clerical matter to divide land, to arrange a marriage, to cast out an evil spirit, to produce a tax, to punish a criminal. But the secular state was beginning to produce pathways—and then roads—into the dominion of the Church.[5] Duplessis would say, "You don't fight elections with prayers."[6] The Québec we see in *I Confess* was a locus of the meeting and struggle of these modes of organization, a struggle engineered by a man who while he "proclaimed the superiority and the desirability of doing things the old way, preserving the old values of Quebec's Catholic society,"[7] yet did not wish to see priests pulling the strings. The protagonist is himself split into a sacred and a secular personification.

We see evidence of an empowered secular class—the Grandforts (Roger Dann and Anne Baxter) and Crown Prosecutor Willie Robertson (Brian Aherne); and of a politically troubled clergy with real affinity for the old days in which clerical moral authority was absolute. Wavering between the two worlds, a sad policeman is caught between his childhood as a true believer and his cynical bureaucratic role in middle life.

The title of this film might seem a nice post-feudal riddle about moral culpability and the social arrangements necessary to sanction it: *I Confess*, indeed, but who is this confessing "I" and who is the receiver of the confession? The conventional critical answer to these questions is based in the presumption that clericism controls everyday life. Moral culpabilities should be confessed for resolution practical and cosmic, and they should be confessed to the Church. If the "I" in this case is taken to be Otto Keller, an immigrant sacristan (O. E. Hasse) who confesses to Father Michael Logan (Montgomery Clift) as we watch, the actual confession within the film can thus be taken to be, or to symbolize, the "confession" of the title. It is worth noting that as regards the society of Québec, such a program of thought is also traditional. The drama of confession, understood in this restricted way, is a religious ritual of cleansing, wholly framed, established, guided, measured, articulated, rationalized, and sanctified in the agency of the Church. But by taking a closer look at this pious and decorous action as filmed, let us see if we can more fully illuminate it.

When Keller is in the confessional booth with Logan, he is not alone. It is a requirement of the mise-en-scène that we should be inside, too, although we may do well to remember that the mise-en-scène has in fact been concocted to make our intrusion a requirement. There are two sides to the confession box, and, at least as the scene begins, we are at home on Keller's. It is as his accomplice, then, and not as Logan's apprentice, that we gain presence. Though at the beginning of the scene we are technically ignorant of the crime that we apparently share with Keller (being sufficiently guilty to be present here)—because as an audience we have not yet heard, apprehended, and digested what he is about to say—nevertheless we affiliate in a general and unsubstantiated way with his culpability. While a conventional critique might suggest this affiliation is a condition of our experience in Hitchcock's audience, I believe Hitchcock believed it was a condition of our lives as moviegoers, perhaps because, as Tennessee Williams put it in *The Glass Menagerie*, we go to the movies instead of moving. As in our personal unease we see Keller about to confess we may think back toward the beginning of the film and discover the following syntactical development:

Presumably returning from an unseen earlier nocturnal and solitary journey to the village of Lévis (directly across the river), where we may have experienced a lovely view of Québec, or indeed having passed through Lévis from a distant point of origin, we now approach Québec by ferry, lulled by an especially haunting soprano melody (composed by Dimitri Tiomkin on an eerie descending scale—this is part of the credit sequence). The rocking of the ferry upon the dark water, the ethereal absence of diegetic sound, the hovering form of the city, all play to our susceptibility to a romantic turn of heart, suggest reflection, and invoke the lingering meditative quality of night. Later on, Michael Logan will turn out to be a devotée of this ferry, and of the night, and of romance, and of meditation. Though we have not met him yet, we are being prepared to identify with him by this pleasant, eerie taste his sensibilities will later echo.

Now suddenly: in the city, and on streets that are notable for their emptiness, we see, in shot after shot, one-way street signs reading in French, DI-RECTION, and pointing right. First we make the most obvious reading, that there is clearly only one direction for thought, action, intention, or fulfillment in this place at this time. This is a rigid one-way society with predisposition toward the political right. But more than a political indoctrination, we are receiving a set of narrative instructions, all of which come from the man behind the camera, who provides "direction." We are being told which way to go on a complicated journey. There is something we need to find—call it purpose, call it meaning—and we are being led on the hunt. We arrive at a window and peer inside. Sure enough, there is something. It is a body. It is dead. Our desire is to linger but at our right is the shuffling of a bead curtain. We hear retreating steps. Out in the street we see a priest stepping swiftly away. In shadow, he takes off his soutane, revealing lay clothing beneath. We follow him. And indeed, we follow him to this place, where now he is about to confess.

Directly, then, we have association with an unseemly corpse; a view of the "priest" as criminal in flight; and a "direction" of thought; all associated with meditation at night upon the river. The film is being couched in terms of elevated, abstracted, even romanticized thoughts about criminality and the priesthood—indeed, about the priesthood as a form of criminality. Perhaps the river suggests perennial flowing, the passage of time and life. As we sit with Keller and listen to his confession, the man on the other side of the grille, listening more actively than we are, is therefore already a little questionable—at least distant—to us. That questionability is a central structural element in the film. As viewers who have proceeded through the narrative to this point, we can be where we are only because we were able to consider a priest (the abstract dark figure escaping down the street) as a potential murderer. Later in the film, this very idea will be suggested by an officer of the law and we must be prepped to accept it early on precisely because it contradicts a certain received view of the priesthood that may well be presumed to be circulating in the audience prior to the film. That view, of course, is the feudal clerical view in which, the Church constituting the law, an association between the priest and criminality is unthinkable. Our very philosophy in this confession box is illegal, then.

But if the man on the other side of the grille is an object of suspicion he is also and at the same time above suspicion, a man who asks probing questions, not one who must answer them. There is the bizarre intensity of his stare, lit to dominate the screen as the confession is made to be swallowed up by it. He is no mere functionary, hearing of a mortal crime. There is something special for him about this circumstance, something implicating. Is he too interested in what he is hearing, too attached to the sin by his attaching presence for us on the screen? Soon later, he meets a beautiful young woman on the sidewalk outside the victim's house and she says to him, "We're free!" A dark suspicion—the French word *soupçon* is apt—that he is not at a complete remove from the murder victim (a human just short of perfect innocence) may now arise.

This scene of confession by Keller to the priest moves us to wonder about Logan and his moral bona fides, but there nevertheless remains here a reinvocation and substantiation of traditional clerical dogma. This looks like a true confession; it occurs in a confession box in a church; the confessor is a priest; and what is confessed reflects a moral issue beyond question. Yet I think that with this confession alone, however palpable it is, we do not find ourselves possessed of enough "material" for a Hitchcock film. Or at least, simply in the idea that a man would have committed a murder and produced a confession to his priest—even if the confession is a conversation that priest has no powers to repeat—is not to be found the sort of construction that would have appealed in and of itself to Hitchcock. To understand *I Confess* as a Hitchcockian narrative we must examine a second confession, which is by far a less intelligible one.

Ruth Grandfort confesses to Inspector Larrue (Karl Malden) that earlier in her life, before her marriage to the renowned politician Pierre Grandfort, she was in love with Michael Logan; and she tells the story of that love. This confession, coupled with the ancillary fact that the murder victim, Villette, had been blackmailing her about this love affair, and the fact that the alibi she provides for the priest does not in fact clear him of the crime, is sufficient to bring suspicion against Logan—a man who has heard the earlier confession of the actual murderer but who has no power to make a statement about what he has heard.[8] If Logan the priest is incapacitated to speak effectively about Keller, Ruth is incapacitated to speak effectively about Logan the lover. Hitchcock thus provides for us a bizarre but relentless mathematics in which Logan the lover seems as culpable as Keller; while Logan the priest seems as innocent as Ruth. Logan is between Keller and Ruth Grandfort, tending toward both culpability and innocence. While Hitchcock often made statements to the effect that he did not much enjoy working with Montgomery Clift,[9] I find the casting impeccable when I consider the teeter-totter quality that was necessary in Logan to situate him believably between these extremes.

But the Grandfort confession is distinct from the Keller confession in a number of vital ways. First, its subject is not murder but love, carnal love. It renders Logan susceptible to the charge of impurity, and so in a sense it murders the priest in order to espouse the man. Then, too, while Keller's confession to Logan is impelled by the murderer's inner psychic need, Ruth's confession to Larrue is compelled by the inspector's technical demand. However, her coerced statement has two interesting ironic corollaries. It appears to free Ruth of a secret that has been poisoning her, to the extent that she can be at rest only when she has finished her long and detailed accounting. To put this differently: she says more, in telling her tale, than Larrue requires. If she would not have made the confession of her own accord, yet she benefits in some important way from the experience of having been directed to make it. And so, of course, do we. Secondly, Ruth's confession is immensely pleasing to us. I shall return to the subject of the Grandfort confession, and the manner in which it is spelled out, but suffice it to say at this point that the contents of Ruth's statement constitute the single symphonic brilliance in an otherwise (and intentionally) somber film. I refer not so much to the voice-over narrative by Anne Baxter as to the style of performance in the silent scenes that play under it, the glimmering lighting, the use of promising angle and exciting movement, the arbitrariness and fragmentation of the cutting that give a sense of impulsion and desperation, of a torrent of feeling.

Beyond darkness and delight, the Grandfort confession, social and legal, is also made distinct from the Keller confession in that Keller's is religious in structure, and thus a manifestation of the clerical power of Logan and the piety of the killer—a piety in no way diminished (though it is made ironic) by the fact that Keller is aware of the tactical benefits that may flow to him from Logan's incapacity to discuss the crime. We must remember a central constant in the perplexing algebra of these social arrangements: while Keller is safe from Logan's betrayal, thanks to the conventions of the Church, he would be safer still if he were to avoid confessing at all. But his confession is necessary *for us*, as a way of openly giving Logan a secret that is equivalent in weight to the one (we will later discover) Ruth bears. Further, the Keller confession removes from the filmic discourse a major potential obstruction to our appreciation of the social, rather than merely the criminal, story in this film—and this obstruction would be the hunt for the killer. In this film, it is only the police who must hunt for the killer, and in truth we are not principally interested in them. Since we are told the identity of the killer early on, we are free to consider the variety of approaches to the case undertaken by various characters. Hitchcock is always interested in acts of character.

Keller's confession also shows remorse to contrast with his later smug manipulativeness. So it yields an opportunity to see the depths of Logan's soulful *tristesse*, since Keller not only troubles but also depresses him; establishes the powerlessness of the (German) "outsider" in an ethnically divided yet xenophobic postwar Québec of the early 1950s; and, for those who are unfamiliar with it from up˜close, produces a fine introduction to the power and formality of the Catholic Church. Very little but Church power is manifested in the Keller confession scene, and so as it commands our attention as a keystone of the narrative it also rings for us peripherally as a profound echo of the feudal past. Ruth Grandfort, however, is acting in a purely secular arrangement as she recounts her love story to Larrue. Because the circumstance of her narrative is a criminal police investigation in a secular society where the justice system is controlled by the state bureaucracy in spite of the Church, she is forced to share her privacies in front of the very man her account implicates—Father Logan has been summoned as well; in front of the Crown Prosecutor; and, the prevailing social arrangements being patriarchal here, in front of her husband, who insists on protecting her symbolically if he cannot in any other way and usurps a chair at her side. To complicate the scene (but not to complicate its probability, since this kind of link would be very easily found among people such as these), the Crown Prosecutor is a close social acquaintance who has taken hospitality from Ruth in front of our very eyes. Both of them are socially embarrassed, then, by a situation that renders her vulnerable to moral disrepute.

The secular confession of Ruth Grandfort is the dominating confession in *I Confess*. It is made emphatic for us in part by virtue of the fact that Larrue is an ambivalent confessor (as is Logan for Keller, although for different reasons), having been raised himself within the precincts of the Church and cherishing into his adulthood a fond respect for the Jesuitical Fathers while yet being a functionary in the secular bureaucracy and having a job to do. The Keller confession places itself in the sanctuary of Logan's church, and in the rectory next door; but the Grandfort confession spreads from the police department, through the streets by means of the police investigation, into the criminal courts, by indirection to the Provincial Assembly where Pierre Grandfort daily holds forth, and thence, in the climactic scenes, to the Château Frontenac. Of course the centrality of the Grandfort tale implies that more crucial to the structure of the film than Keller's hidden malevolence is Logan's hidden masculinity. The meaning of Ruth's story is that under the pristine clerical mask Logan wears—a mask in which he properly denies Keller help but also promises silence, a mask he is willing to wear to the point of self-condemnation[10]—there resides a self so compromised he will reveal it only to prevent Ruth's honor from blemish: and this is the human self. The secret of the priest is that his priesthood is only skin deep. He has not only sensitivities but passions; not only passions but romantic fantasies; not only romantic fantasies but—unthinkable in a professional of the cloth—innocence.

Implied, too, in the importance of the Grandfort confession is this less than utterly salient fact: the "I" in *I Confess* is apparently *not* the subsidiary character, Otto Keller, a man who at some moments and in some ways appears to have sprung straight from Hitchcock's *Lifeboat;* a pathetic alien who has killed for money so that his beloved wife, never having had to work, can be spared labor now; but instead a woman who now already does not have to labor, Ruth Grandfort, wife of a Member of the Assembly,[11] friend of the Crown Prosecutor, embodiment of civilization and light. And the confession referred to in the title is a love story.

I Confess really was a film the Church would have wanted to control sight of. More than an exploration of a crime as openly venal as murder, of an activity tawdry as blackmail, a business as sordid as policing, it is an elaborate recounting of how a woman can take the legal vows of matrimony while retaining passion for another man, how a man can commit himself to the principles of the Church while underneath he longs to be "free" with the woman of his heart: the principled skin and the troubled corpse. When marriage is clerically sanctioned—Michael's to Jesus—it occurs in the presence of the Deity and sentiment is inextricably wedded to ceremony: in a startling moment we are shown Logan among a group of bridelike young men proceeding toward the altar in their ordination. When marriage is civil—Ruth's to Pierre—it is a contract supported by the state, which is ultimately an assemblage of mercantile interests. One's alliances are intended to make profit, in one way or another, and the interests of the flesh find a strict rationalization in the counting house. Ruth Grandfort's confession, her love story, is thus at once an affront to the dignities upheld by the Church and a threat to the organization of the economy. As a vulgar tale, it is a perfect metaphor for the free play of mercantile forces Duplessis had organized to taunt, harass, undermine and ultimately disempower clerical power in Québec— perhaps too perfect a metaphor, since it provided a woman far more agency than Duplessis and his burghers wanted to offer. And it is a confession to displace confession boxes, and priest-confessors who hide passionate men inside their robes.

Let us see the opening of the film once more, but from Ruth Grandfort's point of view. The voyage across the river is played out with a haunting romantic melody, the same melody we hear when (in her own accounting of the beginning of her love affair) Michael sees her descending the curved *casse-queue*[12] in front of her childhood home in a magnificent white dress, glowing through a diffused lens, and in slow motion. The melody, *pianissimo sempre*, is termed by Christopher Palmer "literally an illustration of the lyrics":

> While the town is sleeping tight
> Comes the music of the night.
> One can hear its lonely beat
> On each dark deserted street.
>
> The dreams and hopes of yesterday
> Sigh and slowly drift away;
> All the sounds of earth unite
> Secretly in the night.

And Palmer goes on, "The magic of the distant solo voice, the velvety, deep-purple key of D flat major (associated with the song throughout the score), the slow, sighing, descending drifts of its melodic profile, the whispered *tenebroso* orchestration—all add up to an evocative tone-picture in miniature, the intent of which is patently to lull the audience."[13] Reflected in this musical motif, Ruth's is the tale of a glimmering romance told in the cool aftershadow by a woman settled (even trapped) in a conventional middle-class marriage, not really unlike the story of *Brief Encounter* (another film standing upon a haunting melody). Focused upon middle-class propriety as a cabinet for confining the grander tinctures of sentiment, it is a very British tale—the

Grandforts are surely Francophones who have made every possible affiliation with the British in Québec—a tale that springs from the horrifying limits imposed upon feeling by routines: of Church bureaucracy and of secularization alike. For Keller, it was action that caused difficulty. But what pose serious difficulties for Ruth are the feelings of attraction she experiences in Michael's presence, because they are incompatible with her status.

Michael's priesthood is an elevation of his elemental humanity, of his friendship and *amour* with Ruth. Indeed, it was only after the love affair that he was ordained. The film is troubling because for all his goodness Michael Logan cannot possibly, in any incarnation, end happily. If after the war he does not become a priest, his dilemma is that he loves a woman he learns (from the heinous Villette) to be married; but now that he has become a priest he must survive somehow with the knowledge that his love was impossibly carnal. In every way the opposite of the Québec where his story is set, he began with secular troubles and now has religious ones. Ruth, for her part, is the modern Québecoise—from Duplessis's point of view—the woman focused on Anglo aspirations, with big money and big money connections, one of the forgers of the new French Canada. We may remember that it is Keller who loves Logan the priest; Ruth has little time for Church affairs, and for her the priesthood, Logan's cloak, is an obstruction. As in her secular power she represents an end to clerical dominance, a harbinger of Québec's Silent Revolution, the subterranean truth of her love saga is that, after he took his vows of betrothal to Christ, Michael waned for her as an object of fascination, as though silently a door had closed.

Clerical power was always Francophone in Québec; and the wealthiest protagonists of the Duplessis régime were Anglophone, like Ruth. The shift in *I Confess* from the tale of Logan and Keller to the tale of Logan and Ruth Grandfort mirrors the secularization of the contemporary Québecois state.

LABORS OF THE EYE
Seems, madam? Nay, it *is*. I know not seems.
   Hamlet

I confess to a certain irremediable ignorance concerning what lies at the heart of *I Confess*. When the preproduction of this film was commencing in February and March of 1952, I was a person entirely unaware of the existence of Catholicism. Having been raised in a Jewish religion and culture, indeed, I conflated Catholicism with Christianity in general until I was in high school, at the earliest 1959. I think it is now true—and perhaps, from some points of view, less than ideal—that I owe a great deal of what understanding I have of the Catholic way of seeing the world to the work of Martin Scorsese, whose focus of interest is of course only a part of the broader array of concerns and practices that can be called Catholicism. And my appreciation of Hitchcock's work in general and of this particular film, to the extent that it touches at all upon Catholic matters, has therefore ironically been colored by one of his most devoted students. All the viewers of *I Confess*, on the other hand, were not expected by the filmmaker to be Catholic.

It is not my intent here to explore in any depth the remarkable connection between Scorsese and Hitchcock—*Cape Fear* is an especially observant and open homage—but Scorsese has taken from Hitchcock, and has inspired me to think about, a deep concern with filmmaking itself as a confession; a concern, therefore, with the relationship between moral confrontation and the labors of the eye.[14] I think *I Confess* may have been an especially Catholic operation for Hitchcock. His life at the time he made it was certainly vitally connected to the Catholic Church, as in January 1952 his daughter, Patricia, all her life a focus of her father's most Catholic devotions,[15] had wed Joseph E. O'Connell, the grandnephew of the late cardinal archbishop of Boston, and during production of this film was pregnant with her first child.[16] As is widely known, too, Hitchcock had received the benefits of a Jesuit education as a boy in London, and had been a sometime churchgoer before coming to the United States. But all of Hitchcock's work is a relentless attempt to lay before us a depiction of a dramatic and morally implicating event that has existence and bearing once he has given it the "telling"—which is to say, the showing. The center of Hitchcock is not merely what happens; it is what is seen to happen. The God of Catholicism can surely read the creative artist's mind, yet the artist is forced by his need for transcendence to work out the vision so that it exists in the domain of the palpable. Otto Keller's account to Logan, then, is no mere admission of wrongdoing; it is an embodiment of an act we are in no position to understand or know until he speaks. It is (like the figuration we hear in the credit sequence) a song.

Consider, for instance, Logan's connection with the corpse of Villette if Keller does not sing to him in our presence. After having been visited by him earlier in the evening (Villette is a blackmailer), Logan has made plans to visit the lawyer in the morning. His discovery then of the murder, joined at once by the recognition that it makes him "free," would leave no trace of sanctity upon him—indeed, he would be a creepy profiteer. Father Logan must be confessed to, in order to remain pure, and thus heroic, in our eyes at the moment the death "frees" him. He is unstained because he has taken a confession, though of course we are not innocent in watching him do that. Let us patiently (more patiently than Inspecteur Larrue) follow the delicate rosary of links from the body of the lawyer to the persona of the priest.

Wandering the nocturnal streets in search of DIRECTION,[17] we find a body and see a man in flight, apparently a priest. Partially disrobing, he becomes an ordinary man. He approaches a church. A second man, who also looks like a priest, is in the rectory, gazing out into the night ("on the lookout"), but the jewel-like glow and steadiness of his regard suggest a personality that aims outward and inward at once. He observes the layman walk into the sanctuary, enters there himself, meets the layman, and ultimately hears his confession, which is in its form nothing other than a spiritual wandering in search of "direction" that alludes to a more sanctified "body" produced by an archetypical "murder." The "body" is also the body of a tale. Turning swiftly away from the "corpus" of this narrative is none other than Logan the priest, a man soon to be disrobed by another confession that reveals him, under his soutane, to be an ordinary man with a human heart. We follow him as he is brought to a locus of opinion and justice, the police department, where a policeman who grew up in the Church is "on the lookout." He traps the "priest" (a man who was, in some sense, pretending to be a priest) and hears his confession (albeit through the mouth of the woman the confession is about). A circular story, a story winding around itself. Both Keller and Logan pretend to be priests, with motives and secrets that differ. Wearing the priesthood is the problematic act in this film.

That our street search for "direction" leads to a body may seem arbitrary: one may find much on the streets of Québec at night. But if the word "direction" is taken to refer not to the orientation of a thoroughfare, but instead to a moral and general state of human affairs, to a quest, then the ultimate aim is in fact the corpus. This is the phenomenological sense of embodiment, nicely reflected in a little paragraph from Borges:

> A man sets himself the task of portraying the world. Through the years he peoples a space with images of provinces, kingdoms, mountains, bays, ships, islands, fishes, rooms, instruments, stars, horses, and people. Shortly before his death, he discovers that the patient labyrinth of lines traces the image of his face.[18]

From this corpus, at any rate, a man is moving swiftly away. From death, life takes motion. One might argue that at this point in the diegesis there is no reason to suspect the moving man guilty of anything, except perhaps that he wears a guilty look. In the most general and universal of perspectives there is hardly another way to see it, however. The mover has survival guilt; the guilt of being left behind to tell the tale. He carries with him the weight of the past, which is to say he is burdened by the corpse that he is fleeing. Why, I find myself asking, does he head for a church? Yet he has to go somewhere, and the Church is also, in its most universal sense, the habitation of the soul. (In the Québec of 1955, indeed, there were churches everywhere, as we see in the police hunt sequence. A church was the one habitation one could be sure of finding.) One could argue as well—I think Hitchcock would have—that the cinema is also a habitation. Keller finding the church is like the viewer finding a darkened seat to watch Keller flee. So we move by "direction" from the hunt in the streets to a body, to an escaper, to a church.

There is surely, however, nothing but coincidence in the fact that at the very moment Keller enters the rectory Logan happens to be gazing out his window. Remember that we do not yet know Keller is employed and resident in this church—he is just a man in flight at night. He goes for sanctuary, for "home"—but not, to our mind, necessarily also *home*—and the irony that the church is the place where he lives will strike only later. A man as responsive as Logan will surely speak to this man if he thinks only what we already think: a lonely stranger is coming to a church late at night. But—and we do not know this yet—Logan knows more than we know and thinks more than we think. He knows it is no lonely stranger but Keller the sacristan who lives under this roof. Aside from the fact that our brief gaze at Logan makes us want him to meet the lonely walker outside, and that, therefore, he descends into the church because we want him to, there is no reason *intelligible to us* for him to do anything when he sees Keller in the street. And why, indeed, does he see anybody? Why is he looking? Why is this the first thing we see of Logan: his standing at a window late at night looking out in wonder and discomfort? If these questions seem like exertions, note that if Logan doesn't gaze, he doesn't see Keller; if he doesn't see Keller he doesn't move down to the sanctuary; if he doesn't go to the sanctuary he doesn't hear the confession. And what then? He can still be arrested for the murder, still suspected, even found guilty. But we cannot know of his innocence. Or the story can take another direction: somebody else goes into the church and hears the confession of Keller and we don't meet Logan at all—at least not in connection with Keller and his ugly story. *I Confess* becomes another film. But no: Logan gazes out of his window, surveilling the night. He keeps watch upon the sleeping world, so that it does not disappear.

But more: Logan gazes out of his window because he is distraught, and because he is a man for whom the balm for pains, the solution to puzzles, the release from anxieties, is outside himself. He is an impressionist, needing the air. The darkness of the streets inspires him; he is a searcher for settings, a filmmaker. Why is he distraught? Theoretically he could as well be drowsy and slipping off to sleep in bed. He is distraught because (as we will only much later find out) just a little while ago Villette has been walking with him, near the river, and has demanded a huge sum of money in blackmail against him and Ruth Grandfort. Logan has decided to visit Villette the following morning and to bring Villette's nefarious activity, somehow, to a climax. He is worried about this meeting, because if Villette is dissatisfied enough to go public with what he knows, Ruth's marriage and his own career as a priest are both destroyed. Therefore he has a lot on his mind. It is possible his life as priest will soon be over. He has absolutely no way to know at this moment that Villette is dead—and dead because a man he happens to know (though we do not know this yet) killed him for entirely unrelated reasons and is even now walking into the church to say so.

So the man who has just come from killing Villette—who targeted Villette—is being encountered optically (targeted) by the man who is planning to go to meet Villette, who is targeting Villette, and neither man knows of the other's exact connection to the object of his attention. Logan has as much to hide as Keller does, but he makes no confession. Is this only because Keller is not his priest? The moral bias of the narrative is constructed in alignment with people's social roles, not the nature of their spiritualities. Spiritually, Logan and Keller are brothers, but Logan is in a superior position technically. How unrelated, in fact, is Keller's motive for killing Villette to Logan's motive for gazing out the window? Logan is considering the moral and practical consequences of possibly losing his priesthood. Through his priesthood he hired Keller and gave him a job in an ethnocentric society where German immigrants immediately after the war had much trouble finding work. But of course, such German immigrants made very little money compared with other workers. Logan is thus instrumental not only in Keller's safety but also in his institutionalized poverty. It is for money that Keller has killed Villette.

There is, then, an extremely subtle and tightly woven fabric of motive, suspicion, implication, desire, and motion that binds Logan and Keller together and Keller's confession is the central feature of this fabric's design. But this account does not do justice to our actual experience of this film, and that is because of a central antinomy in human experience that Alfred Hitchcock was more concerned with than any plot, character, or story content in his work. I refer to the troubling liaison between sight and sound. The Catholic God, for instance, sees everything, even, presumably, the inner and contrite heart. Yet it is necessary to recount to him, as to a child, the story of one's transgression, to register morally questionable activity by means of a confession that embeds it in His matrix of testimony and redemption. In *I Confess*, the formula works in reverse. Though the plot may mundanely require that characters narrate their states of reality to one another, still it is fundamentally necessary to Hitchcock (because this is not an illustrated radio program) that he, and therefore we, should see, that we should explicitly be shown. We should recognize, we should take note, we should (like Father Logan) surveil, keep vigil, and keep vigilant.[19] How, then, along what stairway, we see a pathway through the tale of revelation and concealment, and how, in the narrative itself, the characters by steps make use of what they see or cannot see to reach their ends, are the great questions here and also the great prize.

SIGHTLINE

Poi s'ascose nel fuoco che gli affina.
    Dante, Inferno

Let us consider some major stopping points in the optical excursion that is *I Confess*. Written synopses have made little if any reference to these, but persons who watch this film will be unable to shake them from memory:

Otto Keller's Eyes. As he sits in his pew waiting for Michael Logan to approach him in the first church sequence, Keller is about to confess one of two sins he has just committed, the murder of Villette, though not the other—that when he did it he had disguised himself as a priest. Subsequently, Father Logan will be arrested and tried for the crime, his subsequent difficulties with the law, given that he cannot break the seal of the confessional to defend himself, constituting one (only one) skein of the plot. Keller's are bulbous, ravenous eyes, eyes that see everything not only analytically but with a certain exigent and cupidinous *Weltschmerz*—Nietzschean eyes, certainly; eyes that incorporate and digest; greedy eyes that strain to limit and possess through definition. As Logan walks nearer, his candle gives more illumination, and also more perspective, to these vulture's eyes, embodies them progressively, nurtures them with—as Goethe said at his death—"more light." Logan's view—his opticality—introduces us to Keller, then: Keller the ultimate spy and ultimate admirer, the craver who is at the bottom of all things, looking up to civilized life.[20]

The Signal, "Watch." During the confession itself, Father Logan's impulse is to bury his eyes. (He will repeat this gesture later, on the street, leaning against a stone pillar, after hunting desperately through the city full of the knowledge that he is soon to be arrested.) We feel at once that the world has been too much with him late and soon, yet this is not why he is covering his eyes. As a priest his function is to hear what people tell him, not judge on the basis of appearances, and so the confessional booth is fixed for optical privacy. That Logan covers his eyes in the confessional is telling. He is not avoiding his client's face—the booth removes it from consideration—but embellishing upon the use of the eye, and the meaning of his signal *to us* is "Watch." Everything in a Hitchcock film, it may seem selfish but is important to remember, is for us. As counterpoint, we have a close shot of Keller's eye, peering through the screen in predation as he reveals his secret to the man inside whom he intends to hide himself.

The Optical Cycle. Other priests live in the rectory with Father Logan, one, Father Benoit (Gilles Pelletier), the possessor of a bicycle and a pair of thick eyeglasses. Ancillary to his myopia is bicycle trouble—he thinks he needs Keller to fix his machine but later discovers that there is nothing wrong with it. In short, he doesn't have the eyes to take proper care of his equipment. But the broken equipment is a pair of wheels, like eyes: his eyes are so bad he can't see whether or not he's got bad "eyes." Ultimately he's a person who isn't looking, the person I suspect Hitchcock thought most of us really are. The bicycle makes it possible for Benoit to get around, as lenses and dolly do Hitchcock, and also Hitchcock's viewer, and his rolling the bike further and further inside the rectory suggests his desire to move all the way to the center of the action himself. Yet Benoit has bad vision, so while his bicycle will make possible a variety of movements his sight will continue to be a problem. Particularly this, of all Hitchcock's films (lacking the thread of thrilling adventure), is a moral about how to watch a film: moving from place to place and point to point won't help if we can't see in the first place. In more theoretical terms, without (Bazinian) depth of perception, the thrust of montage is doomed to be interrupted by our impotence.

The Back of the Head. Alma Keller experiences an optical crisis as she serves the priests at the breakfast table. She has learned from her husband what he did to Villette, and how he confessed to Father Logan. She must keep her lips stitched. Alma's optical crisis reflects the moral, emotional, and tactical crisis in her life occasioned by her knowledge and her fear, but it also speaks to our own situation, insofar as we are watching her, since we, like Alma, are "married"—to this film. She is standing behind Logan, desperate for a vision of his face that may inform her as to his intent. Might he be considering an approach to the police? Being European and old-fashioned, she regards herself as an adjunct to her husband and is prepared to interpret Logan's potential signals to her as indications of his alignment toward Keller, an alignment to which she should be privy. But Logan's purview is the vast and mountainous landscape of the human condition, not the cloistered court of social nicety the immigrant Kellers know in their blood. Facial expressions are irrelevant to the larger—and longer—*and higher*—purpose his gaze is forever fixed upon: moments do not make eternities, and only eternities matter. He will not turn around for her, then, and leaves her only the back of his head to decode. To us—in order that we may taste her moment fully—in the mirror behind her back as she serves him is left her back.

This scene beautifully explicates how it is with us, fearful and desperate, in a world architected of visions and visual possibilities, when we do not have eyes in the back of our heads for seeing everything everywhere; and when we cannot count on others having eyes in the back of their heads, for revealing to us what we cannot see upon their faces. What we can know is tightly bounded by where, and who, we are.

Much later, as he bypasses Keller holding a bundle of dying gladioli, Logan gives further expression to this lofty, wholly abstracted moral position. Keller is now desperate on his own part to have a clue as to what Logan is thinking, what he plans to do. But Logan sweeps past him without so much as a hello. Logan is a man of the cloth, guided by both conventions and religious dictates. Regardless of the interactional demands of the moment, he is bound to silence as regards the confession, and his binding is legal, moral, general, and supreme, unrelated to his attitudes in respect of any predicament or his sentiments in regard to any person. From behind his back in the breakfast room, then, Alma is seeing all she needs to see of Logan at this pressing moment; namely, that he is a priest. She is seeing the whole man, his ineffable sum. But she is too panicky to realize this fact or what it implies.

Gazes Holding Gazes. Keller is nothing if not a virtuoso at hiding. As he makes his way to secrete himself inside the sheath of his regular labor in the garden of Villette, "ignorant" that the man is dead, Alma momentarily deters him in a rectory window. They have a brief conversation, fixing each other's faces and attentions with rigidly staring eyes. She is panicked about what Logan may have told the police. Keller intones with Prussian authority, prefiguring Professor Lindt in *Torn Curtain*, "They know *noth*'ing." Hitchcock intercuts between the two to emphasize the way they are holding one another's gazes with gazes. Each is watching like a hawk for something to happen. They perform surveillance upon one another, openly, in the air. But they cannot see to the interior of the situation, to the true locus of the decision as to what Logan will do with Keller's confession.

Keller does not understand the church he has been using, and in this he is not alone. To make a central point bluntly if harshly, Keller, looking upward to Logan in his authoritarian secular piety, is akin to the Premier of Québec in his secularity looking down upon, ultimately fearing, the self-serving romanticism of the Church. As much as Keller needs Logan, both tactically and spiritually, he reviles him; and as much as Logan is committed to approximating himself to Keller—by hearing him, by holding his secret in his heart—he is alienated from the secular world Keller represents. Nor, in a society where Church power is eroding all around him, is this alienation of Logan conveniently resolved at the film's end. As we ferry nostalgically away from the city we can know that even if Ruth goes back to her husband, even if Keller is dead, all the characters who represent the Church remain in a tormented limbo: Father Benoit not quite fixing that bicycle; Inspector Larrue guilty of having punctured the confessional seal; and Logan, unable to reconcile human evil with his own desire for moral purity in the world.

Keller, at any rate, relies upon his gaze to probe Father Logan, and his reliance is a sure sign that for him the world is a set of appearances. This is a conception inconsistent with Catholic practice, and Keller's clear self-revelation as a man who uses his gaze to control, coupled with his insistence on confessing to Logan, can lead us to see him as a man who is manipulating the agency of confession to set himself up with an airtight protection. He's not a true believer. Wearing the priesthood during the murder was one form of protection and control but in confessing he makes it possible for himself to wear the priesthood more generally and with greater safety. Keller's confession has two sides, however, because his confessor also does. The Logan who is in the confession box has no interest in the appearance of the world, and will therefore make no signals through appearance to trap Keller. But the Logan who meets Ruth on the ferry is an ordinary man who became a priest. It is as though Keller, who knows nothing of this *affaire de coeur*, nothing of the ordinary man beneath the priest, is concerned that some ordinary man inside will speak even if the priest remains silent. How can Keller be so doubtful of Logan's commitment to Church convention, so fearful of his unknown—second and secular—self? The answer inheres in another question. Which is exterior—available to sight (Keller's and ours)—in Logan: his manhood or his priesthood? As we look at the film there can be only one answer.

Logan, historically a man who was ordained, is nevertheless in his filmic form a priest wearing the surface of a man, and not a man wearing the surface of a priest (as he would no doubt see himself). When he was ordained, that is, he was true to his deeper self, because in his heart he is a priest. But he looks for all the world like a man in torment. Keller sees this man—indeed, himself—in Logan much more than he sees an agent of Divinity; and he knows he must keep an eye on him because all ordinary men are untrustworthy. Logan's outside surface (all that Keller can see) may reveal to Larrue what Logan's inner self would never give out. Inner purity is without value if the skin is blemished (as, indeed, Keller's is, just a little, that we may take note). The other priests do not need to be watched. Whatever there is of them that is human and frail, it is inner and has been covered by the carapace of the Church. They will wear no expressions to give away personal moral sentiments. Logan, however, wears upon his sleeve something Keller points to in discussing him, and that in 1952 Montgomery Clift, at the apex of his career and the beginning of his great torment, was very well equipped to display, "a private distress." It is a quality never for an instant absent from Clift's performance, and indelibly beautiful for the viewer. This is one of the reasons Hitchcock would have needed to cast him, an actor he had never worked with before and whose strange reputation for self-doubt and anxiety on the set would surely have preceded him.

The Optical Gun. Keller immigrated from Germany just after World War II and so he is a man used to the police and who has learned police technique. Having been under surveillance, he can surveil. As Larrue interrogates him at Villette's house the morning after the murder, Keller knows Larrue's professional gaze and how to return it. And while speaking with Keller Larrue keeps his eyes on his victim's face: in his years of forgetting the choirboy he once was at Sainte Marie's, Larrue has learned not to lower his eyes modestly, not to turn himself from the outward fashion of the world for spiritual grace, but to devote himself to superficial business in a secular devotion, a secular piety which is the bureaucratic apotheosis of police business. Suddenly, however, we move behind Keller's head and see Larrue's right eye slide out from the proscenium provided by Keller to stare directly into the lens.[21] This eye is like the mouth of a gun barrel (a tunnel we will look into as Keller prepares to shoot Alma): blunt, remorseless, final, unstoppable. But if Larrue is not looking at Keller, what can he be looking at? For an instant, I take him to be looking at me, and am startled and frightened. Thus it is that a second later, as Hitchcock provides a reverse shot to follow Larrue's line of sight, I see its content with some real chill, a dramaturgical necessity of the instant. It is Logan, moving on the sidewalk, in the sunny street: *dans la rue.* (Logan is in Larrue.) He is a mundane passer-by here, to be sure, but the shot as placed in the film is not mundane at all. My first reaction is to be filled with a tremendous relief—relief that the relentless Larrue has looked past me; relief that I am safe from the glare of his condemnation; relief that somebody else will suffer his investigations in my place. For he seems both devoted and unbridled, a man who will penetrate until he finds (or until the object of his penetration is destroyed). Although the person he is fixing in his eye is a figure I have come to trust and admire—because of his feelingful concern for the pain of Keller, his physical beauty, his delicate voice, his purposeful manner—yet I would rather Larrue interested himself in sweet Logan than that he looked any longer at me. So, I am made a culpable conspirator. To relieve my guilt at this, I project it outward: *What is this that Logan is doing?* (This is precisely Larrue's take.) *He is meeting a woman!* As Larrue would not find this sort of behavior appropriate for a priest I do not, either. The puzzle of seemliness is confounding, because although the encounter of Logan and Ruth Grandfort is staged as a romantic tryst, here in broad daylight, later it will be evident it is a cover, a mask, for a romance not of the present but of the past.

The Eyes of the Witness. In his office, Willie Robertson, the Crown Prosecutor, is playing with a coin and a pair of forks over a glass of wine, bringing into a secure balance two matched and incompatible structures by the application of money. This vertical game has as object the prevention of the profane token from falling down into the sacred wine. It is the perfect glyph for conveying the complexity and deftness of Anglophone power in the Québec of 1952, where big business saw itself as above the Church, yet prone to being subverted by longstanding ecclesiastical power: the coin balanced above the wine. And the forks, once again, are the competing forces grappling for the coffers of the Province over the blood of the citizens: on one side we have the Jesuitical and paternalistic interests of the Church, on the other the liberal and contemporizing demands of burgeoning big business. Money reconciles their disparate—their conflicting—positions. We may recollect, in this regard, Pierre Grandfort's speech to the Provincial Assembly, in regard to the necessity of increasing the wages of female schoolteachers, a proposal that would never have sat well in the patriarchal eyes of the Church.

Interrupting Robertson's game, Larrue has arranged for some "girls" to come in and be interviewed in the presence of this august, and somewhat haughty, superior. Robertson's eyes open wide in anticipation of female fun, but he is immediately let down to discover that the girls are *little* girls, about eleven years old. Those eyes of his, spontaneous to gesture and yet professionally irresponsible, draw our attention to ocularity. Now, the sister babysitters will themselves turn out to have a purely ocular significance.

They were walking past Villette's house, they say, at the time the murderer emerged into the street. They followed him. From a camera position across the street, indeed, we watched them do this. The logic of their observation reveals these girls to have fashioned an extra-diegetic affiliation with me as, behind Hitchcock's camera, I stood across the street watching them watch, an affiliation and even an identification, since before they were following the furtive man, in truth, I was. He was unmistakably a priest to me when first I saw him, also to the girls. Now in Larrue's office they unmistakably identify him as such, in a citric Franglais that rings like a bell: "'*E was a priest!*" One of the girls clearly dominates, though she has less to say. She is virtually blind, equipped, like Father Benoit,[22] with a pair of profoundly thick eyeglasses. She it is who has certainty the man on the street was clergy, although Hitchcock makes emphatic her ocular difficulty—one of her eyeglass lenses reflects like the Hope diamond on the wall between the girls. The witness's tale is not truth but itself a currency, a glittering coin of the realm, that unites and binds the French cop and the Anglo lawyer in their disparate value systems and conflicting energies.

A Critical MacGuffin. In this film the "MacGuffin," the object without which the business of the plot would not take place, is a person, the lawyer Villette. We barely meet him. But when we do, it is impossible to avoid considering the obsequious malevolence in his eyes, and their strange, somewhat alienating, Charlie Chanish quasi-orientalism. By contrast, since it is to her that he most often presents himself, Ruth Grandfort's eyes are small and narrow and there is a porcelain opacity to her gaze, a rarefied and polished exoticism. Is it the Mandarin somnolence of comfort and power that causes her optically to withdraw, or the fright she must be experiencing at Villette's hands? Just before the conclusion of the film she tells her husband to take her home, and at this moment her eyes are bright, even merry, with resolution now that Villette is gone and his death completely resolved. What is interesting about Villette's gaze, however, is that it is essentially a grasping one, like that of the viewer, who takes every social display laid out for optical consideration as an opportunity for gathering evidence, for amassing the pieces that can be assembled into the puzzle of the meaning of the film. Villette, too, is a fan of puzzles, though he is morally contemptible because he puts the pieces together for profit, not for satisfaction. Is he, perhaps, a critic?

Pantomime. In a flashback love scene in a country gazebo (that they do not know belongs to Villette), the morning after a rainstorm, Logan, not yet a priest, stares into the eyes of Ruth, whom he does not know to be married. But to show this moment, the camera is positioned directly in front of his face, so that he is looking into the viewer's eyes. The cover story of the scene is a tryst, involving denunciation and redemption, but the mise-en-scène is about knowing by seeing. It is not really Logan and Ruth Hitchcock is watching but film, the medium in which actor and audience connect by way of the gaze. Hitchcock's loyalty to film leads him to respect the play of the world that Logan's Catholicism, Ruth's jadedness, Robertson's Machiavellianism all turn away from: that it appears, that it is consumed by sight. I am certainly made momentarily self-conscious by Clift's attentions—Clift's, not Logan's, because when my eyes see his I know that Logan is Clift. There being nothing to my experience (as filmgoer) beyond the visible surface, this visible surface, I am awakened to a finer, more exacting reading of its many characteristics. This capacity is given test almost at once, because in the ensuing confrontation scene between Logan and Villette, I must read the nuances of the interaction entirely through the actors' mime, their surface of constructed appearance. Ruth's narration helps only a little, as it is in English, while Villette silently mouths his lines in French and Logan remains mute.

The gazebo scene is the culmination of the love story of Michael and Ruth, but all that story is itself a kind of pantomime acted out for us to see—and decode by seeing—while a very skimpy narrative accompanies it perfunctorily. While the denuded facts of the case (as presented to Larrue, for instance) might have led to a moral denunciation of Michael (such as is ultimately provided by the judge in his verdict), there is yet sufficient innocence plainly visible to the viewer—the soft lighting, the composition of the screen in pleasing mid-tones, the beauty of the gazing faces—for us to acquit not only the priest but also Ruth, a woman whose self-knowledge and knowledge of her lover's innocence cannot force in her a disloyalty to the feeling she inspired before she wedded Grandfort. So the moral position of Logan and Ruth, vital to the outcome of the film, can be established only if Hitchcock holds appearance and visions as a preeminent reality. In a film the moral *is* the aesthetic.

The Police Eye. The police must ultimately hunt for Michael Logan. But to them—bureaucrats separated from the clergy—every priest looks like every other priest. A sequence of shots of priests interrupted in their everyday duties, and then apologized to as it is seen they are not Logan, nicely catalogues the police eye as undiscriminating, alienated, classifying, and brutal. This brutal police eye is also Larrue's, dedicated to the purposes of justice, until in the courtroom and at the point of verdict he recollects that he owes a duty to a higher Jurisprudence.

THE SKIN OF SALVATION

If *I Confess* is constructed essentially as a sightline, a chain of visual stresses and invitations, and if it brings us incessantly to optical experiences and significations of sight, in short, to the labors of the eye, it is also true that its central thought is the relation between sight and salvation. To what extent is our world coextensive with, and dependent upon, the visible impression it makes? And thus, are we being absolutely real and absolutely pure when we are seeming? Seeming, of course, is acting.

The film is full of seeming. The man in the nocturnal street outside Villette's house seems to be a priest; yet he is not a priest. He is an actor playing the role of a priest, much as in Robert Houdin's view, as Orson Welles informs us, a magician was an actor playing the role of a magician.[23] (I refer to Keller-the-actor, not the actor O. E. Hasse who played him.) Larrue is certainly a man playing the role of a police inspector, not a police inspector by nature, because in the courtroom it is evident his deeper concern is for Logan's soul, health, and career. Willie Robertson, we learn at Ruth Grandfort's party if we have not intuited it earlier from a more general knowledge of political appointees, is a bored and ambitious man playing the role of a dispassionate prosecutor—a blithe man at that, even a roué. Ruth has been a woman of passion playing the role of a dutiful wife; even as her husband is a man of delicacy, privacy, and cavalier sensitivity playing the role of a cool husband in a marriage that is largely performance, and the role of a cool, even modern politician in charged public debate. I think it can be argued that Keller plays the role of a contrite sinner making confession, in order to gain material security; and that in that confession he plays the powerless underling from a position of psychological strength. And I have suggested earlier what Logan's confession to Ruth on the Lévis ferry makes fairly plain: that he is a priest playing the role of a man (playing the role of a priest).

The Catholic logic underpinning the film affirms the eternal reality of the inner self and denies the truth or importance of surface presentations. Equally available for our consideration is a governmental, bureaucratic logic that is exactly the opposite, a relentless attachment to the façades people put up for dealing with the business of life in a circumstantial way. It is civil, bureaucratic pressure that forces Logan's trial as a common man and Ruth Grandfort's display of herself as a cheap adulteress, civil pressure because in Québec at this time the Church and Church values were declining in the face of a politic of accommodation and development. The logic of the diegesis, therefore, puts the inner world of the characters under attack from their own skins, an envelopmental crisis. Surfaces being paramount, the imposition called social identity supercedes subjective experience unless a formula is found for looking into the human heart. Surfaces are paramount even when they are the focus of disregard, a response called for by the trial judge whose personal opinion it is that finding Logan innocent of the murder of Villette (as the evidence might lead one to do) is a miscarriage of justice. When the judge instructs the jury (the viewer) to take no notice of the fact that the defendant is a priest, he believes himself to be pointing to a man inside: merely civil, ordinary, transgressive, since for the judge Logan is first like anyone, and only later specialized to the Church. In treating Logan as essentially such a person, we are apparently to choose the bureaucratic road, refrain in a completely secular engagement from giving special consideration to his clerical status as would have been done traditionally in rural French Canadian culture to date.

However, what the judge means in terms of that strange vertical hierarchy in which the telling surface lies above the inner substance is this: Logan looks like a priest, but beneath this guise he is a man like you and I. His looks, and only his looks, are sacred; his nature is secular. As a corollary, his priestliness is only in his looks, a matter of garb, a skin. Penetrate, we are urged, to his secular essence and judge him there. Like Logan, in our most essential selves we are secular beings. Disattend the Church altogether, in fact, says this priest of the secular temple of law. See Logan as a common man amorously struck by Ruth Grandfort, then motivated by his relation with her. See him as being vindictive with regard to Villette because of that carnal attraction and Villette's threat to it. That his failure to give over vital information (from the confession) could have moral origins must be beyond notice; see it as self-serving. We are being told, in short, where to place the focus of our gaze, what we should consider irrelevant, what we must avoid seeing altogether. But I think that because Logan is a priest pretending to be a man, not a man pretending to be a priest, we must give the judge's words a new reading.

Putting aside Logan's priesthood and focusing on his common humanity requires not the dismantling of his surface—as the judge suspects—but a special attention to it, because his humanity is on his sleeve. His humanity is the apotheosis, the blossoming, not the contradiction, of his priestliness. That Logan is a priest first and a man second is the reading opened by the film. Any other actor than Montgomery Clift would have had less success conveying exactly the sense of dislocation and tremulousness necessary to build on the screen the telling image of a deeply moral man caught in an avaricious world.

In film, there is nothing given but what is food for the eye. Everything is composition, construction, display, movement, space. Our world is itself a mise-en-scène. We must find equivalents for our deepest sensations directly on the screen. Logan's fragile humanity is discretely visible in his sustained agony. Keller's puerile malevolence is in the unwavering brazenness of his gaze. Alma's infidelity is in her slouching posture. Ruth Grandfort's ability to prevail is in her command of postural line—the way she holds herself as she gazes at Robertson balancing water on his forehead. The optical problem of the film is not merely to see that things are not the way they appear to be, because here, really, they can only appear to be. The problem is to accept that things must appear, and to see enough. All things really are exactly as they look, yet we tend not to look at them. Logan really looks more natural in his soutane than in his civilian clothes, as though he is proclaiming that moral radiance is exactly what every human being should work for. For Logan, atypically in 1950s Québec, human beings aren't the pretexts for priests and priests don't constitute a special case. But on the other hand, one doesn't have to disregard the priestliness, as the judge does, to get at the humanity. One disregards morally unconscious humanity to achieve morally conscious priestliness. What the little girls saw on the street—what the little girls really saw on the street—was not a priest; it was a man dressed as a priest. They were too young to know that the priesthood is not in the costume alone but in the manner of wearing it. Larrue comes to know this truth, but too late to do Logan any real good.

PAIN

Our principle concern . . . at the present moment should be the re-establishment of the temper or disposition of mind which can look at a gap or chasm without shuddering.

　　T. E. Hulme, Speculations

No more elegant or simpler statement is given of the optical paradox of the film than in the sequence of scenes devoted to that elementary configuration of opticality, the painting of the rectory lounge. Here we have nothing but surfaces and coverings; essences and images; substance and appearance. And because the philosophical problem to be entertained and resolved here is a very old and venerable one, it is fair enough to say with Father Milet that our search is for an "antique white." It is, of course, a hopeless search; any white will do. And in using "antique white" as he paints, Logan becomes a kind of Tom Sawyer, at least in the sense that Keller cannot stop himself from wetting his own brush at the prospect of the great transformation he is watching upon the walls. Let us look.

The painting sequence occupies part or all of three different scenes, making it notable as thematic material though the typical critique of *I Confess* does not mention it at all. In the first scene, Father Milet is discussing with Father Logan an enterprise Logan has entered into some time ago with Keller's help: repainting the priests' sitting room. In the second, we see Logan at work painting, and he is accompanied at various moments by Father Milet, by Keller, and by Alma Keller. In the third, Detective Murphy (Judson Pratt), Larrue's assistant, has been waiting in the rectory for Logan to escort him to the police station for questioning; but Father Milet takes advantage of the opportunity to make a wry comment about the paint that is covering the walls.

I want to emphasize that in none of the three scenes is there any action vital to the ostensible plot of Villette's murder and Logan's arrest for it, so that from the point of view of the murder-confession plot they constitute totally extraneous, indeed fluffy, transitions and the director who insisted on including them can be seen as little more than an undisciplined and self-indulgent eclectic. In order for Father Milet to lead Father Logan to breakfast in the first of these scenes he has no need to stop and chat about a painting project that we, in our turn, do not need to know exists. In the second scene, in order for Keller to walk in on Father Milet and inform him that Villette has been murdered (something we already know), and that he, Keller, has found the body (something we have already heard him tell Larrue), it is not necessary that they be standing together in a room Logan is in the process of painting. Nor is it necessary for our understanding of the judicial drama being played out that we be informed Keller consigned himself to assist Logan in this decorative practice. We do not need to observe him seeming prone to delinquenting himself from the painting work because of his distress over his crime. The paintwork, in short, need have no place in this story. Inspector Murphy, moreover, can attend Father Logan without standing in, of all places, the priests' sitting room, so that the third and concluding scene in this sequence is not technically necessary either. Murphy can wait on the front steps. He can wait in the kitchen or the dining room. He can wait outside in his car. He can arrive, indeed, after Logan has presented himself and avoid waiting altogether.

Yet Hitchcock does not engage himself with decorative samplers, self-indulgence,[24] fluff, or inconsequential screen action, as a substantial body of critical work has shown.[25] In order to understand why the painting sequence is so vital to his purposes, we must examine its mise-en-scène. Then we will see that there is something intrinsic to the film here, to such a degree that the film can finally be seen as more about surfaces, painting them, covering, keeping up a face, and whitening than it is about murder. The murder story, indeed, is the situational pretext that makes it possible to bring the problem of surfacing to the surface.

1. The Smell of Pain

A strange little scene. The congregation for early mass is departing the church of Sainte Marie, Wednesday morning. Keller has gone off to work Villette's garden—his cover because he must give no hint that he knows Villette will not be there to pay him. Having completed the service, Logan and his altar boy are disappearing behind the altar at the rear of a long shot. We cut in upon a medium shot of the two, as they retreat into the vestibule. A large cross is outlined in white on the back of Logan's chasuble. The changing room is wide and airy, taken up with an immense vestment chest of shallow drawers that strikes us immediately, because of the assuredness in which he moves around it, as the altar boy's territory. Through a window at the back we see a tree waving in a strong wind. Logan and the boy bow, and then he removes his biretta and hands it over. He draws off the chasuble. Now, as they stand side by side, the boy is in a dark suit with a white surplice covering the top; Logan's dark soutane is entirely covered by a long snowy alb with lace at the bottom. As he lays out his chasuble to fold it on top of the chest, we dolly in a step or two, Logan's entire body filling the screen, but before we can reach Logan, and before he is able to reach the apogee of his movement, we dissolve to:

A medium shot, a few brief moments—even seconds—later in film time. Now we see Logan from the waist up, and *his alb has disappeared.* He is dressed in his black soutane. "Bonne journée," he says to the boy, and walks out.

Was Hitchcock incapable of realizing this disrobing in a single fluid shot? Inconceivable. The dissolve is an intentional visual emphasis, a play with our sense of time through a visualization of unfolding or peeling. The focal content of the scene is the penetration of layers, layers that are black and white. The removal of the chasuble is the preparation for removals, for strippings, so that in a moment, when we see Logan without his alb we will focus not so much on the fact that the alb is not there as on its seeming to have vanished into thin air. The cross embroidered on the chasuble is there to catch our sight immediately, lead us to the garment, prepare us for the preparation that is its removal. The delicate ritual of the folding elaborates that preparatory act for us, refines it, embellishes its meaningfulness as a skinning, a masquerade.

We watch Logan retreat to a homey and bright room where morning sunlight streams through a long window with a Venetian blind. A ladder stands next to the window. Furniture is draped in white sheeting. Logan stands with his dark back in front of us, looking around the room. We are in medium shot. Milet (Charles André) enters from left, with a somewhat perfunctory "Good morning." This is a man who takes no pleasure in pleasantries. "Will it take you and, um, Keller much longer to finish the painting in this room?" he asks. This is our first chance to hear him use English at length. He is fluent, with a tendency to put extra stress on his final syllables sometimes: longer is LONGer, but painting is PAIN-TING. Because the answer to this matter-of-fact question is far from matter-of-fact—for Logan certainly but principally for us—we now cut to a close shot behind Logan as he says in reply, "I don't know."

"I only ask," continues Milet, "because the smell makes one quite ill, really." As he continues, smiling, the two men turn and head across the hall into the breakfast room. "You know, I read some advertisement [pron. ad-VER-tice-m'nt] about paints and of course one should not judge on so little evidence but, uh, uh—one finds it difficult to believe that there *are* paints . . . but no smell. Do you know of any paints that do not smell, Father Michael?" Logan says he doesn't, whereupon Milet puts the icing on the cake as the two men, now seated, cross themselves: "Don't think of it. Doesn't matter." That Hitchcock should have a character inform us that something he has just said is not relevant is, of course, the clearest possible signal that it is.

I have given details of this scene in order to reveal something of what I take to be its alluring perversity. Milet is the only person in the film who calls Logan "Father Michael." It is a charming, naturally patronizing action, calling our attention to the older man's comparative wisdom and to Logan's youth. Of course, analyzed in terms of realistic social dynamics, the conversation about the paints is small talk, an especially graceful way of navigating the two men, sociably and efficiently, from one room to another without breaking a flow of meditation. But in this particular story, there is no necessity for Milet and Logan to be in the sitting room in the first place or, for that matter, for them to arrive in the breakfast room ultimately; or to speak any words at all as they move from the one room to the other. Hitchcock does not happen to come upon his characters carrying on their lives and dutifully record what they happen to do. The characters do what he intends they should, and the sitting room that needs painting is an attraction for the director, not for the priest. Further, if we listen carefully to Milet—his message and also his voice—we hear that the uneventful scene is full of troubling riddles.

Milet is speaking, first of all, about paints. The most elementary rationale for the conversation is the apparently ongoing project of painting the sitting room and the fact that Milet is not particularly happy with the long time it is taking. But as we regard it we see that the sitting room is clean and airy and does not seem in need of paint—except that its current state indicates a painting job is already underway and must therefore, for closure, be continued and terminated. The furniture, draped in white sheets, reminds us unavoidably of the priest himself, albed in the vestibule, in the scene that immediately preceded this. He, too, looked clean and welcoming, yet he was draped for a reconstitution. The dissolve in that scene made his white alb literally dissolve before our eyes, suggesting a tactile yet evanescent surface that both intrigues and defines—the surface of the world.

Milet now liaises paint and smell, since it is the *smell of the paint* and not the paint itself that is irritating him. But he has read in an advertisement of odorless paints, and wonders if Logan has ever heard of them. Paint is, in its simplest essence, a cover-up, and Milet is asking, with a kind of prescience his wisdom and relative age make believable for us, about the relation between noxious moral problems and strategies for covering them up that are noxious in themselves. He has heard (from *ad-VER-tice-m'nts*) that there are ways of covering up that do not smell, but Logan has no experience of them. Since Logan is presently involved in a cover-up of sorts, albeit an institutionally sanctioned one, the conversation is directly and deeply meaningful (to him and to us). The seal of the confession has rendered odorless the protection Logan is now offering—of necessity—to a murderer, but this case and this odorlessness he is in no position to discuss, even with his superior. The conversation between the two priests is spiced by our awareness that Alma is present in the breakfast room, reminding Logan with every toneless gesture that her husband's life rests in his continuing silence. But my reading so far is only a flat and literary analysis, possible in large measure from study of only a script. The thrill of watching Hitchcock is experiencing his scenes, not just following the action as though it were nothing but caught routine. Experiencing this scene takes me into much headier climes.

Milet comes upon Logan just after Logan has interacted with his altar boy. The teams in the two scenes are paralleled, an older man affectionately addressing a younger one in each. As he leaves the altar boy, Logan reaches out and touches his shoulder. In exactly the same kind of fraternal and pedagogical tone, Milet is now reaching out to "touch" Logan. As a linguistic subject (something Hitchcock's characters frequently are), Milet establishes himself in two dimensions for us, quite swiftly. First, he is relatively expert in English pronunciation (though he does not flawlessly demonstrate this): *Ad-VER'-tice-m'nt*, for example, is an upper-class British usage. Secondly, he has no trouble forging a neat, syntactically correct English sentence, as opposed to the sort of charmingly awkward transliteration one has come to expect Francophones speaking English to use in Hollywood films: *I only ask because the smell makes one quite ill, really*. In Father Milet's natural French this would be, roughly, "Je pose la question seulement parce que l'odeur me donne vraiment mal au coeur." The adverb "really" is an appendix in English, but would be an interior pivot in French; and a man who had been raised in French and whose English was merely a dependent subtongue would have said, instead, "I ask only because really the smell makes one quite sick." Milet's English is capable of the same pristine (and stylish) expression, then, as Logan's. I take his line about the smell making him ill to have been worded as it is precisely to suggest that Milet is a man who can say precisely what he means to say. Now, after he asks in preparation about PAIN-*TING* this room, what we actually hear coming out of his mouth is this:

I read some advertisement about *pains*,

and then,

One finds it difficult to believe that there *are pains*, but no smell,

and finally,

Do you know of any *pains* that do not smell, Father Michael?

—three comments, each containing the word "paints" pronounced unmistakably as "pains."

Although I should like to disparage Father Milet's English pronunciation, and affirm that he is trying to say "paint" but cannot and must drop the final "t," I find myself obstructed in this plan by the knowledge, gained just previously—and thanks to Hitchcock's artful device of having him flawlessly use a British sentence construction—that Milet has no trouble at all speaking English. He is saying, then, exactly what we are hearing, and it is what he intends to say: pain. I suggest, then, not precisely that this conversation is about *pain*—too bold a thesis, surely—but that as much as it is about paint it is also about pain. Milet is old enough to be reading advertisements about pains. And he is astute enough a moral advisor to be wondering about paints that are inherently pains; cover-ups that are agonies in themselves.

The comment about it being hard to believe there are pains but no smell I take to mean that any pain of the sort Logan must now be experiencing—because it is evident he is in discomfort—is totally natural; natural, that is, subject to the kind of (smelly) putrefaction and development one could find with any other living process. Pain is organic. One need not fear, nor feel anxiety about, the derangement that comes with pain because pain normally brings derangement and the derangement—the smell—is in God's world, part of life. A still deeper reading suggests to me something about the character of that derangement, and thus about the nature of what brings it: pain is rank, because the word "smell" has a chthonic connotation the words "odor" and "scent" do not. Rankness is in God's universe, just as majesty is. It's impossible to believe, then, that Logan's pains, his secrecy and fidelity, are not avenues of corruption, or that corruption is foreign to the lives we lead on—and ultimately in—the earth.

But an alarming and fascinating reading emerges if I do not penetrate the surface of Milet's language at all, if instead of hunting for metaphor I take it to mean precisely *and only* what it states. *One finds it difficult to believe there are pains, but no smell.* One does not find it difficult to believe there is smell: smell is evident, smell is manifest (for "smell," read decay, growth, time). What is difficult to believe is pain. One's sense of one's own pain may be a complete misapprehension—what subjectivity may not?—and one's ability to be sure of pain in others can depend only on faith, not belief. Though we cannot trust in the appearance of the world, Milet is teaching his pupil, we must yet have faith that the world exists. Though it is difficult to accept the pain of others on face evidence, yet we must believe it if we are to sympathize. So he is addressing our ability to have certainty about the innermost of worlds in the face of layerings of camouflage, garbings of half-truth, albs and white skins and paints that can make things vanish and pains that can vanish. And of course, if the essence of the purest pain is faith, it is the metaphysical opposite of the essence of smell, which is perception and contact. Pain does not smell.

With his third comment, the question "Do you know of any pains that do not smell, Father Michael?" he puts Logan to the true test. Does Logan have the capacity to believe in what he cannot sense? But no, Logan does not yet know of pains that do not smell. The world that is beyond the senses—Susan Sontag wrote that understanding "starts from not accepting the world as it looks"[26]—is not yet accessible to him. He is coming to know, however. He is ready. This film is the story of his journey.

2. Covering Crime

If the sanctity of pain is the opening gambit in the painting sequence, the closing gambit is the relationship between Church and state.

We watch from deep inside the priests' salon at the rectory (looking outward toward the door as any meditating priest might, of a quiet evening) as Father Milet sits in deep conversation with Detective Murphy. He admits he is unaware of where Logan was on Tuesday night, or what he may have done, yet he is "perfectly sure it's all right." As Logan now makes his entrance (through the door that has been opened for him by none other than Keller), Milet speaks to him across Murphy's intentful gaze: "I believe this room has given this gentleman from the police department the idea that we hide grime with paint." On the last four words, we are in close shot on Logan's peaceful, interested face. "But it is not so, Mr. Murphy," continues Milet, "We have made certain that the walls underneath are spotless."

Milet is sitting on the sofa that was draped in a white sheet when first we saw it; now it is dark, just as Logan was dark under his white alb. The choice of the word "spotless" cues us to the centrality of the Immaculate. Milet is suggesting openly that under its façade, which is applied by human hands, the world made by God is Immaculate, spotless. He does not say they have cleaned the walls, but that they have made certain the walls are spotless. This firm postulation of the potential inner purity of the world is what mobilizes and underpins our sorrow for Keller at the conclusion of the film, even as what scant sympathy we may find in ourselves for Villette is, at least potentially, mobilized by his journey to the gallery of the Assembly to implore Ruth Grandfort for her husband's help with his mundane tax problems (photographed as a scene of amorous courting on a balcony). Both Villette and Keller are in private distress. But the mechanisms of the state are unconcerned with the inner world of faith, fragility, and fidelity. The state enacts laws, which reference and mandate strict windows of action and applications of judgment; and which rigorously subject their violation to a jurisprudence that weighs, dramatizes, dispenses, allocates, apportions, reduces, contains, and defines. Larrue and Murphy are agents of this process. The state's function is to locate and bound action as "crime," and to render it—indeed, bake it thoroughly—in light of law. The function of the Church is to keep purity from the harmful radiation of this light; to create and preserve sanctifying darkness. Milet recognizes, however, that there exists a conflict between the Church and the state for power in Québec, that the inner world sanctified by the Church is a domain regarded by the state as covered, and therefore, discoverable. The Church and the state working at cross-purposes, what the former covers over for its own best reasons the latter must strive to bring to light. If we listen very carefully to Milet, we will hear that what he actually says to Murphy is exactly this: "This room has given this gentleman from the police department the idea that we hide *crime* with paint." Crime, not grime. Paint, not pain. Crime, after all, is whatever does not meet the eye, whatever one must dig for—from the policeman's point of view.

The police, as Father Milet casts them, expect to find the church covering crime. Or: the police take the view that what it is that the church covers is not just the unseen world, but the criminal one. The police, then, for Milet, aim to bring the inner world into the rigorous institutional light of justice, to turn private distress into public nuisance. With this in mind, we can look again at the silent ballet of brief tableaux in which agents of the police confront priests in their rectories, on the streets, at the police department, searching for Logan. Again and again in a little filmic dance we find profound and meticulous respect among the police for the ostensible power of the clergy to hide crime with paint. The scenes all show policemen confronting clergymen, and preparing to "strip" them of their "protections."

The third and central paint scene—indeed, it strikes me as one of the central scenes of the film—needs a very close analysis to reveal its richness. It is wedged nicely between the breakfast room "smell of pain" conversation and the sitting room hint of "covering crime." Keller has been questioned by Larrue at Villette's house, has "dutifully" finished his gardening there, and is returning to the rectory. He makes his way to the hallway outside the sitting room, where he hears Logan in conversation with Milet: Milet would have preferred an old-fashioned white, but an old-fashioned white, according to Logan, is exactly what this is; or at least what it is supposed to be. Milet notices Keller, and we take up Keller's point of view looking into the sitting room. . . .

JACOB'S LADDER

All men constitute one humanity by nature.

> Laberthonnière, *Études de philosophie cartésienne et premiers écrits philosophiques*

Here begins a glorious play-within-a-play that reasserts, within a "set" being "finished" by an "actor" who is one of its characters, all the essential themes of the film in which it is contained. Logan (backstage of his priesthood, in his casual clothes) is atop a ladder, painting with concentration, and we are looking down at the room from a point very near his position.

KELLER: Good morning, Father.

MILET: You're back early, aren't you? Is Mr. Villette's garden flourishing?

KELLER: Mr. Villette is dead, Father.

MILET (*Uncomprehending*): Dead?

KELLER: He was murdered, Father.

MILET: M——— Did you hear that, Father Logan? How dreadful!

KELLER: I discovered the body! I called the police. Then they came and asked me a lot of questions. Lots of people were outside the house. Then the inspector told me: I could leave.

MILET: What a terrible thing! A *very* terrible thing! (*He walks out.*)

KELLER (*Urgently, to Logan*): Father? Why did you come to Villette's house this morning? Father . . . I must *speak* to you! I *know* what you must think of me . . . But I *can't* give myself up, I CAN'T! THEY WOULD *HANG* ME! Hasn't God forgiven me, thanks to you? But the police never would.

LOGAN (*A little coldly*): I don't know what you're talking about.

KELLER (*Climbing up to get nearer to him*): But it was *I* who confessed to you! It was *my* confession! I want you to *speak* to me about it! (*Logan stops, turns, looks at him.*) You must tell me what to do! . . . I can't give myself up . . . You must tell me some other way . . .

LOGAN (*Gesturing helplessly*): There . . . there *is* nothing I can add to what I've already said.

KELLER (*Imploring, his German accent extreme*): Aren't you human? Haven't you ever been afraid? You are so cold! (*Snidely:*) It's easy for you to be good. (*He reaches with his left hand to touch Logan's arm.*) Have you no pity for me?

ANNA (*Off-camera, approaching*): Otto!

KELLER: Oh, Anna!

ANNA: Otto—Father Benoit asked earlier . . . would you please mend the tire on his bicycle? (*Conspiratorially she glances up at Logan, whose head is down.*)
KELLER (*Slowly he turns to look up at Logan*): But the . . . tire *wasn't* flat after all, Alma . . .
(*We can see Logan's eyes staring forward at the wall as he paints it. We can see Keller's and Alma's eyes nervously fixed on Logan. Dissolve.*)

No other filmmaker would have included such a scene; Hitchcock would never have done without it. As with everything else in the film, protagonists openly prate about one thing when they are clearly meaning to invoke another. And the issue at the innermost heart of the riddle is theatricality itself, the play of surface, our capacity to know from a view. Alma and her husband are playing out a charade about Father Benoit's bicycle and whether it needs repair, for example; but the very soul is in mortal danger, and the repairman on the ladder has no power to mend it.

What is both exquisite and extravagant about this scene is that not a word is said that informs the audience of anything it does not already know. Mr. Villette is dead, Father. He was murdered. I discovered the body. The police came and asked a lot of questions. I am the one who made the confession, Father; it was my confession. As information regarding the plot the scene is empty, exquisitely so. Yet what a world it shows the patient eye. We can consider the fact that because we are never made thoroughly familiar with the internal shape of this room, because Logan is up on a ladder; and because Keller is a nervous wreck, we are never quite certain who is looking at whom until the final shot, where Logan is expressly *not* looking at Keller. Often, Keller's gaze is directed off-camera and up at an angle, but we do not see its resting point. His look is generic and reflective, as in prayer. Is he, in fact, praying as he is preying?

We can sense the amazing transformation of Father Milet, early on a mentor who is paternal and instructive—certainly superior—to Logan but now, in the unanticipated presence of Keller, a consciousness reduced to a neutral, almost insentient, force. His sentiments about the murder are entirely appropriate, yet completely undramatic as played out.

The choreography around the ladder—which is, of course, Jacob's ladder (Logan has folded wings—*épaulettes*—on the shoulders of his work shirt [it was once part of his military uniform] as he stands atop it while beneath him the tragic Keller, morally unconscious, "sleeps")—is only slightly less deft than the cinematographic position from which, with hardly a nudge of the camera, we can see everything necessary as actors glide into and out of the shot. Logan moves in and out of the shot by raising or lowering his head, by dipping his paintbrush or holding it frozen in the air. Thus, for Logan, to load up with paint is to vanish and reappear—a superhuman gesture. Keller is trying to climb up, yet is deeply mortified in front of his wife to show that he desires proximity to the priest. And why, in the end, will Alma be angered to see him reaching for Logan? She is convinced, yes, that Logan is on the verge of spilling the beans and that any provocation may tip him to it, but why is ascent an attitude to shirk from, as Keller manifestly does when she enters the room? He believes she will want him to be clutching in this way at her, not at Logan, that his desperation for Logan will make her jealous. Then, there is something if not erotic at least erotophoric about the Keller-Logan connection. If, as Truffaut suggested, Hitchcock filmed his murders like love scenes, might not a scene like this, in which a murder is recollected in tranquillity to someone who has been implicated in it, be played like a tryst about a tryst? [27] Father Milet knows enough to leave the room, because something is going on he should not be party to. Yet it is not a confession, so he has no practical excuse until he can snatch at his mail. Throughout the scene, Logan is to Alma what the illicit lover is to the loyal wife: the competitor; the fantastic object; the enemy swathed in modesty.

Our final position as viewers here is within the wall itself, watching as we are painted: we see what no one else in the room can see, all three faces. Keller, fixated upon Logan in hopes that Logan will give a sign, cannot for a second turn to look at his wife lest he miss the brief moment of his salvation. Alma, afraid of what Logan will do if he knows that she knows—because her knowledge is both a sin and a crime and she has *not* confessed—cannot take her eyes from him to study her husband. And for his part, Logan dare not turn away from the wall—from us. He has no conversational pretext, for one thing. Turning would reveal to Alma that he has knowledge that transcends the surface of the conversation in the scene. But his own deep knowledge is sealed. And because he cannot talk to Keller outside confession about the matter confessed, he is in no position to reveal what he told or did not tell the police, what he does or does not remember, what he can or cannot believe.

It is a scene in which all of the talk can be only sociable surface paint to cover the wound, the crime, and the grime. But the director's relentless focus on this material surface, on the construction of attitudinal verisimilitude through mimic detail, is nothing other than a study of theater. As the husband-wife acting team perform daintily for Logan, he covertly attends to them—we can see this in the shadow that covers his eyes. So if, for me, the screen is a stage, Logan is the onstage audience and the Kellers are on a stage-within-that-stage. The performance Alma and Otto are giving is one that is palpably easy for me to see through—all plays-within-a-play are patently constructed like this—and the tinnier the Kellers seem, the more securely Logan's presence as their captive audience is solidified and reified.[28] The play-within-the-play is Keller's domain: he is its "star" to the degree that he clings to a hope of using it as a gateway for escaping punishment and covering his crime in a masquerade, and Logan is the linchpin upon which this hope is fastened. We must believe in the actuality of Logan, and of his moral view, if we are to see Keller prostrate before it; and the more that prostration is caricatured, while Logan looks on, the realer Logan seems, looking. Viewers are certainly capable of detecting Keller's abject and self-serving fakery, his hypocrisy, his cardboard thinness. And if here the inner stage he plays on is an invisible, conceptual one, later, in the climactic scene of the film at the Château Frontenac, the fleeing Keller is in a ballroom that has a real stage, a stage he is at that point no longer equipped even to mount, let alone strut upon. First he tries to cling to its apron, then finally he steps away and is shot as soon as he leaves its margins.

To the extent that the Kellers seem to have little in them but surface life (we can note the repeated exaggeration of perspiration and reflectivity in the photography of Keller's face, or the pallidity of Alma's), Logan's existence, relative to theirs, is pure depth. To the extent that the Kellers are civil, mannered, grammatical, bureaucratic, hierarchical, mechanistic, opportunistic, and grimy Logan is spiritual, awkward, poetic, passionate, communal, organic, unaggressive, and disturbingly clean. Under his army shirt, he wears (antique) white. If we have wondered how, in the beginning of beginnings, he could have met Ruth Grandfort, we may now come to realize, watching his restraint, his peace, and his fervor, that when she walked out of her apartment into the dazzling sunshine, when she swept down the vortex of stairs in her snowy gown, he had always been waiting for her.

OUT OF THE DEPTHS

The ladder scene is also interesting because its graphic construction so finely symbolizes the architecture of the film as a whole. Here we mount to the apex of meaning and evocation, even floating for desperate, dominant moments over Logan's head. And Keller, far beneath our moral aerie, snatching at space to be near us, is in our judgmental power.

That Hitchcock should have centered his film with so expressive, so intensely visual a pantomime—emphasizing the structuring and molding power of the lens, the camera's position, and the camera's movement and participation—is not surprising, and in fact there is no American film in which he failed to create a mise-en-scène of this type, voluminously revealing, while appearing only to decorate, the central plot. To give only a few of many possible examples: the scene in Rebecca de Winter's bedroom in *Rebecca*, similarly not a central requirement of the "official" plot, is similarly informing about the texture and structure of the new Mrs. de Winter's fear—this due largely to Hitchcock's placement of action in social space. In *Rope* we have the provocative conversation about the theater from Mr. Kentley's aged sister. We can cite the long and involved dinner party in *The Man Who Knew Too Much*; the dinner table conversations in *Frenzy*; the general store art sale in *The Trouble with Harry*; the coroner's inquest in *Vertigo*, which gives the viewer not a jot of information he does not already have, except that Scottie Ferguson is not found guilty of a non-crime in which there can, in fact, be no guilt. In every one of these scenes, and in many more, there is something absolutely vital to the deeper considerations of the Hitchcockian story and yet uninformative as regards the surface "plot."

What is perhaps most central of all in *I Confess*, as we can learn from watching ourselves watching Michael Logan paint, is verticality. In this film Otto Keller is very low, almost bestial. Logan is very high. We are still higher (and must be, to have an estimation of Logan). Ruth Grandfort is at an incalculable distance from the ground, seeming to float untouchably. Grandfort himself is a statue upon a plinth. Larrue is falling.

Altars are elevated, and the worship in which we fix them frames a verticality of regard. Québec City is a vertical territory, the perfect one to ground Hitchcock's modeling of the vertical play of the moral gaze. Very little, ultimately, is not vertical in this film—as profound and sociologically precise a cinematic portrait of Canada as I know.[29] This is a society built on status and privilege, not ethnocultural affiliations and pioneers' dreams. And so *I Confess* begins with our view of the towering Château Frontenac Hotel, built in 1892 by architect Bruce Price[30] (and at the turn of the century the showpiece of the Canadian Pacific chain), looming upon the heights of Dufferin Terrace over the glimmering St. Lawrence River.[31] We pass to a low-mounted, upward-directed, wide-angle shot of some of the gables of this hotel, and then immediately plunge to the lower city, *la vieille ville*, today—tidied and gentrified—a substantial tourist attraction but in the early 1950s an undeveloped and distinctly impoverished section of town. Here, close to the port, lay the dank narrow streets and stone buildings calling up the centuries of French settlement that followed Jacques Cartier's scurvy winter in 1535, his ships frozen offshore with four fingers' breadth of ice above and below decks.[32] Directly below the Château, our gaze ascends a steep flight of steps. From 1879 until October 12, 1996—when at 3:50 in the afternoon the device was damaged in a crash—this was the location of William Griffith's funicular car.[33] As we look upward, with the clouds scudding in the sky at the top of the screen, we see, walking briskly from right to left along Dufferin Terrace at the top of this "stairway to heaven," Hitch himself. It is the upper town he celebrates with his presence, and we look up at him to see this. The upper town is the seat of the legislature, which at this time was controlled by Duplessis's Union Nationale. One of his members would surely have been Pierre Grandfort, arguing that increasing the pay of female schoolteachers would absolutely *not* imperil the entire economy—an anticlerical sentiment if ever there was one since the Church was no leader in advancing equality for women. To be sure, Duplessis was a staunch enemy of the Church by this time. The villain Villette's house is in the lower city, the quartier du Petit-Champlain, like the ferry to Lévis where Father Logan and Ruth Grandfort secretly meet. Our descent is a kind of visual echo of the melodic pattern of Dimitri Tiomkin's haunting theme. But the police department, the court, the house of the Grandforts, the church of Sainte Marie where Logan works—all of these are "up" and "looked up to." Duplessis, who had entered combat with the Church, himself resided in a suite at the Château Frontenac,[34] where it is told he spent his bachelor evenings in celibate enjoyment of recorded music and his favorite television programs—just the sort of distractions we may imagine are fetching his attentions as Keller is being shot downstairs in a mezzanine ballroom. "Le Celibataire," people called him.

As Duplessis—who was simultaneously premier and attorney-general—looked down on the Québec he controlled from his chambers in the hotel in real life, we look down in this film: at Keller the abysmal abuser of the church, at Grandfort the cuckold in the Assembly, at Villette knocked to the ground on the morning after the rainstorm. Or, in a romantic trance, we look up: at the gables of the old city, at the altar of the church, at Ruth sweeping down her *casse-queue*. Verticality is embedded subtly in the structure throughout: in the Assembly, Villette approaches Ruth in the upper gallery, threatening to make her husband's career fall. Robertson the parvenu balances a water glass on his head, playfully looking up through it at Ruth's party. Logan comes down off the altar to meet Keller for the confession, after having come down to the church from his upper-level room when he sees Keller coming in late at night. After his trial, Logan goes out of the court and down into the street, where he points his eyes upward. There is the obvious vertical play of the wall-painting scene, and the many variations on vertical play that are obtained by the use of tall actors in the company of shorter ones: Karl Malden and Brian Aherne loom over the two little girls who witnessed at the murder scene; Father Milet is looking up at a towering Murphy when he makes his comment about the paint job hiding g(c)rime.

The extremities of the vertical axis represent not only Anglo- and Francophone Québec—the upper and lower *villes*—but the secular and religious moral systems espoused in and symbolized by each. The intensely Catholic belief that an inner world of truth and goodness supercedes a superficial skin of deceptive appearance and scintillating reflection reflects lower Québec: the world of the river, the alleyways, the peaceful and profound tranquillity of the innocent countryside where love is consummated in the rain. From the point of view that privileges inner verity, the world's appearance is an antic disposition laid on. On the other hand, the Anglophone power base of modern French Canadian society calls for carefully structured marketing; relentless upkeep of appearances; good impression management; and successful bureaucratic role-play, all regardless of deeper feelings or histories. The priestly class seems to be wise and earthy, simplistic, old-fashioned, while the bureaucracy is transparent and heartless: witness Robertson's scathingly rude performance to Ruth as he interrogates her in his public capacity about what he is quite willing to tolerate in private. The questioning is a brutality performed by an arrogant member of the Anglo power structure upon a Francophone woman who has allied herself with the English but who lacks the cachet of being able to claim she is English by birth.[35]

It would seem that because for Hitchcock the purity of belief is better than the sham of situated duty, the audience is given an opportunity to choose Michael Logan over Ruth Grandfort when, on the ferry, she attempts to seduce him; and, ultimately, to sympathize with the deeper needs of Alma and Otto Keller instead of being concerned with what seem the more superficial needs of the Grandforts. This is a moral view achieved by the viewing audience, not supplied to them. For most of the film, indeed, the audience is placed "low," aspiring upward, instead of resting upon a moral promontory. We are brought into the film upon the river, and allowed to retreat upon the river when the film is done. If the Château Frontenac is a dramatic object of interest, nevertheless we see it from below, from the clerical depths, never taking to ourselves the high positions reserved for secular government.

However, because this story is cinematic, because Hitchcock is not a preacher or a writer but a filmmaker, the issue of representation and the simulacrum can hardly be left far from our hearts. He was to filmmaking, indeed, what Henry James was to the novel, the artist whose mastery was complete and who knew of his audience that as much as they might wish to believe in a comforting moral dimension they could not see, in film they were still—and always—pinioned to sight. Therefore, in film morality must be lit. All of our firmest belief must be kindled by nothing more than appearances, however superficial and secular. Appearances must ultimately connect with—and then sway—us. Appearances must rule.

So it is that this voyage we have taken, first with Otto Keller and then in spite of him, then apart from him, then against him, then in loathing of him, then in anguish for him, and finally with him again—this voyage has been only a sighting. It is a vision of him that we must live with—creeping down the moist dark cobbled street; gobbling Michael Logan with his eyes before confessing to him; seducing Alma in a snakish whisper; coyly striding off to work in Villette's garden; obsequiously kowtowing to Larrue; straining out of his skin to climb that ladder—not his words as he asks, "Aren't you human? Haven't you ever been afraid?" or as he marvels, "You are so cold!—It's easy for you to be good." Whatever he says and however he says it, we see the beads of sweat popping out of his brow, his cupidinous mouth, his desperation. We are locked in a visual interpretation of a moral world. And it is a dramatization of life that we are given to read, not life: the stench of life, not the pain; the act, not the feeling; the secular expression, not the confession of faith; the bureaucratic mime, not the priestly agony. Hitchcock has filmed the priesthood, which is to say, he has compelled an exposition of a moral universe that, in his hands, is entirely visible. Even the invisible is visibly invisible. Such depiction is possible because, although words must rest flat upon a page, a camera can look down. We can look down upon Keller, as Logan does at the beginning of the film, and also look down upon this looking down. Upon Logan himself we may look down, as Ruth did when she saw him waiting for her in the street. Looking down, we may also look in. There in the depths, at any rate, deeper than did ever plummet sound, we may drown our book.

What can we accomplish by saying, "I confess . . ."? I think it likely that because he gives us the tale, the director is indeed, in a manner of speaking, confessing. His confession is everything that we can see by virtue of the characters "confessing," the entirety of the film: its angles and luminosities, its metaphors and games, its parallels and oddities of speech, its religiosities and crimes. It is Hitchcock's testament as a filmmaker, coming at a time in his life when he would commit himself in a new way to the belief in filmmaking. For a filmmaker to make the confession of a film is, of course, to look—to look well—and in a Hitchcock film looking is the ineffable act, the testament of the director himself and, indeed, the testimony he finally demands of his viewing audience. If, as Paul Giles has suggested, "in Hitchcock, cinematic events exist in two realms simultaneously: on the immediate surface of the world, but also within a realm of 'divine' truth, or demonic evil," [36] this "divine" realm is the screen, to which by 1953 he had devoted himself with a new energy and vision. Now the cinema is Hitchcock's cathedral; the screen his altar; the editing room his sacristy, the cutter's guillotine his crucifix. And the actor is his altar boy. It is no inconsequent accident, then, that in this film Montgomery Clift not only confabulates with an altar boy but looks like one himself.

Very soon, Hitchcock would make *Rear Window*, a treatise on stages and staging, viewfinding and viewers, the enchanting impotence of sight. The world itself would be the confessional box, the man with the lens the silent, helpless priest.

Gabriel's Horn:

Vertigo and the Golden Passage

Ah, but only one is a wanderer. Two, together, are always going somewhere.

FIRMAMENT

The Fall is into Division; and the Resurrection is to Unity.
Norman O. Brown, Love's Body

Begin with division. The screen, a pallid and blurry field, is bisected by a clearly defined, darker, horizontal bar. The field's tonality is of crepuscule, but then again, of meteorites; its indeterminacy suggests Nature in flux, the ether. But the dividing bar is purposeful and metallic, dully glowing, sharply and technically defined, a social product. The field may be nullity and empti-ness, the nothing out of which nothing will come.[1] Dramaturgically, it is the waiting stage. The bar is a first entity, an essential substance that we come to see, in both filmic and cosmological terms, after the birth of light,[2] its exis-tence prompting and revealing the first division. Matter comes straight upon light, and the First Matter is nothing but the firmament, the splitting and bounding intrusion that makes up "up" and down "down," that splits the ris-ing heaven and sinking earth. It is the rigidity that establishes dimension and consistency and duration, that permits navigation and narration, that implies a constructed world. Also: the portentous radiant gravity of the bar, the en-

veloping milky matrix of the field—all of this is in shades of gray, in the relative abundance and scarcity of light. There is no movement and therefore no setting. There is no color and no moment. This is how the first shot of *Vertigo* begins.[3]

Under this vision is a vibrato of non-diegetic music, rising above and falling below a ground line in simulation of the path of a sine wave: ~. The music, indeed, is not only non-diegetic but *absolutely* non-diegetic, a pretext for this or any other story, and cannot be otherwise, since if there is yet no invocation of action or of humanity to produce action, still even without action there is the happenstance of potency. Because of the potency, we are riveted in the business of distinction, making the separation between the figure and the ground, trying to understand how the simple geometric bar can have meaning, and thus placing ourselves hungrily in relation to the extreme abstractness of this view. Then, swiftly and without warning, from beneath, and fully laden with living color, a hand invades the scene, touching, grasping, possessing—getting a grip on—the horizontal bar and naming it in a flash as a rung of a ladder.

Two initial elements, then, juxtaposed and conflated: flesh and the climb.

This is still the first shot. The hand is extremely large in frame, and so we understand that we are in extreme close shot. Of Hitchcock's theology we learn: that in this territory both primordial and biblical man rises from below, aspiring to (and struggling for) height; and that human experience—indeed the human body experiencing—is the source of color. We may examine this film—all of Hitchcock's color films—in depth without finding artificial or mechanical color, the color of Jacques Tati, Vincente Minnelli, or Douglas Sirk.[4] The hand both strong and desperate suggests at once—since we need direction—concerns both heroic and problematic.

Now a second hand joins the first. We see a man pulling himself upward, and begin a backward move that opens a greater field of vision to our awareness. We are on a rooftop;[5] a city is below and in the distance (therefore prior). The man who now appears at the top of the ladder climbs over the parapet where the ladder is fastened and runs past us off-camera, panicked and swarthy in a pleasant cream-white shirt and beige trousers. He is clearly fleeing, not approaching—a reading carefully prepared by the director, since filmic motion does not directly imply a vector: this could be approach or avoidance;[6] the urgent force of that first grip on the rung, the thrusting action of the man as he hauls himself up, the way he turns his head a little—not quite taking the leisure of looking behind him, yet nervous to look behind— all suggest flight. The fugitive, by the way, is vaguely Mediterranean, calling up memories of Louis Bernard racing through the Marrakech marketplace for his life in *The Man Who Knew Too Much*.

But the novel that sired *Vertigo* itself concludes in Marseilles, in fact with a criminal. So this first shot begins where *D'entre les morts* ends, with the issue of flight and capture and the setting of the cosmopolitan, secret city. We are in medium shot, with plenty of perspective and a matching capacity for estimation. The attitude of the runner has already suggested he is pursued, so one is not surprised when a uniformed policeman, armed, rises from the ladder in the man's wake. The surprise is that before this shot—still the first in the film—ends, a third man appears in the policeman's wake, slimmer, wearing a dark brown suit and fedora: even the hunter is hunted. This man's eyes are white with avidity. We manage to recognize James Stewart, but swiftly the shot is gone. This third man presents a double suggestion: that the pursuing cop is himself chased after, just as the swarthy man is chased by the cop; and also that if the fugitive is running *from* and this third man is clearly running *to*, the cop, intermediate and also indeterminate between them,[7] is both running from *and* running to; going nowhere. We may discover soon that, existentially and cosmologically, all these presentiments, carefully established by this initial mise-en-scène, echo shockingly in the turn of events.[8]

But as those hands come upon the rungs and we gain our wider view, how precisely is it that we retreat?

GOODBYE, DOLLY

The thing that interests me most of all is a change of perspective within a shot.

    Hitchcock, to Jean Domarchi and Jean Douchet (1959; my translation)

There is no filmic element more vital to Hitchcock's work than choreography, and his camera was one of his dancers.[9] Our movement backward in this first shot could have been accomplished, assuming that a single-minded, fluid continuity of movement was desirable, through a *reverse dolly*—like the celebrated one in *Frenzy*, which backs us down a flight of stairs, out of a building, and across a street—or through a *reverse zoom*. Although in general Hitchcock eschewed the zoom lens, focusing his use of it on the most demanding aesthetic problems, this shot is in fact a zoom-out, as is evident in its rapidity and in the maintenance of pictorial perspective from the close to the wide aspects of the shot. It is not the only reverse zoom in *Vertigo*.

The reverse zoom differs from the backward dolly in three significant ways. First, through the careful manipulation of focus and the use of focal ring extensions, it is possible to produce a fluid zoom that occurs rapidly, more rapidly than a dolly (shifting as it does from one end of the focal space to the other in, say, less than a second). Thus, our movement from the proximate to the distant position in a reverse zoom shot can be with stunning speed, to such an extent that we are left unable to detect the movement as being outside of, or distinct from, our very impulse to produce it. In this case, for example: the blurriness and indiscreteness of the opening position causes us to desire more focus, to want to move back; but the fixed theater seat (a feature of the economic arrangement whereby audiences are made accessible to film producers) makes such a relieving retreat impossible. Instantly, then, we are placed in a potentially conflicted and dependent position with respect to the filmmaker, who is now in a position either to gratify or to frustrate a desire he has forced us to have. (Hitchcock is generally gratifying.) Even our fleeting awareness of the *desire to move back* is itself disengaging from the business of the screen. To the extent that a camera's backward movement is produced through a mechanism that is methodical, even laborious, and thus noticeable, the viewer is put to work knowingly collaborating in activity that produces his own satisfaction. In this way, the bounty of the satisfaction is reduced by the extent of the demand for focused consciousness implicit in the method of the move. The zoom, on the other hand, being almost instantaneous, makes possible a very tight affiliation between the viewer's impulse to back away and its resolution, and so it produces for that viewer a sense—apparently emanating from the screen but in truth resolved upon it—of actuality. In a shot like this one, the zoom-out has greater actuality and gives greater pleasure than the reverse dolly. As I watch, I affiliate so much with the camera that I become it. The camera becomes me.

The second element of zooming that differentiates it from dollying I have already mentioned: the maintenance of pictorial perspective between the long and short focal length positions at the extremities of the shot. By contrast, a rather elegant use of a reverse dolly, coupled with a pan, appears a little later, as Scottie Ferguson (James Stewart) is shown drinking at the bar in Ernie's and we pull back from him and move our eyes across the dining area to discover, at the same time he does, Madeleine and Gavin Elster (Kim Novak, Tom Helmore) at a table near the back. With that shot, the change in perspective produces a minute sensation of disorientation for the viewer, leading to a continuous, if modest, struggle to establish location and navigational power. Lost for a moment, then, and trying to find ourselves in order to remount the narrative, and then finding ourselves and remounting it, we experience a delicate secondary flurry of emotion—a thrill of achievement—that can accentuate the narrative moment. Every dolly incorporates for the viewer a thrill of some magnitude, since every dolly is displacing and confounding to some degree. In the case of this shot at Ernie's, the thrill takes the effect of a gradual appreciation of detail, beginning with the diners and moving to their clothing, the scarlet-flocked wallpapers, the modulated softness of gestures as people sumptuously eat, and the repetition of nuance in the women's gowns around the room, and then climaxing in Gavin and Madeleine in repose at their table: as we see all this we are more and more secure in our placement, and therefore happier and happier, and Madeleine comes into focus at the peak of our *jouissance*. Here on the roof, however, this first shot of the film is complex and suffers the indelicacy of having been prepared by nothing else. Therefore the viewer's stability of orientation is a critical reserve, to be guarded and not squandered. Using the reverse zoom allows for movement without any flurry of positional reestablishment in our emotions, a reestablishment that, here and now, could be ruinous. The zoom-out is therefore more parsimonious than the reverse dolly.

For me at present, however, the most important aspect of the reverse zoom is something else. On a number of emotional and intellectual levels, as I hope I have shown in these essays, we are informed deeply and complexly by the structure of Hitchcock's screen. It happens that a fact that subtly comes to my attention in the reverse zoom, and that I am left free to consider as the film develops, is this: the "camera"—a leading protagonist for me—not only knew where I would want to be at the end of this shot and quickly moved to put me there *but in fact was there already*. Technically: what as a viewer I casually think of as the "camera," the agency by means of which film is produced that I can watch in a particular way and to a particular end, is in this particular instance not a camera at all but a lens mounted on a camera; the motion I detect is a trick of light produced through a certain usage of a certain lens, not through actual movement of the camera at all. Further, the camera is not a servant. Its body is not pulled back during the shot as a response to my imperious need, but was pulled back long before I arrived in readiness for a state of anticipation and desire. The long lens (close-up) distortion of the first part of the zoom (the reduction of focal planes, the resultant loss of depth of field) tricks my perception and suggests to me that I am (that the camera—my loving factotum Hitchcock's obedient factotum—is) near the subject of the shot, when I am not.

More: since, in effect, I am the camera, it is I who have been withdrawn. Though I am convinced I am seeing from up close, the truth of the reverse zoom is that I am seeing—innocently—from a distance. My distance from the subject matter of the shot, and therefore, perhaps, from the subject matter of the film, is not what I think it is. The vertiginous pleasure of the shot lies in a discovery—my discovery, during the zoom-out—that I am not where I thought I was (upon a precipice), but instead resting at a remove, a remove entirely uncalculated because entirely undreamt of. That I might be led to think myself waiting upon a precipice when in truth I am grounded is chilling. With Gloucester, I may ask, "But have I fall'n or no?"[10] How much more chilling is the opposite, also possible if such deceptions can be carried off at my expense: that I might really be lingering at a narrative height while thinking myself safely grounded!

The zoom-out reveals the potential of the camera bearing the potent lens to be elsewhere than where we imagine it; indeed, to have taken placement prior to our knowledge of its existence; to have prepared for us in advance of our experience of needing preparation. We can have the deeply troubling sense of there being more to heav'n and earth than is dreamt of in our philosophies.

A slightly more prosaic contemplation will flesh out this horror. While the very diffuse opening of the reverse zoom shot at the beginning of this film provides no statement of narrative and topographical position, yet suddenly, at its end, I discover that I am not just comfortably positioned, that is to say, perched to see the action as it develops, but also perched in a very specific place: upon the roof of a building overlooking a city that spreads out languidly beneath and at a distance. I am off the ground, though the initial presentation of space did not hint at this. So the reverse zoom makes it possible to focus the viewer, swiftly and without extraneous disorientation, upon the discovery that he is at a height—an eerie experience for a viewer who thought himself secure in a theater seat. To put this differently: all films suffer the problem of causing the audience to make an intellectual transition out of what Goffman calls "theatregoer" status to that of "onlooker"[11]—from being people in the world where theaters exist and tickets must be purchased for entering them to willing participant-observers in whatever dramatic fantasy is at hand. But in this case the transition is as shocking as it is fluid: not only did we unwittingly achieve elevation, of all conditions, but our need (and willingness) to be high was known before we felt it. We were elevated both before we knew it and before we knew we could know it; before thought and desire. Or: we are higher than we thought we were.

This is vertigo.

The vertigo that Scottie Ferguson "feels" in the picture is felt by us at the beginning, and consists not simply in occupying a height; nor in occupying a height while being afraid of heights; but in suddenly seeing that we are occupying a height we did not knowingly climb to. (It is so easy to forget, at the moment when Scottie is hanging in cold sweat from the eavestrough after his companion has fallen to death, what an eager and focused shine of avidity and purpose was in his white eyes as he mounted to this roof and raced after his prey in this opening shot, oblivious to everything except his momentary purpose, free of even the memory of the ladder that brought him here.)

And occupation of height is narrative improbability, the beginning of a fall through a story.[12] Our elevation is related to powerlessness, not power, to the cognition that we can have been lifted, treed, shot up, and not to some skillful achievement of tactical advantage. Hitchcock is showing that no height is as frightening in itself as the knowledge that someone else can have known us without our knowledge, can have preestablished our physical conditions. The narrative specifically plays with this knowing manipulation of the unknowing: Gavin Elster, after all, sets up the climb to the top of the tower in San Juan

Bautista. The fugitive whose hands we first see, and who has led the police to the rooftop at the beginning of the film, sets up Scottie's precarious positioning at the rain gutter. An important aspect of vertigo is our emotional response to a situation that is propelled outside our control. As watchers, we experience what Roger Caillois called *une sorte de panique voluptueuse*,[13] seeing displayed before us a world the outplaying of which we are impotent to direct, as we were impotent to produce it and our own current involvement.

In the ninth shot of the film, trumpets blaring dissonantly, I peer straight downward with Scottie into the street over which he hangs from that rain gutter. As I establish my orientation, a reverse zoom suggests that even here, clearly above the ground, I am in fact higher than I thought because suddenly the ground drops away. Here, by the way, I am lifted out of Scottie in a narrative division (that reflects the division suggested in the first shot) so that I may look down not only upon the street but also upon him looking down upon the street. Adjustment is made impossible for me by a swift cut to Scottie's reaction (a substitution for my own inaction) that is now quite extreme, his eyebrows arching in a panicky rictus and his cheeks twitching uncontrollably as he closes his eyes to escape the sight.[14]

In our feeling of vulnerability (produced through the reverse zoom in this shot and originating in our discovery that we are further from the ground than we thought) is an anticipation of the moment of Scottie Ferguson's introduction to the action of the story in the next sequence (a year later in diegetic time). Using her step stool, he is attempting to demonstrate for his former girlfriend, Marjorie "Midge" Wood (Barbara Bel Geddes), that he has recuperated from the debilitating vertigo of the rooftop chase. His theory is that (contrary to the appraisal of a doctor Midge has been consulting on his behalf) he can overcome his debility "one step at a time." With each step upward, he repeats a little mantra: "I look up, I look down. . . ." But when he has reached the top he falters—having discovered that he is further from the ground than he thought he would be—and tumbles from the stool into Midge's arms. We are given opportunity to establish that Scottie is in control of his perception of vertical distance until this last step, because at each previous step he looks up and looks down successfully and we can see that the steps are evenly spaced. In that last step upward, however, there is an imperceptible essence, a spatial *geist* hidden in the rise, that brings him to a zone he cannot have anticipated and that is further than far, higher than high. In the ascension to it he moves through an experiential transition that is made palpable for us in an analogous reverse zoom.

In Midge's studio there is a fascinating planar analogue to this bizarre vertical discontinuity between the top two steps in the stepladder. Midge's walls, where they are not set with high windows looking out on Russian Hill from Telegraph Hill,[15] are painted yellow; and the step stool she fetches from the kitchenette and sets up near her working table is yellow, too. We can cover the breadth of cinematic space by establishing connections between similarly colored objects and planes. That the stool is the same color as the room could give it, and all the action that is organized around it, a harmonious and continuous relation with the other objects in the space and the action realized in terms of them: for example, the stepladder action could seem tightly integrated with the room design so that when Scottie climbed the steps we would have, on his behalf, the secure feeling he was moving through a space continuous with the cozy studio in which cheery Midge (in a yellow shirt) worked at her comforting bra ad (near some yellow flowers).[16] But the yellow of the walls does not match the yellow of the stepladder, or the pale chiffon yellow of Midge's shirt, or the platinum yellow of her hair. The walls are a dark and soothing mustard—art director Henry Bumstead mixed his yellow paint with gray[17]—but the step stool's naugahyde is a vivacious, alarming, cautionary lemon custard. Scottie will hardly fail to find alluring the surface of that top step he finally comes to stand on so vulnerably. And from that yellow spot, the view downward into the different yellow of the room will be discontinuous, unharmonious, provocative, challenging. In the sense that by its very nature the stepladder is blatant (I think we can take the nature of Hitchcockian objects to reside in their colors) while the space in which it is housed is relatively tranquil and retiring, we can say there is a break between the studio and the device, reflecting the discontinuity between the space and Scottie's climbing action. The color discontinuity is disarming. Indeed, in Scottie's culminating "vertiginous perspective" from the stepladder as he says, "I look up, I look down . . . ," the shot is tinted to leach out a full range of colors while retaining yellow (as though the experience of vertigo at this instant is intrinsically "yellowing") and to muddle the depth possible through color contrast as well as all other depths.

Generally, the use of lateral space in this scene prefigures the verticality that will come to be central to it. If the break in consciousness that Scottie experiences on that stepladder is a sudden one, we were prepared for discontinuity by his moving away from Midge's desk. He also does not warn her of what he is about to do. Until he has the stepladder we cannot discern the purpose of his motion—so action is severed, for a moment, from purpose. The fact of his coming upon the object so suddenly and its blazing, fresh, even audacious yellowness provide us already with a shock of excitement. But the suddenness is entirely in our experience; Scottie saw the whole space off-camera and the stepladder was in his thoughts and sight before it was in ours. So we are temporarily broken away from Scottie. The stepladder, put in place near the window, stands boldly, broken away from the harmonious integration of the visual space by its flamboyant—even outrageous—color.[18] The stool is to the room as the top step is to the other steps: at a remove further than far, higher than high.

Two more tiny preliminaries. Scottie's vertigo is manifested as a balance problem—we see him literally careen off the stepladder into Midge's arms. But technically, balance is an operation of the inner ear. As the scene fades, Midge is murmuring to him, "Oh Johnny, Johnny . . . !"—whispered words that plummet all the way down and all the way in as the screen fades to black. We have the feeling that hearing is central, perhaps not just to this encounter. Too, after this pietà—Scottie helpless in Midge's embrace—what is to happen next, the meeting with Gavin Elster, will set the action of the film in motion. To punctuate this moment, Hitchcock makes his cameo appearance.

SPRINGWORKS OF ATTACHMENT

Men in ships traveling at sea behave quite differently from automobilists. With watery depths below, sometimes as great as five miles, humanity is constantly reminded by many dramatic factors that it can fall into the sea at any moment and thence from the rough and hazardous water's surface into the multi-fathomed, lethally suffocating depths.

Buckminster Fuller, "Vertical Is to Live—Horizontal Is to Die"

But it would be an error to conclude that the vertigo in *Vertigo* is exclusively about physical height. The paradigmatic fall here, after all, is not the one experienced by the anonymous policeman (Fred Graham) at the beginning of the film but the one experienced by Judy Barton at the end. Intermediate between these two drops, in many ways, is the fall of Madeleine Elster at the end of the first act. The policeman has been amicable (he stops and comes back to help Scottie) but he is a dramaturgical cipher, a mere weight that can drop. To Judy and Madeleine, Scottie has become attached, or has tried to: I will have more to say about this directly. His attempt at attachment with the policeman—attachment, one might say, of a purely mechanical kind—was a complete failure. With Madeleine and Judy he fails again to connect, but with greater sentiment and for reasons that have less to do with his physical than with his philosophical position.

Flavières, the hero of *D'Entre les morts*, the Boileau-Narcejac novel purchased by Hitchcock as the basis for the screenplay here, is initially more reticent to assist his friend Gévigne by observing his wife, Madeleine, than is Scottie Ferguson to follow Gavin Elster's lead to follow his. But Scottie is a character in a film, subject entirely to the pressures of dramatic action. In text, we have the opportunity to experience stasis, hiatus, caesura; and so Flavières's commitment can develop more slowly. In the end, he comes to fall in love with Madeleine, quivering at the very thought of her in his quasi-inebriated trance of vulnerability and confusion.

With Scottie the attraction is more complicated still, and is reflected in our own response, since we see Madeleine through his narrative position exclusively. First we are swept away by her style and radiance (as she dines at Ernie's, stands from her table, moves past us). Then we skeptically follow her on that first day's assignment, finding her mysterious or at least oblique (as she shops for a bouquet at Podesta Baldocchi, visits the cemetery of the Mission Dolores, studies a painting at the Palace of the Legion of Honor, and stops at the McKittrick Hotel). Then we come to fear for her (when she drives to Fort Point and falls into San Francisco Bay). Then we are moved to tenderness (as she wakes innocently in Scottie's bed, lifting herself from his yellow blanket). Later, in the redwood forest, we are moved to philosophical meditation, existential trembling, and profound aesthetic sensitivity by her musing about life, time, and the cosmos. At Big Sur National Seashore we feel her desperation, and the tumult of passion sweeps over us as waves crash upon the rocks in pathetic fallacy. Soon after this—much too soon after this—at San Juan Bautista, we grope hopelessly for her when already she is swept onward toward her death. The point of the structure of the narrative so far is that both Scottie and the viewer are brought to a point where the attachment to Madeleine is broken before it is resolved. Wanting more of her, we forget that at the inception of the story we were hesitant to become engaged at all. Finally we go on a hunt, hoping to find her again. But whether we find her or do not, in fact, the hunt is a commitment to rebuilding her image and entrenching it in the territory of our consciousness.

To say that Scottie is hooked on Madeleine—or that we are—is to state a kind of truism in the catalogue of aesthetic reaction. She fascinates him; he loves her; he is attracted; he is stunned; he is transfixed: all of these estimations have in common the presumption that the viewer, settling his attention on an object, can be affected sympathetically by the action of that object.[19] And this sympathy is at the root of all aesthetic perception, all our experience of the cinema, to be sure. That as Scottie clings to the rain gutter desperately afraid to fall we share his fear and the precariousness of his suspense; that as Midge desperately prays her Mozart will bring Johnny back from the psychosis of his nightmare and stares helplessly and frustrated into his glazed face, we pray and stare with her; that as Madeleine tumbles into the waters of the Bay and Scottie throws himself in after her, we join him—all credit and substantiate our involvement with the dramatic action and our feeling of pleasurable attachment to the characters who strut and fret upon the stage before us. We are caught, in short, by dramatization.

The investment of our emotion in the action taken upon an object we see can lead us to cathartic engrossment, but it will never keep us in safety. For this reason, dramatic engrossment is itself vertiginous. William James wrote of our perception of reality that it invokes a vertiginous pleasure. All attraction is a form of love, and all love is a falling. Fixed upon someone, we plunge into a life, become trapped in the implications of a history and the tactics of a plan. If we ask why it should be, if this is the case, that Midge Wood, having fallen in love with Scottie and still feeling attached to him, should significantly fail to experience vertiginous symptoms in his presence, we may note, further examining the scenes in which we find her, that she is in fact cast by him into a flurry of emotional distraction, a nervous unsettlement, a pretense of mothering. While Scottie has no vehicles for carrying his vertigo, Midge does; she can displace her sensation of groundlessness into a set of romantic roles dictated and maintained by her culture: the distraught "female," the doting mother, the bitter ex-girlfriend abandoned for someone new. Empowered by the same culture that keeps Midge and other women subject to men, and therefore presumably in no need of structural help himself, Scottie is in fact without guideline and without assistance in his debility—a common problem for men: his vertigo overwhelms him, leaves him spinning. The spin is a side effect of his dominance.

Johnny/John-O/Scottie is sucked into the vortex of "Madeleine's existence" and we follow him in his passage downward somewhat in the way that finally accelerating toward the roof of the chapel at San Juan Bautista in his animated nightmare (designed for the screen by the artist John Ferren) he follows himself. In the above sentence I use ironic quotations marks— "Madeleine's existence"—because just as for us neither Scottie nor Madeleine actually exists (other than as characters in this filmic tale), his love-object does

not exist for Scottie other than as a character in a tale-within-our-tale—
but he doesn't know this, being innocent not only of his own existence as a character but also of his own proclivity to spectatorship: what we understand to
be a tale, he takes to be reality; and what we can see as his unwitting involvement, he thinks the spontaneity of his existence. The real vortex of our consideration is in the springworks of his attachment (and of our own), his
engagement with the fiction that absorbs him. Our pursuit is an adventure
of the eye.[20] I mean by this to suggest both that Hitchcock moves us
through a story in a passage that is relentlessly visual and that the relentlessly
visual movement is downward, although the downwardness is not always
apparent.[21]

It is worth examining some of the filmic treatments given Scottie's vertiginous fixation upon, and vertiginous pleasure with, Madeleine. Full-blown or
anticipatory vertigo, we will see, is not merely a condition experienced at the
top of a tower, on a roof, or on the top step of a ladder. Indeed, to see the real
vertigo in *Vertigo* we should attend less to what happens in the film than to
how the happenings are shown. I will consider seven aspects of verticality in
this film: the social class position of Gavin Elster, Scottie Ferguson's low status as an unattached male, San Francisco as the locus of a dropping narrative,
the verticality of Madeleine's "attempted suicide," the fall into Judy Barton's
performance experienced by Scottie and by us, the redwood forest and our
fall into the past there, and the fall of resemblance from surface characters to
actors underneath them.

Upward with Elster. The adventure of the tale-within-the-tale that is
the Carlotta plot begins in Gavin Elster's plush, scarlet leather-upholstered
office in the Mission District. The walls are richly laid with framed landscapes and riding prints. An immense model freighter reposes inside a wood
and glass case.[22] Through the windows we see cranes in operation[23] as Elster
discourses on his career in the shipping industry, his happening to have married into wealth. The content of his personal narrative notwithstanding,[24]
what the decor and mise-en-scène demonstrate directly is present bounty, position, the gravity of power, and social superiority. Elster is clearly conscious
of the (vertical) social distance between Scottie and himself,[25] and in this
scene is modulating his facial expression in a perceivable way to avoid slight-
ing Scottie. If Elster here is positioned above Scottie, in the previous conversation scene between Midge and Scottie in Midge's studio he was described
as an old school friend now having telephoned Scottie from a number in the

Mission District and thus probably having fallen upon bad times and residing in a relatively shabby section of town because he is "down and out." The shipping office scene is therefore a revelation to Scottie that Elster is "higher" than he thought, and that in bringing himself to alignment with Elster in the conspiracy to observe Madeleine he is climbing further off the "ground" of casual non-alignment than, just earlier, he expected he would be. Since Madeleine is associated with Elster, Scottie's excursion to eye her is, in effect, a climb the magnitude of which he has had no occasion to anticipate. Given that with his inadequate preparation for Elster and Elster's world Scottie carries himself with notable aplomb in the luxurious precincts of Elster's office, we may note that here, as with the yellow stepladder and in the opening rooftop scene, ascent itself is easy: his discomfort, indeed, is not with ascent itself, but with realizing too late where it leaves him standing. Using an abstracting and generalizing view here, of course, I am anticipating the precise statement Hitchcock makes at the conclusion of the film.

To venture even further with this thought: Hitchcock situates Madeleine Elster—and thus commences Scottie's hunt—near the "top of the Mark [Hopkins Hotel]," a San Francisco landmark and high point. Though he must have journeyed upward to find her, as Royal Brown put it, "orphically,"[26] he will have nowhere to go once she makes an appearance, but down. In fact, the action of the plot has here raised Scottie more than he expected to be raised, and he will be seeing not only Madeleine but also the world of the narrative from something of an unanticipated height. Vertiginousness is the basic experience of the narrative from his point of view within it.

A Loser. At Ernie's[27] we discover Scottie having an amicable drink at the bar. As he turns to survey the room, we dolly back from him and our vision glides across the plush space crowded with diners in formal attire. The walls are red, with damask wallpaper. There is very little color at the tables—the diners are in black tuxedoes and pallid dinner gowns. Non-diegetic romantic music, tender and hesitant, softly begins. (A woman crosses the camera, dressed in one of the gray suits Scottie will later reject at Ransohoff's.) But in the left distance the camera discovers a magnificent female creature in a flowing black gown garnished with a shawl-cape in black satin that is lined with brilliant turquoise! Madeleine allows Elster to pull back her chair, stands, and comes toward the bar. As we withdraw to a position very close to Scottie's eyes we see her glide before us and then stop, her face in perfect profile. As she proceeds off-right, the scene fades.

In this scene we can note both the presence and the distinct absence of elevation. It is absent in the sense that the entire movement is shot from the same camera height, roughly that of Scottie's shoulder in standing position. The movement is forward and back, and also lateral, but not vertical. Thus, regardless of the position Madeleine occupies in some vertical hierarchy as Elster's wife, for the duration of this introductory scene Scottie has come to be her equal. The technicality of his surveillance maneuver dissipates the social class distinction between them and, making them occupy a single vertical plane, opens to Scottie the distinct opportunity of relationship with her. That such a relationship develops and that it becomes spectacular can distract us from recalling that it was the physical design of this scene that made intimacy between Scottie and Madeleine imaginable. Scottie himself has no justification for presuming upon Madeleine's intimacies, except that a democratic sensibility may bring him to an egalitarianism of perspective; yet Elster, with his British accent, dominates and defines the situation in hierarchical terms, from a social pinnacle he is sharing with his well-born wife.

It is in a hidden hierarchy of need and satisfaction that verticality does come into play at Ernie's. In the previous two scenes, some pains have been taken by Hitchcock and his writers to establish Scottie as a single male. He is thus, in a particular sense, lonely by the time we find him sitting at Ernie's bar. His sexual and emotional isolation will receive some extensive comment later, as we are shown his awkwardness with Madeleine in his apartment, for example, or his petrified solitude in the hospital, or his clumsiness and anguish at the Empire Hotel. And his sexual isolation has been treated already in Midge's marginal maternalism and Elster's slightly charitable tendency to become familiar in his raconteurism.

But Elster, placed with Madeleine in the restaurant, is to Scottie's eyes everything Scottie is not, happy, married, well-off, socially engaged, and in control. He has a partner whose chair he can cavalierly withdraw, whose dinner bill he can cavalierly pay, whose elegant dress he can charge to his account. He is not drinking alone at the bar, preparing to occupy a table for one, or even committing himself to a demeaning course of surveillance in the service of another man wealthier than he. In the scale of social values wherein conventional bourgeois married life occupies a paramount position, a scale persistent in the background of this and the earlier scene, Scottie is a loser and Elster represents every kind of success. And it is the presence and behavior of Madeleine that places Elster and Scottie in these particular positions with respect to one another. As it will turn out, Elster has risen but little, if at all, above Scottie's social standing, and estimating him in this scene Scottie has already climbed (without knowing it).

Falling Along. Scottie begins his surveillance of Madeleine a little querulously, sighting her as she leaves her home at the Brocklebank Apartments, 1000 Mason Street, near The Mark Hopkins. She leads him on something of a goose chase, stopping first at the florist Podesta Baldocchi, 224 Grant Street, but entering by way of a back door situated in an alley;[28] and then visiting the cemetery of the Mission Dolores at Dolores and 16th; then sitting in Gallery 6 of the Palace of the Legion of Honor.[29] This is a route that would take a real voyager both down- and uphill, the florist being beneath the summit of Telegraph Hill where the journey begins but the Legion being itself on one of the high vantage points of the city. Indeed, Kraft and Leventhal note that Hitchcock cuts to "Scottie following Madeleine going west on 17th Street toward a steep hill. Although not the fastest route, the 17th Street hill is one of the most dramatic slopes in San Francisco."[30]

But as our passage is portrayed on the screen, all of the uphill portions have been excised, so that the journey is essentially a downhill one. When we consider that Scottie is ignorant of Madeleine's intended destinations one by one and that through insert shots of him as he drives we are positioned to experience the trip from his point of view, we see that the very unfolding of Madeleine's itinerary is itself a kind of tale-within-the-tale-within-the-tale, a sequential development of intentionality—an archetypical tale structure, indeed, our movement from the beginning through to the conclusion being nothing other than a fall: a story begins with potential (at a height) and drops inexorably to its conclusion. As we move onward, probability increases and so does gravity, that is, we have less potential for falling since we are closer to "ground." Scottie has been saddled with the mystery of Madeleine and Carlotta Valdes and, with the viewer as companion, he proceeds downward to get to the bottom of it.[31]

So it is that our fear of falling is coupled with a systematic, gentle, and inexorable passage down a diegetic hill. And the inner meaning of our vertigo is that we resist coming to the end of a tale. In this particular respect, Scottie hanging by his fingernails in the opening sequence represents any devoted viewer suspended between the beginning and end of a narrative. As the finale beckons, then becomes inevitable, the viewer defends against it with a love of the story (which is to say, a love of the pleasure of encountering the story) that makes him want to continue unchecked (possibly forever) as its recipient.

Scottie's later attempt to "rediscover" the dead Madeleine is also a ploy to bring back a story that finished too soon, to reenter the pleasure dome of a narrative too prematurely dissipated in the bitter press of mundane life.

All movement in this film is downward, toward the resolution that is the ultimate grounding. All procedure is a loss of potential. Even a character's ascension to a height—as with Scottie's position at the top of the stepladder or up in the Legion of Honor—is a narratological stepping down. What Scottie learns as he climbs the yellow steps at Midge's is that he is less invulnerable than he thought, that the end is near. At the top of the stepladder he knows the peril of tumbling. At the Palace of the Legion of Honor he is caught by the spiraling riddle of Carlotta Valdes's hair and her disorienting gaze (in the portrait) and led into a downward excursion that terminates in a grave, hers at first and then in a dream his own. *Vertigo* is Hitchcock's vertical play of the cinematic narrative against topography—that we fall through time, though we may mount towers to do so. If going up can be confounded with going down—if the way up and the way down are the same— the relation between the experiences is iconicized in the forward dolly/reverse zoom of the "vertigo shot" in which we seem to move in both directions at once.

Courbevoie. It is from the Seine at Courbevoie that Roger Flavières rescues the body of "Madeleine Gévigne" in the novel, in a scene that has little or no ostensible verticality. The waters are neither turbulent nor especially menacing in this "banlieu sans grâce," a suburb bordering the river on the west side of the Île de la Grande Jatte. "The quays," Roger muses, "were so much nicer in Paris! Was she trying to get away from the crowd? Did she have some need, for reflecting or for dreaming, to follow the passage of slower waters?"[32] Indeed, when he plunges in after her, it is only the forward groping of his hands that causes him the sensation of the river sifting through his fingers like grasses. And we may remember that as she walked toward her encounter with the river with him tailing behind, her eyes unceasingly fixed upon the water, she was very much the distracted figure of Seurat's famous *La Seine à Courbevoie, 1885* (although his figure is on the Grande Jatte): a *péniche* glides by on the mirror surface of the Seine and the tiled houses of Courbevoie are filled, perhaps, with silent watchers in the distance.

It is here—in the novel—that the detective first realizes the pleasure of his surveillance, that in a way he has been seduced and is himself the target of "quelque chose d'un peu grisant, d'un peu louche, qui l'obsédait"—"Something a little intoxicating, a little fishy, that obsessed him." When he has lifted her out of the water, he guides her across the road to a small bar where the patronne can minister to their needs. This one walks out of some back kitchen, carrying an infant in her arms:

"We had an accident," explained Flavières. "You wouldn't have any old clothes to give us, would you? It doesn't matter what—we're completely soaked."

He laughed nervously, to reassure her.

Suddenly the baby started crying. Its mother soothed it quiet.

"He's teething," she said.

"Just something to change into," Flavières insisted. "And then I'll call a taxi. I have to find my jacket . . . I left my wallet. . . . Could you give madame a glass of cognac—something strong!"

But when Flavières returns with his jacket and sees Madeleine in the borrowed clothing, he is in for a shock. The patronne had nothing to offer but a pair of overalls, and now "it was another Madeleine—not intimidating at all." The overalls presented to his eye are far too large, and stained with grease. The two women have a good laugh at his expense (that he should imagine masquerade as being beyond their sex), affronting his sensibilities so that his "joy goes to pieces" and his anger returns; he is ready to tell Gévigne to get somebody else to protect his wife.

The bucolic, even narcotic, tranquillity of this scene, its aura of rustic bonhomie, its topographic flatness—across the bridge to Courbevoie; along the border of the Seine; briefly to a café to write a letter, then tear it up; across the street; into the placid, gelid river; back to the café—and the relaxing comic relief provided by the teething child and the dungarees, are all systematically transformed by Hitchcock as he moves the scene to San Francisco Bay off Fort Point, directly adjacent to the San Francisco pylon of the Golden Gate Bridge. If the Boileau-Narcejac is a flat narrative, its motions lateral and navigational, the Hitchcock is a narrative in depth, a tumbling. We are prepared not by a leisurely stroll but by a visit to the Legion of Honor, a building on a very high vantage point. The close shot of the coil of hair on Carlotta Valdes's head in the painting is matched against Scottie's perspective of an identical coil on Madeleine's, and both coils are like golden whirlpools that suck at our attention and threaten to pull us under. Or like the flowers called golden trumpets, horns of Gabriel, leading into, even as they stick out toward, our consciousness. We are then subjected to further careful mobile tracking, as Scottie follows Madeleine's Jaguar in his DeSoto, moving through the Presidio and slightly downward toward water level. At Fort Point, Madeleine's long moment of standing by the water's edge both frames and exaggerates the abruptness of her disappearance off the pier. Her move downward, made eminently detectable in this way, is central to the film since it represents the occasion for Scottie's commitment to full engrossment in her activity. He is sucked *in* even as he follows her down into the waves. The Bay is turbulent, because we must see both the desperation of her circumstance and the passion of his approach as directly experienced (where Flavières's sensibility can be described metaphorically from without).

Most fascinating, however, is the dénouement of the sequence, as we discover the pair in Scottie's apartment near Coit Tower. The fires of passion in Scottie have not yet quite been kindled, though he is warm enough to her. Scottie has showered and is now comfortably dry, sedate, upon his sofa, in a dark teal sweater that connotes the alluring distance of the sea without implying the direct irritation of wetness. His quietness and the line of Madeleine's clothes hanging to dry in his distinctively modest kitchenette inform us not only that Madeleine is presently sleeping but also that Scottie lives alone, untended by a companion (who would surely want and have a full kitchen) and apart from female presence in general; and that he has undressed her. There is no sexuality directly implicit in his action under these circumstances, only kindness and consideration. Yet the construction of the scene implies an acute sexuality: she is beautiful, she has begun to intrigue him, and we have ourselves already fallen for the entrancement of her grace. The surface rationale that she is recuperating in his apartment is thus at odds with the underlying provocation of her nakedness in his bed. That one's feeling can be so misaligned with propriety is another exemplification of the discontinuity in the vertigo we are made to feel with Scottie. Madeleine in Scottie's bed is at once, then, a vulnerable and attractive sexual object and the victim of a horrifying accident. We are desirous as we watch her, yet uncomfortable and uncertain in our desire. She is the focus and cause of our vertiginous pleasure. And she is also tucked beneath a yellow blanket, narcissus yellow, reminiscent of the steps of the ladder that was Scottie's nemesis early in the picture. Flavières, his ancestor, also had trouble with women, and a young roué advised him, "Speak to them as though you have already slept with them." Neither he nor Scottie has worked out the moves, however. With Midge and Madeleine

Scottie is stiff, awkward, uncertain. By the time he can bring himself to certainty, it will be too late.

And looking at Madeleine with Scottie the camera places us near his face, so that we are aiming down. She herself is the ultimate condition into which we are in danger of falling.

Phantom from the Past. "What bothered him the most was the scent, that phantom from the past," Boileau and Narcejac write of Flavières, "le parfum, ce fantôme du passé." In this film we are prone, and conscious of being prone, to experiencing the seduction of our sensibilities, being engaged and then engrossed, therefore distracted, therefore ultimately confounded by what we see. We are caught believing in a thing, as William James put it in a description of the work of Renouvier, "for no other reason than that we conceive it with passion," and this is *mental vertigo.*[33] "Other objects whisper doubt or disbelief; but the object of passion makes us deaf to all but itself, and we affirm it unhesitatingly." That our conviction in the verity of a thing should be couched in this description as a sensitivity of the ear is fascinating, and we will return soon enough to a consideration of heard authenticity and deafness toward all that is beyond credibility. Indeed, the vertiginous pleasure is capable of producing the kind of alarm that often accompanies a disturbance in hearing.[34]

But what we take to be a true state of affairs is often only an artful construction made to facilitate that taking. "Madeleine Elster" is in fact Judy Barton, but we must not fault ourselves for having been sucked in: Barton is, after all, a competent actress, and the scene has been constructed around her to support every facet of her performance. In the conclusion of the film, as Scottie drags Judy up the tower at San Juan Bautista, he is explosive with anger and his anger is directed toward her, but in fact what he has been misled by is the construct of theatricality itself. The vertigo that he is narratively posited to suffer, one that reaches forward from his history, cripples his present, and offers him up as the perfect lamb for this dramaturgical sacrifice, is a debility we share with him as creatures socialized to a complex arrangement of spectacles and displays. Any viewer taken in by Judy's performance is no more or less than a plant cultivated to be taken in, and the reason Hitchcock retrospectively reveals the first act of the film as a performance *early* in the second act is exactly that he wishes to focus not on attributes of this performance but on aspects of any viewer's vulnerability to performances in general. "Bring this performance to an end!" is what Scottie is really crying into

Judy's ear as he says, "Did he train you? Rehearse you? Teach you what to say and what to do? . . . And you were such an apt pupil!" To dissolve his anxiety—in Scottie desire is thoroughly mixed with fear—the film momentarily does seem to end as, in a moment of triumph, he manages to take himself all the way to the top of the tower. We may compare Scottie in this respect to Roger O. Thornhill, who has existential problems with acting: that others keep inferring he is doing it when, unwitting, he does not see the performance he is engaged in or even admit that there could be a performance.

In the Redwood Forest. The shots in which we observe Scottie and Madeleine walking into—and ultimately out of—the forest at the Big Basin Redwoods State Park were made by William N. Williams, Wallace Kelley, and Irmin Roberts under the direction of assistant director Daniel McCauley and associate producer Herbert Coleman, and using doubles.[35] The viewing audience is here unaware, of course, that the person who looks like Kim Novak portraying Madeleine Elster is in fact someone else (and there is only enough contrivance on the part of the production to foster the maintenance of this lack of awareness). The crime Hitchcock is getting away with, using a stand-in director, a stand-in cinematographer, and two stand-in actors, is the production of a double cinematic fiction: that characters, not merely actors playing characters, are in the forest; and, once this fiction is penetrated, that actors, not merely stand-ins pretending to be those actors, are playing the characters.

The cinematography of the redwood forest makes possible an exploration of depth and fear that we have not experienced articulately as yet in the film, although it has been invoked. I am referring to the relation between age, memory, and rapture; in short, falling through time. Madeleine's attachment to Carlotta Valdes, and to herself, is a romantic one, looking backward for grounding. Scottie's relation to Madeleine mimics this. As the redwood trees have grown thicker at the trunk, centuries have flown by, and the needles have climbed higher and higher off the ground. This is the "shaggy Arcadia" Schama describes in *Landscape and Memory*, not only "a dark grove of desire" but also "a labyrinth of madness and death."[36] We are given to experience the height of the forest visually by means of the shafts of palpable darkness through which bars of sunlight run. The taller the trees, the more the forest blocks light. Made possible by the nature of this structure (and the structure of this nature) is the hide-and-seek game in which for an instant Scottie can fear that Madeleine has utterly disappeared. So old are the trees, so dark is the place, he cannot see her there. Achieving the visual quality of the forest was a logistical nightmare for the production, since, available sunlight being minimized by the dense growth, all the light had to come from hidden arc lamps powered at a distance. Particularly fine Japanese lenses were used with the apertures wide open,[37] a method that normally reduces the depth of field. Therefore, to create the extraordinary sense of depth in this sequence, a great deal of light was necessary in the rear planes of focus. To the degree that the forest clearing can seem hidden away from the regular flow of light, that is, to the degree that lighting technique and copious supplies of electricity can make it discernable and yet not exactly bright, it feels abstracted from the everyday and from the continuum of history, so the moment seems locked in a bubble in time.

Elster's claim for Madeleine, however, is that she is also withdrawn, sealed away, in a kind of bubble. The conditions in the forest perfectly characterize her putative experience: that Madeleine and Scottie are not in the twentieth century as they converse here but floating in and above all time, indeed that the endlessly extending vivacity of this place *is time itself*.[38] In the voices and dialogue there rings something medieval. "Here I was born. . . . Here I died." But although we can be induced to believe in the chronology Madeleine is suggesting, both narratologically and historically it is false. As she mouths these words she is not Carlotta Valdes in fact and has not already died. Says Flavières in the book, in a voice that is nothing more than a whisper, "I've always been afraid of dying."

He speaks for the viewer of *Vertigo*, Goffman's "onlooker." He does not consider his mortality in his day-to-day capacity as a citizen who can buy a ticket to see a film and make his way to a theater. It is in his role as an engrossed citizen of the fictional world that he takes so meditative a position; and the life he cannot resign himself to ending is his life as a viewer, his vertiginous life. We cannot imagine the vertigo ever stopping, because we do not—at least as yet—wish it to stop, this because the performance has not been given away, because it has been a successful performance. When the wrong necklace suddenly appears upon the pallid neck of Judy Barton, we recognize (just as Scottie does) that the focus of our attention is not a personage but an actress paid to simulate one. At that moment we feel ourselves to be, if not lost in the story of Scottie and Madeleine—Scottie and the memory of Madeleine—then trapped in a metafiction where actors and actresses roam. Scottie has the same feeling. (It is Novak's great art that immediately surprises us through the fullness of its rendition of Barton; so that we feel

Barton the actress is a *person* [one like Scottie] rather than just another role being played by the same actress who was once Madeleine and whom we will never meet. The hunger, the green desperation, the shallowness of Judy are incontestable.)

The forest as given to us—by means of the tree cross-section in which we can see nicely delineated the Battle of Hastings, the Magna Carta, the discovery of America, the signing of the Declaration of Independence—is also unreal historically, since our knowledge of it as a narrative topography is constructed by artificially designed shots even as our vision of the cross-section is carefully presented through a duplicity. What has grown over the centuries, the location that is transformed into the setting, now has a nar-ratological duration, a scene length, an effect on cinematic memory. "The forest" becomes for us a scene in the film, not a perduration. Also, the synec-dochical cross-section is not real, but was created for the production by Henry Bumstead.[39] It is a double of a cross-section, invoking the consider-able doubling in the film. As the filmic "forest" doubles for the real Califor-nian one (unequipped with arc lamps) Madeleine's "real" passion for her past doubles artificially for a different, actual past. And in every doubling, every sham, a surface on which our attentions stand is actually a platform from which we can fall to a reality underneath.

Inheritance. The cataract of performance, in which actors tumble into characterizations, is in some ways like the processional of generational con-tinuance. As children are born from parents, characters are born from the actors who make them. How do we account for the qualities in a child's per-sonality—that they are inherited from the parents? From the grandparents? How do we explain the qualities of a character—that they belong to the ac-tor who plays her? The tale Gavin Elster hands Scottie, that Madeleine is ob-sessed with her great-grandmother Carlotta Valdes and is prone to inheriting that ancestral life, is hardly far-fetched in view of our tendency to attribute personality characteristics through the formula of inheritance. That children are in some vital ways *not* like their parents and ancestors is the mystery in this film. The Madeleine we meet has *not* inherited her personality or behavior from the great-grandmother we see depicted; indeed, we are in a position where it is necessary to historically reconstruct the character of the great-grandmother whom we see depicted from the behavior of the Madeleine whom we meet if we wish to maintain our belief in "inheritance." The real ancestors are the scriptors, Alec Coppel and Samuel Taylor, invisible and unknown, their diegetic counterpart and mask the "composer" Elster whom they have created. Madeleine is the way she is because of the operations of Gavin and Judy, yet Judy, we discover in the vital second act of the film, is in every conceivable way *unlike* the Madeleine she plays. Must actors resemble the characters they play? If so, is acting only a set of claims to identity and nothing more?

But the more we examine others, the more we fail to see our relation to them in some critical way, indeed, the more we can fail to see their relation to themselves. As Flavières puts it to himself, "Who can tell how it is that we are ever certain of recognizing anyone?"[40]

On Guard

Whence, indeed, comes this certainty that we have seen someone *before*? It is a fundamental question, as regards our conception of time and therefore our appreciation of filmic narrative. That we can recognize implies that we can remember—that we can position in a context utterly historical the object that looms before us now in a context utterly aesthetic. Uniquely human is the ability to historicize, to watch time go by, to hurry, to see again. Madeleine resents the giant redwoods because for her the fluid passage of time that is vital, but relentless, is only a solid, capacious, unchanging moment for them. "I don't like them . . . knowing I have to die." Only a few moments later she addresses—through a metonymy-within-a-metonymy—nature itself, by invoking a cross-section of one tree for the forest; and the forest for all natural growth: "Somewhere in here I was born . . . and here I died . . . it was only a moment for you . . . you took no notice." This is the Berkeleyan account of experience so much in accord with cinematic construction: that what we can denote, is, and that what is hidden, must be brought visibly onto the surface in order to be. Hitchcock had committed his working life to this premise, most simplistically stated, perhaps, in his television episode, "Breakdown," in 1955,[41] but given elaborate, even baroque, treatment here.

If the redwoods have been blind to Madeleine/Carlotta, or at least unattending, and if they remember nothing, Scottie Ferguson has a quite different consciousness, and this is his problem. For him, vertigo is connected to an inability to forget. Recollect that looking down from Midge's ladder he remembered, he measured the perceived distance against a distance he had experienced before, that separated a rain gutter from a street. His disaffection for Midge is concretized at a moment when he chooses to look at her self-portrait, recalling what she looked like *before* (but also *beside*, because she is standing in his peripheral vision) the painted vision he sees now. His entrancement with Madeleine is related to the fact that he subjects her not merely to surveillance but to the appreciating gaze. She is for him the optical object that calls up a history of feeling, not merely a contemporary source of information, although Gavin Elster cannily never suggested Scottie might find her worth actually looking *at* when he proposed Scottie should look *after* her. But he sees her against a memory of the other women in his life, certainly of Midge. In the nocturnal apartment scene, we are left to suppose that he has been doing a great deal of this retrospective kind of looking at Madeleine while undressing her and slipping her into his bed (later we are given to know that while he did all this, she was in fact conscious and puissante, but inactive). At the Palace of the Legion of Honor, he assembles the pieces of the puzzle of her relation to Carlotta Valdes by concentrating his optical force on the tonsorial vortex; the bouquet; the (tree-like) posture—his concentration is mimed in Hitchcock's close-ups for our benefit—in every case coming to knowledge by seeing now in light of the memory of something seen once before. And, of course, after Madeleine falls to her death, he spends his waking days searching for her everywhere with his hungry eyes—literally looking for what had once been looked at, before time flew by.

Here is how Boileau and Narcejac's Flavières experiences the crisis of his attachment to, and memory of, Madeleine Gévigne. He is in Marseilles near the Vieux-Port, a flavorful, frenetic, passionate part of a city that is already the epitome of flavor, bustle, mercantilism, and warmth, as contrasted with the spacious, almost classical precincts of Paris where the first part of the story was set. Here he has encountered a woman named Renée Sourange, who reminds him immediately of the dead Madeleine. Hitchcock's adaptation colors Judy's clothing, her hair, her face, her posture, her voice, her attitude, and her bearing with the mercantile vulgarity we find in Marseilles; even as the gowns, the grace, the hauteur, the translucence of Madeleine (embodied in Ransohoff's) were Parisian. Scottie's approach is to redecorate Judy, to use her physique as the basis for a physical reconstruction. Flavières is not beyond this kind of operation but he does not undertake it until he has done an interrogation, which leads him to muse, "My word, I've been questioning her as though she's done something wrong!" Finally, at his wits' end, he confesses to her, "I am tortured by memories. . . ."

What has been bothering Flavières is not just that Madeleine threw herself from the church tower, but that in so doing she was running away from something—something vague, indefinite, and haunting. The chilling image of the *vis a tergo* is thus invoked, the unknown ghost that is pushing from behind, the motive, the origin. And worse, it is something even further in the past than the nightmare he cannot bring himself to forget; because it is *behind* that nightmare, urging it onward into existence. "I've always been afraid to die," Flavières goes on, his voice hardly more than a whisper:

> Other people's deaths always overwhelm me, because they announce my own.
> And my own. . . . No, I can't resign myself to it. I have not succeeded in bringing myself to believe in the God of the Christians . . . because of the promise of resurrection. This corpse, buried in the depths of a cave; the stone rolled in front; the armed soldiers on guard [*veillant*]. And then, that third day. . . .
> When I was a kid, whenever I thought about that third day. . . . [Flavières has spent his childhood among the quarries near Bourgeuil, near the Loire.] I would sneak out to the quarries and let out a great shout, and my shout ran off far underground, but nobody answered. . . . But it was still too soon. . . .
> Now I think my cry was heard. I want so much to believe it!

It is the word *veiller*, to sit up and watch, that gives us surveillance. We keep watch over the dead, sitting at their side. The soldiers have not been sufficiently armed at the sepulchre, however. They need opticality, and Flavières, in their place, has come to provide it. His attention to Madeleine is nothing short of a vigil. Scottie Ferguson, too, is optically sensitive; and Elster has good vocational reason—as well as healthy avocational motive—for employing him. Scottie may be the perfect foil for Elster's planned crime, not just because he will never make it to the top of the tower but also because he will take a sincere view of his own optical powers and convince others he has seen everything accurately. He is, after all, principally a man who has been trained to stand lookout. Because we can identify with his perceptual strength we can be brought through the first, twisting part of the narrative of *Vertigo*, where facts are displayed before our eyes that we must assemble before anyone says anything to help us place them in context: what Madeleine appears to be, what her husband leads us to suspect, where she goes, what she must be doing there, how she feels, what she fears—all this is given as visual information before we have a frame for arranging it.

That Ferguson is a man of some serious optical power—a power that must be firmly established in order for us later to take seriously his optical failure—is suggested twice very early in the film, once directly, and once by way of buried reference. Directly, it is the queasy first "vertigo" shot, as he looks down into the street, that should inform us of the liveliness, the animation, and the urgency of his vision. He could close his eyes, after all, and end the nightmare for himself, yet he opts to see. But in a more indirect way we are given clues in the next scene, where, just as Midge sketching her bra reminds him of the Midge he used to date (or as Judy Barton, later, outside Baldocchi's, reminds him of Madeleine), Scottie reminds us of someone we have met before. By "we" I mean, of course, filmgoers in 1958, happy to spend a Saturday evening entranced by Alfred Hitchcock. Scottie is the reincarnation—if I may use that word—of someone who enchanted filmgoers only a few years before, looking almost exactly the same as he does in this scene (as he sits on Midge's sofa leaning against her yellow wall with his tipsy cane): another man with a cute nickname, a professional sidelined from his serious work by a physical injury, tall, dignified, handsome—exactly the way that movie stars like Jimmy Stewart are handsome; a man, indeed, the memory of whose attraction for the audience then would have constituted in 1958 one of the principal reasons for seeing *Vertigo*. I am referring, of course, to Jeff Jefferies in *Rear Window*, the first of the trilogy of 1950s films made with Stewart by Alfred Hitchcock.[42] Jefferies was in a leg cast and couldn't scratch himself; Scottie is laced into a "darn corset" that "binds." Just as Jefferies is counting the days until his cast comes off—a source of our perverse pleasure when, at the film's conclusion, he finds himself in two casts—Scottie gloats, "Tomorrow . . . This corset comes off tomorrow. I'll be able to scratch myself like anybody else. And this miserable thing [his cane] goes out the window. I shall be a free man."[43] But Jefferies's dominant characteristic was optical power, his use of a lens. Through indirect association with him, we are made to feel emotionally close to Scottie, his double, his mirror image, the repository of a lingering residuum of speculation and sight. We find him a little funny as we did Jefferies, we sympathize with (while finding pleasure in) his debility as we did in the other case, and above all, we value his optical powers. These powers, too, are obsessive and centralizing, like those of the lens; they eliminate peripheries, grappling with a central object of adoration as though it is all the world.[44]

And then, as on the stepladder he collapses, we are reminded of the fracturing effect of optical trouble. Every instance of vertigo in the film is displayed for us as an optical collapse. Indeed, every pretense at success is an optical wonder. "How can I see her, to know her?" is Scottie's opening gambit to Elster, a question so central to filmmaking as a process that he could be Hitchcock as he asks it, wondering about how any dramatic nuance will be made manageable for the screen.

For his own reasons, then, and also for Elster's, Scottie is subjecting Madeleine to a surveillance. If the surveillance is to be true, a vigil, there can be nothing surprising about the fact that she seems unlike herself, entranced, half-dead, and in fact marked for death. I suspect that in the interval represented by the coroner's inquest, Scottie's delirium at having failed in his vigil causes him to fall from his observation post; so that we are obliged to mount it in his stead. Now we watch Scottie, lest he be marked for death; and as soon as Judy comes into view we inherit roughly the sense about her that he had about Madeleine to begin with—she is fated. In the end, she will die that he may live.

What led Flavières to consider God more seriously—what may indeed have led Scottie, and what may lead us—is what happens on that third day. The stone rolled away. The body gone. Something taking place that the eyes cannot catch. It is on the third day that Scottie's meticulous surveillance of Madeleine is disrupted as, first in the redwood forest and then at Cypress Point, he falls in love with her. From this point, time seems to collapse. Every moment seems, as Madeleine puts it, "too late." Soon, as at the end of a slide, Scottie is standing upon the bell tower with the great bell ringing, his hands open in supplication and emptiness, his eyes scooped out with remorse and confusion. The surveillance is a technical game, often a stunt, but not a way. The soldier at the cave is fooled, in this awkward case, by the ghostly figure of an advancing nun who says, of all things, now at the finale, "I heard voices." [45]

CHOSEN

On the whole, people tend to trust too much in the evidence of their senses; if they should happen to see a deceased acquaintance in public, they would sooner believe in a resurrection than admit to their own insanity.

    Stanislaw Lem, Tales of Pirx the Pilot

It is not, of course, Madeleine Elster that Scottie is interested in, or that we are, and the precarious architecture of this film is poised upon this very small fact. Madeleine Elster we never, but for an embarrassing moment, meet, and even then she is a glyph in the memory of someone else. That moment is macabre. As in so many of his other films, the director playfully establishes his viewer as a person quite prepared to commit the most hideous crime if only love and pleasure can await at the dénouement—in *Saboteur*, for instance, we root for Barry Kane to escape from Tobin's ranch, though he has abducted a toddler to use as a shield; in *Torn Curtain*, we can hardly wait for Gromek to be murdered, and once he has been partially debilitated, and has fallen semi-conscious to the floor of the farmer's cottage, and we have looked across the room toward the oven, we cry to ourselves, "Yes, yes! Put him in the oven!"—and here we join Gavin Elster in tossing from the top of the tower a somewhat tawdry personage who can do nothing but obstruct our desire that "Madeleine," her radiant replacement, and sympathetic Scottie, should fall in love. That victim, insensate as a dummy, was the true Madeleine, and in truth we are nothing but glad to be rid of her, sharing Elster's sentiments even if our moral outrage prompts us to take a dim and dismissive view of him. It is not the person but the image of her that we meet and surveil, that we adore, that we hope to find again. Our attachment, in the end, is photophilia.

And this is the root of a great puzzle. After he is relieved of the anguish of Mozart, and we are freshened by a breezy pan shot across the sunny perspective of San Francisco in the spring, Scottie brings himself once again into society, and it is our immediate conviction that his immediate conviction is the hunt for, and reestablishment of, the beautiful Madeleine whose death has undone him. He wants to undo the past—narratively, change the beginning of the story from a point within it. This project Stanley Cavell deliciously pronounces a "quasi-hallucinatory, quasi-necrophilic quest in the realm of the subjunctive."[46] At the Brocklebank Scottie spies the familiar green Jaguar in the outer court, and then—because with his look he is intending to?—he sees, emerging, *her*. This is at once shocking and rewarding, but—she has not changed! Boileau and Narcejac take us into Flavières's mind as he waits near the Bois de Boulogne outside the Gévigne apartment. "She would come out because he was waiting for her." But now we must admit it is true that her pace is too quick, even too dowdy, the pace of someone with legs too short; and we see—as we carefully pan with the woman's movement toward the car—that it is someone else (Lee Patrick), older, a woman of bourgeois consequence. Indeed, she is no stranger to the tale of Gavin and Madeleine Elster in which we have ourselves been enmeshed, announcing of the car, "Why . . . I bought it from a man who used to live here, in this apartment building. Mister Gavin Elster. I bought it from him when he moved away. . . . You knew him! And his wife? The poor thing. I didn't know her." Impossible, we sigh as we look at this woman, to find Madeleine again, and this augmentation of despair is what makes us strain to search with all our powers of vision and reconstruction, in what follows. The reconstitution of Madeleine that occupies the second act of the film is no mere neurotic exploitation, but a spelling-out in an interpersonal dramaturgy of the dynamic of our hunger for the image of beauty—Rohmer calls it *le goût de la beauté*—which is our search for the past. What he may imagine Madeleine yearned for as she gazed at the "Portrait of Carlotta" Scottie now yearns for, seeking out Madeleine.

He moves next to the Palace of the Legion of Honor, where, on the same marble banquette Madeleine had graced studying that mirroring portrait of Carlotta Valdes (painted by Henry Bumstead),[47] a young girl (Nina Shipman) sits and stares forward, dressed in the same gray suit, her blonde hair pulled back in the same way. We look from a distance, playing the role of Scottie's shadow, and once again both he and we are swept into the past in hopes of a substantiation for a belief in the resurrection. He turns away and the woman walks on.[48] Now, with some hesitation, Scottie takes himself to Ernie's again. He sits—where else?—at the bar. This time "Madeleine" (Dori Simmons) stands up from her table—the same table—and turns to face him. With her escort (Jack Richardson) she moves forward, in a hazy cloud, wearing the same dark gown that Madeleine wore, with the same stately bearing. As, passing close to him, she draws to a stop—just in the way the other had done but surely for different reasons—we see that she is someone else, plain, thoughtless, without purpose, without aura.

But he who seeks may find. The search bears fruit, because Scottie is sufficiently desperate that it should and because, after these three very close failures, *so are we*. We are affiliated with Scottie because, like him, we have lost someone who enchanted us and who disappeared from our lives much too soon after we met her. As if to drive home this construction, Hitch directs the scenes with the three "mistaken identifications" (as they are often called in the unofficial cast lists) in such a way as to make us hunger for the disappearance of these lesser entities just as soon as we come near them. They are too gabby, or too vapid, or too self-flattering. They do not merit our attention, either because they seem to seek it or because, too much, they don't, and so we wish ourselves rid of them; yet we linger psychologically near the traces of Madeleine, precisely because she was such an object of estimation and so pleasantly bore the challenge of being esteemed. But the giggling girl Scottie's eyes fasten upon, as she walks up Grant Avenue with some friends, is hardly "Madeleine" at all. The noxious green of the dress (hardly, as Raymond Durgnat rhapsodizes, "the colour in which stage ghosts are bathed, presumably through association with green as the colour of the fairies and therefore of the non-Christian supernatural in general")[49] emphasizes her bulk; her flat shoes emphasize her classlessness and cause her walk to be labored; her lipstick is not just "much more makeup," as the September 12, 1957, script called for, it is garish, as though she is technically incompetent at image construction, whereas Madeleine was a skilled professional.[50] On closer inspection we see now, and will see again later, that her hair and eyes are decorated violently and not seductively. And she carries herself with a lumpen acquiescence, a stance from which the world is always visible only as material, as obstruction, not as a haunting image. Yet we look past this, thinking it possible to find the spirit of Madeleine within or to find, at least, the substrate upon which the image of Madeleine might be fashioned once again.

A descent past the surface that is laid upon a structure that is hidden is one of the deep themes of this film, and is itself a vertiginous passage in and down. As Starobinski says, "It is my hunger to see more, to repudiate and transcend my provisional limits, that impels me to question what I have already seen, to hold that it is a misleading decor."[51] We will see much later that our fear of falling—our fear of making an illuminating penetration—led us to take Gavin Elster, who establishes "Madeleine," at face value, though under his image was something less glowing, less comfortable with uncertainty, than he presented to us. All through this narrative are clues to the uneasy relation between the surface of things and the deep structure, clues that play on our fear of depth and our chill at recognizing how far we are from the ground of situations: the coroner's (Henry Jones) scathing insouciance as from a bureaucratic remove he skims the surface of events we have witnessed from closer vantage; the beauty of San Francisco Bay when seen from a distance, placed against its turgidity as Scottie and Madeleine float in it; the troubling, discomforting suggestion of Madeleine's erotic self *beneath* Scottie's prurient protective blanket—that blanket being a mask of vulnerability and need that covers her audacity; our continuing feeling, as we meet Madeleine and listen to Scottie talk with her, that there is something central she is not saying, something we do not wish to hear (something, indeed, that would ruin the love story for us, as, ultimately, it does); our distinct sense that Midge is keeping secrets about her feelings for Scottie. "But even to herself she has to cover," the script says, describing Midge's ironic smile as she watches Madeleine depart Scottie's apartment. Midge is a palimpsest of covers, a chameleon. She smears her painting, literally putting layers over layers, but only when Scottie is not there to see. "Oh! Marjorie Wood! You fool! Stupid! Stupid!" Anxiously she raises her arms and pulls back her hair from her face—

the way Johnny will later demand Judy should to become Madeleine again. Can this not mean that under her façade, Midge is Madeleine waiting to emerge—a woman falling into, and also out of, the past?

The ultimate surface, however, is neither a skin nor a presentational style; it is a *story*. I think we can see *Vertigo* as a tale about the relation between characterizations and essences, between characters and actors. It is as a figure in a tale of personal woe that Scottie and Flavières both first meet Madeleine. Flavières's seduction is ephemeral, glowing, Gévigne having cued him: "I would like you to keep an eye on my wife. She is odd [drôle] . . . she bothers me." Droll, indeed. But for Scottie the come-on was all darkness, what is below and yet to come: "I want you to follow my wife. . . . I'm afraid some harm may come to her." If he will be watching Madeleine, I, in my turn, will be watching him watch and, as Goffman puts it, "Watching is doing."[52] Fear of height is Scottie's. But vertigo is mine, beyond the screen, in my need to know what cannot be seen.

Echo

A recurring theme in *Vertigo* is recurring themes. This is perhaps the ultimate treatment in film of the idea that an essence can be brought back, revivified, lifted out of one setting in time (or mise-en-scène) and reset in another. And that idea is the filmic idea *par excellence*. We are regaled with accounts of not only hauntings but also nostalgias, not only memories but also aspirations and hallucinations. Every fall leads to the hope of a fall, which is to say, a height. And if we imagine this Möbius space set in historical terms, we are speaking of a relation, or co-presence, of historical moments, of eras.

The museum is an archetype of the conviviality of eras. What once was, in its own gone time, lives again before our eyes and along with us, as in the present life we examine its perduration, estimate its shape by our own measures, find shock in the imagination that it is still real although now all those who shared it before are dead. The museum, then, is a mechanism for a kind of immortality. Our chill as we look at artifacts there is in knowing they are relics of another world. Likewise the stable-museum at San Juan Bautista with the old carriages; the Palace of the Legion of Honor with the old Carlotta Valdes graced by the "haunted" stare of the great-granddaughter; the museum-like Argosy Bookshop, where the past life is made new again in the tales of Pop Leibel (Konstantin Shayne); the museum-like dungeon of Gavin Elster's office, its walls papered with visions of the old San Francisco contexted against the action of the shipbuilding crane outside. Or Midge Wood's studio, where old love is measured against present passion.

It is easy enough to show character and setting without positioning the camera to record background detail, yet Hitchcock persists in such positioning. When Scottie meets the first "incarnation" of Madeleine at the Brocklebank the camera is positioned to show, perhaps half a mile behind her, a truly garish new skyscraper. It speaks very much of the present age of the city (1957), and is in point of fact the only visual subject in the entire film that can be said to so brutishly do this. The woman, on the other hand, wears a coat Madeleine may have worn, has her hair as Madeleine had her hair. The effect is to mingle a cutting sense of presence—"Here we are, and here now, in this present place"—with the flood of memories washing over Scottie. The past is pulled forward into the present and the present is drawn back into the past.

This happens as well among the redwoods, as Madeleine muses upon the tree cross-section. The Magna Carta is made alive again in this present; and we are transported back to the twelfth century. Or: "Who shot who in the Embarcadero in August of 1879?" is a question given sudden relevance, as Scottie pours a scotch in Midge's kitchenette: assume Madeleine's mother delivered her in her early twenties, and that her grandmother delivered her mother at the same age; then 1879 is also just about the time Carlotta Valdes had her baby—Madeleine's grandmother—and was "thrown away." Who, indeed, did shoot whom in the Embarcadero,[53] and why might it be a pressing question for Midge to joke about now, or for Scottie to muse upon? Or: Madeleine in present time stares longingly at the old portrait of Carlotta, who has been dead herself many years. That Madeleine's Carlotta is a dramatic fiction fashioned by Elster and utilized by Barton upon Scottie does not diminish the fact that for Scottie Carlotta is quite real: real enough to live in his dream. Or: the visit to the graveyard at the Mission Dolores is itself a kind of museum trip, where the present is conjoined with traces of the past. Or: in Midge's studio, she works assiduously on a project involving a new design for a bra (advanced technology) while Scottie prods her about their long-gone college love. Or: after the scene in the hospital, to establish a new season emotionally, Hitchcock gives us a slow right pan across the entire city from Telegraph Hill; but the depth of field is held a little out of focus, so that this is the everlasting city, the past city alive with the present city. The San Francisco Bay scene is played with the relatively new Golden Gate Bridge[54] abutted as background against the older—for Madeleine, romantic—Fort Point. The present is united to the past. The rebuilding of Judy Barton is a step-by-step process of drowning the present, resurrecting the past. We can look at the presentation of the inquest. Much attention has been focused on the sententiousness of the chief coroner and the extreme ambiguity of his summary comment—relieving Scottie of blame officially while slathering it thickly upon him by innuendo. His sere old-time magistrate's drawl of vitiated wisdom echoes in a "town hall" setting with wooden decor, as though a pioneer saloon has been set up for a town meeting in the wild West. Again, the judiciary concerns of the present are drawn back into the tonal configurations of the past; the tonality of the past brought forward to meet the jurisprudence of the present. The design of the McKittrick Hotel, contrasting strongly with the church we are clearly shown across the street as Scottie arrives there, marks it as another ghost drawn up from the past, convivial with our presence.[55] And throughout the film, sometimes in a laborious way, Scottie is shown in the act of driving through the present continuum of the diegesis, of all vehicles, a DeSoto, bringing up to the surface of our experience the deeply buried history of a man who discovered the Mississippi (thus making possible "the West"); and also drawing our movement now back through time.

All these conjunctions of present and past are crystallized in the vision of Judy Barton in her jarring green dress, prancing down the street with her girl-friends. Essential to our process of coming to terms with this shot is the experience of recognition. Do we know her? Do we not, in fact, know her? Are we seeing in her now, again, someone we have seen before? She takes us back into memory and also brings our memory forward into experience. And for Hitchcock, this experience of recognition, which is a realization of history and its persistence, is vertiginous. This pulling forward of what lies at the bottom of the well of time and pushing backward what lies at its lip constitute the essence of his elaborate trick shot, as Scottie stares down the stairwell at the old church.

For the deeply sentient person, daily life, fully experienced in its unfolding flow and yet also thoroughly embedded in and springing up from memory, is continually a stunning banquet of confusion, a *vertige*. We understand by remembering—in short, by seeing ghosts. Midge Wood is made problematic for Scottie because of the acuity of her perception—in short, because of her eyeglasses. She focuses, she makes draftsman's drawings, she absorbs and analyzes the details of a scene without feelingfully moving in it subject to the gravitational pull of memory. When he stands gazing at her painting he sees those glasses for the first time. Further, the rhetoric of Midge's image, and the fact that we see it through our memory of the "Portrait of Carlotta," give us access to those lenses for the first time, too. Earlier, the eyeglasses framed for us the expressiveness of her eyes, but now they are configured as disruptions of a romantic flow of feeling Scottie has been swimming in, ever since his first vision of Madeleine at Ernie's. What Hitchcock has managed here is a demonstration of how it can be true that Scottie can find one woman appealing, but another not. While for most of us such matters belong in the domain of the personal, the interior, the aesthetic, for Hitchcock they must be mechanically, grammatically demonstrable. First, Madeleine = the painted Carlotta in "Portrait of Carlotta." Then, the painted Carlotta ≠ the painted Midge as "the painted Carlotta in 'Portrait of Carlotta.'" The painted Midge = Midge. And therefore, Madeleine ≠ Midge.

There is another interesting twist. If Madeleine is the emotional substrate beneath "Carlotta" in the "Portrait of Carlotta," she is not the model. The model, presumably, because the portrait is as "authentic" as anything else represented in the catalogue of the Palace, was the "real" Carlotta. She is real to the diegesis, though only diegetically real, unlike, say, Coit Tower, which is diegetically real and geographically real, too. This authentic Carlotta, whose portrait does not appear in the actual collection of the Palace of the Legion of Honor in San Francisco, appears to us only once in the film, as a character in Scottie's nightmare: she stands at the window after the coroner's inquest, between Gavin Elster and Scottie. From her striking resemblance to the portrait (not the portrait's striking resemblance to her), we may conclude—I believe we do conclude, though on an infra-diegetic plane—that the actress who plays this Carlotta-of-the-dream (Joanne Genthon) worked also in Hitchcock's production as the model for the painting diegetically titled "Portrait of Carlotta." Our credence, at any rate, in the Carlotta beneath the portrait and beneath the dream—that there was such a woman living in the late nineteenth century near and in San Francisco—is established entirely by tales: Pop Leibel's tale to Scottie, which we overhear; and Elster's reprise.

The impressionistic quality of the canvas itself, parodied by the more hyperrealist style of Midge's painting (which is to say, by the style of the artist who produced the canvas ostensibly "painted" by Midge), softens its referentiality, so that we are capable of entering what the diegesis posits as Madeleine's consciousness—Madeleine's oneiric consciousness—and imagining that she has reason in aligning herself with the Carlotta there represented. But there are so many torturous windings to this path! As we have no knowledge, directly, of the Carlotta represented—indeed, as this Carlotta is, inside the diegesis, purely a narrative one—we can have nothing to say about the softness of the representation, or even about whether there is representation at all. We can merely note that Scottie believes there is, because when he dreams of Carlotta—after having seen the portrait—he dreams this "painted Carlotta" as his own. Who, then, configures Carlotta for us? Madeleine, Pop Leibel, Gavin Elster, or Scottie himself? And for what reason, aside from an intense desire to believe, does Scottie believe in Carlotta at all?

If Midge, standing next to her own canvas, is surely the model for it physically, she is a stranger to it nominally, because she identifies herself—the painter—(and only at this juncture) as Marjorie. She is herself, then, a little distanced from the representation in the canvas, just as Carlotta may well be. But when we try to examine the relation between the painted Carlotta and Madeleine we can only be confounded, because in truth it is not Madeleine Elster who is in reverie before the canvas, it is Judy Barton (in the performance of a "Madeleine" having a "reverie"). As we have not made the acquaintance of Madeleine Elster, we are in no position to declare that the canvas stands for her in any way. The canvas stands for the textual figuration of Madeleine: for Elster's construct, purchased wholeheartedly by Scottie. Scottie's beloved Madeleine is therefore nothing but his own creation—which is to say, his reading of the character limned and offered up by Elster. It is Scottie's estimation that Madeleine can be equated with or linked to Carlotta, real or painted. The only "factual" statement connecting those two women, that Madeleine is Carlotta Valdes's great-granddaughter, originates in Elster, a man we can rely on, finally, as a deceiver.

So the actual—by which I mean diegetically "actual"—Madeleine Elster is, like George Kaplan in *North by Northwest* and Dr. Anthony Edwardes in *Spellbound*, like Marion Holland and Mary Taylor and Martha Heilbron, whose Social Security cards are in Marnie Edgar's purse, like old Mrs. Bates in *Psycho*, like Harry with whom there is *Trouble*, a characterological black hole. She is there for us only once, and then dead (so not there)—indeed, as Elster had broken her neck *before* throwing the body off the tower, we *already do not meet her*. The narrative is an embellishment upon what once was in what is now an empty space. Madeleine is therefore in her very essence an echo for us, a recession. Madeleine therefore causes us vertigo while Midge—like Mozart—does not.

ALL EARS

I can only wait for the final amnesia, the one that can erase an entire life . . .
  Luis Buñuel, quoted in Oliver Sacks, "The Lost Mariner"

In a scene in *Saboteur* (1942) drawn in part from a scene in James Whale's *Frankenstein* (1931), the protagonist, Barry Kane (Robert Cummings), in flight from the law, seeks shelter from a torrential rainstorm in a mountain cabin inhabited by a blind pianist named Phillip Martin (Vaughan Glaser). Martin benefits from the exceptional sensitivity to sound that is legendary among the unsighted. "You, uh, live here alone, do you, sir?" asks Kane, and Martin replies, "Yes. Except I really don't think of it in that way. You see, sounds are my light and my colors." It is significant that in the elaboration of this scene Phillip Martin's exceptional acoustic sensitivity to "color" and "light" permit him, though he can see nothing, to make the most delicate moral discriminations about our hero, and ultimately to make it possible that Kane's life should be saved. *Saboteur* is, of course, one among many Hitchcock films where the operation of the ear is given narrative play, notwithstanding the paramount quality of the ear in any Hitchcock mise-en-scène (after *Blackmail*) simply because of the way music and sound are used to help establish and further the action.[56] *The Lady Vanishes* turns upon a melody, as does *The Man Who Knew Too Much; The 39 Steps* is brought to crisis around a public recitation. The austere speech of Maxim de Winter (Laurence Olivier) and the incapacitated shy silence of his new wife (Joan Fontaine) are like a pair of cricket wickets between which the action of *Rebecca* vacillates madly. We may consider as well Philip's (Farley Granger) pianism, and pianistic paralysis, in *Rope*, and the finale there of the gunshot into the street. Or Jefferies's paralysis in *Rear Window*, when he can see Lisa Fremont (Grace Kelly) invading Thorwald's apartment, see Thorwald (Raymond Burr) discover her there, but not hear the critical words they are saying to one another. We can hear Jeff muttering to Stella (Thelma Ritter) in his panic and this sound, coupled with the fact that we are deaf to the vulnerable Lisa, is maddening. In *Marnie*, a critical scene involving the protagonist's psychopathology is played out as she robs a safe in the direct presence of a floor-cleaner who turns out to be deaf. And Roger O. Thornhill's adventure as George Kaplan would never happen if in the Oak Room of the Plaza he didn't *give the impression of hearing* something he has not, in fact, heard at all.

In *Vertigo* the auditory riddle has been carried to its ultimate extreme, as befits a tale in which the primary impulse of the two protagonists—for different reasons—is to attempt to hear the message of the dead. Indeed, all of our vertiginous experience in this film is in some way linked to our deep desire to be spoken to, sounded out, by those who lie beyond the world that is merely apparent to us. As theatergoers, we wish for some ultimate contact with the actors beneath the characters. As passersby on the street, we see strangers and wish to make contact with the real humanity turning beneath their controlled exteriors. When Scottie meets Madeleine he wants to know what motivates her odd behavior. When, later, he meets Judy, he wants to know what inner spring—what inner *silent* spring—can nourish his reconstruction.

But Madeleine's identification with silent waters has been established directly for us, and much earlier, three times. First, as she falls into the Bay we hear the waters make no sound. Later, as she kisses Scottie by the crashing surf at Cypress Point, the surf is silent until the kiss. Among the redwoods, in the script of September 12, 1957, she is suddenly brightened by a sight to take her eyes off the looming, uncaring trees:

MADELEINE: But I like the stream! It's a lovely stream! But it makes no sound! Listen! Do you hear anything?
SCOTTIE (*shaking his head*): Only silence. It's always like this.
MADELEINE (*wondering*): And no birds sing.
SCOTTIE: No birds live here.

Scottie is discomfited by the fact that "It's always like this." Like Phillip Martin's niece Patricia (Priscilla Lane), who visits him in his cabin once a year but who, after staying a month, is driven mad by the silence, he cannot tolerate not hearing the voice of that (inner) spring. It represents the answer Flavières had been hoping for as a boy, when he shouted into the quarries and heard no reply. It is the answer Flavières desperately wants to believe he is hearing now, that says, "We live again."

Scottie Ferguson, of course, has a hand up on Roger Flavières, because Alfred Hitchcock is by his side. If the man who cannot see, Phillip Martin, can be saved by the power of his ears, it seems entirely reasonable to suspect that the man who cannot hear what he needs to hear, Scottie Ferguson, can be offered salvation through the powers of his eyes. If sound can be colors and light for Martin, why could light and colors not be sound for Scottie Ferguson? Conceive how we are treated to a canvas, not by Midge but by Hitch. The delicate depth—constructed entirely of the play of colors—of the bouquet Madeleine purchases at Podesta's, miniature pink roses and blue forget-me-nots,[57] that seem to echo Don Quixote in Williams's *Camino Real:* "Blue is for distance. Distance is blue." The autumnal explosion and earthy richness of the architecture, pond, leaves, and lovers as Scottie and Judy amble beside the Musée des Beaux Arts to Bernard Herrmann's enchanting love theme. The stunning silver of Madeleine's silk suit. The Neptunian provocation of the turquoise in her gown at Ernie's and the inflammation produced by the flaring and dipping of illumination upon those scarlet flocked walls. Scottie's ethereal teal cashmere sweater, and his sincere chocolate suit. Elster's seductive, ruby office upholstery. The tedious blue of Scottie's sweater in the sanitarium or sensuous dusty rose of Judy Barton's hotel room walls against the vexatious green of the EMPIRE HOTEL sign outside her window. The clear terrifying blue of that final sky.[58]

And what a choir are the many yellows in this film! Yellow-haired Midge's paintbox full of provoking, direct yellows, the yellow licence plates, yellow flowers, the yellow Chevrolet in front of Scottie as he begins to tail Madeleine. The embarrassment of yellow and the delirium of yellow, the yellow of Midge's stepladder, the yellow of her many lemons, of her walls; the yellow cushions Scottie puts beneath the disoriented Madeleine before his fireplace; the yellow blanket under which he had her sleeping; the yellow boxes from Ransohoff's beside Judy Barton's yellow dresser. Like these yellows, the vertiginous attraction is a vision we cannot escape. It plagues us yellow, riddles our perspective, it lures and shames, it never ceases to attract or to render impossible the relieving embrace. Yellow, it warms us but also leads us obsessively to fall in, or to want to fall. What color more speedily, more instantaneously, affects us in its very existence and self-referentiality—in the fact of its being a color—than yellow, the cautionary yellow, the sad yellow, the fading yellow, the yellow of the yellowing of time, the delirious throbbing blood yellow of the dream-vision of Carlotta Valdes.

Turn for another moment to Carlotta, not as envisioned by Madeleine but as adjudged by Midge—Carlotta the sibyl Midge considers only so much hokum: "The idea is that the Beautiful Mad Carlotta has come back from the dead, to take possession of Elster's wife? Ah, Johnny! Come on!" We must remember that well before Midge makes these disparaging comments, she has herself been established for us as the model of earthwise practicality, the woman who gave up the imaginative career as a painter for the pedestrian and mundane vision of the commercial artist. She has her feet firmly planted (in a warm yellow studio)—utterly rational, indeed, she is inutile to Scottie. Though she has the knowledge and prescience to turn him on to Pop Leibel, it is also fairly clear that she is less entranced by Pop's storytelling about Carlotta than Scottie is, that Pop and his tall tales are not her sort of fluff. Midge is politically savvy, emotionally contained. Our most practical selves, then, are addressed in a most appealing way by her, and we begin by taking the position, on her lead, that Gavin Elster's claim about his wife must be nonsense, that Scottie's curiosity is little more than infatuation.

To tease us from this carefully established position, Hitchcock carefully inserts the disturbing scene in Gavin's club, where we learn with Scottie that the entire story of Carlotta and her history is unknown to Madeleine, and also the bizarre scene at the McKittrick Hotel, where we learn with Scottie that Madeleine herself can move in unheralded ways through physical space; and also the chilling scene in Scottie's apartment early the morning after the visit to the redwoods, where Madeleine recounts having had her recurring nightmare about the curious Spanish village the night before and Scottie suddenly says to her, "It's all there! It's no dream!" How, we wonder a little superciliously, would hyperrational Midge explain all this? So we begin to move away from Midge, that narratological buoy to which we had affixed ourselves but from which we can now create distance as on our own strength we negotiate the plot.

Gradually, through Madeleine's discomfiture and our own attraction to her, and just as Scottie does, we are led to attribute reality to the notion that she is being haunted. The story of Carlotta begins first to seem not quite so unbelievable, and then to appeal. Soon enough, we will be ready to see Carlotta ourselves, to wonder if the everlasting gold of the bun of her hair has moved through time to appear again, whole and chilling, on Madeleine's head. But we have already been prepared even for that propensity to belief. Carlotta is first introduced as the occupant of a grave Madeleine visits in the old cemetery of the Mission Dolores. Though it is certainly not conventional for us to form emotional attachments to the unseen inhabitants of graves that other people visit, this particular visitation has been cued by the carefully arranged string of events that precede it—Scottie's injury, our concern for Scottie, the gradual rehabilitation of this Scottie whom we are happy to see feeling better yet whose recidivism to debility we fear and therefore for whom our feeling is more complexly and thoroughly bound; the visit of this Scottie from whom we cannot part to Elster and our concomitant interest in him; Scottie's soirée at Ernie's, courtesy of Elster's direction and resulting in our own stunned interest in Madeleine; Scottie's tranquil pursuit of Madeleine the next morning (with our eager complicity), Madeleine's visit to the florist, the winding streets, the slow descent, the pulsing music, the antiquity of the Spanish church, the out-of-focus cinematography in the cemetery garden, the gliding quality of Madeleine's approach to the grave, Scottie's furtiveness lest, noticing him, she flee and be unattainable for us, the overall silence, the lambent sunshine, the comforting yet awakening yellow flowers.

The yellow flowers! Peeking into the camera frame every time Scottie appears in the cemetery, and announcing themselves in f 2, the frontmost plane of focus, these are *Allemanda cathartica*, or "Golden Trumpets," suggesting at once the seductive and the acoustic. This is a scene, however, in which we hear no evidence. Everything is relentlessly visual, and yet mysterious, and the silence is palpable. There is a pronounced sense in which Scottie does not belong, in which he is confined to the shadows. But this highlights Madeleine and her quest, making her even more desirable and untouchable. By the time Scottie can walk up to the grave and examine it, she has already vanished and he is desperate to be gone after her. So the grave gets little attention, as we will later (too late) discover both she and Elster knew it would.

Our own commitment to the reality of Carlotta Valdes is the hook that catches us into the story and keeps us there, because if we do not believe what Madeleine believes she will very swiftly become a bore. As we are briefed on the Carlotta story by Pop Leibel in the Argosy Bookshop (built on a stage at Paramount), the lights around him begin to dim, placing us, as it were, in the darkness around a glowing fire where in childhood we heard a primordial tale. The fiction occupies the stage and presumes wholly upon our credulousness. Midge is, of course, the level by means of which our own rationality is hoisted away. She tells us, soon after leaving the bookshop, that the tale of the haunting is preposterous. Then we see Scottie save Madeleine out of pure heroism and selflessness. Then we see the same down-to-earth Midge—in her car, watching Madeleine leave Scottie's house in the street—come straight to the conclusion that Scottie is a man with ulterior, if not confused, motives. Because we love to watch romance and she clearly does not, we begin at this point to reject Midge—although she is quite correct in her assessments, both of Scottie and of the Valdes tale—and the door is now open for us to reject, as well, the sum of her judgments, including the preposterousness of Valdes. Carlotta Valdes becomes real even as Midge zooms away angrily in her car. Later, when Scottie sees that the Carlotta Valdes tale had been but a bait to lure him, he is already a step ahead of us: we have not acknowledged yet that we, too, were lured; and that Scottie was the bait for that.

Vertigo, then, is a film to which we are listening, even—perhaps most— when we use our eyes. It is a film in which from the title sequence onward our experience is cochlear, spiral, auditory. We experience a dizziness and excitement that are, more than anything, auditory disturbances. This is why the "vertigo" shot is coupled with a musical alarm. Because we always want to hear more than we are hearing, because we hope for a statement that never comes fully enough, there is a particular sense in which, watching *Vertigo*, we experience what it is to be deaf.

Two final observations, then, in the light of this sonic trouble:

The Side of a Face. The photography of the scene at Ernie's in which Scottie first sees Madeleine is entirely peculiar. While I can certainly drum up an explanation for its awkward action—her moving toward him and stopping in front of his face; Scottie regarding her; Madeleine not noticing that she is being regarded; Scottie observing that she is not noticing, during all of which the background redness is flaring with heat and intensity—an explanation, indeed, congruent with the surface requisites of the plot (Madeleine knowing nothing of a man keeping an eye on her at the bar, she waits in patient grace for her husband to have his word of business with the maître d' and join her for the "opening at the opera"), still I cannot help noticing a number of shots that a plain story of a man falling in love with a woman would not require. Scottie has had his vision of Madeleine, after all, and whether or not she now pauses in front of him—in a moment exaggerated by the flaring of the background lighting—he will be sure to recognize her later, which is all the meaning this scene is ostensibly designed to convey. But when I look at these interruptive shots directly and with no particular expectation, I see the side of a face—her face, his face, her face, his face—lit in a very particular way, key lights trained on, of all possibilities, the ears. Scottie's head, indeed, is tilted just a little, so that his ear will present itself squarely in the frame. It is a moment of conversational nullity; perfect silence; and they are using their ears to reach out to the world. Or: it is by means of the ear that the world enters them. Also true: what Brill calls the "dominant geometric figure of *Vertigo*, the spiral,"[59] is also the structure—the inner structure—of the ear.

Other points in the film become newly accessible now. The policeman on the rooftop called out, "Give me your hand!" but Scottie did not hear him. The nun-killer of the finale (Sara Taft) "heard voices." The sententious coroner reminds his jury—which surely includes us—of what they *heard:* "You *have heard* that Mr. Elster was prepared to take his wife to an institution. . . ."; "As to Mr. Ferguson: you *have heard* his former superior, Detective Captain Hansen, from that great city to the north, testify. . . ." Midge expostulates on therapeutic tape recordings to Scottie in the sanitarium, promising that the Mozart she is playing will be "the broom that sweeps the cobwebs away,"[60] but she also wonders, given the availability of precise music for a vast array of precise afflictions, what would happen to all those disturbed folk yearning for curative music "if somebody mixed up their files"? "Johnny-O" isn't particularly listening to this question. Indeed, because he makes no response to Midge, because he gives all appearances of not *hearing* her—from his point of view she is not saying anything—she thinks he does not know that she is there, that because he is functionally deaf to her presence she has no presence for him.

More acoustics: we can note the silence of the redwood forest. We can note the silence of the banter in Elster's office, the noisy outside world blocked out by his picture window (crane 24 moves without a sound). In general, we can note the overwhelming silence of the film itself until Judy Barton steps in. It is as though Scottie is trying to discern the smallest voice in the greatest wilderness of voicelessness. There is no traffic noise as he follows Madeleine, nor any sound in the cemetery, and a resounding silence in the Palace of the Legion of Honor. At Baldocchi, seen from Scottie's point of view, there were vast and floral silences—silence was a flower. Or, it could be said the sumptuous floral arrays visually shriek—but our ears hear nothing. Against this general early background of silence, Judy's whining voice and the sudden voice of the nun in the tower are shocking.[61]

The presence of ears, then, the presence of silence, and the measured acoustic constraint of the film all colorfully signal a focus on the human need to be told, to hear, to make continuance of vital meaning. It is through sound that we remember, through the voice that we string the narrative of the past. So it is that Scottie avidly and frantically persists in beckoning from Madeleine and Judy not only the revivification of the past but its articulation in a present confession: Madeleine must tell him her fears; Judy must tell him her sins. Thus, too, Pop Leibel's extravagant vocalization, emphasized with a manipulation of the background lighting, as he presents with a raw and concocted ambiance a tale that seems to possess a genuine fictiveness but that, within the context of the story, the story as "real," is the only nonfictive element:

> POP LEIBEL: She became the Sad Carlotta. Alone in the great house . . . walking the streets alone, her clothes becoming old and patched and dirty . . . the Mad Carlotta . . . stopping people in the streets to ask, "Where is my child? . . . Have you seen my child?"

Scottie is like some lost wanderer who cannot find his roots, a man without a past—indeed, the archetype of the typical film character. He must

find a way to go in and back,[62] yet he is terrified of what he may find there
except height again, the potential for another story—that vertiginous moment both luring and paralyzing. When Oliver Sacks describes his patient
with Korsakov's Syndrome as a "lost mariner,"[63] perhaps "condemned to . . .
a meaningless fluttering on the surface of life," a bobbing upon the ocean of
time and experience without awareness that he is experiencing a moment and
without connection to other moments, he could be speaking of Scottie,
whose desperate passion it is to connect himself with something so that he
will be able to lose the incessant fear of falling, which is to say, the incessant
need to fall.

With ears, echoes. We do well to remember that, from the point of view
of Scottie's experience, Madeleine is herself only, and profoundly, an echo.
When first he encounters her, she is a fictive element in a tale being spieled
out of Elster's reticent mouth, at best a fabular echo and representation of a
woman as yet unseen. Her essence, in short, is that she is a character, and
when he sees that character actually embodied at Ernie's it is both his failing
and his glory that he denies the narrational frame, enters freely into the role
the storyteller demands he occupy, and takes her as real. She is real because
he has *heard* about her. And she is real because he is dying to hear what she
will tell him. "Why did you jump? . . . What was it inside that told you to
jump?" There is no wonder that her voice is a melody in itself, fluid as a
brook, articulate without being pompous, gentle and urging yet never hungry. More amazing is that even before she speaks—and it is some great distance into the film that she does, in Scottie's apartment—we feel we hear her
because of what we believe we have heard *about* her. But we have heard relatively little. We have been listening instead to what Madeleine tells us by the
color and illumination with which she moves and lives. We have been seeing
her voice.

Scottie's desire to hear Madeleine positions him for us in a particular way,
within the existential field. He is rendered passive and open to influence. His
capacity to be led, influenced, directed, stimulated, and acted upon is emphasized: we can note the way he leaps over the rocks to follow Madeleine down
to the surf at Cypress Point, the way his "wanderings" seem naturally to
follow hers, the intensity of the passion of his response to her murmurings in
the forest. Hitchcock went so far as to say that "in the second part of the film,
Scottie starts acting the way Madeleine did in the first."[64] But what this suggests is that in the first part of the film, as Madeleine moves through the city
in her trance, she is listening for the beckoning and directing voice of Carlotta; and that Scottie, later, is listening for her. The condition represented

by Madeleine's circumstance early in the film, then, at least as it is fictionally established for Scottie and us by Elster, is that of susceptibility to inspiration. She is affected by the world, empathetic. Scottie's ability to believe in her at the beginning is one of the by-products of his own capacity for such susceptibility: a capacity we do not see fully realized until she is "dead." What comes *From Among the Dead*—the provisional title for the film—is the call to fall (into belief), the gravitational lure. To experience it, we must first be raised to a height, since the ground does not appeal to us until we stand above it. And that raising, for Hitchcock, was implicit in the mechanism of suspense.

Upward into suspense we have taken ourselves as a species—and the voyage has been human civilization: points of vantage; social standing (Elster); upstanding character (Scottie); taking a stand (Midge); and stand-offishness (Madeleine). We have used the cantilever to cause high masses to support themselves against gravity by their own weight; the bra Midge is drawing will work this way, bridges are built this way, and hearing about it Scottie is already cantilevering himself against her walls. Along with points of vantage and their tools, we have certainly used money—the entire first section of the film is an essay on Gavin Elster's capacity as producer. We have used sheer might—note the force in those hands climbing that ladder in the first shot. But we may have left intellect behind, since our experience at the top of the tower is one of panic, disorganization, emotional extremity, helplessness, and loss.

Himself. My last observation is wee, and yet bizarre, centering on the presence within the film of Hitchcock himself. Taking his signature cameo shot as a direct and concise statement of his own engagement, I note that in this film he appears along the sidewalk outside the entry to Gavin Elster's shipyard, walking briskly from left to right. He carries a little case. What is in it? *Vertigo* is constructed to provide clues (but only clues), even as this little scene has been constructed as a clue (and only a clue) to *Vertigo*. The film is about the quest for meaning beyond what we can see. Just as our sighting of a surface often has to substitute for a buried object of desire that declines to manifest itself, perhaps a voice, so a story of an encounter may replace an encounter. Wanting to hear a story, listening as I might, I can never be sure I have heard enough. Wanting to hear is at the epicenter of experience. What I listen for exceeds the visible, present moment. I am attuned to history, to possibility, to everything over and beyond the present. I am interested in vortices, spirals, cochlear structures in general, because hearing is a twisting fall to the interior of *something*. As the story penetrates to my interior when I listen, it is also a passage through which I can fall, a basis of attachment, and a foundation for my belief that *there exists something the interior of which might speak*. With the trumpets of our ears we conceive a world. A told story engenders belief in its subjects and in its very telling.

In this tiny scene we are on a mission to Gavin Elster's in the Mission District, where a key story, if we can hear it properly, will set us in motion. We care enough about hearing and the inner world it represents to need "equipment" to help us. Let us call this equipment the narrative surface: without it, the world is a cacophony. To protect our "equipment" we find as beautiful, as economical, as sturdy a shell as possible: let us call that shell, the film. We can approach inner experience only through the imagination affected by a tale of the inner experience. At this particular moment, Scottie has just finished plunging from Midge's stepladder as the words "I look down," yet unspoken, echo in his thoughts, and, holding him, Midge has lovingly whispered his name. And he is heading toward an encounter in which the adventure of the fall will begin (again). Between what has happened and what is to come, walking past the shipyard where the yarn will be born is a man with a beautiful little protective case, and since this man is Alfred Hitchcock, he projects himself into the position of the audience—we who wish now, or soon will wish desperately, to hear and who will therefore, because light and colors speak, take pains to see. The little case has a very polished exterior and an interior that we do not, that we must not, see. Metaphorically, the outside is form, the form of this film, form that symbolizes and beckons, form that suggests and invokes, form that is everything except our desire. And inside . . . ? Inside is the organism of hope, that voice from beyond the boundary, the murmur from the cave.

All this, to be sure, is metaphor. But beyond metaphor, or far below it, once we have fallen like Icarus into the practical world, we must be tickled by a practical question: What is the only object that can possibly be inside this silent man's beautiful, trumpet-shaped, little case? I might answer coyly, "All of *Vertigo* except this moment." And what is *Vertigo* but the journey down and in, a fall from a height, from a height not always recognized as a height, into a story not always recognized as a story, a story that is a resolution of the improbability of the past, the past that we must use our eyes to hear. But insofar as this is a real moment outside a real shipyard as well as a metaphorical one, insofar as Hitchcock is not only a diegetic "passer-by" but also a real man as he parades past the camera (a real man, yet not even, at this moment, a real

filmmaker), insofar as that is a real case under his arm, what is the only real thing that can be inside, a thing that might, indeed, *suggest* everything of the interior world because it absolutely cannot, does not, come out to speak— that might seduce our appreciation of the immense spiral of concentration, dream, and imagination that is this film, or any film, that might help us to hear that faraway voice?

On this note, because Hitchcock himself is silent, I must close.

Notes

Introduction: His Master's Voice

1. Norman O. Brown, *Love's Body* (New York: Random House, 1966), 56.

2. Genevieve Taggard, *The Life and Mind of Emily Dickinson* (New York: Knopf, 1934).

3. John Belton, "Technology and Aesthetics of Film Sound," in Elisabeth Weis and John Belton, *Film Sound: Theory and Practice* (New York: Columbia University Press, 1985), 63.

4. Ina Rae Hark, "Revalidating Patriarchy: Why Hitchcock Remade *The Man Who Knew Too Much*," in *Hitchcock's Rereleased Films: From Rope to Vertigo*, ed. Walter Raubichek and Walter Srebnick (Detroit: Wayne State University Press, 1991), 209ff.; Robert J. Corber, *In the Name of National Security: Hitchcock, Homophobia, and the Political Construction of Gender in Postwar America* (Durham, N.C.: Duke University Press, 1993).

5. "For those who want it I don't think films should be looked at *once*," Hitchcock told Ian Cameron and V. F. Perkins. "I think they go by too fast." Sidney Gottlieb, ed., *Alfred Hitchcock Interviews* (Jackson: University Press of Mississippi, 2003), 50.

6. In the face of cinematography itself, in fact, Freud described himself as an old child and said, "I usually remain spellbound." See Sanford Gifford, "Freud at the Movies, 1907–1925: From the Piazza Colonna and Hammerstein's Roofgarden to *The Secrets of a Soul*," in *Celluloid Couches, Cinematic Clients: Psychoanalysis and Psychotherapy in the Movies*, ed. Jerrold R. Brandell (Albany: State University of New York Press, 2004), 147–167.

7. Harvey Roy Greenberg, "*Psycho:* The Apes at the Windows," in *Screen Memories: Hollywood Cinema on the Psychoanalytic Couch* (New York: Columbia University Press, 1993), 111–143; Slavoj Žižek, "The Other Must Not Know All," in *Looking Awry: An Introduction to Jacques Lacan through Popular Culture* (Cambridge: MIT Press, 1992), 71ff.

8. See Laura Mulvey, *Visual and Other Pleasures* (Bloomington: Indiana University Press, 1989).

9. William Rothman has taken us furthest in understanding this. See his "The Villain in Hitchcock: Does He Look Like a 'Wrong One' to You?," in *BAD: Infamy, Darkness, Evil, and Slime on Screen*, ed. Murray Pomerance (Albany: State University of New York Press, 2004), 212–221.

10. John Russell Taylor, *Hitch: The Life and Times of Alfred Hitchcock* (New York: Da Capo Press, 1996); Donald Spoto, *The Dark Side of Genius: The Life of Alfred Hitchcock* (New York: Ballantine Books, 1984).

11. Dan Auiler, *Hitchcock's Notebooks: An Authorized and Illustrated Look inside the Creative Mind of Alfred Hitchcock* (New York: Avon/Spike, 1999).

12. Pat Hitchcock O'Connell and Laurent Bouzereau, *Alma Hitchcock: The Woman behind the Man* (New York: Berkeley Books, 2003).

13. Truffaut, letter to Hitchcock, June 2, 1962, in François Truffaut, *Letters*, trans. Gilbert Adair (London: Faber & Faber, 1989), 179.

14. To Rui (Ruy) Nogueira and Nicoletta Zalaffi in 1972 Hitchcock said, "When a critic is not very deep—which is the case less rarely than one might think—he limits himself to retelling the story of the film that he sees." Gottlieb, *Interviews*, 120.

15. Lesley Brill, *The Hitchcock Romance: Love and Irony in Hitchcock's Films* (Princeton: Princeton University Press, 1988); Robin Wood, *Hitchcock's Films Revisited*, rev. ed. (New York: Columbia University Press, 2002).

16. Robin Wood, "Looking at *The Birds* and *Marnie* through the *Rear Window*," *Cineaction* 50 (1999): 84.

17. On chiaroscuro see José Ortega y Gasset, "On Point of View in the Arts," in *The Dehumanization of Art and Other Essays* (Princeton: Princeton University Press, 1972), 107–130.

18. Brill, *Romance*, 202.

19. William Rothman, *Hitchcock—The Murderous Gaze* (Cambridge, Mass.: Harvard University Press, 1982), and *The "I" of the Camera* (New York: Cambridge University Press, 1989).

20. Fredric Jameson, "Reading Hitchcock," *October* 23 (winter 1982): 15–42, quoted in Jane Sloan, *Alfred Hitchcock: A Filmography and Bibliography* (Berkeley: University of California Press, 1995), 36.

21. Rothman, *"I" of the Camera*, 173.

22. Sloan, *Hitchcock: Filmography*, 37.

23. Jean Narboni, ed., *Alfred Hitchcock* (Paris: Éditions de l'Étoile/Cahiers du cinéma, 1980), 38, quoted in Sloan, *Hitchcock: Filmography*, 37.

24. Although not all Canadians agree. Peter Clandfield is in tune with the negative key of much current criticism when he describes *I Confess* as displaying "cinematic colonialism." See his "Bridgespotting: Lepage, Hitchcock, and Landmarks in Canadian Film," *Canadian Journal of Film Studies* 12:1 (spring 2003): 4.

25. His claim to Bogdanovich that the decision sprang from his desire to have a country church with a tower, which was available in a California mission near San Francisco, hardly begins to explain. Interesting details of Hitchcock's use of San Francisco, here and in other films, can be found in Jeff Kraft and Aaron Leventhal, *Footsteps in the Fog: Alfred Hitchcock's San Francisco* (Santa Monica: Santa Monica Press, 2002), but these questions are not addressed.

26. "I have a horror of what I call the passport photograph: shooting straight in," said Hitchcock to the American Film Institute in 1972. Gottlieb, *Interviews*, 95.

27. See note 20.

28. In his "Journal of *Fahrenheit 451*," for Tuesday, May 3, 1965, printed in *Cahiers du cinéma* soon after that film was completed. See François Truffaut, *La Nuit Américaine et le Journal de tournage de Fahrenheit 451* (Paris: Seghers, 1974).

29. Jean Starobinski, *The Living Eye*, trans. Arthur Goldhammer (Cambridge: Harvard University Press, 1989), vii.

30. Ibid., viii.

A Great Fall: Action North by Sincerity Northwest

(A small part of this chapter appeared as "The Consumer Perversity of Roger Thornhill," *Quarterly Review of Film and Video* 17:1 [Spring 2000]: 19–34.)

1. See for example Tom Gunning, "Tracing the Individual Body: Photography, Detectives, and Early Cinema," in *Cinema and the Invention of Modern Life*, ed. Leo Charney and Vanessa R. Schwartz (Berkeley: University of California Press, 1995), 15–45.

2. Not written as such, but in many ways an excellent general introduction to the films of Alfred Hitchcock, is Garfinkel's "Passing and the Managed Achievement of Sex Status in an Intersexed Person," in *Studies in Ethnomethodology* (Englewood Cliffs, N.J.: Prentice-Hall, 1967), 116–185.

3. A New York advertising executive, Roger accidentally falls into the hands of a gang of agents seeking a mysterious "George Kaplan," is interrogated by them and nearly killed. His escape takes the form of a perilous journey from the United Nations Building in New York, by train to Chicago and environs (where in a rural cornfield another attempt is made on his life), and thence to Rapid City, South Dakota. On the way he meets an engaging woman, Eve Kendall, who at first seems to be involved with the spies but later is discovered to be a secret government agent. Roger saves her from the spies on Mt. Rushmore in the finale of the film.

4. A note for Hitchcock aficionados who like small riddling things: the mysterious being named George in this film is almost universally spelled K-a-p-l-a-n by scholars and writers. This is how we find him, for example, in James Naremore's excellent *North by Northwest, Alfred Hitchcock Director* (New Brunswick: Rutgers University Press, 1993) and even in Ernest Lehman's published screenplay (London: Faber & Faber, 1999) as we read through the shots of the film. Lehman's "Introduction," however, mentions researching "the adventures of Roger Thornhill, a.k.a. George Kaplin" (ix).

5. Still in the late 1950s one could routinely send a telegram for hand, rather than telephone, delivery.

6. "He was extremely defensive about class." Jay Presson Allen, interviewed by Patrick McGilligan, *Backstory 3: Interviews with Screenwriters of the 1960s* (Berkeley: University of California Press, 1997), 24.

7. The newspaper addressed to Lester Townsend on the desk in Long Island is still cleanly packaged, pure, and so Roger can inspect the address label and come to believe the man he is talking to is Lester Townsend. Roger also reads his own material: as he gets into the taxicab with Maggie at the beginning of the film, he opens his paper

directly to the stock quotations at the back; but through advertising, he has in some measure authored the business values here quoted.

8. On performance and identification see Stanley Cavell, *Themes Out of School: Effects and Causes* (Chicago: University of Chicago Press, 1988), 155.

9. Grant brings a certain sophisticated daffiness to the neo-aristocratic role, without compromising grace or command. See, for an elaborate discussion of his performance here, James Naremore, *Acting in the Cinema* (Berkeley: University of California Press, 1988), chap. 12.

10. In his analysis, Cavell pays extended and strict attention to marriage as a central organizing theme, a piety I find intriguing but do not here completely share. He finds Roger lifting Eve up "directly from the isolation of the monument's ledge to the isolation of the marriage bed," the goal of the protagonists, in his view, being "the legitimization of marriage." Were I putting forth an argument about Thornhill and Kendall as essentially romantic subjects, I might contend they are actually not passionate about one another but that allegiance, self-knowledge, and orientation are more important to them than lovemaking as a source of erotic involvement. On the issue of romance in this film, see as well Lesley Brill's interesting essay, "*North by Northwest* and Romance," in *The Hitchcock Romance* (Princeton: Princeton University Press, 1988), 3–21.

11. He is not the only professor in Hitchcock, and possibly a professor only in name. He has the look, but not the curiosity. See, for other fascinating examples, *Spellbound*, *The 39 Steps*, and *Torn Curtain*. In the essay on the latter in this volume, there is further discussion on the professoriate in Hitchcock and elsewhere.

12. Tania Modleski, *The Women Who Knew Too Much* (New York: Routledge, 1989), 90–91.

13. Naremore, *North by Northwest*, 163.

14. Shot 1224 itself is very short, but in the urgency produced by the running and the music we are thinking rapidly and it therefore feels longer than it is.

15. Jessie Royce Landis was actually a year younger than Grant, reveals Paula Marantz Cohen in *Alfred Hitchcock: The Legacy of Victorianism* (Lexington: University Press of Kentucky, 1995), 142.

16. An agent of the controlling classes, Roger is equipped with personally monogrammed matchbooks. He is terrified, therefore, that Vandamm or Leonard will see the matches at Eve's feet; indeed, *Leonard does*. Roger is saved, and so is Eve, precisely because, though Roger continues to think of himself in sincere terms as Roger O. Thornhill, Leonard knows him as George Kaplan and therefore the R•O•T monogram is for him nothing but a design (or a word). Another version of this staging is in *Spellbound*, as Constance finds a letter under her door while threatening forces are standing there; and still another is in *Torn Curtain*, where Manfred sees a note that has been slipped under Sarah Sherman's East Berlin hotel room door, bends down, and graciously hands it to her.

17. If this is a comment on Eve's vulnerability and Roger's manipulativeness—in short, gender politics—let it be said that Hitchcock, and not this author, is making the comment. His portrait of Eve is *in the context of* a portrait of Roger, and highlights—

rather than glorifying, reveling in, or camouflaging—her problematic position. The view of many critical viewers that Hitchcock's films are inexorably sexist needs serious reevaluation; perhaps they point to sexism.

18. Hitchcock at the American Film Institute. Sidney Gottlieb, ed., *Alfred Hitchcock Interviews* (Jackson: University Press of Mississippi, 2003), 85.

19. Hitchcock reconstitutes social disarray as a device in the ballet scene in *Torn Curtain*, while, to strains of Tchaikovsky's *Francesca da Rimini*, Michael Armstrong engineers a social catastrophe.

20. This is a scene with a significant amount of dramatic excitement, to be sure, yet not the sort Hitchcock had in mind when he told the *Evening News* in 1931 about an auction scene he had just completed for *The Skin Game*: "We were able to flash from bidder to bidder, while the auctioneer's voice was heard, showing how the drama of the mounting sum affected each person." Here the drama must be seen primarily to affect— and respond to—Roger. Gottlieb, *Interviews*, 9.

21. On which status see Edwin M. Lemert, *Human Deviance, Social Problems, and Social Control* (Englewood Cliffs, N.J.: Prentice-Hall, 1967).

22. Slavoj Žižek, "How the Non-duped Err," in *Looking Awry* (Cambridge: MIT Press, 1992), 69–87.

23. Formally, the well-bred Roger is referring to a "chromolithograph," suggesting that the so-called canvas is in reality a mass-produced photoreproduction. For a discussion of lithography as the beginning of Benjamin's age of mechanical reproduction, and hence of popular instead of high art, see Martin Jay, *Downcast Eyes: The Denigration of Vision in Twentieth-Century French Thought* (Berkeley: University of California Press, 1994), esp. 120–122. The chromolithograph was often considered "the antithesis of true art." See Tom Gunning, "Flickers: On Cinema's Power for Evil," in *BAD: Infamy, Darkness, Evil, and Slime on Screen*, ed. Murray Pomerance (Albany: State University of New York Press, 2004), 28.

24. Though we will not ourselves see the film contained on that film. The figurine is the MacGuffin of this plot: a "MacGuffin," said Hitchcock, is "something that the *characters* worry about but the audience does *not*." In Peter Bogdanovich, *Who the Devil Made It* (New York: Alfred A. Knopf, 1997), 502.

25. For some other interesting analyses of this theme in film, see David Desser and Garth Jowett, eds., *Hollywood Goes Shopping* (Minneapolis: University of Minnesota Press, 1999).

26. Donald Spoto, *The Dark Side of Genius: The Life of Alfred Hitchcock* (New York: Ballantine, 1984), 208.

27. Alfred Hitchcock, "Murder—With English on It," *New York Times Magazine*, March 3, 1957, reprinted in Sidney Gottlieb, ed., *Hitchcock on Hitchcock: Selected Writings and Interviews* (Berkeley: University of California Press, 1995), 134.

28. Karal Ann Marling, *As Seen on TV: The Visual Culture of Everyday Life in the 1950s* (Cambridge: Harvard University Press, 1994), 1.

29. See William Rothman, "*North by Northwest*: Monument to the Hitchcock Film," in *The "I" of the Camera* (New York: Cambridge University Press, 1989), 181.

30. Brill, *Romance*, 7.

31. Following Hitchcock's lead, indeed. "Ernie Lehman and I decided . . . to make a picaresque thriller with lots of locales for the chase," he told Charles Thomas Samuels, while to the American Film Institute he confessed, "*North by Northwest* is a nightmare." Gottlieb, *Interviews*, 151; 104. And, "*North by Northwest* is an adventure film treated with a certain lightness of spirit," he told Jean Domarchi and Jean Douchet. "*Vertigo* is much more important to me than *North by Northwest*, which is a very amusing divertissement." *Cahiers du cinéma* 102 (December 1959): 17. See also Donald Spoto, *The Art of Alfred Hitchcock: Fifty Years of His Motion Pictures*, 2nd ed. (New York: Doubleday Anchor, 1992), 301. Robin Wood describes *North by Northwest* as "a comparatively relaxed film, a divertissement; that is to say, one must not demand of it the concentrated significance, the extraordinarily close-knit organization of *Vertigo* and *Psycho*. Nevertheless, it has a coherent and satisfying development, a construction sufficiently strong and clear to assimilate the occasional charming but irrelevant little *jeux d'esprit*" (*Hitchcock's Films Revisited*, rev. ed. [New York: Columbia University Press, 2002], 32). Thomas Schatz comments, "The story was an ideal melding of romance and geopolitical intrigue, with its Cold War spy story gradually yielding to the courtship between Grant and Eva Marie Saint" (*The Genius of the System* [New York: Henry Holt, 1996], 486–488). For David Sterritt, *North by Northwest* is "at once too whimsical, too frenetic, and too peripatetic" (*The Films of Alfred Hitchcock* [New York: Cambridge University Press, 1993], 65); John Russell Taylor suggests the film pays "a price in shallowness for what [it gains] in surface glitter and busyness" (*Hitch: The Life and Times of Alfred Hitchcock* [New York: Da Capo Press, 1996], 128); and Raymond Durgnat suggests that in making it, Hitchcock reverted to a "familiar, lighter and regularly successful format" (*The Strange Case of Alfred Hitchcock* [London: Faber & Faber, 1974], 299). Lesley Brill calls it a "comic romance . . . the relatively fabulous kind of narrative that we associate with folklore and fairy tale" but also does recognize that "critics of Hitchcock's films have [called it] 'entertainment'— 'mere' entertainment if they are hostile, and 'superior' entertainment if they are friendly" (*Romance*, 5); and Stanley Cavell muses that "many people think, or think they think, that *North by Northwest* is a light comedy" ("North by Northwest," in *Themes Out of School* [Chicago: University of Chicago Press, 1984], 152–172).

32. Peter Bogdanovich, *The Cinema of Alfred Hitchcock* (New York: Museum of Modern Art, and Garden City, N.Y.: Doubleday, 1963), 6.

33. See Jean Domarchi and Jean Douchet, "Entretien avec Alfred Hitchcock," *Cahiers du cinéma* 102 (December 1959): 17.

34. Naremore, *Acting in the Cinema*, 217.

35. The instances in which Roger *does* transact with cash in this film are each strange. In the opening sequence he buys a newspaper in the lobby of his office building, but reaches behind the kiosk to do this so that we do not see money leave his hand. He bribes his mother with fifteen dollars to get the key to Room 796 of the Plaza, but rather than a transaction this seems a coy and oft-repeated game, both a mother-son ritual and also a gender transaction not very dissimilar from his necking with Eve in the train compartment; he himself establishes the link between Eve and his mother at the Ambassador

East as Eve takes his jacket off: "You know, when I was a little boy, I wouldn't even let my mother undress me." He tips the valet in the Plaza room, *but as George Kaplan*, and it is as Kaplan that the valet thanks him. After dining with Eve on the train he pays for the meal, but in such a rush he seems barely conscious of spending money; the money he drops down, in fact, is just paper to him. The red cap in Chicago has been paid for his uniform, but not definitely by Roger. And he has been paid too much—this is clear from his amazement as he counts the bills; the money has been used not so much to purchase as to force a moment to its crisis. Roger puts personal valuables, perhaps including money, into his pocket in the hospital room, though the shot does not make clear what the valuables are for a man like this, beyond his handkerchief. He pays the cabbie who drives him to Vandamm's house, but the mise-en-scène suggests the money is an inducement to make the man drive away without coming too close to the door. And he tosses coins to get Eve's attention at Vandamm's house, thus revealing that money is nothing to him but a substitute for a pebble. In all this, he certainly has funds to dispense; yet he never spends to involve himself in what members of the consumer society call consumption. Money is simple utility, action. In many cases where Roger's transactions can be dramatized money-free without him seeming socially disconnected, they are.

36. In this he in some ways reflects Ben McKenna, who is introduced to us in *The Man Who Knew Too Much* sitting *with his back to* an emergency exit on the Casablanca-Marrakech bus. All his woes, and all the plot of the film, ensue because he does not turn and use it.

37. Not, I think (as Cavell suggests), a way of saying that Roger *is*—or is a surrogate for—Hitchcock. Hitch, at the beginning of the film, *can't get on* the bus; Roger can, but won't. The bus, if it symbolizes at all in its robustness, stolidity, reliability, and movement, is the director himself. See Cavell, *Themes*, 164.

38. A line contributed to the script by Hitchcock himself, as he admitted to Ian Cameron and V. F. Perkins. Gottlieb, *Interviews*, 50.

39. "Can't say it is, 'cause it ain't," is the man's elegant and spartan claim.

40. Central Greyhound Lines schedule no. 234, Oct. 27, 1957.

41. The shots of Roger holding his hands up to stop the massive vehicle were made through a glass plate. Roger's paralyzed stare as he confronts the advancing vehicle that is visible to us in the intercut shots, like his stare of disbelief and wonder as the cropduster heads directly for him, makes an eloquent contemporary example of what Tom Gunning calls the "looming response": a "divided and vertiginous spectator is caught between invoking phantasmagoria (via technology) and awareness of reality." That Roger's "awareness of reality" is not so sharp as it may seem is evidenced by his ending up under the bumper, though unscathed. Gunning, "Toward a Cultural Optics," paper presented at the Society for Cinema and Media Studies, Minneapolis, March 2003.

42. Brill, *Romance*, 4.

43. Not, as Fredric Jameson repeatedly claims, the "new" Seagram Building on Park Avenue. See "Spatial Systems in *North by Northwest*," in *Everything You Always Wanted to Know about Lacan (But Were Afraid to Ask Hitchcock)*, ed. Slavoj Žižek (New York: Verso, 1995), 52.

44. Norval White and Elliot Willensky, *A.I.A. Guide to New York City*, 1978.

45. The Metropolitan Club was a "stronghold of late nineteenth-century exclusiveness." *The WPA Guide to New York City* (New York: Pantheon, 1982), 230.

46. These are the beneficiaries of what Marling calls the "new American leisure," inheritors of the forty-hour week, the two-day weekend, "a three-week annual vacation, daily lunch and coffee breaks, and early retirement on a pension." Marling, *As Seen on TV*, 51.

47. "The cinema is an invention with no future." The Lumières are quoted on a set at Cinecittà in Rome, thus in Italian.

48. Reprising Grant's earlier role for Hitchcock, John Robie the "Cat," in *To Catch a Thief*.

49. When this shot was made, however, it would have been impossible for Hitchcock to indulge his taste for authenticity of location, since after June 14, 1957, East 60th Street was restricted to eastbound traffic (it is a westbound cab), and Madison Avenue handled traffic in both directions. The scene was very likely shot at a nearby corner where traffic could flow westerly. With many other locations in the film, pains are taken to achieve verisimilitude, though often sets are constructed, like the celebrated soundstage fakes of the Rapid City monument. Hitchcock's mise-en-scène is an index of his precise social reference, suggesting his tales are not just social fictions but also social commentaries.

50. A similar analysis of the breaking-and-entering trade is provided by Mary McIntosh in "Changes in the Organization of Thieving," in *Images of Deviance*, ed. Stanley Cohen (Harmondsworth: Penguin, 1973); economic "perversity" is seen as sensible in terms that are themselves unconventional.

51. A lovely self-reflective turn of Hitchcock's here, played out in many of his films: the absence of Roger's ticket is a diegetic one; because all the riders on that train are without tickets nondiegetically, though they are not without seats (and for many of the shots it is a real train, not a studio set).

52. David Cronenberg pays homage to this scene in *The Fly* (1986), with Seth Brundle, a man of many suits, acknowledging as sartorial mentor Albert Einstein. But Hitchcock, too, had his suits duplicated. In 1964, for example, according to Spoto, "His closet held six identical dark suits (made to order at $300 each), six identical pairs of shoes, ten identical ties, and fifteen identical shirts and pairs of socks. 'I am,' he told an interviewer that season, 'a creature of habit and order'" (Spoto, *Dark Side*, 505). In being such a creature, Hitchcock had placed himself sartorially in close affiliation to his friend, mentor, business partner, agent, and eventual boss, Lew Wasserman, who began his career in Jules Stein's office "in a suit that Stein considered tasteless" and moved on to become the ultimate Hollywood mogul, leader of a pack of agents at MCA who lived by a "rigid" dress code: "dark suits, white shirts, dark-blue or gray ties" (see Connie Bruck, "The Monopolist," *New Yorker*, April 21–28, 2003, 136–155).

53. On the importance of the off-camera voice, see Michel Chion, *The Voice in Cinema*, trans. Claudia Gorbman (New York: Columbia University Press, 1999).

54. Also potentially lost to viewers is the point of the nearly deaf floor-cleaner

who continues to mop during a heist in *Marnie*. In both cases, the point of the preparation is to provide sufficient illumination for the real development, which immediately ensues. In *Marnie*, the issue is thinking one has cleanly succeeded in problematic activity when one hasn't, and all because of an acoustic clue: Mark Rutland finds her at Garrod's because he remembers something she said at the race track; in short, he has been quite intently listening to comments she has been making merely in order to fill conversational space; and the floor cleaner sets us up by dramatically *not hearing* a shoe drop.

55. Grant's contract called for an outright $450,000 plus a profit percentage equal to Hitchcock's, plus a per diem bonus. James Stewart "pleaded" for an idea of the script, and Hitchcock avoided mentioning he "had Grant in mind." See Spoto, *Dark Side*, 436–439. Grant had a particular value for Hitchcock: "The value of having Grant, the film star, is that the audience gets a little more emotion out of Cary Grant than they would from an unknown, because there is identification. There are many members of the audience who like Cary Grant, whether they know about his character in the scenes or not." Gottlieb, *Interviews*, 92.

56. On viewing as acquisition see Susan Sontag, *On Photography* (New York: Farrar, Straus & Giroux, 1981).

57. I here cull *Gourmet* for 1958.

58. On references to *Hamlet* in this film Cavell is not the only author who has made comment, but his analysis in *Themes* is especially insightful.

59. Maggie is being dispatched four blocks from the Plaza, to a breathtaking "Parlor" of Sweets at 700 Fifth Avenue (at 54th Street), where Blum's of San Francisco has only months before (February 19, 1958) opened its first New York store. As the advertisement in the *Times* put it, "Oh! Happy Day! Blum's is here, and Fifth Avenue Never Had It So Sweet!" Since 1891, Blum's had been selling candies to the very discerning from a number of shops in San Francisco, Carmel, Beverly Hills and other spots, at least one of which, near Union Square in San Francisco, would have purveyed to the likes of Gavin Elster and his beautiful wife Madeleine. One of the specialties was a four-pound dose of chocolates in a Limoges porcelain box ($150). See Elizabeth Squire, *The New York Shopping Guide* (New York: M. Barrows and Co., 1961), 154–155.

60. Because, in true vaudeville style, calling up a famous George White routine from *Ziegfeld Follies* (1946), he would not "Pay the Two Dollars."

61. Lyric by Stephen Sondheim, © Stephen Sondheim. I am grateful to Suzanne Meyers Sawa at the Edward Johnson Music Library of the University of Toronto.

62. A particularly entertaining account is Luc Moullet's review "La Concierge et le bûcheron" in *Cahiers du cinéma* 102 (December 1959): 52.

63. Cavell, *Themes*, 155.

64. "In cinema," Paul Giles paraphrases Geoffrey H. Hartman, actors "are always physically absent." *American Catholic Arts and Fictions: Culture, Ideology, Aesthetics* (New York: Cambridge University Press, 1992), 327.

65. Erving Goffman, *The Presentation of Self in Everyday Life* (Garden City, N.Y.: Doubleday Anchor, 1959), 17ff.

66. Hollywood legend has it that Irene Sharaff's costumes for Sammy Davis Jr.'s performance as Sportin' Life in Preminger's *Porgy and Bess* (1959) fitted to the skin in this way.

67. Published in *Cahiers du cinéma* 102 (December 1959): 17.

68. My translation.

A Bromide for Ballantine: *Spellbound*, Psychoanalysis, Light

1. For comparison see also the discussion below regarding Lieutenant Cooley's mother's health.

2. Coleman was Hitchcock's longtime collaborator, from *Rear Window* through *North by Northwest* and also for *Topaz*.

3. Jack Whitehead to Donald Spoto, November 7, 1981, in Donald Spoto, *The Dark Side of Genius: The Life of Alfred Hitchcock* (New York: Ballantine, 1984), 164.

4. Geoffrey T. Hellman, "Alfred Hitchcock, England's Best and Biggest Director, Goes to Hollywood," *Life*, November 20, 1939, quoted in ibid., 223.

5. Truffaut likens Hitchcock to James, in fact, invoking "The Beast in the Jungle." See his "Hitchcock par Henry James," in *Alfred Hitchcock*, special edition of *Cahiers du cinéma* (Paris: Éditions de l'étoile, 1980), 39.

6. "Those film fans of the twenties who took their cue from psychoanalysis," writes Siegfried Kracauer, quoting first Dr. Allendy and then Jacques Poisson, "were confident that the cinema was predestined to 'express the most profound mechanisms of our soul' and 'penetrate the caverns of the unconscious.'" *Theory of Film: The Redemption of Physical Reality* (New York: Oxford University Press, 1965), 189.

7. Consider, for instance, *Suspicion:* it all comes out of the dark.

8. Leonard J. Leff, *Hitchcock and Selznick: The Rich and Strange Collaboration of Alfred Hitchcock and David O. Selznick in Hollywood* (New York: Weidenfeld & Nicolson, 1987), 115.

9. And of *Rebecca* and *The Paradine Case*.

10. Leff, *Hitchcock and Selznick*, 116.

11. Otto Friedrich, *City of Nets: A Portrait of Hollywood in the 1940's* (New York: Harper & Row, 1986), 225.

12. An interview with Patrick McGilligan in *Backstory 3: Interviews with Screenwriters of the 1960s* (Berkeley: University of California Press, 1997), 24.

13. When, with Josef Breuer, he wrote about a mechanism of hysteria.

14. Sigmund Freud, *Collected Papers*, vol. 5, trans. and ed. James Strachey (London: Hogarth Press, 1950), 378–379.

15. At the Green Manors psychiatric facility, the director, Dr. Murchison, is retiring and his replacement, Dr. Edwardes, takes up the job with a huge advance reputation, since his book on the guilt complex has overwhelmed one of the residents, Dr. Constance Peterson, and infatuated her with him. It soon becomes apparent that "Edwardes" is an amnesiac imposter, however, and that the real Edwardes has been found dead. "Edwardes" flees, and Peterson, convinced he is innocent, follows, leading him to her wise

old teacher, Dr. Brulov, who psychoanalyzes him and brings to light enough information so that the identity of the murderer of the real Edwardes can be known.

16. Alexander Michael Doty, "Alfred Hitchcock's Films of the 1940's: The Emergence of Personal Style and Theme within the American Studio System" (Ph.D. diss., University of Illinois, 1984), quoted in Jane Sloan, *Alfred Hitchcock: A Filmography and Bibliography* (Berkeley: University of California Press, 1995), 28.

17. See Leslie A. Fiedler, "The Moor as Stranger," in *The Stranger in Shakespeare* (New York: Stein & Day, 1973).

18. See Peter Gay, *Education of the Senses* (New York: Oxford University Press, 1984).

19. Kirk Varnedoe, *Vienna 1900: Art, Architecture & Design* (New York: Museum of Modern Art, and Boston: New York Graphic Society/Little, Brown, 1986), 17.

20. Peter Gay, "Introduction," in *Berggasse 19: Sigmund Freud's Home and Office, Vienna 1938—The Photographs of Edmund Engelman* (New York: Basic Books, 1976), 31–32.

21. Jonathan Crary notes that Charcot used "a method of standing behind so-called hysteric patients and whispering to them while they appeared to be preoccupied and inattentive to their surroundings." "Unbinding Vision: Manet and the Attentive Observer in the Late Nineteenth Century," in *Cinema and the Invention of Modern Life*, ed. Leo Charney and Vanessa R. Schwartz (Berkeley: University of California Press, 1995), 58.

22. Sigmund Freud, "Charcot," in *Collected Papers*, vol. 1, trans. Joan Riviere (London: Hogarth Press, 1949), 10.

23. Sidney Gottlieb, ed., *Alfred Hitchcock Interviews* (Jackson: University Press of Mississippi, 2003), 21.

24. Gay, "Introduction," 30.

25. Ibid.

26. François Truffaut, *Hitchcock*, rev. ed., trans. Helen Scott (New York: Simon & Schuster, 1985), 269.

27. Ernest Lehman, quoted without reference in Spoto, *Dark Side*, 440.

28. Gay, "Introduction," 31.

29. Truffaut, *Hitchcock*, 282.

30. Gay, "Introduction," 27.

31. See Murray Pomerance, "The Skin of Our Teeth: The Man Who Knew Too Much Dines Out," *MacGuffin* 25a (December 1998). Further discussion of dining in this film was given in my paper "The Man Who Ate Too Much," at the meeting of the Society for Cinema Studies, West Palm Beach, Fla., April 1999.

32. Roland Barthes, *The Pleasure of the Text* (New York: Hill & Wang, 1975).

33. The film, in fact, was originally titled *The House of Dr. Edwardes*, following the 1927 novel by Francis Beeding that had been its source; eventually the name was Americanized to *The House of Dr. Edwards*, but Selznick preferred something punchier. Before Ruth Rickman, a secretary in the studio, came up with *Spellbound*, both *The Couch* and *Hidden Impulse* were tested. Leff, *Hitchcock and Selznick*, 160–161.

34. Joseph Breen, of the Production Code Administration, wanted Selznick to "please take care to avoid any characterization of Miss Carmichael as a woman sexually obsessed, or anything bordering on nymphomania" (Breen to Selznick, June 1944, quoted in Leff, *Hitchcock and Selznick*, 142). But whether because Selznick decided to stand up to him (as Leff suggests), or because Breen delegated the picture over to the slightly more understanding Geoffrey Shurlock, or for reasons unknown, we find Mary Carmichael's uncontrolled sexual passion and borderline nymphomania not at all stifled in the release print.

35. In earlier treatments, the doctors themselves had been fashioned in more perverse terms than we see, but there was fear on Selznick's part that he would be denied approval from the American Psychoanalytic Society.

36. Thomas J. Scheff, "Audience Awareness and Catharsis in Drama," *Psychoanalytic Review* 63–64 (Winter 1976–77).

37. A metaphorical "contact," to be sure, since the "stageline" in cinema makes for a boundary that cannot be crossed. A typical preparation was offered audiences five and a half weeks before the film opened nationally, in a full-page advertisement in *Life* magazine that read in part, "Incomparable Ingrid Bergman, First Lady of The Screen . . . Magnetic Gregory Peck, screendom's newest star . . . *together* to hold you irresistibly spellbound" (November 19, 1945, 21).

38. For just a few examples: Sarah Sherman (Julie Andrews) is watching Michael Armstrong (Paul Newman) in *Torn Curtain;* Lydia Brenner (Jessica Tandy) is watching Melanie Daniels ('Tippi' Hedren) in *The Birds;* Inspector Oxford (Alec McCowen) is pointedly *not* watching Bob Rusk (Barry Foster) in *Frenzy,* and therefore, over his shoulder, as it were, we are. Mark Rutland (Sean Connery) is watching Marnie Edgar ('Tippi' Hedren) in *Marnie.* And so on, not to mention the case of "Jeff" Jefferies in *Rear Window,* a quintessence of surrogacy.

39. The Hitchcockian irony: she still hasn't. If the author is the creature actually at work in the moment of creation—say, the being the writer becomes in order to write, analogous to the character that the actor becomes onstage—our only way of "discussing" the work with him is the reading *itself.* For a fascinating discussion of this dynamic, and one in which what I am calling the "author" is labeled the "speaker," see Walker Gibson, "Authors, Speakers, Readers and Mock Readers," *College English* 11 (1950): 265–269.

40. Glen O. Gabbard and Krin Gabbard, *Psychiatry and the Cinema,* 2nd ed. (Washington, D.C., and London: American Psychiatric Press, Inc., 1999), 149. Gabbard and Gabbard's interest in *Spellbound* as a romantic film, and in the trope of lovebound psychoanalytic relationships onscreen, somewhat follows from popular observations of the film when it was released. Noting Bosley Crowther's claim in the *New York Times* that the film showed love conquering all, Frank S. Nugent called *Spellbound* and *Notorious* "bulletins from the romantic front." Gottlieb, *Interviews,* 17.

41. "A man kisses a woman," Hitchcock told Frank S. Nugent in 1946. "Everyone in the audience expects him to follow it up with 'I love you' or 'I think you're wonderful.' Or to say something which shows that he has his mind on his, shall we say, work. In real

life it is far more likely that his mind is elsewhere. He might be noting the time, or wondering what's cooking for dinner." Gottlieb, *Interviews*, 19. The man who is doing the kissing, of course, is wondering where he is—as, for a moment, are we, when the symbolic doors start opening.

42. "I asked Ben Hecht to find out for me the psychiatric symbol for the beginning of love between two people, and he came back with the doors," Hitchcock told Peter Bogdanovich. Quoted in Bogdanovich, *Who the Devil Made It* (New York: Alfred A. Knopf, 1997), 512.

43. In *Citizen Kane*, Orson Welles had used a similar construction for the opposite effect, when Susan Alexander Kane is shown walking out on her husband in Florida. As these doors open, we feel a movement *out*, as Susan liberates herself from the bondage of Xanadu.

44. Kracauer, *Theory*, 285.

45. Eric Rohmer and Claude Chabrol, *Hitchcock: The First Forty-four Films*, trans. Stanley Hochman (New York: Ungar, 1979), 112, quoted in Paul Giles, *American Catholic Arts and Fictions: Culture, Ideology, Aesthetics* (New York: Cambridge University Press, 1992), 326.

46. Because of cinematic depth of field, the further something is from us—in this case, the more interior—the "deeper" it is. Also, technically: the further something is from the camera the more light is required to show both it and its distance.

47. On the diagnostic gaze see Michel Foucault, *The Birth of the Clinic: An Archaeology of Medical Perception*, trans. A. M. Sheridan Smith (New York: Vintage, 1975), 107–173.

48. The sets were built to Dali's designs by James Basevi and shot, finally, by Rex Wimpy (Spoto, *Dark Side*, 292, and Leff, *Hitchcock and Selznick*, 140–142). The dream sequence as originally planned—"It opened with four hundred human eyes glaring down at [Peck] from black velvet drapes," said Ingrid Bergman (quoted in Friedrich, *City of Nets*, 225)—was to last twenty minutes, but Selznick insisted on abbreviating it.

49. Bogdanovich, *Devil*, 515–516.

50. Erving Goffman, *Frame Analysis: An Essay on the Organization of Experience* (Cambridge: Harvard University Press, 1970).

51. It was photographed by Nestor Almendros. See his *A Man with a Camera* (New York: Farrar, Straus & Giroux, 1984), 253–258.

52. Hitchcock to Bogdanovich in Peter Bogdanovich, *The Cinema of Alfred Hitchcock* (New York: Museum of Modern Art, 1963), 26, quoted in Spoto, *Dark Side*, 292 (emphasis added). Later, with the same conversant, Hitch went further, explaining that the problem stemmed from the fact that George Barnes was what was conventionally known as a "woman's cinematographer," one who produced soft close-ups that would pass detection by using the cadge of softening his focus *through the whole film*. Given this strategy, the exceedingly crisp high-contrast and deeply focused exterior shots Hitch wanted to make of Dali's drawings would have compromised the visual quality of the rest of the film. Bogdanovich, *Devil*, 512–513.

53. *Film Profiles: Alfred Hitchcock*, interview with Philip Jenkinson for BBC TV, n.d.,

quoted in Nathalie Bondil-Poupard, "Such Stuff as Dreams Are Made On: Hitchcock and Dalí, Surrealism and Oneiricism," in *Hitchcock and Art: Fatal Coincidences*, ed. Dominique Païni and Guy Cogeval (Montreal: Montreal Museum of Fine Arts/Mazzotta, 2000), 156.

54. Salvador Dalí, *Dalí News*, November 20, 1945, 2. Quoted in Bondil-Poupard, "Such Stuff," 159.

55. For more on this see Jean Starobinski, "Poppaea's Veil," in *The Living Eye*, trans. Arthur Goldhammer (Cambridge: Harvard University Press, 1989), 1–13.

56. Truffaut, *Hitchcock*, 263.

57. Made at about the same time, for example, were *Double Indemnity* (Billy Wilder); *Gilda* (Charles Vidor); *The Big Sleep* (Howard Hawks); *The Blue Dahlia* (George Marshall); *The Killers* (Robert Siodmak); *Leave Her to Heaven* (John M. Stahl); *Mildred Pierce* (Michael Curtiz); and *The Woman in the Window* (Fritz Lang).

58. Thomas Schatz, *Hollywood Genres: Formulas, Filmmaking and the Studio System* (Philadelphia: Temple University Press, 1981), 115.

59. Paul Schrader, "Notes on Film Noir," in *Film Genre Reader II*, ed. Barry Keith Grant (Austin: University of Texas Press, 1996), 216.

60. Herbert Read suggested precisely this formula for understanding surrealism, and thus, by implication, the Dali dream sequence as a structural center of this film, when he aligned the surreal with the organic:

From the moment of its birth Surrealism was an international phenomenon—the spontaneous generation of an international and fraternal *organism* in total contrast to the artificial manufacture of a collective *organization* such as the League of Nations.

"Surrealism and the Romantic Principle," in *The Philosophy of Modern Art: Collected Essays* (London: Faber & Faber, 1952), 106.

61. A theatrical metaphor for the process of general illumination is suggested by Wolfgang Schivelbusch. "The whole stage was lit up, including those parts that had previously been in semi-darkness." *Disenchanted Night: The Industrialization of Light in the Nineteenth Century*, trans. Angela Davies (Berkeley: University of California Press, 1995), 199. The theater, writes Schivelbusch, was "the place with the greatest appetite for light in the nineteenth century" (50); now, it seems reasonable to suggest, that place is the cinema.

62. See William Rothman, *Hitchcock—The Murderous Gaze* (Cambridge: Harvard University Press, 1982), and also "The Villain in Hitchcock: Does He Look Like a 'Wrong One' to You?" in *BAD: Infamy, Darkness, Evil, and Slime on Screen*, ed. Murray Pomerance (Albany: State University of New York Press, 2004), 212–221.

63. I will here forgo listing other problematic mothers in Hitchcock and Freud, who are legion, but in all six films analyzed in this volume a mother plays a critical role. In *I Confess*, the mother is the Church.

64. Walter Benjamin's extended essay, *Charles Baudelaire: A Lyric Poet in the Age of*

High Capitalism, trans. Harry Zohn (London: Verso, 1997), is an appealing example that conveniently brings us round to the Paris that anticipated Charcot.

65. Simon Schama, *Landscape and Memory* (Toronto: Vintage Canada, 1996), 473.

66. The civil danger of police inquiry and the formal similarity of police hunts to totalitarian practices had been explored in a very explicit sequence in *Saboteur,* where a blind man chides his daughter for being too eager to help the police.

67. *Julius Caesar,* I.ii.184-187, 195-201.

68. "Lining up the 'trick shot' close-up through the raised glass required over an hour, rehearsing it forty-five minutes, and shooting it one and one-quarter hours," Leff reports (*Hitchcock and Selznick,* 155). Leff also suggests (157) that one of Hitchcock's motives in spiking the milk in this scene was to make response to an earlier critical reaction by the National Creamery Buttermakers' Association to *Foreign Correspondent's* implicit suggestion that "milk drinking is an object of ridicule."

69. Viewers surprised to find that the milk is drugged may kick themselves for forgetting that in *Suspicion* this exact trick was neatly set up.

70. Hitchcock shared his pain with Peter Bogdanovich (*Devil,* 508): "One day he asked me to come back and do a shot of Jennifer Jones selling war bonds. It was a waist shot. He got the best cameraman, Gregg Toland, who had shot *Citizen Kane,* and me to direct—a waist shot, mind you, of Jennifer selling a few war bonds. So I said, 'Well, let's go, come on,' and the [script] girl said, 'Oh, Mr. Selznick must see this.' I said, 'OK, send for him.' Next door was a huge empty ballroom that had been used in a picture and there was one Bentwood chair. I put it right in the corner of the ballroom and sat in it. Suddenly I heard, 'Where's Hitch? Where's Hitch?' 'Oh, he was here a minute ago—I think he went around there.' And Selznick looked in and saw this great empty ballroom and this figure sitting in a corner. I said, 'All ready for you, David—All ready.' 'No, no,' he said, 'I was just wondering if it's ready for you. Come on.' That was the biggest pictorial hint I could ever give."

71. Leff, *Hitchcock and Selznick,* 143. May Romm, nevertheless, approved heartily of *Spellbound,* finding in it "no technical inaccuracies." Eileen Johnston, a college graduate who had majored in psychology and been named technical advisor to the picture along with Romm by Selznick, to Selznick, August 21, 1944, quoted in Leff, *Hitchcock and Selznick,* 159.

72. Tom Gunning's work on the "looming response" is apposite here. See above, "Action North by Sincerity Northwest," note 41. The *locus classicus* of this paralysis can be seen as "Jeff" Jefferies, trapped in his wheelchair, watches helpless (through a telephoto lens, no less) as his friend Lisa Fremont is brutalized by the murderer Lars Thorwald across the courtyard in *Rear Window.*

73. Spoto, *Dark Side,* 293.

The Tear in the Curtain: *I forbid you to leave this room*

(A small part of this chapter appeared under the title "'I forbid you to leave this room': Mind/Power in *Torn Curtain,*" in *Closely Watched Brains,* ed. Murray Pomerance and John Sakeris, 2nd ed. [Boston: Pearson Education, 2002], 153-168.)

1. Robin Wood, *Hitchcock's Films Revisited*, rev. ed. (New York: Columbia University Press, 2002), 198.

2. Donald Spoto, *The Art of Alfred Hitchcock: Fifty Years of His Motion Pictures*, 2nd ed. (Garden City, N.Y.: Doubleday/Anchor, 1992), 354.

3. Kathleen Kaska, *The Alfred Hitchcock Triviography and Quiz Book* (Los Angeles: Renaissance Books, 1999), 136.

4. This is the tale mastered by Henry James, and called by Leslie Fiedler, in *The Return of the Vanishing American* (New York: Stein & Day, 1968), the "eastern." See for variations *Foreign Correspondent*, *The Man Who Knew Too Much*, *Topaz*, and *Notorious* (the action moves to South America but is set within a German cadre there).

5. I am grateful to Barry Keith Grant for reminding me that a showier and more classical dance routine is enacted in the cemetery dance of Mrs. Joseph Maloney and George Lumley in *Family Plot*, not to speak of the Francesca da Rimini ballet sequence late in *Torn Curtain*. The gavottes I invoke are structural, not scenic.

6. François Truffaut, *Hitchcock*, rev. ed., trans. Helen Scott (New York: Simon & Schuster, 1985), 345.

7. It is also, at least for Robin Wood, an elemental statement about Hitchcock's meaning and concerns, since it highlights "the seemingly hopeless incompatibility of male and female viewpoints within our socially constructed arrangements of gender and sexuality. This—and the attempts to move beyond it—seems to me the core of Hitchcock's work, and of his importance to us today." "Looking at *The Birds* and *Marnie* through the *Rear Window*," *Cineaction* 50 (1989): 82.

8. Sidney Gottlieb, ed., *Hitchcock on Hitchcock: Selected Writings and Interviews* (Berkeley: University of California Press, 1995), 306. The cinematographer John Warren also very frequently used bounced light instead of arc lamps, in the manner of the *nouvelle vague*. For a very clear description of the kind of photography that is evident in this film, see Nestor Almendros, *A Man with a Camera* (New York: Farrar, Straus & Giroux, 1984).

9. Norman O. Brown, *Apocalypse and/or Metamorphosis* (Berkeley: University of California Press, 1991), 4.

10. In Roman Polanski's homage to this film, *Frantic* (1991), the shower scene preceding the excursion to the Elmo Bookshop is reprised as pretext for a kidnapping.

11. Donald Spoto, *The Dark Side of Genius: The Life of Alfred Hitchcock* (New York: Ballantine, 1984), 536.

12. The arrival at, and entry into, the Kunstmuseum is yet another "reading," at least for us, since we see a full-color reproduction of the building in Armstrong's tourist guide and as we focus on the image the photograph dissolves into the filmic "reality." This tiny essay—which occupies no more than two seconds—is an exploration of cinematic representation as (narrative) truth.

13. A thorny issue: Michael is not an "official" spy, and so his performance training is perfunctory and in fact hardly better than Sarah's. As we shall see, the aspect of performance for which Michael is expertly prepared is secret-keeping; and what makes him better than Sarah at doing this is his position in the academic establishment.

14. Most of the shots are principally constructed of mattes.

15. Gromek, sincere, has a memory that is flawed—indeed glazed—by nostalgia. In 1966, 88th Street met Central Park West, not its downtown extension, 8th Avenue. Or could Gromek be lying?

16. *Torn Curtain*, screenplay by Brian Moore, Sept. 27, 1965, shot 131, revised Oct. 26, 1965–Nov. 4, 1965.

17. Peter Bogdanovich, *Who the Devil Made It* (New York: Alfred A. Knopf, 1997), 542.

18. It seems clear that he is not operating for the CIA, but he is operating with CIA assistance on behalf of interests at the Defense Department.

19. John Maynard Keynes, *Essays in Persuasion*, 370, quoted in Norman O. Brown, *Life against Death: The Psychoanalytic Meaning of History* (New York: Vintage, 1959), 108.

20. Erving Goffman, *Frame Analysis: An Essay on the Organization of Experience* (Cambridge: Harvard University Press, 1974), chap. 5.

21. In an article entitled *"Torn Curtain's* Futile Talk," Christopher D. Morris makes the argument that the title of the film allegorizes problematizations of reading, speech, and language (*Cinema Journal* 39:1 [1999]: 54ff.). This view of *Torn Curtain*, centering to some degree on "Armstrong's belief in meaning," seems to me a good example of the "absence of the political" in recent Hitchcock criticism that irritates Robin Wood ("Why We Should [Still] Take Hitchcock Seriously," *Cineaction* 31 [1993]), although it contains a discussion of Hitchcock's heteroglossia in this film that is truly fascinating.

22. Spoto, *Art*, 356; Wood, *Revisited*, 198.

23. Sidney Gottlieb, ed., *Alfred Hitchcock Interviews* (Jackson: University Press of Mississippi, 2003), 131.

24. In one of my very first lectures as a premedical student fresh out of high school, I sat in exactly such a seat in exactly such a room. I felt nauseated and overwhelmed with not only ignorance but hopelessness at ever knowing anything. When, with the insouciance of Lindt, the professor started calling on students by name (having memorized our photographs before this first class), I thought I might not survive the hour.

25. Hitchcock told Claude Chabrol, "I pay attention to the setting for credibility." Gottlieb, *Interviews*, 42.

26. On the *Narrenschiff*, see Michel Foucault, *Madness and Civilization: A History of Insanity in the Age of Reason* (New York: Vintage, 1973).

27. The original intent had been to use a selection from Ravel's *Daphnis et Chloë*, but Ravel's estate was uncooperative. By October 22, 1965, the Tchaikovsky had been found as a substitute. See Viola Hegyi Swisher, "Toumanova in Hollywood," *Dance* (March 1966). I am grateful to Larry Billman of the Academy of Dance on Film and to Kristine Kreuger of the Margaret Herrick Library of the Academy of Motion Picture Arts and Sciences, Beverly Hills.

28. The shooting script in fact ended the film with a close shot of this ballerina, piqued at being upstaged in Sweden just as she had been upstaged earlier in East Berlin. People looking at academic spies instead of artists, indeed!

29. Congenial, note, not red-blooded. Because he is likeable, Newman will cause us pain as his resentment gets the better of him. Because he was a known Method actor, who had played ignoble characters, his character was not above this kind of behavior. Thus, at once we could believe with Sarah and feel her despondency, too.

30. Guy Davenport, "On Reading," in *The Hunter Gracchus and Other Papers on Literature and Art* (Washington, D.C.: Counterpoint, 1996), 25.

31. The European academy is a fountainhead of male dominance.

32. A useful analysis of the power relations implicit in this social structure is given in a discussion of *potlatch* in Marvin Harris, *Cows, Pigs, Wars and Witches: Riddles of Culture* (New York: Vintage, 1974).

33. Harold Garfinkel, *Studies in Ethnomethodology* (Englewood Cliffs, N.J.: Prentice-Hall, 1965), 146. There is an elaborate discussion of it in "Action North by Sincerity Northwest," in the present volume. William Rothman suggests to me, in personal correspondence, that the teacher-pupil sequence in this film may be a gloss on the Truffaut-Hitchcock conversations of August 1962. *Torn Curtain* was made not long after that significant event. See Truffaut's letter to Hitchcock, June 2, 1962, in François Truffaut, *Letters*, trans. Gilbert Adair (London: Faber & Faber, 1989), 177–179.

34. Phenomenologically, "truth" is not a characteristic quality but a reading or attribution, and thus a framing. When I say "true" identity, I am certainly raising more questions than I am answering, but it will be sufficient if we understand that beneath the masquerade there is presumed to be an agency whose actions are not ultimately to be understood as play. A helpful guide is Goffman, *Frame Analysis*, chap. 3.

35. Garfinkel, *Studies*, 137ff.

36. I suspect the required immodesty, stunningly portrayed by Newman, is one reason so many critics of the film claim to deplore his performance. He had established himself in many films as modest, retiring, even shy; and so "Armstrong"—at least while he is operating upon Lindt—is a very atypical Newman role, given his recent exposures as Hud, as Chance Wayne in *Sweet Bird of Youth*, as Ram Bowen in *Paris Blues*, or as Ari Ben Canaan in *Exodus*.

37. As professors they are colleagues, but Manfred the escort is controlling Lindt for the state police.

38. Other interesting professors can be found in *The 39 Steps, North by Northwest, Foreign Correspondent, Rope,* and *Spellbound,* but only here is professing itself professed.

39. Of the many descriptions of Hitchcock himself that are mirrored by this comment of Lindt's—that he reveled in conceiving, even drawing, scenes but was relatively uninterested in actually shooting them—none is perhaps so dramatic as André Bazin's description of him during an interview in Nice on the set of *To Catch a Thief*: "Did he ever do any improvisation on the spot? None at all. He'd had *To Catch a Thief* completely in his head for two months. That's why he seemed so relaxed. Otherwise, he said with a pleasant smile and getting up from his seat, how could he have given me a whole hour in the middle of shooting if at the same time he had to think about his film?" *Cahiers du cinéma* 39 (October 1954): 32 (translation mine).

40. In a critique of Daniel Dayan's transposition of Jean-Pierre Oudart's conception of the "suture" system, in which a shot implies a being called *l'absent* whose axis of vision frames what is seen and who appears and resolves the absence in the subsequent shot, William Rothman interestingly argues for an essentially triadic structure, in which (i) a character, present onscreen, looks off at (ii) a field we are given in a second shot, before we see (iii) the character again, in verification that they have seen. Rothman uses Melanie Daniels's sighting of Lydia Brenner's house from the middle of Bodega Bay; but here in *Torn Curtain*, Hitchcock has given the same construction a fascinating twist: Armstrong is seen looking at the board; we are shown the board he is looking at; and we see his ocular response. But *for us*, mathematical ignorami, what he is looking at—and therefore, what he desired to look at and later took pleasure in having seen—is unintelligible. William Rothman, "Against 'The System of the Suture,'" *Film Quarterly* 29, 1 (1975): referrring to Dayan, "The Tutor-Code of Classical Cinema," *Film Quarterly* 28, 1 (1974); Jean-Pierre Oudart, "La Suture," *Cahiers du cinéma* 211–212 (1969).

41. Hitchcock's casting is invariably flawless, and one must never pay too much attention to comments he made in public about this or that actor being unsuitable for this or that reason. There is no evidence Hitchcock was ever comfortable with interviewers or said anything but what would get the interview done with. The truth about his relation with his actors is spoken on the screen.

42. Walter Benjamin, *Charles Baudelaire*, trans. Harry Zohn (New York: Verso, 1997), 41.

43. From the name of the cruise ship onward, it is possible to read the film in terms of fire symbolism, but here I forgo this option.

44. Brown, *Apocalypse and/or Metamorphosis*, 5.

45. In *Bande à part*, filmed in 1963, Jean-Luc Godard had parodied the tourist's deprecation of high art by showing his protagonists scurrying through a ten-minute tour of the Louvre, much as here Michael Armstrong moves through the Kunstmuseum without really appreciating it. Gromek later reproaches him. Armstrong's museum-going is not a race, however; he uses the scene as a forest of symbols in which to hide his tracks and destination. What both directors share that should interest the present reading is an interest in the distinction between concentration on content and concentration on the frame in which it is contained, since in both scenarios a devoted attention to paintings is incompatible with navigation through the museum space. This division of thought is longstanding in Hitchcock. In much the same way as Armstrong moves through the Kunstmuseum, for instance, we move through the scenes of J.B.'s dream in *Spellbound* in order to find our way through the film.

Once in Love with *Marnie*

1. "A spellbinding portrait of a disturbed woman" is the epigram on the recently released DVD (Universal 20587).

2. "When the girl goes out after their first meeting in the office, she may just glance at him—but it doesn't mean anything. The main purpose of this scene is that this

man was attracted to her right in that office when he gave the nod to hire her." Hitchcock quoted in Donald Spoto, *The Dark Side of Genius: The Life of Alfred Hitchcock* (New York: Ballantine, 1984), 496.

3. I say this notwithstanding some elegant critiques, such as Robin Wood's, in which the film is posited as a reading of Rutland's own character and personality flaws and problems. See *Hitchcock's Films Revisited*, rev. ed. (New York: Columbia University Press, 2002), chap. 8, esp. 185ff.

4. See Erving Goffman, *Frame Analysis: An Essay on the Organization of Experience* (Cambridge: Harvard University Press, 1974), chap. 4.

5. I here and throughout follow the shooting script of October 29, 1963 (with additions), by Jay Presson Allen (unpublished). A shot added to the script on November 21 gives Mark hearing Strutt's voice in the back of his mind: "*You* remember her! I pointed her out! The little witch! Always pulling her skirts down over her knees as if they were a National Treasure!"

6. Jay Presson Allen recounted to me (in personal conversation, January 2001) the circumstances of Connery's hiring. "'I've been sent some footage by these people who are doing this James Bond thing,' Hitchcock said. 'They've got this Scottish actor that everybody is very enthusiastic about.' This was the first James Bond movie. They were still shooting. He'd never been seen. We sat there in the dark looking at this guy with this *extreme* Scottish accent to play a Virginia gentleman and the light went up and we looked at one another and we said, 'Let's go with him,' and we just howled at what we intended to do."

7. "He was always a voyeur. He was never in. He never knew it from the inside. . . . He was outside looking in, he was a keen observer" (Allen, personal conversation).

8. François Truffaut, *Hitchcock*, rev. ed., trans. Helen Scott (New York: Simon & Schuster, 1985), 306.

9. I am grateful to Eric Schramm for pointing out that in a trailer for *Marnie*, Mark and Marnie are shown separately descending the contrasting staircases of their parents' houses. Hitchcock notes in his narration how different the two persons are and specifically indicates the unequal size and splendor of the two "homes"—both, of course, meticulous set constructions by Robert Boyle.

10. This line in the shooting script of October 29, 1963, was slightly modified in performance.

11. "The close-up is so tight, the frame filled so fully with pressing lips, that the tone is virtually pornographic," writes Spoto (*Dark Side*, 500).

12. "Feminine sexual panic" was the theme for Penelope Gilliat in the *Observer*, July 12, 1964. For Laura Mulvey, Marnie's "guilt" leads her to "masquerade" as the "perfect to-be-looked-at image." *Visual and Other Pleasures* (Bloomington: Indiana University Press, 1989), 24. "Lesbian desire" is Marnie's problem for Lucretia Knapp in "The Queer Voice in *Marnie*," *Cinema Journal* 32:4 (1993): 6—23.

13. Using a series of false identities, Marnie Edgar has been committing a string of robberies and taking flight. She visits her ailing mother in Baltimore and then takes a

job at a Philadelphia publisher, Rutland's, where the scion of the family, Mark, falls in love with her. They marry when, having caught her stealing, he offers himself or the police. On the honeymoon voyage she cannot bring herself to consummate the marriage, and back home she takes to robbing the company safe. Her husband brings her to her mother's house where in a flashback remembrance she reconstructs a long-buried moment in her childhood when she killed a man who had sexually attacked her mother. Able now to let go of her past, Marnie goes off with Mark toward a more open future.

14. Wood, *Revisited*, 192.

15. The title cards were produced at the "best classic printers" that could be found, Stellar Press in Hertfordshire, for £300, according to Tony Lee Moral, *Hitchcock and the Making of Marnie* (Lanham, Md.: Scarecrow Press, 2002), 135.

16. Truffaut, *Hitchcock*, 304.

17. Baker's diegetic position between Mark and Marnie reflected onscreen something realer, suggesting Hitchcock was no stranger to the complications of human relationships. Tony Lee Moral suggests that while shooting the film Baker thought "it was difficult being in the middle between Hitch and Tippi" and that the actress "found herself retaliating" against an awkward "competitive triangle" that included Hedren, Hitchcock, and herself, since she was often invited to lunch with the director in a party from which Hedren had been excluded, and was the secret recipient, against her will, of negative comments by Hitchcock about Hedren. Moral, *Making of Marnie*, 121.

18. Joe McElhaney, "Touching the Surface: *Marnie*, Melodrama, Modernism," in *Alfred Hitchcock Centenary Essays*, ed. Richard Allen and Sam Ishii-Gonzalès (London: British Film Institute, 1999), 99.

19. And invoked explicitly in the dining car sequence of *North by Northwest* when Eve Kendall wonders why Roger Thornhill thinks he has to conceal his desire to make love to women. James Naremore, *North by Northwest*, *Alfred Hitchcock Director* (New Brunswick: Rutgers University Press, 1993), 85.

20. See, for an analysis of repeatable and situated comic turns, Mel Gordon, *Lazzi: The Comic Routines of the Commedia dell'Arte* (New York: Performing Arts Journal Publications, 1983).

21. Allen, shooting script, October 29, 1963, pp. 44–45.

22. Just one time more than Marion Crane in *Psycho*, and one fewer than she'd like: Mark prevents her from going at Howard Johnson's. (I am grateful to Eric Schramm for pointing this out.) To a number of actresses over the years, Hitchcock confided that when using a public toilet, if another man entered the room, he would quickly raise his legs within the stall "so that no one could tell there was anyone there." Spoto, *Dark Side*, 415n.

23. "He was extremely pleased with the script," said Allen. "But that doesn't mean that everything stays in a script. . . . You can't write for the movies if stuff like that's gonna bother you" (personal conversation).

24. The emphasis is on the location and on the shoving; not on the nickels: all payment at the automat was by means of nickels.

25. See William Carlos Williams, "The American Background," in *Selected Essays* (New York: New Directions, 1969), 134—161.

26. I am grateful to Ann Dooley for the translation.

27. The screenwriter was not thrilled by the character of Old Rutland. "I thought the father was so phony. He was comical, pathetic, totally unreal—cast unreal, performed unreal. I never met anybody like that in my life. That's a movie character, doesn't have anything to do with the real-life character" (personal conversation).

28. On Hitchcock's anticipation of his audience: "I wrote that Mark drove in a beat-up old pickup truck," Allen told me. "Hitchcock couldn't *tolerate* that. 'But Hitch, that's the way it is.' 'But the public doesn't know that, they won't buy it.' But it wasn't just the public, it was Hitch himself who didn't go for that beat-up old truck" (personal conversation).

29. The recipes were straightforward and the exceptionally high customer turnover guaranteed exceptional freshness in the food. In Philadelphia, where old Mr. Rutland would have routinely fed his secret but acceptable vice, the automats were fed twice daily from the central Horn & Hardart commissary; though it is likely the Rutland household would have been catered from one of the waitress-service restaurants in the suburbs. Joseph Horn and Frank Hardart, having founded the automated restaurant in Philadelphia in 1902, owned restaurants, automats, cafeterias, and "Less Work for Mother" Retail Shops by 1960.

30. On do-it-yourselfism in American life of the 1950s, see Karal Ann Marling, *As Seen on TV: The Visual Culture of Everyday Life in the 1950s* (Cambridge: Harvard University Press, 1994), 51ff.

31. "Glittering chrome-and-glass art deco glory" is the descriptive phrase used by Bethany Kandel, "Last Automat," for the Associated Press, n.d., n.p.

32. There was a "nickel girl," since payment was accepted only by means of coins of this denomination; her job was to change money into nickels all day long, and on the first day of operation of the first automat in New York, 8,693 nickels were amassed. By 1987, only one automat was left, at 42nd Street and 3rd Avenue in Manhattan; by then the slots took quarters (ibid.).

33. "One of those who holds the secret [of how they get the food in there] is 64-year-old Melvin Matterson of Brooklyn, who's worked for the Automat since 1947. He wears a black bow tie and starched white hat and apron as he fills the rows of windows.

"'People always try to peek to see who's behind the doors, but I keep them guessing,' he says" (ibid.).

34. "There was continual speculation on who was behind the glass boxes, secretly refilling them. 'Are there little gnomes with long beards and green union suits who scamper about, placing a creamed chicken in this box and a ham on rye in that, like mail sorters in a country post office?' one newspaper writer asked" (ibid.).

35. Wood, *Revisited*, 189.

36. Psychological realism is the key to numerous readings of this film, and Donald Spoto's is notable in this respect: "Larceny is often related to sexual pathology, and so

the film uses three classically Freudian images to make the connection." *The Art of Alfred Hitchcock: Fifty Years of His Motion Pictures*, 2nd ed. (New York: Doubleday, 1992), 346. More recent readings are more particular, and go further: "Marnie's hair is dyed; her purse, the repository of stolen money; her jewels, the emblems of her captivity; and her desirable feminine appearance, the envelope for a passionless body," writes Paula Marantz Cohen, in the process of arguing that Mark is as disturbed as she is, in "Beyond the Family Nexus," in *Alfred Hitchcock: The Legacy of Victorianism* (Lexington: University Press of Kentucky, 1995), 154–155. Lesley Brill takes a softer approach, writing that "Hitchcock's handling of Marnie's story suggests that art has a curative role to play in helping us to bring our personal pasts into harmony with the present." *The Hitchcock Romance: Love and Irony in Hitchcock's Films* (Princeton: Princeton University Press, 1988), 250. More explicitly, Tania Modleski states that the message of Marnie is this: "The bond linking the man and the woman is his knowledge of her guilty secret (guilty, that is, in patriarchal terms), that the union is founded on the man's ability to blackmail the woman sexually." *The Women Who Knew Too Much* (New York: Routledge, 1989), 30.

37. "Hitch loved working with strong women" (Allen, personal conversation).

38. The French version, we may remember, was called *Pas de printemps pour Marnie* ("No Springtime for Marnie"), an invocation of the season of regeneration.

39. Wood, *Revisited*, 189.

40. A point made bluntly by Kenneth Anger's description of Lupe Velez's unfortunate end: "Juanita traced the vomit trail from the bed, followed the spotty track over to the orchid-tiled bathroom. There she found her mistress, Señorita Velez, head jammed down in the toilet bowl, drowned.

"The huge dose of Seconal had not been fatal in the expected fashion. It had mixed retch-erously with the Spitfire's Mexi-Spice Last Supper. The gut action, her stomach churning, had revived the dazed Lupe. Violently sick, an ultimate fastidiousness drove her to stagger towards the sanitary sanctum of the *salle de bain* where she slipped on the tiles and plunged head first into her Egyptian Chartreuse Onyx Hush-Flush Model Deluxe." Anger, *Hollywood Babylon* (New York: Dell, 1975), 339–342.

41. On Hitchcock's "toilet privacy" see Spoto, *Dark Side*, 415; on his fascination with "toilet silence" see Spoto, *Dark Side*, 523; and on the general relation between civilization, social arrangement, and alimentation see Claude Lévi-Strauss, *The Raw and the Cooked* (Harmondsworth: Penguin, 1986); Alain Corbin, *The Foul and the Fragrant: Odor and the French Social Imagination* (Cambridge: Harvard University Press, 1986); Wolfgang Schivelbusch, *Tastes of Paradise: A Social History of Spices, Stimulants, and Intoxicants* (New York: Pantheon, 1992); and Dominique Laporte, *History of Shit* (Cambridge: MIT Press, 2002).

42. "Hitch 49," *Cahiers du cinéma* 154 (April 1964): 51.

43. Robin Wood, *Hitchcock's Films* (London: A. Zwemmer Ltd., 1965), 158.

44. "The Marnie picture," he called it in 1963, "the story of the compulsive thief." Sidney Gottlieb, ed., *Alfred Hitchcock Interviews* (Jackson: University Press of Mississippi, 2003), 53.

45. On May 1, 1963, Evan Hunter learned that Jay Presson Allen had replaced him as screenwriter on this film. He was not surprised, having taken Hitch aside three months earlier to complain about plans for the honeymoon rape scene, which utterly displeased him:

> I told him that I did not want to write that scene as he had outlined it. I told him we would lose all sympathy for the male lead if he rapes his own wife on their honeymoon. I told him we can see the girl isn't being coy or modest, she's terrified, she's trembling, and the reasons for this all come out in the later psychiatric sessions. I told him if the man really loved her he would take her in his arms and comfort her gently and tell her they'd work it out, don't be frightened, everything will be all right. I told him that's how *I* thought the scene should go.
>
> Hitch held up his hands the way directors do when they're framing a shot. Palms out, fingers together, thumbs extended and touching to form a perfect square. Moving his hands toward my face, like a camera coming in for a close shot, he said, "Evan, when he sticks it in her, I want that camera right on her *face!*"
>
> Many years later, when I told Jay Presson Allen how much his description of that scene had bothered me, she said, "You just got bothered by the scene that was his reason for making the movie. You just wrote your ticket back to New York."

Evan Hunter, *Me and Hitch* (London: Faber & Faber, 1997), 75–76. I suspect Hunter of having signally failed to appreciate this aspect of the gender politics of the film; and thus, of having misread Hitchcock altogether, when he balked at writing that honeymoon scene. It is Marnie's experience Hitchcock wanted to reflect in that close-up, not Mark's experience inscribed upon her.

46. Moral, *Making of Marnie*, 116.

47. See, on substance, Kenneth Burke, *A Grammar of Motives* (Berkeley: University of California Press, 1969).

48. The particular children's rhyme was selected by the screenwriter, Jay Presson Allen, because it was "funny and amusing" (Moral, *Making of Marnie*, 138). Psychoanalytic theory likens the purse to the vagina and a critique in this vein draws the rhyme into the organization of the film as a treatment of Marnie's psychosexual pathology. However, the "lady with the alligator purse" is also wealthy, capable, and positioned, like the doctor and the nurse but not like the "I" who sings of being ill.

49. "Alfred Hitchcock devant Marnie," *Cahiers du cinéma* 157 (July 1964): 39.

50. Ecclesiastes 10:19 (King James Version).

51. Jacques Rivette, "L'art de la fugue," *Cahiers du cinéma* 26 (1953): 50.

52. We can remember his pride in boasting to Truffaut that the studio wanted $50,000 minimum to get the "vertigo" shot in *Vertigo*, yet he managed it for $19,000 (*Hitchcock*, 246).

53. We might well have been prepared for this structuring by the anticipatory verse 18 of Ecclesiastes 10: "By much slothfulness the building decayeth; and through idleness of the hands the house droppeth through."

54. This line was changed in performance to "No. Not after what I have to tell them."

55. A fascinating Marxist reading of this film is given by Michele Piso, "Mark's Marnie," in *A Hitchcock Reader*, ed. Marshall Deutelbaum and Leland Poague (Ames: University of Iowa Press, 1986), 288–303. "Mark's control is everywhere visible," she suggests, accurately I think, if neglectful of his gentility, kindness, and genuine affection.

56. I have read some of his casting and scripting memoranda, and it was not uncommon for him to negotiate among as many as thirty names for a character, rejecting many that to another eye would seem indistinguishable from those on the final list.

57. These resemble just a little the locations George Kaplan inhabits in *North by Northwest*. He, too, in an odd sort of way, steals.

58. McElhaney, "Touching," 92.

59. Allen, shooting script, October 29, 1963, p. 2.

60. A Union parody of which is given at http://www.pcola.gulf.net/~vbraun/FlaStar/songs/ dixie.html, with these lines: "I wish I was in Baltimore / I'd make Secession traitors roar."

61. On secret scriptures, see Leslie A. Fiedler, *Love and Death in the American Novel* (New York: Criterion, 1960).

62. Allen, shooting script, October 29, 1963, page c.

63. A link between this film and Douglas Sirk's *Imitation of Life* (1954).

I Confess and the Men Inside

(A small part of this chapter was delivered at the Society for Cinema Studies in Ottawa in May 1997 as "Alfred Hitchcock's Stairway to Heaven: *I Confess* and the Labours of the Eye.")

1. Jean Starobinski, *The Living Eye*, trans. Arthur Goldhammer (Cambridge: Harvard University Press, 1989), 11.

2. Quebec City, 1952. In a confession to Father Michael Logan, the sacristan Otto Keller confesses that he has murdered a lawyer, Villette—coincidentally the same man who has been blackmailing Logan about a love affair in his youth with the married Ruth Grandfort. Because the killer was seen disguised in a soutane, suspicion falls upon Logan, and the investigations of Police Inspector Larrue culminate in his trial. Bound by the seal of the confessional, Logan can say nothing about what Keller revealed to him. But on the witness stand the details of his affair with Ruth are broadcast. In the end the priest is found innocent of the murder due to insufficient evidence. In the Château Frontenac, Keller is found hiding and is shot by police. Ruth goes back to her husband and Father Logan is left to somehow continue his life.

3. Gérard Pelletier, *Years of Impatience: 1950—1960*, trans. Alan Brown (New York: Facts on File, 1984), 49.

4. That Hitchcock shot *I Confess* under the aegis of a man who lusted for control is especially intriguing in light of Paul Giles's comment that "the culture of Catholicism in Hitchcock's American films promotes the representation of a world dangerously out

of control." *American Catholic Arts and Fictions: Culture, Ideology, Aesthetics* (New York: Cambridge University Press, 1992), 330.

5. See, for an interesting example of secularization, institutionalization, and anti-clericalism Natalie Zemon Davis, Jean-Claude Carrière, and Daniel Vigne, *Le Retour de Martin Guerre* (Paris: R. Laffont, 1982).

6. Pelletier, *Years*, 50.

7. Robert Bothwell, *Canada and Quebec: One Country, Two Histories*, rev. ed. (Vancouver: University of British Columbia Press, 1999), 87.

8. Given that the making of statements in a moral-legal case such as this is the quintessential form of action in a civil society, the priest is paralyzed, much like John Ballantine in *Spellbound*, who twice in his life sees a mortal accident occurring in front of his very eyes yet is impotent to affect the chain of events. See "A Bromide for Ballantine" in this volume.

9. To Arthur Knight he recalled that "working with Montgomery Clift was difficult because, you know, he was a Method actor, and neurotic as well. 'I want you to look in a certain direction,' I'd say, and he'd say, 'Well, I don't know whether I'd look that way.' Now immediately you're fouled up because you're shooting a precut picture. He's got to look that way because you're going to cut to something over there. So I have to say to him, 'Please, you'll have to look that way, or else.'" Sidney Gottlieb, ed., *Alfred Hitchcock Interviews* (Jackson: University Press of Mississippi, 2003), 173.

10. The original shooting script called for Logan to be convicted and executed; the Catholic Church refused to stand for it; the ending was rewritten, perhaps with a view to the limitations on exhibition that may well have been imposed otherwise by the Catholic Legion of Decency.

11. It has been suggested Grandfort is modeled on Premier Duplessis himself (but for the action of this plot it is unnecessary for us to see him this way). See Jean-Claude Marineau, "Hitchcock's Quebec shoot," *Cinema Canada*, March 1985.

12. The *casse-queue* ("bust your ass") is an external staircase leading from the second story of a Québec house to the street. As an architectural innovation it was hugely successful both in Québec and Montréal, freeing interior space although imperiling very old and fragile residents in the icy winter. Hitchcock was an exceptionally astute observer of cultural fact, and his decision to make special use of the *casse-queue* in the film shows his concern to show details of Québecois life of which typical tourists would be ignorant.

13. Christopher Palmer, *Dimitri Tiomkin* (London: T. E. Books, 1984), 96—98. "The singer," Palmer notes, is "very distantly recorded—so distantly, in fact, that the words are barely distinguishable. The effect is that of a poignant reminder of long-lost happiness."

14. This is written on the day of the funeral of Diana Spencer. The critic Martin Lewis, commenting upon television images of the hearse bearing her casket out of London, remarked that he was reliving an experience of childhood—that of believing the revered object would in fact disappear if he took his eyes away from it for a second. And

so he was spellbound. There is plenty of homage in that thought to Alice and the Red King, of course, and further back to Berkeley, and further still to the primitive consciousness we see reborn in children. And it may be that the fascination Diana held for so many as an object of vision in her later life was in truth predicated upon viewers' terrible fear they would lose her if they did not look, look, look, and continue to look at representations of her being; this notwithstanding the fact that without those images, she could not have become a person that a very large audience would fear losing. Images exist in two ways: they signify and embody (and thus make famous), and also appear and radiate (giving us a basis for believing in the powers of the gaze).

15. Donald Spoto, *The Dark Side of Genius: The Life of Alfred Hitchcock* (New York: Ballantine, 1984), 129.

16. Ibid., 353—355.

17. An amenity offered again, a few years later, in *The Man Who Knew Too Much* as Ben McKenna navigates a passageway to meet Ambrose Chappell; and, later, with arrows painted on a wall, in *Frenzy*.

18. Jorge Luis Borges, "Epilogue," in *Dreamtigers*, trans. Mildred Boyer and Harold Morland (New York: Dutton, 1970), 93. My thanks to Blake Fitzpatrick.

19. Not unlike the chimerical *griffin*, a symbol of optical perspicacity and featured protagonist on the Coat of Arms of the Comte de Palluau et Frontenac, which was carved on stone over the main exterior entrance of the Hotel Château Frontenac, in which the finale is set. "Its purpose was to guard valuable treasures, among them the Pearl of Wisdom and the Jewel of Enlightenment." Joan Elson Morgan, *Castle of Quebec* (Toronto: Dent, 1949), 157.

20. Some who have written about *I Confess* have expressed the thought that Keller is intended to signify "Killer," but no such usage is further from the *modus operandi* of Alfred Hitchcock. If he were going to play sound games with characters' names, he would have been quite precise. And Keller in fact does have meaning quite on its own. In German—the operative language, since that is the one Keller himself speaks—there are two Kellern, one masculine and one feminine (just as in the film). But even Keller himself can be seen to have a masculine and a feminine side, just as his wife can be seen to have a feminine and a masculine one. With Alma, Keller is a male Keller, which is to say, a cellar; as far down as one can go; the bottom; the dank underworld; the nether abode. But with Logan, Keller is a female Keller, which is to say a sow-bug or wood-tick, an insect crawling beneath rocks, slimy, grasping, vulgar, plain, and poisonous.

21. In John H. Auer's *City That Never Sleeps*, made at the same time as this film, there is a remarkably similar set-up in which William Talman peers out from a proscenium provided by the body of Otto Hulett at Tom Poston standing with a woman in a hallway. Auer's camera set-up bears only a mechanical similarity, however; Talman's eye and that of Karl Malden bear entirely different relations both to the role of vision in the respective films and to the characters they are looking around and at.

22. And like one of a pair of girls who gawk at a visiting prime minister in the lobby of the Albert Hall in *The Man Who Knew Too Much*, which Hitchcock filmed soon after this.

23. In *F for Fake* (1973).

24. Some viewers consider Hitchcock's cameo appearances self-indulgent, but a careful reading of his films will reveal that the cameo is always well integrated thematically. For further discussion, see "Gabriel's Horn: *Vertigo* and the Golden Passage," in this volume.

25. For a healthy listing of this work see Jane Sloan, *Alfred Hitchcock: A Filmography and Biography* (Berkeley: University of California Press, 1993), perforce no longer definitive but sumptuous nevertheless.

26. Susan Sontag, *On Photography* (New York: Farrar, Straus and Giroux, 1977), 23.

27. François Truffaut, *Hitchcock*, rev. ed., trans. Helen Scott (New York: Simon & Schuster, 1985), 345.

28. Erving Goffman, *Frame Analysis: An Essay on the Organization of Experience* (Cambridge: Harvard University Press, 1974), 475.

29. See John Porter's much-acclaimed book, *The Vertical Mosaic* (Toronto: University of Toronto Press, 1965), for a picture of 1950s Canada.

30. The father of Emily Post.

31. Where once had stood the Chateau Haldimand, part of the seventeenth-century Fort St. Louis. The hotel was originally projected as The Fortress, and letters patent were issued for the formation of The Fortress Hotel Company in 1890 with a capitalization of about $200,000. But the hotel would cost substantially more; and so leaders of Canadian Pacific Rail, including William Cornelius Van Horne and Thomas Shaughnessy, joined with friends to form the Chateau Frontenac Company in 1892. See Morgan, *Castle*, chap. 14.

32. James Trager, *The People's Chronology* (London: Heinemann, 1979), 177.

33. See "Le funiculaire en chute libre," *Le Soleil*, October 13, 1996.

34. See Pierre Laporte, *True Face of Duplessis* (Montreal: Harvest House, 1960), and Matthew Fraser, *Quebec Inc.* (Toronto: Key Porter Books, 1987).

35. Ruth's French accent when she speaks to her maid suggests she may be Parisian.

36. Giles, *American Catholic Arts and Fictions*, 349.

Gabriel's Horn: *Vertigo* and the Golden Passage

(Some of the material in this essay was delivered to the Society for Cinema Studies in San Diego, April 1998, as "Vertigo in *Vertigo*," and a small portion was included in "The Man Who Wanted to Go Back," in *The End of Cinema as We Know It*, ed. Jon Lewis [New York: New York University Press, 2001, 43–49].)

1. Lesley Brill suggests that this blank screen is "a radical declaration of the director's power to show us nothing beyond what he wishes," and concludes, "Nothing seems possible in *Vertigo*, and only nothing." *The Hitchcock Romance: Love and Irony in Hitchcock's Films* (Princeton: Princeton University Press, 1988), 214, 221.

2. Robin Wood, in his inspiring essay on this film, pointed to "a single object

against an undefined mass." *Hitchcock's Films Revisited*, rev. ed. (New York: Columbia University Press, 2002), 110.

3. San Francisco, 1957. John "Scottie" Ferguson, a retired detective, has acrophobia, which gives him vertigo. An old chum, Gavin Elster, hires him to follow his wife, Madeleine, who has been "behaving strangely": she believes, for example, that she is possessed by the suicidal spirit of her great-grandmother, Carlotta Valdes, whose tomb she repeatedly visits and in front of whose portrait in an art gallery she sits for long hours. One day she jumps into the Bay; Scottie rescues her, then takes her driving to the redwood forests and an old mission at San Juan Bautista. They fall in love. But she says it is "too late" and races away to the top of a bell tower. He tries to follow her but because of his consummate fear of heights he must stop on the stairs short of the top. Suddenly he hears a scream and her body plunges past him, crashing in death. Considerably later, he happens to meet a shopgirl who resembles Madeleine, Judy Barton. Soon we see that earlier she had pretended to be Madeleine Elster in order to assist in the real woman's murder. As Judy and Scottie spend more and more time together her anxiety builds. Scottie, ignorant, insists on making Judy over with new clothes and new hair style and color until she looks disarmingly like Madeleine. But one night, dressing for dinner, she inadvertently gives away her secret, attempting to lock "Carlotta's" necklace (a souvenir from her days with Elster) around her neck. In a frenzy of awareness, Scottie brings her to the Mission tower and succeeds this time in climbing to the top, where Judy is startled by the voice of a nun and falls to her death.

4. As used in Tati's *Playtime* (1960) [the gowns in the nightclub], Minnelli's *The Band Wagon* (1954) [Fred Astaire's socks], and Sirk's *Written on the Wind* (1954) [Dorothy Malone's negligee].

5. The long shot was taken at twilight, in fact, August 26, 1957, between 7:50 and 8:05 P.M. See George Turner, "Hitchcock's Acrophobic Vision," *American Cinematographer* (November 1996): 86–91. According to Turner, the close shots in the roof sequence were done on Paramount's process stage by John Fulton; and additional shots to be used for augmentation were made in Los Angeles.

6. The Kuleshov effect, discussed by Hitchcock with François Truffaut in *Hitchcock*, rev. ed., trans. Helen Scott (New York: Simon & Schuster, 1985), pp. 214ff., in relation to *Rear Window:* "Let's take a close-up of Stewart looking out of the window at a little dog. . . . Back to Stewart, who has a kindly smile. But if in the place of the little dog you show a half-naked girl exercising in front of her open window, and you go back to a smiling Stewart again, this time he's seen as a dirty old man!"

7. As John Fiske would put it, "anomalous." See "Reading the Beach," in *Reading the Popular* (Boston: Unwin Hyman, 1989), 43–76.

8. Jean Douchet wrote of Hitchcock's creative principles, "L'Idée chez notre cinéaste, précède l'existence et la fonde" (With this filmmaker, the Idea precedes existence and defines it). "Le Troisième clé d'Hitchcock," *Cahiers du cinéma* 99 (September 1959): 47. For his own part, Hitchcock said something not dissimilar to Claude Chabrol: "For me the screenplay is nearly secondary. I make the film before knowing

the story. It comes to me as a form, as an impression of a whole. Afterward I develop a script and make it correspond to what I have in mind." Sidney Gottlieb, ed., *Alfred Hitchcock Interviews* (Jackson: University Press of Mississippi, 2003), 42.

9. In this it can be said he followed in the tradition of Busby Berkeley. "I did my cutting with the camera. . . . That is, the cutter had to put it together the way I shot it." Berkeley, in an interview with Mike Steen in *Hollywood Speaks: An Oral History* (New York: Putnam, 1974), quoted in Ronald L. Davis, *The Glamour Factory: Inside Hollywood's Big Studio System* (Dallas: Southern Methodist University Press, 1993), 183. "[Berkeley] was clever with the camera," affirmed Harry Warren. "He was the daddy of that." Anne Baxter saw the liveliness of Hitchcock's camera while shooting *I Confess:* "He did not care so much that the actors acted—he wanted the *camera* to act." Paraphrased by Donald Spoto, *The Dark Side of Genius: The Life of Alfred Hitchcock* (New York: Ballantine, 1984), 361.

10. *King Lear* 4.6.56.

11. Erving Goffman, *Frame Analysis: An Essay on the Organization of Experience* (New York: Harper & Row, 1974), chap. 5.

12. On narrative development and probability, see Paul Goodman, *The Structure of Literature* (Chicago: University of Chicago Press, 1954).

13. Quoted in Goffman, *Frame Analysis*, 380.

14. The subjective downward view was one of the small number of narrative and design elements that Hitchcock insisted upon for this film. There were always, according to Henry Bumstead, one or two things Hitch particularly wanted in a film he was working on—things he would go to considerable trouble to achieve. In this case, the crew scouted downtown Los Angeles, where in 1957, as today, the buildings were not especially high, until they found a pair of suitable structures to convey the effect. A wooden bridge was erected between the two buildings across the alleyway that separated them, and the camera, mounted in the center, shot directly down. But the effect was insufficiently dramatic. In the end the artifice was accomplished through a matte shot. (Henry Bumstead, in conversation, December 1996.)

15. See Jeff Kraft and Aaron Leventhal, *Footsteps in the Fog: Alfred Hitchcock's San Francisco* (Santa Monica: Santa Monica Press, 2002), 80.

16. For a fascinating retake on which, see Martin Scorsese's *Cape Fear* (1991).

17. Conversation, October 30, 1996.

18. In order to have a full taste of the yellowness of this scene, and especially of the precocious stepladder, it is necessary to view a clean, faithful, new print of the film, such as the 70mm restoration by James Katz and Robert Harris.

19. "If the onlookers laugh when the clown suddenly finds himself falling like a stone it is because they had all along been projecting their musculature and sensibilities sympathetically into his walk and now find that their leaning into his anticipated conduct, into the anticipated guidedness of his doings, their framed prediction of what is to come, is disordered." Goffman, *Frame Analysis*, 381.

20. Should we be prone to neglecting this vital insight, Hitchcock signals us in the

opening credits (designed by Saul Bass) to consider (a) the aperture and (b) the human body, especially the eye, in relation to one another.

21. Though Brill argues it is "always true of Hitchcockian irony" that "the physical descents of the characters are matched and intensified by camera placements that push them down optically," I think we often see in *Vertigo* a narratively downward passage that is emphatically not an optical descent. Midge's departure from the sanitarium is one example that comes to mind: her hopes for Scottie have fallen completely, but the shot has no vertical architecture and she recedes down one side of a long corridor.

22. In an early plan for his cameo in the film, Hitch was to have carried such a model ship. François Truffaut, "Hitch: Vertigo," *Cahiers du cinéma* 84 (June 1958): 43.

23. The largest and nearest of which bears the number 24, while itself rotating at 24 frames per second.

24. It includes reference to the fact that the shipping money is from his wife's family, who own another yard in Baltimore. Hitchcock will make reference to that more explicitly in *Marnie*, situating what might well be one of Madeleine's family's ships at the end of Mrs. Edgar's little street; this setting has very often been criticized for its blatant two-dimensionality, its open fictiveness, but by the time *Vertigo* is done we have enough information about the Gavin Elster whose wife is from the east to wonder not only about him but also about her, her family, and their ships. In the context of this intertextuality, the open fictionality of the Baltimore street scene *qua* scene seems not entirely without purpose.

25. Elster's social dominance could have been demonstrated by placing him in various occupations, however. That he is involved with shipbuilding adds to the texture of the narrative an invocation of the peculiar and terrifying gravitational challenge of the sea. As Fuller put it, "Most of the ruination of the great B.C. Greek architecture was caused by centuries-apart earthquakes. Seaquakes occur daily and the designers of ships have to anticipate them. Thus great engineering had its beginning in ships." "Vertical Is to Live—Horizontal Is to Die," *The American Scholar* (Winter 1969): 27–47.

26. Royal S. Brown, "*Vertigo* as Orphic Tragedy," *Literature/Film Quarterly* 14:1 (1986): 32–43.

27. The exterior and interior are studio reconstructions by Henry Bumstead. See Kraft and Leventhal, *Footsteps in the Fog*, 85ff.

28. Ashburton Place, a dead-end delivery alley, was replaced in the production, according to Kenneth Clopine, by Claude Street behind Sloane's (quoted in Donald Spoto, *The Art of Alfred Hitchcock: Fifty Years of His Motion Pictures* [Garden City, N.Y.: Doubleday Anchor, 1992], 270); but according to Kraft and Leventhal by Claude Lane, a narrow alley nicely showing "the architecture and density of traffic which characterize the area surrounding Union Square" (*Footsteps in the Fog*, 93).

29. Shot on location.

30. Kraft and Leventhal, *Footsteps in the Fog*, 102.

31. The reader will note, perhaps with a query, the spelling of the sad Carlotta's last

name. While many critics make it "Valdez," thereby (like the concierge at the McKittrick Hotel [Ellen Corby]) attributing to her Spanish, or at least Mexican, nationality, the screenplay for the film and the gravestone at the Mission Dolores spell the name with an "s." "Valdes" is a Portuguese spelling, suggesting that Carlotta's ancestry may be Portuguese or Brazilian—in either case she is of distinctly higher social standing than we may have presumed. Elster is British, certainly British middle class. We can have reason for imagining he has married upward (as we keep in mind that Carlotta Valdes is in dramatic truth connected to his wife). The story recounted by Pop Leibel of Carlotta's fall is given more resonance as we understand that in class terms, as well as personal ones, she has been dropped from a height by the man who threw her away.

32. All the translations here are my own.

33. William James, "The Perception of Reality," in *Principles of Psychology*, vol. 2 (New York: Dover, 1950), 309.

34. Hearing "phantasmal voices" when the movement of lips and faces can be seen is one recurring phenomenon. For a broad discussion of deafness see Oliver Sacks, *Seeing Voices: A Journey into the World of the Deaf* (London: Stoddart, 1989).

35. This sequence reflects a similar treatment with Joan Crawford and Jack Palance, in the same location, in David Miller's *Sudden Fear* (1952). The production information is given in Turner, "Acrophobic Vision," 88.

36. Simon Schama, *Landscape and Memory* (Toronto: Vintage Canada, 1996), 517–522.

37. Hitchcock in Charles Bitsch, "Alfred Hitchcock entre trois films," *Cahiers du cinéma* 92 (February 1959): 25.

38. We may contrast with this setting the lambent and metrical forest clearing of *North by Northwest*, where the conversation is practical, fleeting, almost a business meeting.

39. Personal conversation, December 1996.

40. Certainly invoked in *Vertigo*, principally through Hitchcock's use of Judy Barton as performer, a cipher for drawing our attention to the indecisiveness of our knowledge of people, is the modernist experience of urban circulation and its relation to authenticity, as discussed by Marshall Berman. Berman writes about Montesquieu's 1721 *Letters from Persia*, in which the observation is raised by wealthy Persian visitors to bustling, varied, fast-moving Paris of the early eighteenth century that the overall condition of compulsion in their Persian harem forced a certain deadening uniformity in human behavior: "We don't see people as they really are, only as they are forced to be." *Lettres Persanes*, 3rd ed., ed. P. Vernière (Paris: Garnier, 1960), letter 63, quoted in Marshall Berman, "Too Much Is Not Enough: Metamorphoses of Times Square," in *Impossible Presence: Surface and Screen in the Photogenic Era*, ed. Terry Smith (Chicago: University of Chicago Press, 2001), 50. In Paris, suggests Berman (without noting that he is pointing to the city in which *Vertigo* was originally set), there was to be found "freedom to expose and express yourself with the fullest openness, with nothing veiled or hidden; or it can mean freedom not only to experiment with yourself, but to consciously veil yourself and deceive other people" (53).

41. Episode 7 of "Alfred Hitchcock Presents," aired on CBS, November 13, 1955. Written by Louis Pollock and Francis Cockrell, "Breakdown" presents the events of a car accident in which the victim is presumed by the attending ambulance crew to be dead when in fact he is not: it is through his point of view that we experience virtually the entirety of the narrative. (For her kind assistance, I am indebted to Jane Sloan.)

42. The second is *The Man Who Knew Too Much* (1956). In 1948 the two had collaborated on *Rope*.

43. In the shooting script, but not in the final performance, Scottie prates on, "I shall wiggle my behind . . . free and unconfined," a remark that plays interestingly on both his attitude toward his own masculinity and the undergarments Midge is sketching as she listens to him with a smile. Alec Coppel and Samuel Taylor, shooting script for *Vertigo*, September 12, 1957, 4.

44. "The camera with its one eye has no peripheral vision," said Gene Kelly. Quoted in Davis, *Glamour Factory*, 191. See as well José Ortega y Gasset, "On Point of View in the Arts," in *The Dehumanization of Art and Other Essays* (Princeton: Princeton University Press, 1968), 107–130.

45. About this figure, Hitchcock made a chilling joke. Charles Bitsch asked him what happened after the last shot: did Stewart fall off the tower himself, or go back down the stairs? "Frankly," said Hitch, "I think he falls. . . . On the other hand, maybe he retraces his steps in order to court the nun!" "Entre trois films," 26.

46. Stanley Cavell, *Themes Out of School* (Chicago: University of Chicago Press, 1988), 180.

47. Personal conversation. In the Fall of 2000, Robert Harris recounted to me how during work on the restoration, he came across another version of this oil at Paramount Studios, with Kim Novak as Carlotta; although he may have meant Vera Miles (who had been cast in this film), because Kraft and Leventhal report (*Footsteps in the Fog*, 103) that he now has that portrait hanging in his California office.

48. In Coppel and Taylor's script of September 12, 1957, 103–104, the scene was written more fully than the version that finally appears in the cut film, ending with Scottie actually meeting and touching the girl.

49. Raymond Durgnat, *The Strange Case of Alfred Hitchcock, or the Plain Man's Hitchcock* (London: Faber & Faber, 1974), 294.

50. Even here, however, there are hidden structures. In fact (and also in verisimilitudinous dramatic recreation), Gavin Elster's wife may very well have stage-managed her own "well made-up" appearance, since her social class permitted frequent use of Elizabeth Arden's in exactly the same cause as moves Scottie to have Judy "redone." The glamour of Madeleine, then, and the relative plainness of Judy are signals of differential access to social capital.

51. Jean Starobinski, *The Living Eye*, trans. Arthur Goldhammer (Cambridge: Harvard University Press, 1989), 5.

52. Goffman, *Frame Analysis*, 381.

53. The Embarcadero in 1879 was very often a setting for rowdiness, given its centrality in the shipping industry and its definition as the port of the city. Anyone who

would be able to say who shot whom there in a particular month of that year would be an expert on San Francisco, indeed.

54. It was but twenty years old when *Vertigo* was filmed.

55. "The [Portman] mansion was torn down in 1959 shortly after *Vertigo* was filmed." Kraft and Leventhal, *Footsteps in the Fog*, 106.

56. See Elisabeth Weis, *The Silent Scream* (Rutherford, N.J.: Fairleigh Dickinson University Press, 1985); and Murray Pomerance, "'The Future's Not Ours to See: Song, Singer, Labyrinth in Hitchcock's *The Man Who Knew Too Much*," in *Soundtrack Available*, ed. Arthur Knight and Pamela Robertson Wojcik (Durham: Duke University Press, 2002), 53–73.

57. Designed, according to Spoto, by Kenneth Clopine. *Art*, 270.

58. Hitchcock did not like blue skies and generally avoided using them.

59. Brill, *Romance*, 205. Brill here gives many non-auricular examples.

60. Spoto informs us (*Art*, 280) that Herrmann inserted the second movement of Mozart's Symphony No. 34 in C, K. 338, but does not suggest why this relatively un-played work, dating from 1780, might have been especially appropriate. This work was written around the time Mozart was disparaged by one of his great admirers, Baron von Grimm, as "'Too confident, too little a man of action, too much ready to succumb to his own illusions, too little au courant with the ways that lead to success.' . . . Disappoint-ment was followed by tragedy: the sudden death of his mother. For the first time in his life Mozart was alone." Milton Cross and David Ewen, *Milton Cross' Encyclopedia of the Great Composers and Their Music*, vol. 2 (Garden City, N.Y.: Doubleday, 1953), 517–518.

61. Durgnat reads Judy's voice as having a different function: "As Judy's outbursts re-mind us, Scottie's relationship with her is one of Hitchcock's astute studies in, not male, but masculine, bullying of the female." *Strange Case*, 288. Typically, critics and scholars who read Scottie's remodeling of Judy as aggression of one kind or another neglect to mention Elster's remodeling of her in the first place, as though Scottie's desperation makes him noteworthy while Elster's clearcut fraud and murderousness make him invisible.

62. We can see this theme rearticulated in Truffaut's *Fahrenheit 451* (1966), as Mon-tag searches through literature for a past his society has denied him.

63. Oliver Sacks, *The Man Who Mistook His Wife for a Hat* (London: Duckworth, 1985), 37.

64. Bitsch, "Entre trois films," 24.

Index

Page numbers in *italics* indicate images.

About the Author

Murray Pomerance is professor and chair in the Department of Sociology at Ryerson University, where he also teaches in the Joint Graduate Program in Communication and Culture with York University. He is the author, editor, or co-editor of numerous volumes, including *Magia d'Amore; Ladies and Gentlemen, Boys and Girls: Gender in Film at the End of the Twentieth Century; Sugar, Spice, and Everything Nice: Cinemas of Girlhood; Enfant Terrible! Jerry Lewis in American Film; Popping Culture;* and *BAD: Infamy, Darkness, Evil, and Slime on Screen.* Two volumes are forthcoming, *Where the Boys Are: Cinemas of Masculinity and Youth* and *Johnny Depp Starts Here.* He is editor of the Horizons of Cinema series at the State University of New York Press and, with Lester D. Friedman, co-editor of the Screen Decades series from Rutgers University Press. He is a member of the editorial board of the Contemporary Cinema series from Editions Rodopi. He has published fiction and criticism in the *Paris Review, New Directions, Kenyon Review, Descant, Quarterly Review of Film and Video, Film Quarterly,* and elsewhere, and is at work on a book about American cinema of the 1950s.